The long wave in the world economy

The long wave in the world economy

The present crisis in historical perspective

Andrew Tylecote

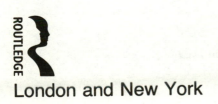

London and New York

First published 1991 by Routledge
11 New Fetter Lane, London EC4P 4EE

Simultaneously published in the USA and Canada
by Routledge
a division of Routledge
29 West 35th Street, New York, NY 10001

Reprinted 1993

New in paperback 1993

© 1991 Andrew Tylecote

Typeset from author's disks by J&L Composition Ltd, Filey,
North Yorkshire
Printed and bound in Great Britain by
Mackays of Chatham PLC, Chatham, Kent

British Library Cataloguing in Publication Data
Tylecote, Andrew, *1946–*
    The long wave in the world economy: the present crisis in
    historical perspective.
    1. Economics. Theories
    I. Title
    338.54

    ISBN 0–415–03690–9 Hb
    ISBN 0–415–03691–7 Pb

Library of Congress Cataloging-in-Publication Data
has been applied for.

To Marian

Contents

List of figures

List of tables

Preface and Acknowledgements

One day in the summer of 1979 my eye was caught by an advertisement in the corridor outside my office. King's College, Cambridge was calling for research proposals on the long wave, with a view to a research fellowship. The long wave? As a student in the 1960s I had come across this implausible idea, that there were recurring cycles of boom and slump in the world economy, about every 50 years – so that, for example, having had mass unemployment in the 1930s, we could expect more of the same by the late 1970s or early 80s. . . . Implausible? Kings did not think so, and nor now did I. I had just finished my book on inflation – the great economic issue of the 1970s – which had treated rising unemployment as a side-effect of disinflationary policies; but the uneasy feeling had been growing, that there was a deeper crisis of which inflation and unemployment were each a part. After a few weeks' reading of the long wave literature some ideas of my own began to form. I submitted a tentative theory and research programme. Kings judged them the best of the bunch but too vague.

This problem clearly required work across the whole range of the social sciences, on all the major Western economies and beyond, and ranging back in time from the present to the eighteenth century. Now there was to be no fellowship, no help. There matters rested, until the autumn of 1982, when on a visit to CEPREMAP in Paris (funded by the Economic and Social Research Council and the Counseil Nationale de Recherche Scientifique), I happened to show my long wave papers to Robert Boyer, who was working in the field. Boyer is intellectually as generous as he is brilliant: he told me I *must* return to the work; and encouraged me to present a paper at a conference on the long wave in Paris the following spring. At least two people there liked my paper: Immanuel Wallerstein, editor of *Review*, who published it; and my old teacher Chris Freeman, who invited me to follow it up as Visiting Fellow at the Science Policy Research Unit (SPRU) at Sussex University, the following year. The Economic and Social Research Council, and the Leverhulme Foundation, provided grants. Suddenly I found myself with the support I needed. There were several people at SPRU working on the long wave and glad to share their ideas – Freeman himself, Luc Soete,

Bengt-Ake Lundvall, and Carlota Perez. I found Carlota Perez's ideas particularly stimulating. Beyond that, SPRU is a Unit indeed. You may learn more there from your neighbour at coffee in ten minutes than from the average library in a day; and SPRU'S library is not average. That summer we travelled to Manchester for a seminar with Rod Coombs, Vivien Walsh and others at UMIST – new allies. Though I was back at Sheffield in the autumn, with a full teaching load, I was now confident that I could produce my own original theory of the long wave.

Originality, on big subjects, is not well received by the scholarly journals, unless perhaps from the already famous. (*Review* is an exception.) Lesser academics are well advised to limit themselves to adding to some pyramid of knowledge, one brick at a time. The rash, and stubborn, have one alternative: they can write a book. I showed an outline to my agent, Anthony Goff, who liked it. We found a publisher, Elizabeth Fidlon of Routledge, who was prepared to take it at our valuation. After that, all we needed was the book. I am afraid it took much longer than intended, and at one or two points I could wish that it had been a little more thoroughly researched. (The job should really have been done by an international consortium of interdisciplinary research institutes.) I could not have managed without the continuing help of Chris Freeman, who (among other things) saw to it that I was invited to present a paper – one of the few detachable bricks – at the Siena long wave workshop in December 1986. At Siena I met Solomos Solomou, who has since tempered successive drafts in the fire of his scepticism (well expressed in his own book), and Louis Fontvieille, who invited me to detach another brick at the Montpellier Workshop in 1987, and helped in discussion. I depended equally on the constructive criticism of John Westergaard, who (having done more than any one else to improve my last book) agreed to take this one in hand. In the later stages I was encouraged by Willy Brown, helped with the text by Marian Tylecote, and with the technology by my late father Ronnie Tylecote, aided in my travels by Sheffield University's Research Fund, and tactfully nagged by Alan Jarvis and Ruth Jeavons of Routledge. I am grateful to all those I have mentioned, and many others, who will certainly disagree with some of what follows, but may perhaps agree with Simon Kuznets, writing in the American Economic Review of 1955, who has the last word:

> For the study of the economic growth of nations, it is imperative that we become more familiar with findings in those related social disciplines that can help us understand population growth patterns, ... technological change, ... the characteristics and trends in political institutions, and generally patterns of behaviour of human beings ... Effective work in this field necessarily calls for a shift from market economics to political and social economy. ('Economic growth and income inequality', p. 28.)

Andrew Tylecote

Introduction

The idea that economies and societies move in a circle is not attractive to the modern West. We march forward, and ever faster: that is our vision of progress, and it is supported by our measures of economic growth. Two centuries ago, in Britain of the Industrial Revolution, national income per head rose by less than 1 per cent per year. Now such a growth rate, sustained over a decade, would be regarded as shameful stagnation in any western country. Our concept of cycles in national income has been adjusted accordingly: 'downswings' are defined as periods of deceleration, of slower growth; they do not often involve an actual decline in national income. Our cycles are 'growth cycles'.

From the perspective of the South, the Third World, this attitude might seem smug. There, where the large majority of the world's population lives, there is no such inevitability to increasing affluence. True, the total national incomes of Southern countries, as conventionally measured, have increased during the last half century by not much less than those of the North. But Southern populations have increased much more rapidly than Northern, over the same period.[1] Worse, among the many flaws of our conventional measurements of national income is one which is, for the South, of ominous significance: no valuation is put upon changes in the value of natural resources.[2] An investment in bricks and mortar, or plant and machinery, counts towards national income, but the *disinvestment* which takes place when a forest is felled, topsoil washed away, or an oilfield is emptied, does not count against it! Since most of poor countries' wealth consists of natural resources, and tropical ecology is far more fragile than temperate, it seems likely that in most their wealth is dwindling; and dwindling fast, per head of population.[3] An odd sort of economic growth.[4]

If a large part of the world's population may be suffering a decline in income per head, we cannot take it for granted that world income per head is on a rising trend. Periods of 'slow growth' may be worse than they seem: 'downswing' may mean just that. This should make us the more concerned to identify cycles in economic growth and their causes. The longer the cycle, the more concerned we should be, for the more prolonged the misery in the downswing. The longest economic cycle – if indeed it exists – is the the Kondratiev cycle, or long wave, of about half a century from peak to peak or trough to trough. The long boom of about 1948–73 has been described as a 'long wave upswing' in the world economy. Before it, the depression of the 1930s would have been part of a long wave downswing (the precise beginning and end of which would be arguable). Since 1973 or thereabouts there has been another period of slow growth – or worse – to which falling living standards in the south, crisis in the east, and high unemployment in most of the west have borne witness. This would be another downswing. If there is such a regular cycle in the world economy, we can expect the downswing to continue until about the end of this decade; whereupon a new long boom will begin.

But does such a long wave really exist? We need an answer, if we are to know our fate, at the end of the millennium; or perhaps I should say, if we are to *master* our fate. Long wave downswings, if properly understood, may turn out to have been unnecessarily long – even unnecessary. If we knew what to do, and what to avoid, we might be able to bring on an earlier, stronger, longer upswing. Such an understanding is the aim of this book. In this it could be described as a contribution to the theory of economic growth and fluctuations. Anyone familiar with this subdivision of economics should be warned, however, that the approach taken is unusual. The argument is presented in plain English, without a single mathematical equation, and the issues discussed extend across and beyond the social sciences and over the history – not only *economic* history by any means – of the world since the late eighteenth century. This merely follows Henry Phelps Brown's injunction to the Royal Economic Society, 'Where an economic problem arises, let us observe whatever seems significant, and follow clues to causes wherever they may lead'.[5]

The book is divided into two parts, the first theoretical, the second historical. (In fact there is a good deal of history in the first part, but it is arranged around theoretical themes.) Chapter 1 gives a (selective) review of the long wave literature, and sets out my own theoretical point of departure. Chapter 2 describes and explains the long wave which appears to exist in the rate and character of technical change. Chapter 3 shows how certain features of political, social and economic structures may interact with economic long waves. Chapters 4 and 5 discuss the evolving interplay between economic growth and (respectively) monetary and demographic factors. Chapters 6 and 7 put forward a highly controversial thesis on the interaction between economic growth and inequality of income and wealth – inequality within Northern countries, between North and South, and within Southern countries.

Part II is introduced by a brief résumé and synthesis of the arguments of Part I. The theory is then applied in a chronological treatment of the subject. Chapter 8 deals with the period 1780–1848, which could be described as the 'prehistory' of the long wave. Chapter 9 follows the history of the world economy – and much else – to 1896, which some have taken as the end of the first long wave downswing. Chapter 10 deals with the period 1896–1945, in which political and economic developments are most obviously intertwined, and Chapter 11 covers the post-war period up to the end of the 1980s. Chapter 12, in conclusion, has three parts: a résumé of the theoretical and historical argument; a predictive section in which the outlook for the next decade is firmly set in its *ecological* context; and finally a prescriptive section. This sets out proposals for resolving what I have argued to be a very deep-seated and acute crisis, so that we may release the economic and social potential of recent developments in technology, and launch a new world upswing without parallel in history.

Part I
Theory

Chapter 1

The long wave debate

THE SHORTER ECONOMIC CYCLES: KITCHINS, JUGLARS, AND KUZNETS

To be sure, the path of economic growth is not and never has been smooth. But are the fluctuations we observe merely *episodic*, due to factors which occur without any regular pattern? Or are they true cycles – and if so, of what kind? A true cycle must show some regular pattern of fluctuation, which may be *endogenous* or *exogenous*. An endogenous cycle is one which is self-generating, so that the downswing sets forces in motion which lead to the next upswing, and *vice versa*. The Kitchin 'inventory' cycle is (or was) one such: Kitchin, writing in 1923, found a pattern of fluctuations of growth rates of three to four years from peak to peak or trough to trough, which appeared to be due to overshoots and undershoots of business inventories or stocks: recovery from recession left firms short of stocks of raw materials, components and finished goods, which they then strove to rebuild. Their efforts to do so increased demand throughout the economy and were thus to a degree self-defeating; which led them to try harder. Suddenly they found they had succeeded all too well, and were obliged to cut back orders and output accordingly; which depressed the economy, and by doing so caused a further involuntary pile-up of stocks...

The advantage of so short a cycle as this one is that there is a relatively large number in a given period – more than a dozen in half a century. It is thus relatively easy to prove their existence and study their character. But the economic and social structures which give rise to cycles are bound to change over any long period of time. Even if we take the existence of 'Kitchins' as proved for the period Kitchin was surveying, we have no reason to assume the same cycle prevails today. Thus if we still find a cycle of roughly this duration in the second half of the twentieth century it may well be of a different character, generated perhaps by the political cycle of four years or so between elections. Before an election a government will reflate the economy to make the electorate feel prosperous, and grateful; afterwards, facing inflation and/or a balance of payments deficit, it deflates, causing a recession ... This cycle, if its causes are as described, is of the *exogenous* variety, generated by forces outside the economy; and the change from the Kitchin short cycle has taken place because of the great increase in the importance of the State in the economy.

Another recognised cycle, discovered indeed long before Kitchin's, is the Juglar or investment cycle.[1] This has, or had, a length of seven to eleven years, and appears to have been driven by investment in fixed assets (plant, machinery, etc.) rather than stocks, but to be otherwise analogous: investment overshoots at the peak, giving excess capacity, and undershoots at the trough. The longer period between peak and trough reflects the slower process of adjustment involved. As with the Kitchin, and for much the same reason, it is unlikely that the Juglar survives today in its old form, though it appears from van Duijn (1983) that there is still some such cycle at work, at least in the USA.

The third and last cycle to be fully accepted by economic historians is the longest of the three, the Kuznets cycle, of some fifteen to twenty-five years duration.[2] This has been most clearly established for the United States before 1914, and has been linked with building much as the others were with other forms of investment. In this case, however, it is rather harder to see how the cycle can be self-generating. Some *exogenous* factor seems to be required, and it used to be found in migration: the Kuznets expansion phases of 1861–71, 1878–92 and 1898–1912 all coincided with heavy emigration from Europe to the United States. This solution was not entirely satisfactory, because there is much doubt and debate as to how far migration really was exogenous to the US cycle: how far did the migrants *generate* an upswing, how far were they attracted by one that was already under way? So far as the US Kuznets cycle is concerned, the argument seems to have been settled by a meteorologist, Robert Currie, who found another determinant which was certainly exogenous: the weather. Currie (1988) found a strong effect of the 'luni-solar tide', which has a cycle of some 18.6 years, on US rainfall, and thus on crop production and the US economy in general: more rain, more crops, more output. The effect was pronounced from 1830 (the starting date for the study) until the early twentieth century, becoming

Table 1.1 Currie's rainfall cycle, USA, 1830–1936

Peaks	Rainfall Troughs
1834	1843
1852	1861
1871	1880
1890	1899
1908	1918
1927	1936

Source: Currie, 1988

weaker thereafter as the importance and vulnerability of agriculture declined.[3] The effects of the luni-solar tide on rainfall, and of rainfall on crops, will not have been the same in other countries as in the United States, but given the importance of the US economy the cycle still has world significance, and we may do well to note Currie's rainfall cycle – see Table 1.1.

Links between cycles: periods and countries

If there are cycles of different lengths, how do they relate to one another? If two are both endogenous, self-generating – as the Kitchin and Juglar seem to be – then one might expect them to be closely linked, with two or three Kitchins to a Juglar. In other words, during the course of each fixed-investment cycle there would be two or three stockbuilding cycles. The peak of the boom would be reached during a Juglar upswing when the Kitchin upswing came; the depths of depression would be touched when a downturn in stockbuilding was added to one in fixed investment. We might go on to accommodate two or three Juglars in a Kuznets; but if we accept that Kuznets cycles are exogenous, we must not expect any neatness in the relationship.

Links between countries are at least as important as between periods. It is for individual economies that cycles have generally been identified, but clearly there must be some effect of one country's cycle on another country to which it is closely related. The most obvious effect is positive, with a lag: thus a boom in America will lead to more orders there for European exports, and thus make for a boom in Europe, a year or two later. As the volume and ease of trade increase, this effect must increase too. But there may be negative effects; there certainly were in the past. In the nineteenth century the migration waves across the Atlantic must have stimulated the American economy, and it has been convincingly argued that they depressed the 'senders' in Europe. Moreover booms in America 'pulled' migrants, depressions in Europe 'pushed' them. For this and other reasons there appears to have been an inverse relationship for much of the nineteenth century between Kuznets cycles in the US and those in some European countries.[4]

KONDRATIEV OR LONG WAVES

Beyond the Kuznets cycle, we cross the frontier, out of any sort of certainty. Kuznets cycles exist, in some countries and periods: after Solomou's *Phases of Economic Growth* (1987) we know they can be found in more countries and periods than previously thought; and after Currie, it is quite easy to see why. The next economic cycle 'up' from the Kuznets, is (if it exists) the Kondratiev cycle, or long wave, of some forty-five to sixty years. If we judge by the passion it has aroused, the long wave is something of an economic historian's Holy Grail. Like the Holy Grail, it has not yet been found for certain; and if it had been, its value would be doubtful. For a cycle can hardly be seen to exist, or shown to do so, unless it repeats itself a considerable number of times. The problem with so long a wave is that we have only had time for about four since the beginning of the Industrial Revolution: there is no point in looking for any before then, for forces that could generate a particular wave in the industrial twentieth century, would hardly have behaved in the same manner in the agrarian eighteenth. Indeed, even 200 years is a very long time for such continuity in economic dynamics.[5] So if we found four 'Kondratievs', or even three, we would be very hard put to explain them. On the other hand, if we found fewer – well, once is happenstance, twice is mere coincidence.

Let us begin with the facts, so far as they are known. During the nineteenth century it became apparent that there was something resembling a long wave in prices (see Figure 1.1). The British economist W. S. Jevons, writing in 1884, found evidence of a long wave in (UK) prices from 1790 to 1849, with twenty-eight years of generally rising prices, to 1818, followed by thirty-one in which they tended to fall. Jevons in turn influenced the Dutch Marxist van Gelderen, who in 1913 looked back on a second long wave in prices, rising from 1850 to 1873, and falling to 1896, when a third upswing began. For van Gelderen cycles in prices were not of great importance in themselves: he and other Marxists were interested much more in 'the slow breathing of the monster', in cycles of fast and slow expansion (or contraction) in the capitalist system they hoped one day to bury. Van Gelderen came to the conclusion that the long waves he observed in prices, of some half a century in length, existed also in growth rates. Nor was either

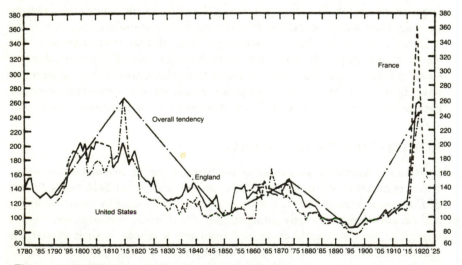

Figure 1.1 Kondratiev's index numbers of wholesale prices (1901–10 = 100)
Source: Kondratiev (1979 [1935]), p. 524

long wave confined to the British economy: he believed that there were more-or-less synchronised long waves in all the main economies, and in the world economy as a whole.

Van Gelderen has had very little credit for his work, until recently. He made the obvious mistake (in retrospect) of writing only in Dutch, and the less obvious one (which will be explained later) of writing during an upswing. As a result, it was another Marxist, the Russian Nikolai Kondratiev, working in Moscow in the 1920s, at first in complete ignorance of van Gelderen's ideas, who gained the title of the 'father' of the long wave. Kondratiev and van Gelderen both cited a great deal of statistical evidence in support of the long wave theory; but while their evidence for long waves in prices, back as far as 1800, was based on quite good statistical series, their series for output and income were far more sketchy and less trustworthy. This was a fault to be expected, and excused, for one only needs records for a few producers or traders to calculate what the *general level of prices* was for a commodity; but one needs records for *all* producers, to know what the *total output* was. Nonetheless, it left the really important question, whether there were long waves in the expansion of output, open.

For the period about which Kondratiev was writing, that question is still open. Up to 1850 and beyond, the problem is still largely one of data, while after 1870 it concerns interpretation. Van Duijn, in *The Long Wave in Economic Life* (1983), declares that 'What emerges [from his presentation of the data] is a near-perfect long-wave pattern' in the world economy after 1866 (his p. 154; see our Figure 1.2 and Table 1.2). Solomou, in *Phases of Economic Growth* (1987), roundly denies it. One reason for the disagreement lies in the treatment of wars. Any major war will depress output while it is going on, and lead to a 'reconstruction boom' some time afterwards. So van Duijn glosses over the disastrous 1913–20 period as a mere 'interruption' in his third Kondratiev upswing; on the other hand, he counts 1866–72 as a 'peak' without mentioning that its fast growth might be ascribed to recovery from the American Civil War. (For that matter, as Solomou points out, much of the apparent long wave in prices in the early nineteenth century can be put down to the effects of the Napoleonic Wars.)

In the sixty years since Kondratiev wrote, the position has been reversed. Growth rates in the world economy have conformed very well to a long wave pattern, with a downswing in the 1930s and early 1940s and again since the mid-1970s, an upswing in between (Figure 1.2). Prices, on the other hand, after falling as predicted until 1933, have since then been 'misbehaving' more and more, with continuous inflation which quickened in the early 1970s, at just the 'wrong' point in the growth cycle (Figure 1.3). It is the apparent long wave in growth which has given vitality to the long wave debate. It was the depression of the 1930s which brought Kondratiev's work to the attention of economists in the west – for he had predicted what they had not; and (what was better) he had predicted also that there would be an

Table 1.2 Growth rates of industrial production in van Duijn's long wave upswings and downswings

	United Kingdom		United States		Germany[a]	
2nd Kondratiev						
upswing	1845–1873	3.0	(1864–1873	6.2)	(1850–1872	4.3)
downswing	1873–1890	1.7	1873–1895	4.7	1872–1890	2.9
3rd Kondratiev						
upswing	1890–1913	2.0	1895–1913	5.3	1890–1913	4.1
	1920–1929	2.8	1920–1929	4.8	1920–1929	
downswing	1929–1948	2.1	1929–1948	3.1	1929–1948	
4th Kondratiev						
upswing	1948–1973	3.2	1948–1973	4.7	1948–1973	9.1
	France		Italy		Sweden	
2nd Kondratiev						
upswing	1847–1872	1.7				
downswing	1872–1890	1.3	1873–1890	0.9	1870–1894	3.1
3rd Kondratiev						
upswing	1890–1913	2.5	1890–1913	3.0	1894–1913	3.5
	1920–1929	8.1	1920–1929	4.8	1920–1929	4.6
downswing	1929–1948	−0.9	1929–1948	0.5	1929–1948	4.4
4th Kondratiev						
upswing	1948–1973	6.1	1948–1973	7.9	1948–1973	4.7

a 1948–73: West Germany
Source: Van Duijn, 1983, Table 9.7

end to it, and a new boom, in time. And here, parallel to the fluctuations in growth, we see an intellectual cycle appearing. During the boom, it is among the Marxists that the theory finds adherents, attracted by the implication of woe to come for capitalism. Capitalist economists mock them for their wishful thinking; but when it turns out right, some of the mockers are converted, remembering, to their comfort, that the same theory which predicted the Slump predicted a boom after that. The converse is also true: some Marxists find it hard to tolerate a heresy which holds that what they are greeting as the death throes of capitalism are not terminal at all. (Stalin did not tolerate Kondratiev: he had him arrested, and sent to Siberia, where he died.) So the idea was taken up by bourgeois economists, notably Joseph Schumpeter, who named the Waves, 'Kondratievs'; but once prosperity returned, the capitalist world duly lost interest. Again, of course, the theory was rescued by Marxists, including one who could only sympathise with Kondratiev's fate at the hands of Stalin – the Trotskyist, Ernest Mandel. By the mid-1960s Mandel was writing regularly and, as it turned out, rather accurately, about the coming long wave downswing. By 1974 he was able to claim, very plausibly, that it had arrived.[6]

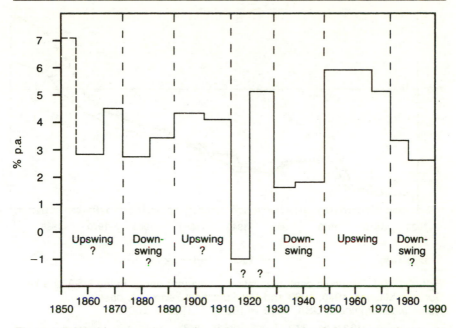

Figure 1.2 World economic growth – a long wave pattern? Juglar growth rates in industrial production
Source: van Duijn (1983) Table 9.5 and *UN Statistical Yearbooks*

EXPLANATIONS OF THE LONG WAVE

Since its adherents have claimed to find long waves in the *world economy*, it is at that level that they have looked for explanations. Van Gelderen's explanation revolved around the relationship between the industrial countries – the imperialist heart of the monster – and the primary producers. So long as the latter provided ample supplies of gold (which kept interest rates down) and raw materials (which fuelled industry directly) capitalist expansion proceeded rapidly. Once the expansion ran ahead of primary product supplies, this led to rises in prices and interest rates which helped to bring the long upswing to an end. During the downswing which followed, low profits and high unemployment in the industrialised countries of Europe drove both capital and labour overseas to the 'new' countries of the Americas and Australias, helping to develop their economies, and to provide gold and raw materials for the next upswing.

Kondratiev, apparently independently, offered a similar explanation, but with one important addition, the claim that long waves involve a 'wave' in inventions and innovations:

During the recession of the long waves, an especially large number of important discoveries and inventions in the technique of production and

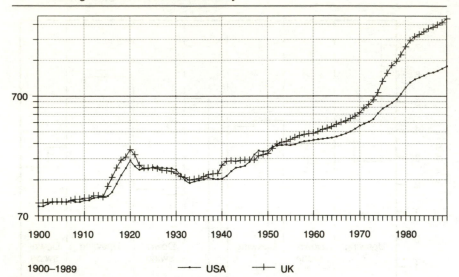

1900–1989

Figure 1.3(a) Twentieth-century inflation: consumer prices in the USA and UK
Source: Mitchell, 1978, 1983 and *UN Statistical Yearbook, passim*
Note: Index numbers: USA, 1913 = 100; UK, 1929 = 100

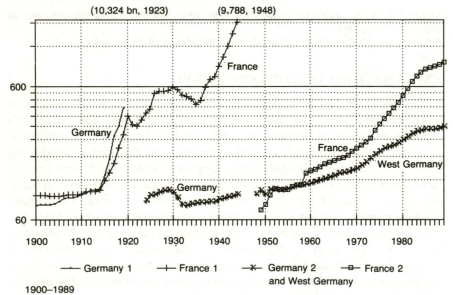

Figure 1.3(b) Twentieth-century inflation: consumer prices in France and Germany
Source: Mitchell, 1978; *UN Statistical Yearbook, passim*
Note: There was hyper-inflation in Germany, 1920–4 and a currency reform in West Germany, 1948.
Index numbers: Germany 1, 1913 = 100; France 1, 1914 = 100; Germany 2, 1929 = 100; France 2 and West Germany, 1953 = 100.

communication are made, which, however, are usually applied on a large scale only at the beginning of the next long upswing.[7]

It was this suggestion which was taken up by Schumpeter (who had already been thinking on similar lines) and made the basis of his own theory of the long wave, which he believed had started with the Industrial Revolution.

The Schumpeterian tradition

Schumpeter and his followers stress the central role of technical progress, in providing opportunities for profits and accumulation. He explains how basic innovations like the steam-engine and the railway, and the 'swarming' of smaller, secondary innovations which follow them, can launch a long wave; he explains how the initial impulse is gradually dissipated, and this leads to the downswing. But what determines the rate and character of technical progress? Early Schumpeter (1934) stressed the independent march of science, following its own logic and its own paths, leaping forward when it was ready; late Schumpeter (1939) had studied the research and development activities of large corporations, and had become convinced that they, and thus economic forces, had a great influence on the changes in technology. Late Schumpeter is richer in possibilities for the theory of long waves: technical change may shape the long wave in the economy, which in turn may shape technical change. But at no point does Schumpeter fill the crucial gap in his theory. If a new upswing is launched by basic innovations, what explains their arrival, in clusters, every fifty years of so?

It was not Schumpeter but one of his followers, Gerhard Mensch, who made the first serious effort to answer this question. According to Mensch (1979), depressions make entrepreneurs more adventurous: 'the prospect of execution concentrates the mind wonderfully' and they become ready to take a chance on new ideas: there is therefore a bunching of radical innovations in the depression, which launches the upswing. It was at this point, and partly in response to Mensch, that Christopher Freeman, with colleagues at the Science Policy Research Unit (SPRU) at Sussex University, took a hand in the game. Freeman was sure that Mensch was wrong; *wrong in fact*, for SPRU could find no bunching of innovations in depressions, and *wrong in theory*, for

Mensch had been looking at the wrong 'swarms'. .... Surprisingly when [Mensch] speaks of the 'bandwagon' effect he is talking about a disparate set of basic innovations. It is very hard to see in what sense the originally quite separate launch of helicopters, television, tetraethyl lead, titanium, etc. in the mid-1930s could constitute a 'bandwagon' in any normal meaning of the term. The swarms which matter in terms of their

> expansionary effects are the diffusion swarms *after* ... a set of inter-related basic innovations, some social and some technical, and concentrated very unevenly in specific sectors.   (Freeman 1983)

This set of *interrelated basic innovations* was crucial to the long wave.

> The important phenomenon to elucidate if we are to make progress in understanding the linkages between innovations and long waves is the birth, growth, maturity and decline of industries and *technologies*. ... Thus we are interested in what we shall call 'new technology systems' rather than haphazard bunches of discrete 'basic innovations'. From this standpoint the 'clusters' of innovations are associated with a technological web, with the growth of new industries and services involving distinct new groupings of firms with their own 'subculture' and distinct technology, and with new patterns of consumer behaviour.[8,9]

Freeman and his collaborators were able to show how the character of technical change had evolved during the course of the last long wave, with a 'swarming' of new *product* innovations in the early upswing, and a gradual change towards more minor 'improvement innovations' in products, and more stress on *process* innovations, improvements in methods of production.

It was easy to see how the new products of the early upswing could stimulate investment, perhaps also consumption. Likewise, the switch towards process innovations – in effect, cheaper ways of providing consumers with what they were buying already – threatened to increase supply without increasing demand, and thus helped to account for the downswing. What was lacking from Freeman *et al.*'s theories at this point (1982), as from Schumpeter's, was an explanation of the upturn in the first place: if it was caused by some set of basic innovations, what caused *them*; and were these innovations enough by themselves to launch an upturn? The gap was filled by drawing on an element of the Marxist tradition, to which we now return.

The Marxist tradition

What Marxists of different schools have in common is a stress on the interactions – the dialectic, they would say – between political, social and economic factors, in a society subject to continuous change. This society, in our period, has been dominated by capitalists who have been continually seeking to accumulate capital and to make as much profit as possible while doing so. These capitalists have had, in some ways, a rather precarious position in a system of social relationships in which accumulation and profitability have been constantly threatened by the demands of the working class – yet have been also at risk if working class purchasing power were insufficient.

It is the first threat – of excessive working-class power – which is emphasised in Ernest Mandel's long wave work.

Mandel's theory goes roughly as follows: capitalists will not invest heavily until the rate of profit is sufficiently high, and can be expected to remain so. This is not so during the downswing (we shall see why in a moment); investment is therefore low, and the economy slides into a depression. This causes a deep social and political crisis, which continues until capitalists can find some way out: they do so sooner or later by winning a decisive victory in the *world class struggle* which opens some new avenue of profitable accumulation. (There is always the hope for Marxists, in each depression, that anti-capitalist forces will solve the problem *their* way.) In the late nineteenth century the victory came through imperialistic expansion abroad; the crisis was resolved at the expense of the conquered peoples, whose territories provided vast new markets and sources of raw materials. In the next depression crisis this possibility was not available, because it had already been used. The crisis of the capitalist 'core' was accordingly deeper, and led to a bitter internal class struggle. The capitalists finally emerged victorious in the late 1940s, in a position now to make full use of the technical possibilities of the capital-intensive, assembly-line methods of production ('Fordism') developed during the last long wave upswing in the United States.

The upswing, once under way, encourages investment and innovation, the two interacting in a virtuous circle (Mandel is receptive to the ideas of the Schumpeterians). But the upswing is doomed by developments in industrial relations and the economy. The working-class movement has now had time to recover from its defeats and takes advantage of favourable conditions on the labour market to return to harass capitalism and reduce its rate of profit. A less obvious nemesis is rising capital intensity, which is a response to rising labour costs, and to the advanced stage of development of the ruling technological system and the corresponding 'scaling-up' of plant and equipment; this too, according to Marxian theory, forces down the rate of profit. Capitalist confidence in the outlook is shaken, investment falls, and we are back in the downswing – which helps to put the workers on the defensive, but does not of itself provide the decisive capitalist victory required. ...

Where Mandel seems to me rather un-Marxist, is in his apparent in-difference to the distribution of income. Capitalist victories in the class struggle are apparently all to the good, from the point of view of the economy – but if they increase the rate of profit, will they not, by doing so, drive down the purchasing power of the working class? Will that not detract from the demand required to propel the upswing? The problem does not arise, in Mandel's story, in the late nineteenth century, for the capitalist victory comes *outside* its own economy; increased demand for capitalist industries can thus come both from the markets of the conquered territories, and from their own working class, who share in the spoils in the form of cheap food, etc. But there is no escaping it in the 1940s, when the victory (we are told) is *inside*, and involves 'a radical change in the overall sociopolitical environment in which the system operates (destruction of trade unions, elimination of bourgeois democracy, atomisation of the working class, impossibility of collective sale of the commodity labour power, etc.')[10]

If this had happened in the late 1940s, would it not have led to a steep fall in real wages and thus in consumer demand? In any case, *did* it happen? I shall argue later that it did not. Similarly, it is very hard to argue, from the historical facts, that the downswings after 1928 and 1973 were in any way precipitated by working-class successes in the class struggle, *world-wide*.

It is a relief to turn to Marxist writers on the long wave who base their work on careful analysis of what actually happened; so careful, in fact, that they have not essayed any general theory of the long wave, but have tended to concentrate on the causes of the 1930s depression, the escape from it, and the current downswing and depression. They are the 'regulationist school', led by the French economists Aglietta, Boyer, Mistral and Lipietz. Their analysis is subtle and complex, and not at all easy to summarise. They deploy two key concepts: the *regime of accumulation* and the *mode of regulation*. The first relates to the capitalist firm, its techniques and methods, the second to the wider society (national and international), its complex network of relationships, of checks and balances. A radical change of technology, such as we associate with Henry Ford and the assembly line, changes the regime of accumulation, but it does nothing to make the mode of regulation change in harmony. It is likely – one might say inevitable – that the necessary harmony will be lost, and that this will cause a crisis, and a depression. Thus the 'Fordist' regime of accumulation involved the growth of large firms, with closer control over their workers, and increased market power. This led, among other things, to the redistribution of income away from wages to profits, and a consequent shortfall of consumer demand, which caused the inter-war Depression. (In ascribing the Depression largely to under-consumption, and this in turn to maldistribution in favour of profits, the regulationists follow the great Marxist economist Kalecki (1954).) The subsequent recovery followed from the gradual growth of a suitable new mode of regulation, which restored harmony; in particular, the operation of the welfare state, and the strength of unions, guaranteed a much more equal distribution of income.[11]

PEREZ'S SYNTHESIS

The regulationists' change in the *regime of accumulation* is clearly not very different from Freeman's *new technology systems* but the regulationist theory offers a more complete explanation of the long booms. By the early 1980s the way was open for a new synthesis by Carlota Perez, who had been working independently on long wave theory in Venezuela and California after her social science studies in Paris. She broadened the regulationist approach and introduced the original concept of 'technological styles' which she described as:

> A sort of paradigm for the most efficient organisation of production, i.e. the main form and direction along which productivity growth takes place within and across firms, industries and countries. The particular historical form of such a paradigm would evolve out of certain key technological developments, which result in a substantial change in the relative cost structure facing industry and which, at the same time, open a wide range of new opportunities for taking advantage of this particular evolution.[12]

Thus the 'Fordist' style had been preceded by innovations which made possible high-performance machine tools, and cheap petroleum products, electricity, and electric motors. On this basis Ford and others developed the assembly line and mass production engineering – that was in essence the new paradigm.

A new technological style would appear during a boom – we shall see why and how in a moment. The new style would cause rapid change in what Perez calls the *techno-economic subsystem*. But this subsystem has to coexist with the other main subsystem within capitalism, the *social and institutional framework*. This *framework* has a 'high degree of natural inertia', all the stronger for the self-satisfaction bred by the upswing. The new style is 'mismatched' with the old framework, and the mismatch leads to crisis and depression. 'The crisis forces the restructuring of the socio-institutional framework with innovations along lines that are complementary to the newly attained technological style ...'.[13] With a new style *and* a new framework, harmony returns, and the blockage to economic expansion disappears. A new upswing follows, and with it comes Freeman's swarming of product innovations.

What then is the origin of the *next* technological style? Perez's general explanation is that the upswing leads to a point 'where the underlying technological style approaches the limits of its potential for increasing productivity'. The new technological style emerges 'to surmount this barrier'.[14] More specifically, we can see the connection between Freeman's increasing stress on process innovations, and Perez's 'substantial change in the relative cost structure facing industry'.

This is a most elegant synthesis of the best of the Marxist and Schumpeterian traditions, and it explains a great deal (see Figure 1.4). Unfortunately, it explains rather too much. According to Perez (and I believe she is right) we have had four technological styles since the beginning of the Industrial Revolution, at roughly fifty-year intervals, and a fifth has just appeared. (We look at these styles in detail in the next chapter.) In that case, if her theory holds, we should have had four long waves in economic growth; but as Solomou and others have shown, we have not. Somehow the relationship

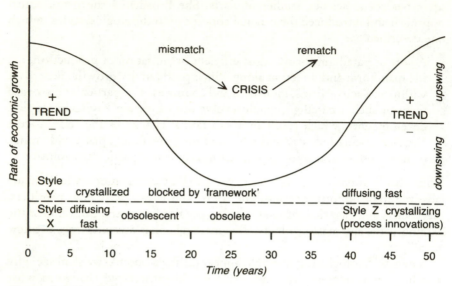

Figure 1.4 The Perez model

between technological styles and the rate of growth of the world economy must be more complex than Perez's model suggests. Let us look, one by one, at some of the complexities she leaves out.

Mismatch and crisis

If a new technological style is 'mismatched' with an old socio-institutional framework, this can in principle cause a crisis in at least two ways. First, let us assume the old framework blocks the diffusion of the new style. This will cause a downswing, leading to economic crisis, and *that* will cause some kind of social and political crisis. We might call this a 'depression crisis', and take the 1930s as an example. Second, we may imagine that the old framework is *not* such as to block the new style's diffusion; perhaps it had been, initially, but has been sufficiently reformed. ... Diffusion and economic expansion then proceed apace – no economic crisis develops, but economic change puts an increasing strain on the old framework at the social and political level. Then we would see a socio-political crisis, with any economic difficulties only arising indirectly. Such a crisis we would call a crisis of the upswing. (Kondratiev argued that 'it is during the period of the rise of the long waves, i.e. during the period of high tension in the expansion of economic forces, that as a rule, the most disastrous and extensive wars and revolutions occur',[15] and we shall see that, *up to his time*, he was broadly right.)

We shall see that these two types of crisis, 'depression' and 'upswing', appear to have occurred, in alternation, during the twentieth century. There is also a third scenario, in which the old framework *partly* blocks the new style. This then diffuses far and fast enough to cause a build-up of social and political tensions, but not enough (perhaps not *evenly* enough) to avoid economic difficulties too: the crisis which finally erupts is then of mixed socio-political and economic origins. We can find examples of this third, *mixed* type of crisis in the late eighteenth and nineteenth centuries.

If crises can vary in their origins, they may also vary in their effects. Perez's crises are wonderfully functional: they produce the required reforms in the socio-institutional framework. Why should they? In the case of the first type, we can see why: since the crisis originates from the unsuitability of the old framework to the economic demands of the new style, all who have an interest in the success of the new style have an interest in reforming the framework in the appropriate way. That does not mean that all or even most of them know at the outset what is necessary. There may be a process of trial and error; but until approximately the right reforms have been made, the crisis will not end. So they have to keep on trying. A *depression crisis*, then, can be expected to produce a well-reformed 'framework', and thus to lead to a long boom.

We can have no such confidence in the cathartic effects of the second type of crisis, of the upswing. The problem posed is not, in the first instance, economic, nor can we assume that the solution produces economic benefits. What is at issue, above all, is power. Low in the social order there will be groups – typically, of industrial workers – whose size and importance have been increasing rapidly as the current 'style' diffuses in the upswing. They find their standing in the workplace and outside it does not reflect their importance, nor does their income; and the boom puts them in a position to do something about it. After a long upswing (as well as after a long depression crisis) there are great waves of strikes, as in many countries in the early 1870s, in 1913–14, and most recently in the late 1960s and early 1970s (see Chapter 6, below). Much higher up in the social order there may be other groups in precisely the opposite situation: they have political power and social standing disproportionate to their declining economic position, and they want to keep it. The classic example of such a social group are the Central and Eastern European aristocracies before the First World War. In alliance with other threatened groups lower down the hierarchy, they may be expected to unleash something more dangerous than strikes. . . . Note that in the most recent crisis of the upswing, in the late 1960s and early 1970s, there were no such groups of this type in western countries. We can put this down to the radical reforms which ended the previous depression crisis, and produced a very up-to-date 'framework' with a unified and flexible upper class. The only social category not 'looking for trouble' are those doing very well out of the upswing and the new style – they, the *nouveaux riches*, are quite contented even if their political position is lagging somewhat behind their economic one. They may well emerge stronger from the crisis – as in general the 'bourgeoisie' did from the 1914–18 war – but they have no programme for reform, and no incentive for allying with that other 'progressive' group, the industrial workers, who have after all been attacking *them*. Any changes to the socio-institutional framework are likely to be made under pressure from an upper class whose current priority is the defence of its power and privileges. As a result, the framework is likely to become if anything *more* mismatched economically than before with the style now diffusing, and its successor.

Our third, 'mixed' type of crisis would have been mixed in its effects. There were no such clear-cut categories of *gainers* from the new style as in the crisis of the upswing. The working class and poor would have been less confident, less ready to use their industrial muscle, and more inclined to try political, and violent, methods. Since the new style was partly blocked by the 'framework', the real gainers from it – e.g. in France of the 1780s and the 1840s, the bourgeoisie – would have been as much prospective as actual. They would have had an interest in reforms which would improve the 'economic match'. How much reform they would have got is another matter: others with different, even opposite interests would have been mobilised too, by the economic hardships accompanying the halting advance of the new style. In general, one might expect a mixed outcome of a mixed crisis, with a modest improvement to the economic match between 'style' and 'framework'.

We have not yet enriched, or complicated, the model anywhere near enough; but the distinction between types of crisis can go some way already to explaining the irregular pattern observed in economic growth. Suppose (as I argue in Chapter 2) that there is a *technological* long wave, with new technological styles arriving, or 'crystallizing', every half-century or so. When style 1 arrives let us assume its mismatch with the old framework is considerable, but not enough to prevent quite rapid diffusion which leads to some upturn in growth rates. The result, at some point, is a mixed crisis which, so long as it lasts, depresses growth rates; once it is over, the modest reforms to which it has given rise allow the diffusion of style 1 to quicken again, with a consequent upturn in growth rates. How marked, and how long-lasting this upturn is, depends among other things on the extent of the reforms. Afterwards, one may expect some downturn, as style 1 begins to be played out, then style 2 crystallizes, and the cycle begins again.

The growth rate fluctuations resulting from this pattern are less likely to conform to a long wave shape than to that of the longest Kuznets or long swing, with two ups and two downs in every (technological) long wave (see Figure 1.5). One could, on the other hand, well imagine a long wave in prices resulting, with a price peak during the crisis, and a trough during the end-of-style downturn. This might, then, fit the nineteenth century record; and as we shall see, 'mixed crises' are typical of that period. In the twentieth

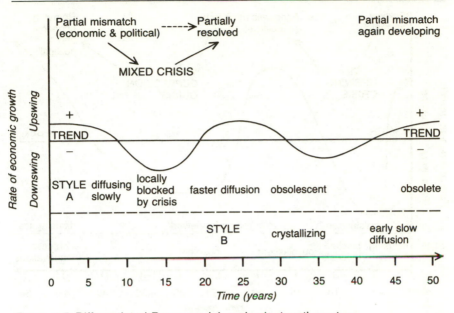

Figure 1.5 Differentiated Perez model, early nineteenth century

century, however, we have had a distinct alternating pattern of crises of the upswing and crises of the downswing. All such a pattern needs, as a point of departure, is a long, strong upswing in which an established technological style is diffusing fast, and a new one is 'crystallising' somewhere. That upswing will lead in due course to a social and political 'crisis of the upswing' – which will be a relatively severe one if the upswing was not preceded by a properly cathartic 'depression crisis'. *Being* a crisis of the upswing, it will not be resolved by radical reform, and the outcome will be a socio-institutional framework which is little, if any, better matched with the new style than before. The stage is then set for a long and severe *downswing*, and for a renewed social and political crisis arising out of that downswing. This, going deeper, takes longer to resolve, but is in the end resolved with radical reform and a thorough 'rematch' of framework with style: the stage is now set for a long, strong upswing. In turn this boom brings about a crisis – less severe this time because the process of reform and rematch had been so thorough; as before, however, the crisis of the upswing leads to a modified, not fully-reformed framework, and the new style now crystallising interacts with this inadequate framework to produce another long, severe downswing and renewed social and political crisis.

If we apply the model to the twentieth century, it fits quite well. We start off with the pre-1914 upswing; the 'crisis of the upswing' is then the First World War and its aftermath. It was severe because there had been no previous 'long downswing' to bring about reforms; and it was not resolved

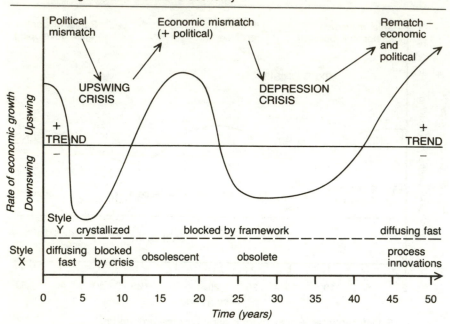

Figure 1.6 Differentiated Perez model, early twentieth century

by radical reform. Meanwhile the 'Fordist' technological style had crystal-lised in the US (see Chapter 2). A long and severe downswing did follow after 1929, with a deep social and political crisis resulting from it; the reforms which ended it were decidedly radical (as we shall see). This gave us the longest and strongest international boom on record, and that in turn led to a (relatively mild) social and political crisis in the late 1960s – of which more later. No really radical reforms resulted, and with a new style appearing (see below) it was time once again for a sustained and serious downswing of the world economy (see Figure 1.6).

We do now seem to be getting somewhere: the Perez model as modified no longer falls at the first hurdle of the non-existent nineteenth century long wave, and the 'interrupted' early twentieth century wave. But it needs further refinement, first to understand crises better, and second to consider other influences on economic growth. In the first task we can get some assistance from an even longer wave than the long wave – George Modelski's (political) *long cycle*.[16]

Insights from Modelski

Modelski's long cycles are cycles of world political leadership,[17] which start not a mere two centuries ago, like long waves, but five, when the world was opened up to European trade, and conquest, by Da Gama's voyage around Africa and Columbus's crossing of the Atlantic. This created what has been called the modern world system, which Modelski sees as dominated by a succession of *world powers* which have fulfilled a certain role of leadership in the world economy, and in international relations generally. (Notably, their control of the sea has guaranteed free trade, in one sense or another – suppression of piracy at a minimum.) The first generation of a new world power's leadership is assured and harmonious; the second is one of *delegitimation*, and in the third it is weakened to the point of *deconcentration*, with a serious challenger emerging – whose power is a regional, land-based one as opposed to the world power's maritime global reach. Then the period of leadership comes to an end, with a fourth generation (approximately) of *global war* in which the challenger is beaten by a coalition which normally includes the old world power; out of this coalition emerges the new world power. Modelski's first world power is Portugal, from 1516 (I think its leadership was shared with Spain, but let this pass); his second, very reasonably, is the Netherlands, from 1609; his third is Britain, from 1714. In both the second and the third long cycles the continental challenger is France, and at the end of the third long cycle the French challenge to British leadership culminates in the Revolutionary and Napoleonic 'global war'. At this point we have an oddity: the new world power which emerges from the wars, in 1815, is none other than Britain – the old world power rejuvenated. But the fourth long cycle unfolds much like the others, with a new challenger emerging (Germany) and its challenge culminating in the 1914–45 period (a global war with a long pause in the middle). The new world power which emerges in 1945 is the USA, its challenger (perhaps) the USSR.[18]

Long cycle theory alone has not provided any really satisfactory explanation of the rhythms of growth in the world economy (for a good try, see Goldstein, 1988). But what it does offer is an invaluable insight into the length and nature of crises. Let us start with our first, touched off by the crystallisation and early diffusion of our first new technological style (the 'water' style, the first phase of the industrial revolution – see Chapter 2). This first (mixed) crisis is the French Revolution, which, transmuted into the Napoleonic Wars, drags on from 1789 to 1815 – twenty-six years. And no wonder, for as we learn from Modelski, this is the 'global war' which ends the third long cycle. We might guess from the rather restrained upswing which followed that this first mixed crisis ended with rather little in the way of reform; and we might explain this, at least partly, by the character of the new world power – not a new one at all, with reforming ideas, but the old one, warmed up. The next crisis, 'mixed' again, is that of the late 1840s in Continental Europe, as style no.2 (the 'steam transport' style) diffuses. We are the less surprised to find this a rather brief affair, when we see that there is no question of global war, British leadership being at this point beyond challenge. By the same token, Britain has no call, this time, to get involved in defence of the *anciens régimes*, and we may expect, accordingly, to see rather more reform at the end of the crisis than in 1815. Such reform might be expected to give rise to a rather long and vigorous upturn. Just such an upturn did follow, in some countries at least, and from that upturn, it may be, arose wars, in the 1860s and early 1870s, which together give more than a hint of a crisis of the upswing. The next crisis was due, according to our model, after the crystallisation of technological style no.3 (the 'steel and electricity' style), which would mean some time in the 1880s or early 1890s. As Chapter 9 shows, we can find a crisis, or crises, during that period, but it seems to have involved little disruption to economic growth, and no major war or revolution. The economic mildness of this crisis cannot yet be explained; the absence of wars can be put down, following Modelski, to the fact that no one was yet ready to challenge Britain's leadership. (The absence of revolutions could be ascribed to the relative prosperity and peace.)

By 1914 time was up again, on the Modelskian clock. A new continental challenger, Germany, was ready to challenge the old leader, Britain. We can help to explain the timing of the new outbreak of global war by treating it as essentially a crisis of the upswing, following the rapid diffusion of technological style no.3. Germany attacked in 1914, not just because it now stood a chance of winning, but because economic development had brought its internal social/political tensions to bursting point (see Chapter 10). But why did the ensuing global war, unlike the last, come in two acts, with so long an interval between? For an answer we may draw again on Modelski's model. Modelski points out that the peculiarity of the 1793–1815 global war was that the old leader, Britain, emerged from it as the new leader. So Britain had no new leader with which to combine against its continental challenger, France; accordingly it took a long time to raise the strength to beat the French on land. Next time it was different: a new leader of huge latent strength was emerging – the United States. As soon as it was induced to throw that strength into the scales in alliance with the old leader, Britain, Germany had no chance: end of first act. However, the US was still most reluctant to discharge its responsibilities, and so began a second act of the tragedy, in which Germany was now joined by Japan and Italy; it ended with the USA assuming leadership in no uncertain manner.

The long interval in the twentieth century's global war had a most interesting consequence for the long wave. While its opening phase represented a crisis of the upswing, its concluding phase came as the culmination of the following depression crisis. This gave the depression crisis a most decisive and cathartic character: not only was it made more intense, but it ended with the United States's definitive arrival as the new world power. It is hardly surprising, then, that the reforms to which it led were, taken as a whole, one country with another, quite unprecedented in their breadth and depth. Accordingly, the upswing which followed was also unprecedented for strength and duration, and the crisis of the upswing was much the milder for the thoroughness of the previous reforms. By contrast, the superficial nature of the post-1918 reforms can be explained, first, by their following a crisis of the *upswing*, second, by the vacuum of leadership as the old world power faded before the new one was ready to take over.

THE TASK REMAINING

We have seen that there is much to be gained by setting our crises in the context of the 'long cycle'. It is also necessary to understand them better from our original perspective: what is it exactly which makes a new technological style, and the 'techno-economic subsystem' it tends to create, *mismatched* with an existing socio-institutional framework? What exactly are the effects of the different sorts of mismatch, and are there other processes which may lead to similar effects? What does it take to restore a good match or more generally to resolve a crisis? How much reform can one expect to arise from a given type of crisis? This is new territory which we have only just begun to explore: the exploration goes further in Chapter 3.

The theoretical model is as yet far from complete. Powerful as the tools are which are already in our kit, we should not neglect any others which may be useful. What we need to look for are factors which may play an interactive role in the 'slow breathing of the monster': factors which are on the one hand affected by growth rates, technological styles or crises, and on the other hand have an effect on growth rates, etc. These factors would then be playing a part in a *feedback process*. Feedback processes of the appropriate kind will tend to generate or intensify a long wave, as in the original Perez model (Figure 1.4): they are *pro-cyclical*. Others will play a spoiling role, weakening or entirely blotting out any long wave rhythm of growth: they are *counter-cyclical*. Whether a feedback process is pro-cyclical or counter-cyclical, will depend on its *direction* and its *speed*. For example, let us assume that fast growth leads to an increase in factor X, and slow growth to a decrease in it. If factor X in turn makes for slow growth, we have

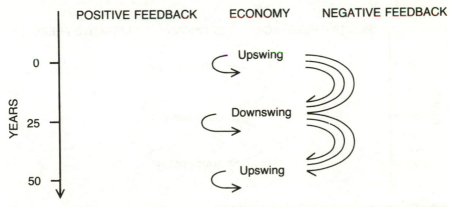

Figure 1.7 Feedback loops for a regular long wave

negative feedback; and that will work pro-cyclically, if the whole process – effect *on* X plus effect of X – takes around twenty-five years: for then a long wave upswing is helping to cause the next long wave downswing, and so on (see Figure 1.7). But if the negative feedback process were much faster – say five years – or much slower, perhaps fifty, then it would be counter-cyclical: a long wave upswing (or what might otherwise become one) would be working against itself, or its successor (see Figure 1.8). We have changed the effect by changing the *speed*. Alternatively, we might change the *direction*: we might imagine that factor X makes not for slow but for fast growth. In that case we have *positive* feedback, which will be pro-cyclical if either very fast or very slow, counter-cyclical if it takes around twenty-five years.[19]

All the endogenous models of the long wave have one or more such factors at work, mostly operating through negative feedback over a period of around twenty-five years. What is objectionable about them – as I have already, in effect, argued about Perez's – is that they take for granted an unchanging direction and speed of feedback. Economic, social and political structures have changed enormously over 200 years. Why, then, without careful study, assume that a particular interaction among them is essentially unchanged? If we give up this rigidity and allow for some change in feedback processes – as I have already begun to do – we may be able to account better for the changing rhythms observed. It might be a change in direction or speed of a particular feedback. If we had a number of feedback processes, some pro-, some counter-cyclical, the change in rhythm could even be produced by changes in their relative *strength*: the long wave would emerge as the pro-cyclical processes got the upper hand.

Let me now briefly introduce the feedback processes which I propose to describe and deploy later in the book.

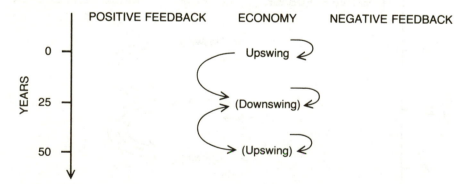

Figure 1.8 'Counter-cyclical' feedback loops

Money

Money may affect the rate of economic growth through its quantity and its price. By its price I mean the rate of interest: few would disagree that a rise in the rate of interest will have *some* depressing effect on economic growth. It is less obvious how economic growth will affect the rate of interest and supply of money. One route, which was suggested by Kondratiev, requires a close connection between the supply of money and the stock of *gold*, and between movements in prices and those in growth rates. An economic downswing then leads to falling prices of goods, except for gold, whose price is fixed in money terms; this increases the relative price of gold. The search for gold is thus carried on more vigorously. More is found, and the rate of gold production soars: this pushes up the stock of money, and the real value of that stock, with falling prices, rises even further. This tends to reduce the rate of interest. Once the upswing is under way, however, this whole process goes into reverse. Fast expansion leads to a rise in prices of goods, except (again) gold. Gold's relative price will now be falling. Gold output is cut back somewhat, and the expansion of the real stock of money reduced even more; so the interest rate rises...

This monetary feedback process is a very plausible one until this century. During this century, however, the link between gold stocks and the supply of money, and later between growth rates and price increases, has become looser. If such monetary feedback has continued it must have taken a rather different form, and have become more dependent on the workings of the institutions which create money. We go into these changes further in Chapter 4.

Population

Population is an attractive candidate for one of our feedback processes because it is easy to imagine that economic growth affects population, and that population in turn affects economic growth: what is more, since human beings have continued throughout our period to take much the same time to grow up and have children, the speed of any population feedback might well have remained roughly unchanged. The problem is that the most obvious feedback process would be counter-cyclical. Thus if we assume, (a) that prosperity stimulates fertility (with perhaps a five–year delay), and (b) that the resulting extra children stimulate economic growth (allowing some twenty years for them to grow up and pay a full part on the labour market), we have about twenty-five years from one upswing to the next. Meat and drink for Kuznets, dust and ashes for Kondratiev.

Richard Easterlin (1961, 1968) and Nicholas Keyfitz (1972) made a helpful change in the assumed determinants of population. Previously demographers had taken it that a small 'cohort' of people of child-bearing age in year nought would make for another small cohort in year twenty-five, and so on. But Easterlin and Keyfitz pointed out that the smaller the cohort the less the competition among them for job opportunities; that might well raise their fertility so much that they had, in total, more children than the larger cohorts before and after them. This might help explain how the small cohort of those born in the depressed 1930s produced, in the late 1950s, a particularly large 'crop' of children. We would then, in the early 1980s, have a baby slump, rather than a baby boom. This would help explain any long wave we might observe in population increase: not only would a depression depress fertility, and a boom increase it, but the after-effects of the last depression would on balance be working to increase fertility in a boom. Such a demographic wave could help to account for the long wave observed in economic growth, if a baby boom like that of the late 1950s turned out to have an immediate stimulating effect, and/or a depressing impact after twenty years.

This sketch of an 'Easterlin-based' pro-cyclical effect only scratches the surface. None of the links suggested is self-evident, nor, if one is found for one period, can it be assumed to hold for another. Nothing has been said so far of the effects of large and small cohorts as they progress through their teens, and later through middle age to retirement and death. Migration, too, may be of importance, and not only to individual economies: world economic growth may be as much affected by people's location as by their numbers. It can be guessed already, and will be argued in detail in Chapter 5, that population feedback is very sensitive in direction and intensity to economic, social and political structures. It helps accordingly to explain the irregularities of the long rhythms of economic growth.

International inequalities

Differences between countries in level and dynamism of technology have played little part in the argument so far. This is a defect which needs a remedy, for it is easy to imagine that such inequalities would affect the long rhythms of economic growth. Moreover, inequalities between nations have increased a great deal over two centuries, and it may well be that this increase has had some influence on those rhythms.

The first inequality is between 'leaders' and 'followers': between the country or countries in which a new technological style crystallises, and other 'advanced' countries, which do not show such dynamism. We can take it that leaders will have a relatively good match, at least in economic terms, between the new style and their existing 'framework'. They may be expected, without any serious crisis or major reforms, to use a new style to launch a sustained 'growth spurt'. That may lead to socio-political tensions, or it may run up in time against some faults in the 'economic match'; but they will have a good run for their money first. It is the less dynamic followers who need reforms more urgently, and are unlikely to show a growth spurt – rather the reverse – until they have had them. The effect of this difference would have been considerable in the 1780–1900 period, with its *mixed crises*. These would have been by far the most acute in the followers – like France in 1789; while their growth was held back by crisis, the leaders would be pressing ahead with the exploitation of the new style. The result would have been to even out the fluctuations in economic growth, at the world level, and take it even further away than it otherwise would have been from a long wave pattern. In the twentieth century the effect would have been less: the closer trading links between advanced countries make it more difficult for one to thrive while others are in crisis.

A much greater difference exists between what is called the *core* of the world economy, and the *periphery*. By *core* is commonly meant the more industrialised countries which export mostly manufactures; the periphery then comprises those which export, in exchange for manufactures, primary products – foodstuffs and raw materials. As we saw at the beginning, van Gelderen made much of the trading relationship between these partners as part of the dynamics of his long wave: when primary production ran short and its relative prices began to rise, this put a brake on the growth of industrialised countries. The much later non-Marxist writer W. W. Rostow (1978) treated the relationship as the heart of his long wave: a period of relatively high primary product prices was his upswing, a period of low prices, his downswing. Like van Gelderen – and in contrast to Kondratiev – he regarded the downswing in primary product prices as conducive to an upswing in growth rates.

I have two main criticisms of Rostow's approach. One relates to what he is measuring, the other to how he measures it. To deal with the latter first, his measure of the relationship between manufactures exporters and primary producers is a ratio of prices known as the net barter terms of trade. Reliable data for this ratio do not exist before about 1870, but until about 1900 Solomou (1987) finds no evidence for a long wave pattern in it. After that, yes, there is a long wave of sorts – high primary prices till about 1920, a trough in the early 1930s, high prices again in the 1940s and early 1950s, after that a downswing, with low prices through the 1960s. Then comes what Rostow (1985) greets as the beginning of the fifth Kondratiev upswing: a steep rise in primary prices, relative to manufactures, in the early 1970s. An odd sort of long wave upswing, even in relative prices: by the end of the decade all that was left of it was the rise in the price of oil, and in 1986 even that was reversed. In the late 1980s the net barter terms of trade of the primary producers were at their worst since the early 1930s. So in practice this measure of the primary exporter/manufactures exporter relationship does not follow much of a long wave rhythm. In theory too, as I argue in Chapter 7, it cannot be treated as a good measure of the relationship.

My second main criticism of Rostow is that his choice of categories is wrong. For each period, he lumps all manufactures exporters into one group, and all primary exporters into the other. The former are a fairly homogeneous group of advanced countries, at least until the last decade or so, when some poor countries begin to creep into the category on the strength of cheap labour, etc. But the primary exporters are split throughout between rich underpopulated countries of European settlement – like the USA, Canada and Australia – and underdeveloped tropical countries with a far inferior technological capacity. It seems strange to treat either the causes or the effects of a rise in primary product prices as the same regardless of whether it accrues to, say, Canada or Tanzania.

I shall argue, then, in Chapter 7 that the core-periphery relationship can be taken to have great importance for the dynamics of economic growth in the world economy, so long as we recognise:

1 That we must define *core* and *periphery* in terms of technological capacity, or level of development, not on the primary/manufactures criterion. We are looking then at the implications of the deepest kind of international inequality.
2 That the core-periphery relationship must be measured by much more subtle means than one set of price ratios.
3 That the effects of the relationship have changed, and become more important, as the world economy has become at the same time more unequal, and more integrated. We now see a slow negative feedback process in which fast growth in time leads to greater international inequality, and this greater inequality leads to slower growth.

I find that the core-periphery relationship did little to help generate a long wave in world growth rates, before this century, but that it has by now become one of the most important 'motors' of the wave.

Internal inequalities

Just as the Marxist tradition, through its concept of imperialistic exploitation, draws attention to the relationship of rich and poor countries, so through its concept of capitalistic exploitation it points to the relationship of rich and poor in one country. We have seen how Mandel took the view that the more of both kinds of exploitation, the better for capitalist growth. Kalecki and the regulationists, on the other hand, argued that excessive capitalist strength, *vis-à-vis* their workers, would lead to a shift from wages to profits which would depress consumption and thus demand, causing recession. As with international inequality, we must beware of too crude a definition of the relationship. There is more to internal inequality than the division between capitalists and workers, and more to measuring it than the division of income between profits and wages. Nor can its consequences be limited to its effects on consumption and aggregate demand. Nonetheless it is plausible – and in Chapter 6 I shall argue that it is true – that internal inequality, in much the same way as international, plays a part in the long wave.

REFLECTIONS

If the arguments so far have seemed plausible, they may have concealed the highly controversial character of the enterprise as a whole. Economics aspires to be a science, and sciences, whatever else they may involve, have theories, hypotheses, models, which set out to describe how certain causes have certain effects. Effect A is alleged to be caused by factors X, Y and Z in some conjunction. If the science is lucky enough to be an experimental one, then this hypothesis can be tested by combining X, Y and Z in the appropriate way and observing whether A follows. Sceptics can replicate the experiment until convinced. If experiment is not possible (as in some natural sciences, like astronomy, as well as most of the social sciences) observation must do instead: one has to find enough cases in which the combination of X, Y and Z is known to occur, and confirm that A can also be identified in them. Now this requirement – as we have already seen – is bound to pose serious problems for any theory of the long wave, for (even if it went right back to the dawn of the industrial age) we would only have four observations, four waves, for the world as a whole. That provides barely enough observations to confirm or deny whether any such phenomenon as the long wave *exists*, let alone a sound statistical basis for testing a theory of it. But I have argued, to make matters worse, that:

(a) There is no regular long wave in the conventional economic sense of alternate fast and slow expansion of the world economy over an (approximately) fifty–year cycle, except for the period since the 1930s – and some approximation to it in the fifty years before that.

(b) We have no reason to expect such a wave over the whole 'industrial' period, because the 'feedback processes' which might give rise to it – which I argue have recently given rise to it – were not, and could not possibly have been, sufficiently unchanging over 200 years.

The last is the fatal blow to any pretension to conventional scientific method. Not only are the observations deficient in number and what they seem to indicate; what is being offered to explain them is not even a *theory* in the conventional sense. No sooner have I argued that X, Y and Z cause A, than I describe this as a unique occurrence, followed by another unique occurrence in which (with some help from A) X, Y and Z evolve into T, U and W and proceed to cause B, which in turn ... 'This is not theory, this is just telling a story' as an outraged biologist has complained. Historians may regard that as a respectable occupation, but economists certainly will not. Story-telling may be interesting and entertaining, even instructive, but if it involves, as this book does, assertions about the dynamics of economic growth now and in the past, how are we to judge their truth?

In fact I am doing a great deal more than story-telling: I am putting forward an *evolutionary* theory. An evolutionary economic theory assumes that the dynamics of an economic system evolve over time as a result of the evolution of its institutions. Its assumptions are therefore changed for each successive sub-period (this is a simplification, since the changes are in reality mostly continuous). What we have then is a sequence of sub-theories, of different explanations for the different outcomes in the sub-periods observed. Two larger structures hold this sequence together:

1 A master or meta-theory whch lays down how changes in assumptions about institutions and their interactions will alter the dynamics between one period and another. Thus it has been asserted that if any 'feedback process' changes from 'fast negative' or 'slow positive' to 'slow negative', this will make for the development of an economic long wave.
2 A master-account of the evolution of institutions and their interactions, which sets out the directions in which they have changed, in a way that is consistent with the detailed evidence cited.

Neither sub-theories nor meta-theory are testable in any conventional sense. Yet I maintain that their construction is a scientific enterprise. Experimental and statistical procedures of testing are means to an end; the end of scientific activity is to bring greater order into our knowledge of the world. Other means may serve. The means employed here are at least open to critical examination: they are based on assertions of historical fact, and the individual elements of the theory – the cause-and-effect relationships asserted – are verifiable or refutable because they apply to a considerable number of different countries, even regions, and often a number of time periods. The overall structure may be judged against the objective – to bring greater order into our knowledge of the world. The making of such judgements must of course be highly subjective, but it is (if Thomas Kuhn is to be believed) a necessary activity nonetheless, in the natural sciences. He argues (in *The Structure of Scientific Revolutions*) that at times of crisis in a discipline, scientists are obliged to choose between competing *paradigms* without recourse to experiment. The paradigm which finally prevails is that which is able, most simply and elegantly, to account for most – not yet all – of the available evidence; in other words, to bring greater order into our knowledge of the world. It is from such a standpoint that I ask the reader to judge this book.

There is one more issue left to discuss, by way of introduction, before we can go in detail into the feedback processes which complete our theory. Much has hung, in the argument so far, on the idea of technological styles, and they will form an important part of what follows; a part which has the rare merit of changing rather little during our period. So far, however, only the concept of them has been sketched. What a new technological style is in principle; what the technological styles have been since the late eighteenth century in historical fact; and why, when and where they crystallised and diffused; these issues form the subject of Chapter 2.

Technological styles

THE NATURE OF TECHNOLOGICAL STYLES

Perez defines a 'technological style' as 'a sort of "ideal type" of productive organisation or best technological "common sense" which develops as a response to what are perceived as the stable dynamics of the relative cost structure'. In other words, the basic techniques of production, and methods of organisation, which are seen as the most efficient and profitable, change in response to the appearance of new key *factors of production* which are:

(a) clearly very cheap, by past standards, and tending to get cheaper, and
(b) potentially all-pervasive.

For example, when (as we shall see) the price of steel plummeted after 1850, this had drastic implications for methods of production throughout the economy. About half a century later, the cheapening of various forms of energy, particularly oil and electricity, played a similar role in the development of the Fordist style. The new 'style' is:

> grounded on the introduction of a cluster or constellation of interrelated innovations both technical and managerial which lead to the attainment of a general level of total factor or physical productivity clearly superior to what was 'normal' with the previous technological style.

The crucial innovations take place in two areas of the economy: the industries which *make* the key factor(s) of production (Perez calls these the *'motive branches'*) and those which *use* the key factor(s) most intensively and are the best adapted to the new organisation of production (the 'carrier branches'). (Thus oil refining and electricity generation were 'motive branches' in the Fordist style, while the motor vehicles industry was a 'carrier branch'.) The motive and carrier branches are the locomotive of the economy, though once they have got the upswing going there is a burgeoning of a third category, the 'induced branches', which provide goods and services for which demand is increasing rapidly.[1]

Once a new technological style has arrived, it starts to fan out across the economy:

As long as the ... evolution of the relative costs of various types of material inputs, various types of equipment and different skills follows the expected trends, managers and engineers will apply what becomes the 'technical common sense' to make incremental improvements along the natural trajectories of the technologies in place, or radical technological changes in those branches of production of goods or services which have not yet achieved the 'ideal type' of productive organisation.

Thus from the beginning of the Fordist style, in the USA, 1910–20, the motor-vehicle industry used Fordist technology, like the assembly line. Improvements to the automobile, and the methods of making it, were (at least until the 1970s) incremental – you had basically the same assembly-line system but you made it faster and more automated. But other industries had to make radical changes in order to come into line.

The diffusion of the new style leads to a restructuring of the whole economy, involving:

(a) A new 'best practice' form of organisation at the firm and/or the plant level;
(b) A new 'skill profile', using different proportions of the various categories of labour, and changing the nature of the skills within them: this in turn has implications for the distribution of income;
(c) A new 'product mix': those products which use the new key factors intensively will make up a growing proportion of the GNP;
(d) New trends in technical change: innovations will be aimed at economising on expensive factors of production through more intensive use of the key factor(s);
(e) A new pattern in the location of production: the new structure of relative costs transforms the pattern of 'comparative advantage';
(f) Heavy expenditure on *infrastructure* of the kind required by the new style.[2]

I think this is enough on technological styles in general. We shall know one when we meet it. Let us now go in search of five such creations in the history of the last two centuries or so. The discussion of each will naturally refer to the changes in structure which were involved, but I will review the organisational changes of all five styles together at the end.

THE WATER STYLE

There were two main hindrances to increasing industrial efficiency in the early years of the eighteenth century, in Britain and elsewhere: the high cost of transport, and the limitations of human muscle-power. Expensive transport meant that all but the most valuable goods (per unit of weight) had to be produced locally and thus in small quantities for which mechanisation would not usually pay; and where it did pay, it could do relatively little to increase productivity so long as it depended on human strength. These were old problems, and there were, in fact, old solutions: transport by water had always been far cheaper than on land (see Table 2.1) and with improvements in ship design (notably by the Dutch) had been getting steadily cheaper. As Adam Smith put it later in the century, 'Six or eight men ... by the help of water carriage, can carry and bring back in the same time the same quantity of goods between London and Edinburgh, as fifty broad-wheeled waggons, attended by a hundred men, and drawn by four hundred horses'.[3]

As for power, the water-wheel had been invented by the Hellenistic Greeks (probably in Asia Minor around 100 BC), had been much improved and diffused by the monastic orders in the Middle Ages, and was by 1700 intensively used throughout Western Europe, particularly in Britain.[4]

So what was the difficulty? It was that you could have water transport *or* water power – not, except for the rarest places, both. Coastal cities like London could trade cheaply with the world, and their own coastal towns, by water; almost the whole of the Netherlands was as well placed. But the same geography which gave them water transport, deprived them of water power.[5] That was, of course, abundant in the hills – but there were not even adequate roads there, let alone waterways. In the space between hills and sea, ran rivers with some fall of water which could be used – but only by blocking them with weirs. Over the centuries, as the demand for water power had increased (particularly in England) the obstacles to navigation had proliferated.[6] At the same time the roads had deteriorated – the splendid Roman network, with little more than hole-filling for a millennium and a half, was decidedly the worse for wear. (As Table 2.1 shows, the pack-horse, for bad roads, was inferior to the cart, for good roads, as the cart was to the boat.) It was an irony that the London merchant of the time of Queen Anne could now send a cargo or a clerk to Bombay; but to get either to Birmingham would be harder for him than for any of his forebears back to the time of King Egbert!

To the problem of inland navigation, the solution, again, was known. Dredge and straighten the rivers (or failing rivers, dig canals) and at weirs (or

Table 2.1 Horse-drawn loads on land and water

	tons
Average pack-horse load	1/8
Stage waggon, soft road	5/8
Stage waggon, macadam road	2
Barge on river	30
Barge on canal	50
Wagon on iron rails	8

Source: Rolt, 1969, p. 1

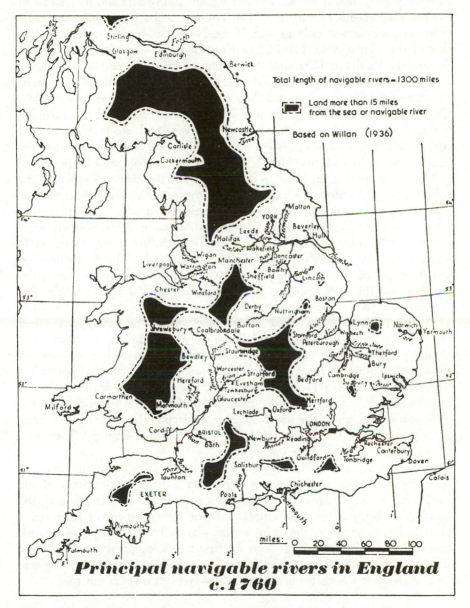

Principal navigable rivers in England c.1760

Figure 2.1 Principal navigable rivers in England, c. 1760
Source: Rolt, 1969, p. 16

changes of level) put pound locks – the type now seen, invented in renaissance Italy, extensively used in the Netherlands, and used first in England on the Exeter Canal in 1564.[7] It was generally much cheaper to make a river navigable than to dig a canal (and rivers were less inclined to run short of water). It was known to the English landowners and merchants of the late seventeenth century that their country had a potentially navigable river network second only to that of the Netherlands, and far better than that of their great rival, France.[8] During the next century they organised themselves, locally and through Parliament, to make it a reality (see Figure 2.1). By 1770 the work was as good as done, and they were turning to canals, to connect the rivers and extend their reach (see Figure 2.2 and Rolt, 1969, Ch. 3). They had also done much to improve the roads, with the turnpike system.[9] (For freight, the horse and cart on local roads were a vital complement to a waterway system which could never reach everywhere; for people, the stagecoach provided, for the moment, incomparable speed.)

There was another problem, in the first half of the century, to which the solution was not known. In England, in many areas, the use of water power was pressing up against the limits of the available supply.[10] Either another source must be found, or water-wheels must be made much more efficient. Newcomen's steam-engine followed the first path, but it was enormously wasteful of coal and better suited to pumping than to the rotary motion mostly required. The second path offered a quicker solution, and John Smeaton led the way along it. Well educated, and trained as a scientific instrument maker, Smeaton carried out a course of experiments between 1751 and 1753 on the vertical water-wheel, using the newly-established technique of *parameter variation*.[11] There were two kinds of water-wheel of similar popularity, the undershot and the overshot: Smeaton was able to show the maximum level of efficiency for each kind, and how to approach it by (among other things) regulating the speed of flow of the water against or into the wheel. His experiments clearly showed the great superiority of the overshot wheel, and also the scope for replacing the undershot wheels already in use by a third type, newly introduced and of similar efficiency to the overshot – the low breast-wheel.

Smeaton was no gentlemanly dilettante, impelled by mere curiosity. He was quickly becoming the most sought-after industrial consultant of the day, involved in numerous canal and navigation improvement projects, the building of bridges and lighthouses, and the improvement of harbours – even the improvement of the steam-engine – as well as his water power work (indeed he has a better claim to have the first technological style named after him than Henry Ford has to the fourth style). When Smeaton said replace your undershot wheels by breast-wheels, watermill owners did so.

It was one of the continual occupations of Mr Smeaton, during forty years, to improve the old water-mills, by substituting breast-wheels for

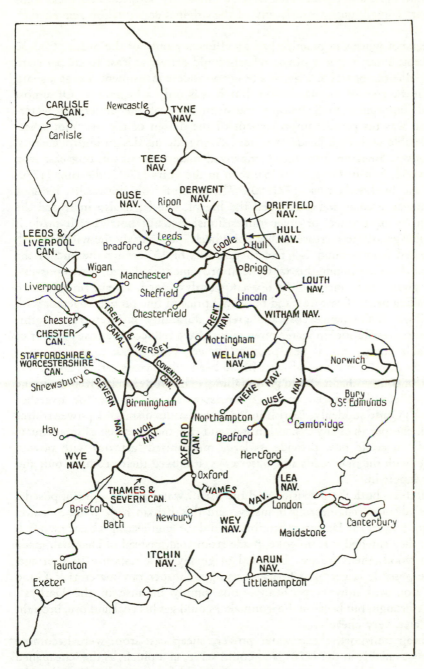

Figure 2.2 The English waterway system, 1789
Source: Hadfield, 1974, p. 81

undershot; and the advantages were uniformly so great, that these mills were copied, until scarcely any of the original construction remained.[12]

Undershot wheels in practice had an efficiency only of the order of 20–30 per cent; Smeaton's low breast-wheels could deliver at least 40–50 per cent.

Double the power at a given site for a modest investment meant a sharp fall in the cost of mechanisation, but it was only a beginning. Of almost equal importance to Smeaton's transformation of the undershot water-wheel, was his parallel improvement of the design of the overshot wheel (preferable with high heads of water). Alongside his design improvements, moreover, Smeaton introduced improved materials, substituting cast iron for wood, first in the axle (1755), then in the gears (1766), the rims (1770) and the bucket boards (1771–80). The use of iron drastically reduced maintenance costs and prolonged the life of wheels; it also increased the efficiency of a wheel of given dimensions; last but not least, it made it possible greatly to increase the size of wheels (particularly the width, which increased from around 2–3 feet to upwards of 15 feet by the end of the century[13]). Combining this with the improvement in design, it was possible on a given site to increase the horsepower developed, several times. Given the falling price of cast iron and the rising price of fine timber, together with the lower maintenance cost and greater durability just referred to, this 'Smeaton revolution' in water power must have reduced the cost per unit of available energy for a 'best-practice' wheel, circa 1780, to a fraction – perhaps 20–30 per cent – of what it had been thirty years earlier; and it was clear, of course, that it would go on falling. (Thus for example Rennie, in the early 1780s, introduced the high breast-wheel to replace the overshot type.[14]) Quite suddenly, British industry had at its disposal a power source much cheaper than any it had known, and (for the time being) in adequate supply: it could now provide its large mechanised factories with power, while (with the new roads and waterways) it moved their products out, and their inputs in.

All this – both the provision and the use of water power – presupposed a quite advanced engineering industry, and this Britain had. What Smeaton did for power, the Darbys at Ironbridge did for engineering's basic material, iron: they smelted it from coke, made from coal, instead of charcoal, made from wood; their process, intended originally as a response to shortage, made possible larger blast-furnaces using a cheaper raw material.[15] Good cast iron was now very cheap – not simply because of the Darbys's breakthrough, but because the ironmaker could get his coal and ore, brought by water, very cheaply.

Cheap transport, cheap water power, cheap cast iron, were becoming widely available in the 1770s, and could serve, at a pinch, as the 'cheapened factors of production', of a new, mechanised-factory technological style. This soon began to emerge, with the new leading industry, textiles, quickly adopting Arkwright's 'water frame' method of spinning. But factory production still faced two difficulties. First, machine-making was inhibited by the physical characteristics (brittleness, basically) of coke-smelted cast iron. Steel, which was not brittle, was still extremely expensive, even after Benjamin Huntsman's development of crucible steel in the 1740s. Henry Cort, in the early 1780s, dealt with this problem, by the 'puddling and rolling' of coke-smelted pig-iron into much more tensile *wrought iron*.[16] The diffusion of Cort's was remarkably fast, as suggested by Figure 2.3. Second, if industry depended on water power, it had to spread out, going where that power was. Fortunately, an alternative to water was becoming available. The decade before, Watt had developed a steam-engine which was much more economical of coal than Newcomen's.[17] It was now possible for the branches of industry which particularly valued the 'external economies' of clustering together in large conurbations, to do so without foregoing cheap power. We should not, however, give Watt too much of the credit for this. A large proportion of the steam-engines installed in Lancashire industry, until the end of the century, were of the relatively primitive Newcomen and Savery types (Watt's patents kept his engines in short supply, and many were taken by the mines of Cornwall, where coal was

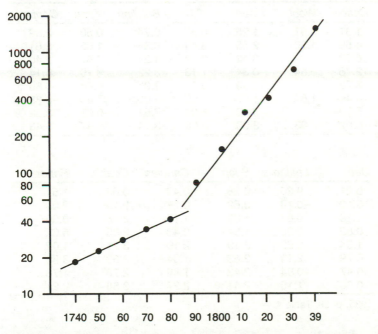

Figure 2.3 Pig iron production (thousands of tons) in England, 1740–1839
Source: Schubert, H. R. (1958) 'Extraction and production of iron and steel', in *A History of Technology*, ed. Charles Singer *et al.*, vol. IV, *The Industrial Revolution, 1750–1850*, Oxford: The Clarendon Press, p. 107.

dear).[18] What was crucial in Lancashire (besides cast and wrought iron, to make the engines) was the availability of cheap coal, brought by water from local pits. Manchester and Birmingham, the twin cradles of the Industrial Revolution in general and the engineering industry in particular, make the importance of water transport very clear – how, without the inland waterways, would they have got either their coal or their food?[19]

Thus, around 1785, we can say the water style took shape, technically; and by the same date the organisational requirements – the development of hierarchical factory management, and the attitudes to match – had, more or less, been met. (One early writer argued that the invention of the water frame was less remarkable than Arkwright's other achievement – 'to devise and administer a successful code of factory discipline'.[20]) In the 1780s and 1790s the two 'leading sectors', cotton textiles and engineering, expanded with great speed (see Table 2.2 and Figure 2.4). The growth rate of industry and commerce overall, also quickened (Table 2.3).

Table 2.2 Sectoral growth rates of real output in British industry 1700–1831 (per cent per annum)

	Cotton	Wool	Linen	Silk	Building	Iron	Copper
1700–60	1.37	0.97	1.25	0.67	0.74	0.60	2.62
1760–70	4.59	1.30	2.68	3.40	0.34	1.65	5.61
1770–80	6.20		3.42	−0.03	4.24	4.47	2.40
1780–90	12.76	0.54	−0.34	1.13	3.22	3.79	4.14
1790–1801	6.73		0.00	−0.67	2.01	6.48	−0.85
1801–11	4.49	1.64	1.07	1.65	2.05	7.45	−0.88
1811–21	5.59		3.40	6.04	3.61	−0.28	3.22
1821–31	6.82	2.03	3.03	6.08	3.14	6.47	3.43

	Beer	Leather	Soap	Candles	Coal	Paper
1700–60	0.21	0.25	0.28	0.49	0.64	1.51
1760–70	−0.10	−0.10	0.62	0.71	2.19	2.09
1770–80	1.10	0.82	1.32	1.15	2.48	0.00
1780–90	0.82	0.95	1.34	0.43	2.36	5.62
1790–1801	1.54	0.63	2.19	2.19	3.21	1.02
1801–11	0.79	2.13	2.63	1.34	2.53	3.34
1811–21	−0.47	−0.94	2.42	1.80	2.76	1.73
1821–31	0.66	1.15	2.41	2.27	3.68	2.21

Source: Berg, 1985, p. 28, Table 4

Table 2.3 Estimates of growth in British industry and commerce (per cent per annum), 1700–1831

	Deane and Cole	Crafts
1700–60	0.98	0.70
1760–80	0.49	1.05
1780–1801	3.43	1.81
1801–31	3.97	2.71

Source: Berg, 1985, p. 28, Table 3

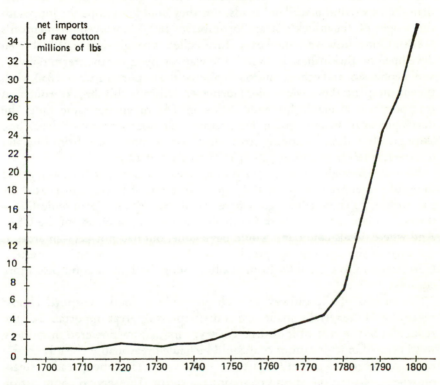

Figure 2.4 Raw cotton used in the British textile industry during the eighteenth century
Source: Pacey (1974), p. 217
Note: Figures are ten-year moving point averages

THE STEAM TRANSPORT STYLE

As we shall see, most of Britain's neighbours and rivals found it extremely difficult to adopt her new style, largely because of its exacting geographical requirements. If you did not have abundant water power and/or coal cheek by jowl with your existing waterways, you must dig until you had; and canals were expensive, in hilly country fearfully so. Not all rivers were suitable, either – they might, like most in the USA, be too fast-flowing for sail and too shallow by the bank for horse-and-towpath.[21] The Americans solved this particular problem for themselves, in the late 1820s, with the paddle-steamer,[22] but the general problem of inadequate transport systems was left to the British, with their incomparable engineering industry, to deal with. They too found the capital costs of extending their canal network too high, and increasingly resorted instead to 'stretching' it with 'tramways' – railways of one sort or another carrying horse-drawn wagons.[23] These railways, made of cast iron, could stand a much greater volume of traffic than the new 'Sand macadam' roads, but they could not cope for long with the weight of Trevithick's steam locomotive (1805), nor even Stephenson's (1818). Once, however, the heavy-duty rolled wrought-iron rail had been developed by Birkinshaw in 1821,[24] the way lay open for the steam railway, and Stephenson and others quickly exploited the opportunity: by 1830, with the opening of the Liverpool–Manchester railway, this breakthrough in transport was available for wide diffusion. (At much the same time, the development of steamships, and the remarkable improvement of the sailing ship, greatly reduced shipping costs: thus (for example) fares from England to America fell from about £20 in 1825 to around £3 in 1852.[25])

Railways brought about a drastic reduction in the cost (in money and time) of passenger transport, and a *generalisation* of lower transport costs for freight.[26] They could go where canals could not (economically) – through upland France, South Germany and the Appalachians of the USA. And where canals could and would have gone, but had not yet – in areas at the edge of the developing core, like the American Mid-West and Eastern Germany – railways could, from the beginning, be built a good deal more cheaply.

The arrival of the railway as a cheap mode of land transport, almost regardless of the terrain, made two contributions of great importance to the reduction of the cost of industrial energy. First, steam-powered machinery was liberated in its location: coal could be hauled reasonably cheaply to any railhead, to provide power for factories of any size. Thus the spread of steam on wheels assisted the spread of stationary steam. The second contribution was more paradoxical: steam on wheels also encouraged the use of water power. For the great inhibitor of the spread of the water style, in France and elsewhere, was the concentration of really suitable sites for water power in remote areas, upland and otherwise; only when the railway made transport to and from these sites cheaper, could they be used competitively. There is no doubt that at the right site, thanks to the continuing improvements of technique (notably Fourneyron's invention of the water turbine in the late 1820s)[27] water power remained highly competitive with steam. Chapman found that even in Britain, where steam was most familiar and the price of coal low, water power was cheaper, as late as 1840, for a 100 to 110 horsepower cotton mill, even when it required relatively extensive auxiliary works (dam and reservoir systems).[28] In France and much of the United States, where there were excellent sites for water power and coal was distant, water power was decisively cheaper at this stage. In the United States:

> Although steam power was used widely in manufacturing by 1870, most of its uses were concentrated in a few industries and it provided the main power for almost none. The direct costs of steam power were higher than the costs for water power, and industries used steam only when the freedom of location gained by using steam was large. In other words, in the years before it became important as a supplier of land transportation, the steam engine functioned as a *substitute* for such transportation, allowing power to be brought to the raw materials when it was expensive to bring the materials to waterpower sites.[29]

Of course, after 1840 the arrival of the railway soon made it a great deal less expensive to bring the materials to water-power sites. As late as 1870 there were still more water-wheels than steam-engines in US manufacturing, and they produced only slightly less horsepower in total (48.2 per cent to 51.8 per cent).[30] In France, where coal was more expensive than the United States, water power remained dominant even longer: in 1856 Alexandre Moreau de Jonnes found that of 734 cotton-spinning mills in France, 478 used water power, 244 steam, with a few using both.[31] The industrial census of 1861–5 showed that steam now led in the textile industry, as in mining, metallurgy and metal-working; but overall, water power led steam by a margin of two to one.[32] Elsewhere in Europe the picture was similar.[33]

Thus the coming of the new style did not involve any clear cut or sudden shift in the source of power for industry. The manufacturer took his pick between steam and water, as he had come to do already; but whereas before the railway his choice was constrained by the availability of water transport, the railway freed him from locational slavery (to a degree: there could not be railheads everywhere; complete freedom had to wait for the motorisation of road transport). There could now be better use made both of water power and steam. One of the greatest gains was the freedom, henceforth, for industry of whatever type to concentrate in large urban areas, regardless of the availability of water power or transport, and enjoy the 'external economies' of being near to a whole range of suppliers and customers.

We have, then, again satisfied our basic requirements for a new technological style; the drastic cheapening of one or more key factors of production. Transport became much cheaper, particularly by land; and while the cost of water power at a given site, and steam power next to a coal mine, both continued to decline steadily, the revolution in transport made the effective cost of industrial energy fall precipitously.

There was another technological revolution which although a little later was a great deal easier and cheaper to implement than the railway, and so diffused alongside it: the electric telegraph. This innovation in communications came as a neat complement to the innovations in transport: following some fundamental advances in the production and use of electricity, Henry in the US (1831), Gauss and Weber in Germany (1833) and Cooke and Wheatstone in England (1837) produced successively more effective telegraph systems, and rapid diffusion was proceeding by the mid-1840s.[34]

On the story so far

It is, it seems to me, very hard to deny the first two technological styles. Of course, technical progress was continuous, but nonetheless there were two rather short periods, which I would set at the first half of the 1780s and the end of the 1820s, when, quite suddenly, one country, Britain, completed a new technological 'package' which had the potential to transform its own, and others', economy. (Note however that the first style was hard for many countries to copy, and the value to Britain of the second was reduced by its huge investment in the first.) Here then is a long wave rhythm in one important area. To explain the length of the 'technological long wave' at this stage – the interval between styles – is more difficult. There was a certain number of steps which had to be taken, and they took the time they took. The wide diffusion of some advances which were part of the water style – like the use of wrought iron – made possible others which were preconditions of the steam transport style – like the rolling of the wrought-iron rail. On the other hand, there were features of the water style – like the canal – whose wide diffusion made people increasingly aware of their limitations, and thus drove them to substitutes, like the tramway, which prepared the way for the next style. Likewise, the growth of canal, road and tramway transport together implied an alarming growth in demand for horses and their fodder, which only the use of steam-powered transport could check. In one case diffusion increases the capacity, in the other it increases the desire, for technical change. It may be, too, that there is a generational effect; the generation who grow up with a technological style are better able than their parents – who introduced it – to see how to go one better. The challenge, later, will be to explain the relative length of the subsequent intervals between technological styles.

THE STEEL AND ELECTRICITY STYLE

The third technological style was unlike both its predecessors in two, related, ways: it was a composite, of two elements which were not very closely linked; and it was brought to birth in not one country but at least three.

What underlay the first element of the new style was the development of cheap steel, pioneered in Britain.[35] The great British engineering industry was increasingly frustrated by the materials available to it. Cast iron was made brittle by its impurities; wrought iron, less brittle, was a composite material, with an iron saved from its inadequacies by fibres of its own glassy slag.[36] Steel was far better, but hopelessly expensive for bulk use.[37] As knowledge of metallurgy improved, it became clear that this was unnecessary: steel was only pig-iron with some of the carbon burnt off and other impurities reduced. In 1854 Henry Bessemer accordingly made the first breakthrough, with his 'converter', in which air was bubbled through molten pig-iron: the process was wonderfully cheap, because it was very quick, and because the burning of the surplus carbon provided the heat required. It quickly became clear that Bessemer steel was excellent for rails, outlasting wrought iron (in tests in England) by six to one, and making higher speeds possible. For other engineering purposes, however, it was deficient; moreover, it required low phosphorus ore – which was available to the British in Cumbria and from Spain and Sweden, but was less easily obtained by their main rivals in the United States, Germany and France. The first problem was solved after the appearance in the following decade of the Siemens-Martin open-hearth process – a slower process, less economical in fuel but more easily controlled and capable of using cheap scrap, which was soon developed to produce steel as high in quality as the crucible type. The problem of phosphorus, however, remained until 1878–9, when Gilchrist and Thomas perfected a method of removing it from the open hearth with a basic (alkaline) flux. From that point on – as the German steel-makers immediately saw – anyone with cheap ore and coking coal could produce cheap steel.[38] Over the same period there was an impressive cheapening of steel's main raw material, pig-iron, as the blast furnaces in which it was made were improved: 'The twenty years from 1856 to 1875 saw the swiftest advances in blast furnace construction and practice since the introduction of coke smelting'.[39]

The fall in the price of steel was spectacular. In 1850 the cheapest Swedish steel cost £50–£60 per ton, and the high quality crucible steel was a good deal more expensive. Wrought iron cost about £4 per ton. By the late 1850s Bessemer steel was available in England at £7 per ton – £1 of that, the royalty.[40] But it took a long time for the process to diffuse, and for the technology of working the new steel, to be mastered. Thus in the first bulk use of Bessemer steel, for rails, their price was still, in 1864, £17 10s per ton, against £7 for ordinary wrought iron piled rails.[41] By 1879, however, steel rails were down to £5 2s 6d per ton, a mere whisker dearer than wrought iron, at £4 18s 3d.[42] Steel took longer to be accepted in shipbuilding (the steel era here is dated from the launch of HMS *Iris* in 1877[43]), and in 1881 it still outpriced wrought iron by £11 per ton against £7 15s, for plates; ten years later the gap was minimal, at £6 10s against £6. Abroad, the fall in prices came later and was even more remarkable: in the United States, for example, the price of Bessemer rails dropped from $106.75 per gross ton in 1870 to $48.25 in 1878 (and $29.83 ten years later).[44]

Cheap steel unchained the engineering industry. Much iron- or steel-intensive equipment which had already been developed, became much cheaper to make and/or better made than before; and the incentive to develop new steel-intensive equipment greatly increased. Thus the highly-efficient triple-expansion steam engine was introduced in 1874, but did not spread until the 1880s, when high quality open-hearth steel plate became available which could withstand its high boiler pressures: by the end of the century it was standard for big plant.[45] Cheap steel must have played a large part in the increasing popularity of the steam-engine, of various types, which finally after 1870 got the better of water power almost everywhere;[46] thus by 1911 it provided 73 per cent of primary power even in France.[47] Likewise, the great age of railway construction, in terms of mileage, came after 1870, almost everywhere outside Britain.[48]

Electricity

It is tempting to treat cheap steel as *the* key factor of production of the new style, as Perez suggests.[49] But there were, after 1870, two sectors, the electrical and the chemicals industries, which were intensely innovative, played a most important part in economic growth, and yet do not seem to fit into a (mere) 'steel style'. They were not *motive* branches for it, providing vital inputs to steel and engineering; nor could they be described as carrier branches for a steel style, for although chemical and electrical engineering naturally used steel, the sectors as a whole were not steel-intensive. Chemicals can, at a pinch, be given the status of an 'induced' branch, since most of its output was for the textiles industry, still fast-growing thanks to rising incomes. The electrical industries, however, made up a new, relatively self-contained network in the economy – going from capital goods like generating equipment to consumer goods like telephones and light bulbs – which grew extremely fast. There is, moreover, no difficulty in finding the new cheap factor of production on which their growth was based: electricity, of course.[50]

Modern electricity generation can be traced back at least as far as the work of Faraday on electromagnetic induction in 1831. By 1858 it had progressed far enough, together with arc lighting, for trials on its use in lighthouses. A succession of improvements during the 1860s brought the cost down rapidly, and when the Belgian inventor Gramme's ring dynamo became generally available in the early 1870s, general purpose arc lighting became economically feasible.[51] In 1873 Gramme exhibited the first electric motor of commercial significance. Soon afterwards, in 1876, Bell in the United States patented the telephone; between 1878 and 1880 Swan in England and Edison in the US invented incandescent filament lamps; and Siemens and Halske in Germany constructed the first public electric railway in Germany in 1881. The following year the first power station for private consumers was opened in London.[52]

The steel and electricity style: overview

Looking back at the narrative, we cannot point to one, more-or-less coherent, technological 'package' appearing in a particular place. By the end of the 1870s there was, if not one coherent 'package', then a pair of two compatible packages, available for adoption. The British made their contribution, mainly in the making and use of steel; the Germans, Americans and others made theirs, mainly in the making and use of electricity.

It may at first sight seem odd that the different elements of the new style appeared, 'crystallised', at about the same time, during the 1870s; but this can be explained by their common root – the response to the diffusion of the old style. As I argued, on the development of the steam transport style out of the water style, each new style generates new needs and new opportunities. The need for cheap steel was much increased by the expansion of engineering. The opportunity for advance, in steel-making and in the making and use of electricity, was enormously improved by the expansion of scientific education and the use of science for industrial purposes – which was due in large measure to the appearance and diffusion of the steam transport style, as we shall see below.

The transition to the Fordist style

The changing character of the engineering industry is the key to understanding much of the qualitative differences between the steel-and-electricity style and both its predecessor and its successor. Engineering had been growing in economic importance ever since the mid-eighteenth century. With this new style its importance grew faster than ever, but its role did not change: it was, as before, mainly a producer of capital goods, goods for the production of other goods.[53] Through the increase in the rate of growth of capital goods production, and of their productivity, engineering in the new style made possible a quickening in the growth of output and income generally.

There was, however, no fundamental change in engineering's own internal, organisational, character. The skilled worker – the 'craftsman' – in engineering was descended, literally and by tradition, from the independent craftsman, and he was still treated, within even a large works, more like a subcontractor, with authority over his own men, than the 'cog in the wheel' which his counterpart in textiles had become. Why? Textiles had long been mainly a mass production industry, and engineering was not yet one, for two reasons: markets and technology. In its nature, there is much less uniformity in the market for capital goods than for consumer goods – for each capital good there is a multitude of consumer goods – and far more demand for quality, since if one capital good is deficient that multitude of consumer goods is lost or spoiled. But even where the market demanded mass production,[54] there was a technological problem. Mass production required interchangeable parts – parts produced with a high degree of uniformity so that a_1, b_1 and c_1 will fit together in just the same way as a_2, b_2 and c_2... This was obvious, and by 1800 Eli Whitney was producing muskets with interchangeable parts.[55] But Whitney's materials were mainly wrought iron and wood. To make machine tools that would cut uniform parts out of steel was a far harder matter. It was only in the 1880s that the open hearth steel-makers achieved steels of a quality and a consistency really adequate to the task.[56]

It is now clear what the next style would do. With machine tools from the new steel, it would turn engineering into a mass production industry; and the main market for that mass production would be the consumer. The steel-and-science style would have provided the consumer products – the automobile, and 'white goods' like the refrigerator – and at the same time, by raising income levels, it would have created a class of consumer able to afford them. The mass market for 'consumer durables' (the term implies that products like Chippendale chairs and tweed suits are 'consumer *perishables*', by contrast!) was reached in the United States long before Europe, for by the 1880s the US was richer per head even than Britain, with a larger population, and a much more homogeneous middle/upper class, and the advantage in size and affluence grew rapidly.

But to seize the opportunity, the power of the skilled craftsman had to be broken. In the 1890s F. W. Taylor, in Bethlehem Steel, showed the way, subordinating craftsmen and their underlings to a planning department staffed by engineers which allocated tasks to semi-skilled workers with a much more specialised division of labour.[57] The task for the engineering firms which followed Taylor's lead was to assign semi-skilled workers each to a 'dedicated' machine tool performing one narrowly-defined operation, and then to arrange the movement of components (in a complex chain of operations) smoothly between them.

The *idea* of the assembly line was obvious enough – the chemicals industry already used sophisticated flow processes, and the Armour Corporation in its Chicago slaughterhouses had by mid-century installed overhead lines carrying carcasses – dis-assembly lines, so to speak. But machine tools needed more than muscle-power. The traditional large steam-engine providing a central source of power was too inflexible for an engineering factory: electric motors, not needing a chimney apiece, were the obvious alternative which the steel-and-electricity style provided. Early in the new century small ones became available, cheaply (they were one capital good which could itself be mass-produced). Meanwhile another type of motor – the internal combustion engine, running on a derivative of petroleum, had been developed which could move the vehicles which were the most important product of the assembly line.

THE FORDIST STYLE

By the early 1900s there existed, in the USA, all the preconditions for the new technological style. There was the affluent mass market, the Taylorist pattern of work organisation, the capacity to produce the appropriate machine tools and motors. There were also the cheap petroleum products required to run the motor vehicles,[58] and electricity – not only cheaply produced now, but available, through the distribution *grid*, where it was needed, to run the motors and 'white goods'. It was time for the crystallisation of the 'Fordist' technological style, which we can date rather precisely, if we like, to the year 1915, when Henry Ford opened his first assembly-line plant. The personalisation of the style – in which I am only following Aglietta, Perez and others – is reasonable enough: Ford was not only the pioneer of the key technological systems of the new age, but the main producer of the key consumer durable, the automobile. As Landes puts it,

> The motor car industry was begining to play ... (by the end of the interwar period) a role analogous to that the railroad in the mid-nineteenth century: it was a huge consumer of semi-finished and finished intermediate products ... and components ... it had an insatiable appetite for fuel and other petroleum pιoducts; it required a small army of mechanics and service men to keep it going; and it gave powerful impetus to investments in social and overhead capital (roads, bridges, tunnels). At the same time, it posed new technical problems in metallurgy, organic chemicals, and electrical engineering, eliciting solutions that had important consequences for other industries as well.[59]

It was, in short, a classic 'carrier branch'. As for the 'motive branches', improvements in electricity generation led to a fall in the average price of electricity in the USA, between 1902 and 1928, of 41 per cent (31 per cent in constant terms).[60] The price of oil fell: from a peak average of $2.00 per barrel during the 1915–20 period, it dropped to an average of $1.35 per barrel, 1931–5.[61] Advances in refining techniques brought the cost of petroleum *products* down a good deal faster. These advances, of course, belonged to the chemicals industry, of which oil-refining ('petrochemicals') had become a branch. The fundamental advance which diffused through chemicals and analogous industries, as the assembly line diffused through engineering, was continuous flow – not along conveyor belts, but through pipes.

The separation of spheres in Fordist production

There are three functions which someone in manufacturing industry has to perform. There is the actual process of manufacture, the physical turning of inputs into outputs; there is 'design', using the term very broadly to include the whole process of generating new and improved products and processes; and finally there is 'co-ordination' – management, again broadly defined. One effect of 'Taylorism' was to take much further than previously, the separation of these functions in practice. The small firm at the beginning of the Industrial Revolution had had little 'design' to do, because technology changed slowly, and little 'co-ordination', because it was small, and both, such as they were, were at least partly the responsibility of skilled workers who were involved in the process of manufacture. Now they were distinct *spheres*, in Kaplinsky's words, and increasingly important ones (see Figure 2.5). The larger firms became – and they grew fast under Fordism – the more 'co-ordination' was required; the faster technology and products changed – and the pace of change was steadily accelerating – the more 'design' was required. There had always been a tendency, in the 'steel-and-science' style, for the scientists and engineers involved in the development of new products and processes to be drawn into the day-to-day problems of production. General Electric and Bell Telephone, in the USA, solved this problem in the 1900s by adopting the system pioneered by the German chemicals industry, of separate research and development laboratories, and this was widely copied in the United States in the 1920s – we can call it part of Fordism.[62] There was little in Fordist technology, once the typewriter and the telephone had been exploited, to raise labour productivity in either sphere, design or co-ordination, so that their share of the labour force, within manufacturing industry, steadily increased.

The limits of Fordism

Fordism – as improved over forty years – offered a marvellously efficient system of mass production. The 'dedicated' machine tool and other machines could be made to require less and less labour and produce at higher and higher rates, perfecting the 'transformation mechanisation' which had begun with the water wheel. Transformation mechanisation, according to Coombs (1983) is only the first stage, the second being *transfer* mechanisation, the mechanical moving of materials between different stages of transformation; well, Fordism, with the assembly line among other systems, had that too. What it still largely lacked was Coombs's third stage, *control* mechanisation: the substitution of machines for the human brain in the direction and supervision of the productive process. That lack becomes apparent in the increasing share of non-manual workers in the labour force of the mass-production industries, and in the relatively slow rate of increase

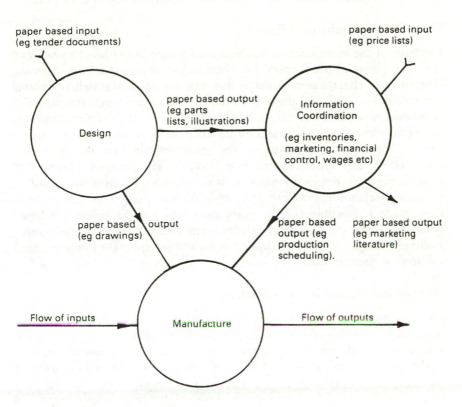

Figure 2.5 Fordist organisation of factory production
Source: Kaplinsky (1984) p. 24

of productivity in burgeoning service industries, like banking. It was also reflected in the difficulties of mechanising those engineering industries, mostly making capital goods, which were limited in volume to *batch* rather than mass production. (In the USA Lund *et al.* (1977) found that over 75 per cent of all metal-working firms were engaged in small batch production, and according to Ayres and Miller (1983) between 50 and 75 per cent of the dollar value of all 'durable' manufactured goods were batch produced.) Finally, it helped to explain the high *energy-intensity* of Fordist technology, which tended, instead of the subtleties of the human brain and hand, to resort to brute mechanical force, and crude on-off choices. What was needed, for control mechanisation, was *machine intelligence*: and that was what the next style produced.

THE MICROELECTRONICS AND BIOTECHNOLOGY STYLE

The microelectronics paradigm

The basis of the emergence of machine intelligence in the last 30 years as a new 'key factor of production' has been technical progress in electronics. The transistor effect was invented by Bardeen and Brattain at Bell Telephone Laboratories in 1947, and after a brief pause this breakthrough was followed by a brilliant sequence of advances, almost all in the United States (which, having the richest consumers and by far the richest armed forces, was doing most of the electronics research). The most notable were the integrated circuit (1961) and the microprocessor (1971).[63] The common currency of these devices, as Kaplinsky puts it, was interrupted electricity, used in increasingly elaborate (and cheap) systems of binary logic (off/on, yes/no). They made it possible for the computers which were being developed already, to be far cheaper, more reliable – and small. With microelectronics, machine intelligence could be applied to each of the spheres of production. I will look at them in turn.

Machine intelligence in co-ordination

Co-ordination involves information: its gathering, storage, manipulation, presentation and transmission. *Manipulation* by machine intelligence (otherwise known as electronic data processing) involves the computer (or, on a smaller scale, the calculator). 'Mainframe' computers were initially used, in the 1950s, in such roles as payroll calculations and stock control, but they were expensive and did not save much labour, at that time, largely because of the primitive methods of information gathering and storage – transcription of data written on paper, on to coding sheets, which were then punched on to computer cards. As manipulation improved – as computers became smaller, cheaper, more reliable and quicker – so information gathering and storage began to make use of microelectronics, so that information could proceed to manipulation without intervening coding and punching. It has, since about the early 1970s, been possible to enter information directly into microelectronic storage networks by humans using computer terminals; in many cases, indeed, it goes in directly from machine to machine, for example, in feedback-control systems in power plants and furnaces. (The next stage is to enter data by voice.) *Presentation* has traditionally been on paper; here the VDU – visual display unit – is the microelectronic contribution, which matches the computer; it is also an essential element of the word processor. More durable presentation is by printer and photocopier, which are now coming to be based on electronic components. *Transmission* is still something of an obstacle: the conventional cable is universally available (in the telephone network) but is woefully limited in its capacity; microwave transmission, for example via satellite, is available, but is still expensive and restricted compared to fibre optics, which is potentially 'the answer' but requires huge 'infrastructural' investment (see below).[64] As a result the linkage of different elements of microelectronic co-ordination – at a distance – is still restricted; but the restrictions are dwindling.[65]

Machine intelligence in design

The early development of the (pre-electronic) computer in the 1940s was stimulated by the need to make the design of shell trajectories more accurate, and in the 1960s computer technology was increasingly applied in the design sphere. The breakthrough to the wide use of what is called computer-aided design (CAD) only took place in the early 1970s, when five recent developments were combined:

(a) The microprocessor, from which microcomputers were produced, which were cheap enough to be scattered around firms. The designer could thus get a microcomputer's undivided attention, and receive an immediate answer to his questions; it could thus be used 'interactively';
(b) 'Virtual memory' techniques, which allowed large CAD programs (in effect the computer's instructions) to be stored in small computers.
(c) 'Structural programming', which allowed these 'instruction packages' to be written relatively cheaply and quickly;
(d) The visual display unit (VDU) (see above); this had just been much improved by the development of low cost 'storage tubes'.
(e) The digitising board – which converted drawings into a form suitable for treatment by binary logic, which could then appear on a VDU.

It was now possible to package CAD know-how into 'turnkey systems', which the 'naïve' user could buy 'off the shelf'. This was duly done, by the 'turnkey vendors' who sprang up. Having started in the defence/aerospace sector, and beginning to spread in the late 1960s to electronics and the motor industry, CAD was by the late 1970s spreading explosively to other sectors (Figure 2.6).[66]

Machine intelligence in manufacture

Not surprisingly, the first application of machine intelligence in the manufacturing sphere was to overcome the restriction of the dedicated machine tool to mass production engineering. General purpose machine tools used by skilled workers were not sufficiently accurate, and it was this which (inevitably in the aerospace industry, and for military requirements) led to the development of *numerically controlled* (NC) machine tools in which instructions were given to the machine via binary logic systems. Work began (at the Massachusetts Institute of Technology) in 1949, financed by the US Department of Defense, and NC machine tools were in use in the US

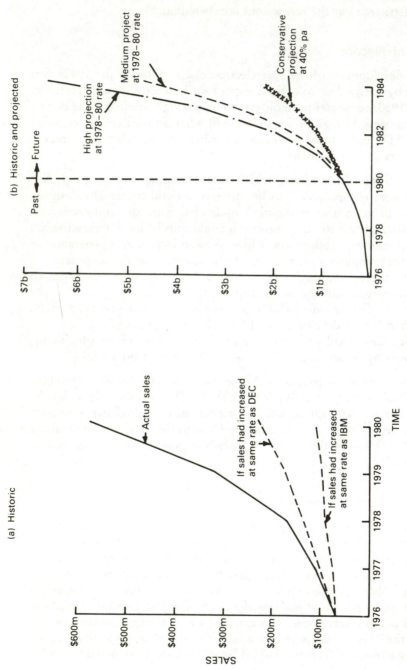

Figure 2.6 Sales of US CAD turnkey vendors – past and projected
Source: Kaplinsky (1984) p. 48
Note: 1976–80 annual rate of 69.3 per cent
1978–80 annual rate of 84.6 per cent

(a) Historic

SALES

$600m
$500m
$400m
$300m
$200m
$100m

1976   1977   1978   1979   1980
TIME

Actual sales

If sales had increased at same rate as DEC

If sales had increased at same rate as IBM

(b) Historic and projected

$7b
$6b
$5b
$4b
$3b
$2b
$1b

1976   1978   1980   1982   1984

Past ← → Future

High projection at 1978–80 rate

Medium project at 1978–80 rate

Conservative projection at 40% pa

aerospace industry in the 1950s. What worked for machine tools clearly had wider applications – to robots, for example. But numerical control as first introduced was inflexible. In the early 1970s computer numerical control (CNC) was introduced, based on the introduction of the microprocessor and the development of minicomputers. CNC was flexible: CNC machine tools could have their instructions changed so as to perform different tasks, and the 'lead-time' involved in the changes steadily dropped. Batch producers could now drastically increase their mechanisation and decrease their labour costs (as well as improve quality); existing mass producers could increase the variety of their products – without proliferation of plant. But one major obstacle to the use of machine intelligence in manufacturing still remained: the lack of suitable *sensing* technologies, which could provide the information the robot or machine tool or other element of an automated system required, before it could go into action.

In the late 1970s two crucial breakthroughs were made, namely the mass production of low-cost sensors for automative control and the linking-up of sensors to microprocessors. The resultant growth of the industry was phenomenal; the market in the US alone in 1981 for 5 million sensors exceeded the total sum of world demand for all sensors in all the preceding years.[67]

It is now, in most types of manufacturing, possible not only to automate the different operations individually, but (in principle) to link them up in the *flexible manufacturing system* (FMS). With FMS, flexible transfer lines direct work in progress automatically to machines which transform or assemble components; these machines use direct numerical control (DNC) in which individual numerically-controlled machines are controlled by a central computer or a hierarchy of computers.[68]

The microelectronics paradigm: an overview

What I have been describing is a process in which machine intelligence was applied, ever more skilfully and cheaply, to more and more individual activities within each 'sphere': what Kaplinsky calls *intra-activity auto-mation*. One can, however, go a step further, and link these up in *intra-sphere* automation: the potential gains from this are much greater than those from the more restricted kind. For example, looking at only one type of gain, extra output due to reduced 'machine downtime', Ayres and Miller (1983) reckoned the increase from introducing robots in US metalworking plants as 11 per cent for mass production, 14 per cent for mid-volume, and 16 per cent for low-volume plants; for introducing intra-sphere automation, the increase in output would be 39 per cent, 55 per cent and 52 per cent respectively. Given that the 'co-ordination sphere' and, to a slightly lesser extent, the 'design sphere', are *based* on information processing, these other spheres can benefit even more than the sphere of manufacture from intra-sphere automation. Even this is not the last step on the road: the goal, which in some sectors is clearly in sight, is full *inter*-sphere automation, as in a new General Electric locomotive plant:

> Starting at the beginning, the design output of the engineering department will be passed on to the manufacturing engineers in electronic form, rather than as drawings, and will then move through materials control, which will automatically schedule and order materials and keep track of stock and production flows. All this information will come together in the factory in the host computer, which will contain in its memory details about how, when and what to produce. This in turn will send instructions to the computer-controlled equipment, such as numerically controlled machines and robots, which will actually do the job. Quality controls, financial data, and customer service records will also be plugged into the same system.[69]

Perez sums up the emerging paradigm as 'the flexible batch production network where all activities ... are integrated in a total information-intensive system to turn out information-intensive products'.[70] To talk of batch production, however, suggests the new paradigm is restricted to manufacturing, while of course it is at least as relevant to service industries: in banking and insurance, for example, it is already very obviously being put to work, while in health and education – both huge and growing employers – its potential has so far only been glimpsed.

About when should we say the microelectronics paradigm crystallised? When was there established 'a new best productive common sense which strives to get maximum advantage of the key factor, across wide families of related or apparently unrelated technologies?'[71] It seems to me from the above account that it was in the late 1970s that the wide relevance and huge potential of microelectronics became apparent, even if there was as yet no example of 'inter-sphere automation' to look to.

The biotechnology paradigm

I have been at pains not to talk about a microelectronics style, rather a paradigm or pattern, and I can now explain why. We can only have one new 'style' at a time, according to Perez's rules, whereas I propose we allow ourselves more than one paradigm, or pattern. We shall have to, because there is another one newly crystallised, which is a complement to microelectronics, as 'electricity' was to 'steel' a century earlier: biotechnology. In fact we should really refer to 'new biotechnology' since 'the technological application of biological science' has been going on for a long time – since the Stone Age, if you count selective breeding and fermentation. The breakthrough, in the early 1970s, was the introduction of genetic engineering into this activity – 'techniques for the manipulation, alteration and synthesis of the genetic material in cells in such a way that the functioning of the cell is modified'.[72]

This sudden development can be dated to 1973, when Boyer and Cohen first used restriction enzymes to cut out, and reinsert, segments of the DNA chain; it combined with more gradual advances in four other areas:

(i) cell chemistry, particularly to do with understanding the role of DNA;
(ii) microbiological techniques for screening, selecting and cultivating cells and micro-organisms;
(iii) techniques for the culture of plant cells and tissues, and their application to crop cultivation;
(iv) development of chemical engineering techniques, for handling fermentation, and extracting, treating and purifying the products of it.[73]

Only the last is clearly linked with the microelectronics paradigm, for it uses new sensors, combined with microelectronic controls.

Clearly we have here a development in biology comparable to that in physics, chemistry and engineering a century earlier: just as those disciplines became available then to transform important areas of technology, so biology has become available now. The biotechnology paradigm has much more limited relevance to manufacturing than microelectronics has – so far it is only being applied to any substantial extent to food and drink, and to chemicals and pharmaceuticals – and more limited still in services, for example to health, and waste-management and pollution control. It is, on the other hand, enormously important for agriculture and other 'primary' industries. The primary sector is a small and declining employer in the developed world; but in the Third World, where most of the human race lives, it is the most important, and likely to remain so for a long time. Since it is the *world* economy with which we are concerned, we have to give biotechnology equal importance with microelectronics, and speak of a new *microelectronics and biotechnology style*.

CHANGES IN ORGANISATION

As we shall see later, one of the principal obstacles to the diffusion of the microelectronics and biotechnology style is that it demands methods of organisation, and attitudes within organisations, which are decidedly different from those typical of the previous style. This has generally, but not always, been true. The water style, as we have already seen, required a new structure of discipline and supervision; the steam transport style, on the other hand, required little if any change from the water style's arrangement of relationships within the factory. With the larger and more complex firms of the steel-and-electricity style, however, it was necessary to introduce the distinction between line and staff functions which had been pioneered by the

American railway companies:[74] there was one hierarchy of control for 'line' or production management, and others for 'staff' functions like marketing, purchasing, etc.

Fordist mass production, as we have already seen, involved the 'Taylorisation' of arrangements within the engineering factory – a big change for engineering, but not dramatic by comparison with what had long been the norm in (say) textiles. There is another change, higher up in the firm, which is associated with Fordism: the shift from the U-form or unitary firm to the M-form or multidivisional firm. The M-form is (even now) only used for large, diversified companies, and was introduced by Du Pont and General Motors in the USA in the 1920s: it involves the breaking up of firms into a number of divisions, each with its own board and its own functional departments (marketing, finance, production, etc.), which in their day-to-day operations are independent of Head Office and the main board of directors, but are controlled by them on the basis of financial targets and reporting of performance.

The development of the multidivisional firm can be seen as a way of improving the efficiency of management, but equally it can be seen as a method of ensuring management's obedience to the wishes of the owners, the shareholders.[75] From this point of view, it is a step in the evolution of the relationship between managers and the owners of the capital they use. That relationship, as a matter of any complexity, goes back to the development of the joint stock company, which in its modern form can be traced back to the 1840s. Note that date: it follows the crystallisation of the steam transport style, as the M-form follows that of the Fordist style. Neither was essential for the basic systems of manufacture involved: Henry Ford, for example, managed very well for a long time without anything like M-form organisation, as his British counterparts in the engineering industry of the 1840s and 1850s had done without joint stock firms. But these were *creators*, moving forward in an evolutionary way at the leading edge of technology. The *diffusion* of a style makes much greater demands on the upper structures of the organisations involved. The German and American firms, for example, which introduced the new metalmaking and metalworking technology in the 1850s and 1860s, had to be built up from virtually nothing to a large scale in a few years. Only joint stock organisation could allow the necessary capital to be raised so quickly. In fact, in Continental Europe the joint stock firm was not enough by itself, since there was no tradition of equity investment by individuals. Large 'universal' banks had to be set up at the same time, on the pattern of the Credit Mobilier (established in 1852) which would put depositors' money into loans and even equity for business. The German banks took care of their own industry, the French banks (and in due course their individual investors) exported capital to the rest of Central and Eastern Europe.[76] Later, in the international diffusion of Fordism, the M-form facilitated the export of technology as well as capital, by providing an ideal form of organisation for multinational firms; it probably helped also in the diffusion of technology between industries straddled by a diversified M-form corporation.[77]

The new style which is now diffusing demands, we can be sure, quite different organisational arrangements from those which suited Fordism. These requirements are so much bound up with the need for constant technological advance, that we shall consider them only after a discussion of how such advance has, historically, been achieved.

The use of science in innovation and diffusion

Let me first clarify the meaning of 'science', in this context: 'technical expertise with a scientific basis, i.e. systematic and rooted in theory'. For all the evidence we now have of the scientific education and interests of some of them, the British inventors and innovators of the Industrial Revolution period did not, for the most part, make progress by applying scientific knowledge.[78] It was not adequate for the purpose, and was not needed: they were familar with the existing 'state of the art', and could progress by trial and error, with some induction from experience. Their American rivals were able to draw on British experience through the skills of emigrants.[79] The Europeans found it much more difficult to get good value from British expatriates, although they had to use them;[80] accordingly, they had to make the more effort to find other means of improving their technology, and the obvious alternative was formal technical training at various levels. In France, the *Ecole Polytechnique* dates from 1794, but few of its 'engineers' went into industry. The *Ecole Centrale des Arts et Manufactures* was set up in 1829 on private initiative to remedy this. '*Polytechnische Schulen*' were set up in Prague in 1806, Vienna in 1815, Karlsruhe in 1825 and Berlin in 1827: there was a rash of other 'polytechnics' in Germany in the early 1830s of the Karlsruhe model.[81] Sweden and Switzerland were also active. The aim was well expressed in the first statutes of the technical university in Stockholm (1826): 'to collect and supply the information necessary in order to run ... crafts and industry successfully'.[82] 'Much of it, in Germany particularly, was symptomatic of a passionate desire to organise and hasten the process of catching up'.[83] But there was, at the beginning, little emphasis on putting the technical education on a systematic scientific basis. That came in Germany in the early 1840s, led by Karlsruhe and Berlin; the other continental countries soon followed. (The Germans – as now – paid particular attention to the training of technicians, in institutions like the technical trade schools.)

In the 1840s and 1850s, the products of the new technical/scientific education were few, but they still made their mark. Werner Siemens pioneered the practical applications of electricity to telegraphy and other uses; his younger brothers Karl Wilhelm and Friedrich went to England and developed open-hearth steel-making and a good deal else. Karl Wilhelm

Siemens expressed the new approach well: 'the further we advance, the more thoroughly we approach the indications of pure science in our practical results'.[84] It was in chemistry that it paid the most obvious dividends, and it was there that German research and education made the most rapid strides. Ironically it was the British who were the first to benefit industrially from German chemistry: the German Prince Albert, Queen Victoria's husband, persuaded the great German chemists Liebig and Hoffmann to teach in London, and in 1856 Hoffmann's pupil Perkin discovered the first of the aniline dyes, synthesised from coal-tar.[85] But the British got what they deserved after Albert's death in 1861, and it was around that time that the still-small German chemicals industry began to marry science with industry. By 1868 the two leading firms, BASF and Hoechst, were systematically hiring research-trained chemists to work in their laboratories, and in the 1870s it was they, followed by the electrical firms Siemens and AEG, who appear to have pioneered the research and development laboratory as an autonomous unit within the firm, isolated from the day-to-day pressures of production.[86]

It would be premature, however, to treat R&D laboratories as the main means by which science was used in industry in the late nineteenth century. It could be done by independent inventor-consultants like Karl Wilhelm Siemens, academics-turned-entrepreneurs like Perkin, or collaboration between firms and universities as in the German chemicals industry. Never mind exactly how it was used – the point was that science had become available and could help transform technology. God help those (like the British chemicals industry)[87] who did not use it in some way. Can we put a date to the perception of this point? So far as chemicals were concerned, it must have been at some time in the 1870s, when the science-based German industry was on its way from supplying a negligible proportion of the world dyestuffs market in the early 1860s to about half by 1880.

The penny seems to have dropped at about the same time in the United States. The development of scientific and technical education in the USA did not lag far behind the Continental Europeans; engineering was taught at a number of colleges from the 1840s and 1850s, and the Massachusetts Institute of Technology was set up in 1861. The following year the Morrill Land Grant Act provided funds for the teaching of 'such branches of learning as are related to agriculture and the mechanic arts' and after the Civil War such education took off.[88]

> Beginning in the period after the Civil War, academically trained engineers were hired in rather large numbers of American firms with interests in machine tools, metals fabrication, transportation, chemicals and electrical equipment. They forcefully brought the content and methods of science to industry.[89]

In 1875 the large and successful Carnegie Steel Company hired German

PhD chemist Ernst Fricke to analyze the process of steelmaking and to determine the preferred composition of ores ... Fricke found that some ores, generally considered of low quality and therefore cheaper, actually produced better iron and steel. He discovered that pig iron could be made at a lower cost by using fly ash and other waste products mixed with 'inferior' ones. Carnegie soon regretted his tardiness in resorting to chemistry and noted in his autobiography: 'What fools we had been! But then there was this consolation, we were not as great fools as our competitors'. In order to keep up with Carnegie, his competitors also turned to chemistry. As a result the industry's efficiency, consistency, and product diversity improved dramatically over the next thirty years.[90]

By the 1880s the commercial successes of (the German chemicals) firms rested predominantly on the results that issued from their labs. This was quite clear to all would-be competitors, including the Americans.[91]

The account so far shows the Americans as imitators. In one respect, however, they were at least level with the Germans, thanks to Thomas Edison.

His use of team research at his laboratories in Menlo Park (from 1876) alerted businessmen to the potential value of science in general and to the profit-generating possibilities of coordinated work by scientists and engineers in particular. Edison's entrepreneurial activities drew financiers into the business of funding research, and his success in a number of ventures demonstrated that there was money to be made in the development and control of advanced technologies... Though American myths about Edison portray him as the cut-and-try inventor with little concern for science, he actually made very good use of both historic and contemporary scientific literature in order to understand the principles of his work. He was, moreover, careful to have on his staff men trained in science and mathematics.[92]

For evidence of the effects of the new use of science we can look to Baker's series for 'significant patents', which shows a remarkable rise above trend from the 1870s to the 1890s (Figure 2.7). These innovations were particularly important in the rise of the chemicals industry – led by Germany – and the electrical industry, led by Germany and the United States;[93] they were also important in the steady development of medium and light engineering industries in all the technologically, educationally, advanced countries.[94] 'Medium' and 'light' in effect refer to the weight of steel per unit of value added. In a ship, say, there is a greater weight of steel per unit of value-added; Britain, which had cheap steel, continued to dominate shipbuilding. In dairy machinery there is a great deal less; the south of Sweden, having made the key innovations, could continue to lead that industry.[95] The automobile, in its early expensive days, was no more than light-to-medium: the French, without cheap steel but with an excellent road network and some brilliant engineers, were able to take up the running here from Germany (which had introduced the internal combustion engine in the early 1880s) and lead the European motor industry.[96]

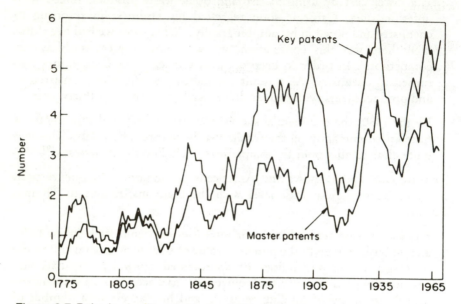

Figure 2.7 Baker's significant patents, 1775–1965, 10-year moving averages
Source: Clark, J., Freeman, C., and Soete, L., 'Long waves, inventions and innovations', in *Futures*, August 1981

Clearly there is a close association between the first systematic use of science, and the development and early diffusion of the steel-and-electricity style: a few crucial innovations in steel and electricity generation created the new cheap factors of production for the style, and as it crystallised it set off an upsurge in innovations across a wide field, as Baker's 'significant patents' show. The next upsurge in innovation, following the crystallisation of the Fordist style, is associated with the rapid diffusion in American industry of the autonomous research and development laboratory.[97] If we can look forward to another upsurge in innovation now that the microelectronics-and-biotechnology style has crystallised, it will again, presumably, be linked with a further organisational advance in the use of science in industry – and I believe that such an advance is already being made. While the last advance, making the R&D function autonomous, liberated it from the day-to-day pressures of production, so that it could take a long view, autonomy meant a degree of isolation which also had disadvantages: it is well known that firms which are successful in innovation are generally those in which R&D is closely co-ordinated with other functions.[98] In an effort to institutionalise such co-ordination, *matrix* structures of organisation have been developed, in which managers are each responsible to more than one boss in different functions. (This originated in the American space programme in the 1960s.[99]) It has however been the Japanese who have taken it furthest so far, with their concept of 'the factory as laboratory'.[100]

The evolution of trade unions

Organisation begets counter-organisation – the response of those who feel that the structures into which they have been brought are not designed and run with their interests sufficiently in mind. The response to the firm was the trade union. In order to be effective, the trade union 'counter-organisation' has to change to match changes in the firm – changes which, as we have seen, tend to be associated with a change of style. However, trade unions, like all other organisations, suffer from inertia: every radical change in firms' organisation makes the prevailing structure of unions obsolete, and it is only after a painful period of ineffectiveness and decline that they reform themselves to meet the requirements of the new style.

Let me sketch this process at work over the last century. We must bear in mind at the outset that although in some sense opposed to hierarchy, trade unions are bound to reflect it: where there is much differentiation among workers – between manual and non-manual, skilled and less-skilled, male and female – the structures of trade unionism will themselves be differentiated. We can observe this in the engineering unions of the steel-and-science style, when (with the growth in size of firms) unions first became important: it was the skilled workers who organised themselves, in the USA and UK at least, to protect their privileged position *vis-à-vis* the less skilled as well as against their employers. Such unions were in a very poor position to organise the mass-production industries, where skilled workers began with much less power and privilege (or had lost it through Taylorism): more egalitarian, inclusive unions were needed there, and in the USA it was not until such organisations appeared (with the rise of the Congress of Industrial Organisations in the 1930s) that these industries were unionised. In turn, the union structures which flourished from the 1930s to the 1950s, began to look outdated as the microelectronics style spread in the 1970s; by the 1980s trade unionism was in retreat almost everywhere in the developed world (see Chapter 6, below). Again, this reflected the obsolescence of union structures designed to cope with the rigidities of the large Fordist plant. In the new style there are fewer workers in each plant and worker initiative is at a premium, by comparison with the old mass production system; so it suits management to pay quite close attention to the feelings and grievances of individuals and work groups, and thus to undermine the appeal of the union. On the other hand, they have much more to lose than before by accepting detailed union interference in such matters as the deployment and manning of new equipment. This is not the place to argue precisely what union response is appropriate, but we may note the general principle, that it must reflect the progressive decline of *hierarchy* within the firm (and of deference outside it) with each change of style.[101]

WHY WAS THE TEMPO (FAIRLY) CONSTANT?

I identify the point of crystallisation of styles (the point at which a new technological pattern or 'package' becomes discernible which is (a) far superior to the established one, (b) relevant right across the national and international economy) as follows:

1 Water style: c. 1785;
2 Steam transport style: end of 1820s;
3 Steel-and-electricity style: late 1870s;
4 Fordist style: c. 1915;
5 Microelectronics and biotechnology style: late 1970s.

There is nothing particularly precise about these dates (the second and the fourth are more precise than the others, partly because the introduction of the steam railway and the assembly line were so important) but it would be hard to shift any of them more than five years either way; perhaps we should restate the dating, to allow for a degree of uncertainty and gradualness, as:

1: 1780–90
2: 1828–32
3: 1874–80
4: 1913–18
5: 1973–83

Taking the mid-points of these periods, we have intervals of:

1–2: 45 years
2–3: 47 years
3–4: 38–9 years
4–5: 63 years

The first point to note is that there is no sign of any general tendency for the tempo either to slow or to quicken over the last two centuries. This should not surprise us. The manpower and apparatus devoted to scientific advance have been increasing, but so has the inherent difficulty of making new advances, when the easier things have been done already, and each new worker in the field has to assimilate them first. The communications network through which new technology *diffuses* has been improving, but the space over which that network has to operate has been growing larger at the same time.

How then can we account for the irregularities in the series? *A priori* we might expect that the new style will arrive the more quickly if it crystallises in one country which was involved in the development of the previous style – and therefore has no catching up to do – and has not lost its dynamism. We might expect the process to take *longer*, other things equal, if there has been a *global war* since the crystallisation of the last style, particularly if countries involved in the development of the new style have suffered heavily in that war.

Now the sole developer of style number 4, the USA, *had* been involved in the development of the previous style, and had most certainly not lost any of its dynamism by the early twentieth century. The 1914–45 global war was only just beginning as style 4 crystallised, and could certainly not be said to have interfered with it in any way. Thus every circumstance was favourable to the rapid development of style 4; and we observe, in its case, clearly the shortest interval. Style 5, on the other hand, had everything against it: the USA had clearly lost much of its dynamism by the time it arrived, while Japan and Western Europe, which made a vital contribution to the new style, had their progress terribly interrupted by the global war. Thus the exceptionally long interval. Styles 2 and 3 are intermediate, for different reasons: 2, the steam transport style, was developed in a country, Britain, which had developed its predecessor and was still dynamic (favourable circumstances); on the other hand there had been a global war in the interim, albeit one which had not had *very* adverse effects on Britain (rather unfavourable). With style 3, steel and electricity, Britain, the developer of its predecessor, had lost much of its dynamism, and a vital role fell to Germany and the USA, which had some catching up to do (unfavourable); on the other hand, there was no global war to interfere with the process (favourable). We would therefore expect the intervals in these cases to be about average; and so they are.

Schumpeter redivivus

I have not offered any formal, quantitative proof of the succession of new technological styles: it is, I suppose, open to anyone not impressed by the account given here to decide that the discontinuities I have claimed to find in technological change are no more marked than others in between. I can merely invite the sceptic to try to find others which are of comparable importance. Meanwhile, it may be interesting to look again at the question of long waves in numbers of innovations or inventions. We saw in the first chapter how Mensch had claimed to find a 'bunching' of (radical) innovations in the downswing, and how Freeman *et al.* had argued roughly the opposite. Solomou, in a later study (1986), found no significant long wave fluctuation in innovations, one way or the other. One problem in such research is to decide the timing of an innovation – the commercial introduction of a new idea. I shall look here only at inventions, which have the merit of a fairly clear dating (to the time of first patent). We have to make a judgement as to which inventions were 'significant' or 'important', and it is clearly invidious for such a subjective decision to be made by someone with an axe to grind; so, following Clark, Freeman and Soete (1981), I will simply accept the selection of 'significant patents' by Baker,[102] since he gives no sign of interest in the long wave debate.

Figure 2.7 shows fluctuations between 1775 and 1965 in Baker's significant patents: in 'master' patents – the first to be economically viable in a series of patents relating to the same basic concept – and in 'key' patents – the most important of the series. Only in the middle years of the period is there a clear long wave pattern, with a pronounced 'hump' in both series around 1840, and another, longer 'hump' from about 1875 to 1905. This would fit well with the very reasonable hypothesis that the crystallisation of a new style sets off a surge of technical advance; the greater length and strength of the surge after 1875 presumably reflects the expanded role of science in industry already discussed, and perhaps also the larger number of countries which joined, after only a slight pause, in the diffusion of the new style. Why then did the periods after the crystallisation of the water and Fordist styles not show such a regular pattern? Because they were both blighted by global wars.

Much has been said about the contribution of war to technical progress, but I believe the discussion has been biased: it is easy to give wars credit for advances they appear to have caused, harder to blame them for advances which they delayed. Thus if we look at the series, expecting a surge after 1780 or so, we find it – but it is cut off prematurely around 1790, when the Revolutionary and Napoleonic Wars began, which disrupted the economic and cultural life of Europe and largely cut the links between Britain and the Continent. The surge resumes, to some extent, after 1805 – displaced by the wars, we may suppose, from its 'proper place' some fifteen years earlier.[103] Again, we might have expected a 'Fordist' surge after about 1915; this appears to have been displaced by the First World War and its aftermath to the period after 1925, and then interrupted by the Second World War. So if we allow for the effects of wars, the rhythm of innovation is consistent with Schumpeter's theory.[104] What is not consistent with his theory, as we have already seen, is the rhythm of economic growth. We return to this problem in the next chapter.

Chapter 3

Integration, disintegration and crisis

THE IDEA OF INTEGRATION

Before exploring the 'feedback processes' to be added to our original model of Chapter 1, we should examine that model more carefully. Perez argued that a new technological style tended to change the 'techno-economic subsystem' so that this then became 'mismatched' with the existing (and unchanging) 'socio-institutional framework'. That the mismatch caused crisis; and the crisis, in due course, led to a renewal of the framework and thus a good match between it and the new style. This in turn led to a long wave upswing and another change of style. I argued that there were three types of crisis. The type which arose in and out of a long wave upswing was due to a *socio-political* mismatch between style and framework when the latter was not (or no longer) preventing fast growth. The type which arose in a downswing, partly causing it and partly caused by it, reflected an *economic* mismatch. (The type which occurred before there were long wave upswings and downswings was a mixture of the first two.) But what is actually *wrong* when there is an economic or a socio-political mismatch? And is it simply due to the inertia of the socio-institutional framework in the face of changes in technological styles?

Inertia can explain a good deal. For example, any major change in technology demands changes in the educational system, to produce workers with the necessary aptitudes and attitudes. It is scarcely likely that the reforms required will take place quickly enough to avoid some mismatch in this (economic) sphere. But equally, one may expect enough 'give', soon enough, in such areas to avoid any really serious problems, were it not for obstruction elsewhere. Where entrenched resistance to change is most to be expected is in those aspects of the socio-institutional framework which are closely bound up with the vested interests and power struggles of social groups. What is more, where power is at stake there is worse to be feared than inertia. *Regressive* change, which makes the framework *less* well matched to a given style, may occur – because it expresses, protects or enhances the power of some dominant group.

What we can find, then, within any socio-institutional framework, is a particular arrangement of power relationships, of links between social groups. The jostling of the various groups is bound, in time, to change this arrangement. The direction of change will depend on circumstances, including the challenges posed by any new technological style, and the effects of its diffusion. For economic growth, and social and political stability, the arrangement needs to be of such a kind as, without necessarily resolving conflicts, contains them in a constructive way. If it is conducive to economic growth, we can then speak of *economic integration*; if conducive to social and political stability, we have *social and political integration*. The key relationships here are essentially *vertical*: for economic integration, they are relationships between the different levels of the hierarchy of work; for political integration, they are those between different interest groups and social classes; and for social integration, they involve the different elements of the family, and the institutions which (may) support it. To the extent that these relationships break down, we have *disintegration*, and we would expect economic stagnation, political instability, social demoralisation. (Note that though the *primary* effects of each form of integration are within its own sphere, it inevitably has *some* consequences for the others: thus if political disintegration leads to war or revolution the economy will suffer.) In each long wave the forms of integration which are appropriate to the new technological style, are different; thus the coming of a new style makes for disintegration until such time as appropriate reforms have been made.

The forms of integration which are appropriate with a given style will differ somewhat among countries. More importantly, the degree of integration actually achieved will vary greatly among countries, as will the balance between economic and political spheres. Two countries might emerge from the same depression crisis with quite different degrees of integration, across the board – in which case we could expect the more integrated to be the more successful and stable in the following long wave. Or *A* might emerge well integrated economically but poorly integrated politically, whereas in *B* it was the other way about – in which case, watch for political instability or aggression from *A*, economic stagnation in *B*.

International integration

International integration, like other forms, involves the 'functional adequacy' of essentially vertical relationships: politically, between the 'world power', other 'great powers' and the rest; economically, between the economic leader(s) and the rest, and between the 'North' collectively, and the South, 'developed' and 'less-developed' countries. (The political and the economic aspects of international integration are particularly closely related, while there is no appreciable social aspect.)

The status of countries – as world powers, challengers or others; as economic leaders, or followers; even in some cases as members of North or South – changes gradually from one wave to the next; so do the forms of relationship required for a high degree of integration. As with other types of integration, the degree achieved varies a great deal over the long wave, particularly over the 'double long wave' of the twentieth century. The difficulty in maintaining integration is not simply that technological styles change, but that (only partly in consequence) so do the relative political and economic positions of countries. Thus before 1914 Britain was in financial, as in other terms, the world power, and 'managed' the gold standard while dominating world capital flows. After 1918 Britain was no longer the world power, and the USA was not yet ready to take her place. Moreover the 1914–18 war was part of a crisis of the upswing, which as we saw in Chapter 1 is unlikely to lead to thoroughgoing reforms. The result was a leaderless international financial system which was much more fragile than before and broke down completely after 1929. The reintegration of the world financial system under US dominance was not achieved until the late 1940s, when at the end of a depression crisis the US took up its responsibilities as world power. A degree of disintegration was evident again in the early 1970s, by which time the US, though still the world power, had lost much of its financial dominance, and another mild crisis of the upswing had (belatedly) arrived.

Similar factors make for integration and disintegration in North-South, core-periphery relationships. The North being far more important to the South than vice versa, these relationships have been most clearly reflected by conditions in the South. We shall see in Chapter 7 how political and economic developments there responded to, and changed, relationships with the North, and how they were affected by technological styles developed in the North, and by crises there.

POLITICAL INTEGRATION

We shall look at political before economic integration because political reforms tend to precede economic ones (while of course responding to underlying economic changes). This is most obvious when a revolution leads to direct state control of the economy – the political is so intertwined with the economic as to be scarcely worth discussing separately. But even in the western core countries, where state intervention in the economy is least, the state's role, direct and indirect, remains of great importance. A deep and prolonged depression crisis is likely to bring about far-reaching political, as well as economic, reintegration. In this country, the classic example is provided by the 'post-war settlements' achieved in most western countries, in the late 1940s or early 1950s. (The main exceptions are France and Italy, for reasons I shall examine in due course; the United States, standing back from the war, had a rather earlier and more superficial reintegration; the Scandinavian countries reintegrated even earlier and rather thoroughly.)

These settlements had common features – the great expansion of the responsibilities and apparatus of the State, including a redistributive 'Welfare State'; the ascendancy of a left wing or centre-left party, with links to a powerful trade union movement which shared or alternated in power and was dedicated to expanding and radicalising the state's role. (In Europe it was Labour or Social Democratic parties which grew stronger, to play this role; in the USA it was the Democrats who (outside the South) moved left to do so.) In other terms, it was the working class (led by the (male) workers in heavy industry) who were being integrated into the political process, much more than ever before. The old right wing conservative parties, representing the social groups which had had to give ground in this shift, accepted it, and when in power made no attempt to reverse it – thus, for example, in Britain the economic policies followed in the early 1950s by the Labour Chancellor Gaitskell and his Conservative successor Butler were referred to as Butskellism.

It is possible also to generalise about the process of political disintegration during an upswing. Regressive changes are, in such circumstances, inevitable: structures which were set up to serve broad social purposes are twisted to serve the interests of those in immediate control of them – the latter, in such prosperous and contented times, being left much to their own devices. At the same time, social change, hurried on by the upswing and the diffusion of the new technological style, creates new needs and problems which the existing structures are not well designed to cope with. The upswing and new style give new shapes to rivalry between and within states, without providing institutional means to contain or resolve them.

As I have already suggested, the crisis to which these new stresses give rise – the crisis of the upswing – will not be severe if a previous depression crisis has led to far-reaching reintegration. Arrangements which were newly designed and well suited for the circumstances of a given period are not *hopelessly* inadequate, twenty years later. They creak, but they serve; and so serving, they are not radically reformed – more's the pity. It is the following downswing which really puts radical reform on the agenda – it is hard to deny that existing arrangements have some responsibility for the growing economic and social difficulties. But what reform? Where moderate 'progressive' reform has been the watchword of the upswing, it tends to be discredited, with the rest. The Right offers reaction, in the guise of reform; the Left, various apparently hare-brained schemes for further 'progressive' changes. Normally, the Right – better organised, with a narrower constituency to rally, and with only the appearance of newness – gets its turn first, while the Left, split between moderates and radicals, seems more interested in its own squabbles than in defeating reaction.

This has certainly been the experience in most western countries during the current downswing since the mid-1970s. The Left in West Germany, for example, began during the late 1970s to divide between Social Democrats and Greens, while the centrist Free Democrats prepared to desert the coalition which had completed the construction of the German welfare state. At the same time, the Right in the United States grew stronger. The British Conservatives under Thatcher, having in opposition prepared a radical right wing programme, implemented it with vigour on their return in 1979. The Labour Party on the other hand, losing office in 1979, was split the following year by the defection of the Social Democrats and the struggles which followed between the remaining 'moderates' and the various factions of the Left. The French Socialist Party, refreshed by a long period out of office, swept into power in 1981 talking of radical change, and within two years had begun a ragged retreat which prepared the way for the advent of a 'new Right' government in 1985.

Just such a rightward swing has happened once before, in the 1920s. Indeed, to anyone with some knowledge of modern history, the resemblances between the 1980s and the late 1920s, are striking – not in the state of the economy (then, briefly, booming) but in the attitudes of policy-makers and those they represent. They were all for monetary discipline then, and interest rates were accordingly kept high; so it is in our time. They were for fiscal discipline too, and managed to keep their budgets in surplus – our governments are mostly in deficit, but (at least outside the US) unwillingly and as little as possible, given the state of their economies.[1] The greatest similarity is in their attitude to the making of money, by those rich already. There was to be, in the late 1920s, no impediment to this activity. In the USA, controls on mergers were left virtually unenforced by the Justice Department under successive Republican presidents; in the UK the new fashion of forming cartels was allowed to flourish. Trade unions, on the other hand, were regarded as obnoxious interference with the market mechanism, and their increasing weakness was welcomed. Money once made, should be kept: rates of taxation on the income of both corporations and rich individuals were low. (In the US, Andrew Mellon's Revenue Act of 1924 had reduced the top rate of income tax from 73 to 46 per cent.[2]) For the 1980s, this description holds almost without modification; there is the single change of detail, that it is mergers rather than cartels which flourish in the UK.

The example of the 1920s suggests that the strengthening, and sharpening, of the Right, may not only be due to the initial effect of the downswing, but also to the crisis of the upswing a little earlier. I argued in Chapter 1 that the outcome of this crisis was affected by the background of prosperity which prevented the development of any broad coalition of interests demanding radical reform. It may also be that the response of policy-makers to this crisis is influenced by 'generational factors' – by the formative experiences of the generation in power, which vary over the course of the long wave.

At what age are experiences formative, for political purposes? I take it, in the transition to adulthood, in about the late teens and early twenties.[3] Childhood is a period of relative shelter from the wider environment, in which the child is exposed within the family to values which are likely to be traditional; even in school, the attitudes picked up from peers and teachers have been formed over a long period of individual and parental experience. It is on emergence from school, into higher education and/or employment (or military service) that there begins a period of intensive 'engagement' with the wider environment, which I take to be the most formative period, so far as environmental influences are concerned. That gives us an age for formation of attitudes of perhaps 20 to 25 (note that the people we are most concerned with here are opinion-formers and policy-makers whose education is likely to be prolonged; working-class attitudes are likely to be formed earlier). The next point which concerns us is that at which our opinion-formers and policy-makers acquire the power to form opinions and make policies. This we may put at some point in their forties. We are dealing, then, with a lag of about a generation – perhaps twenty-five years – between, so to speak, input and output. Not, let me stress, that our -formers' and -makers' views are set in concrete from their twenties onwards. On the contrary, they evolve and change in response to the new situations and intellectual currents to which they are exposed on their way up the greasy pole. *But* (and this is crucial) their choice among alternative responses to these developments is conditioned by the basic attitudes established at this formative period.

Let me now give some examples. The British Tory, Harold Macmillan, had served in the trenches in the First World War alongside his working-class contemporaries. When he and his generation came to power in the 1940s and 1950s, it would have been deeply repugnant to them to have engaged in any conflict with these men, and their trade union leaders, which could decently have been avoided. Their deepest instinct was for social harmony. (It may be that one element in the different attitudes in US politics and business at this time was the lack of men who had had such experiences.) A rather later generation, that of J. F. Kennedy in the USA and Edward Heath in Britain, came to adulthood during the Great Depression or just afterwards, during the Second World War. For them, the conclusion drawn was likely to be that the market mechanism, so much beloved of their fathers, could not be left to rule the economy without extensive government intervention whenever and wherever it seemed necessary. Thus, in their period of power, in the 1960s and early 1970s, they resorted freely to welfare programmes, fiscal reflation, incomes policies, etc. In this generation the right-wingers are moderate and cautious.

This latter example relates to the adolescents of the downswing, who rule in the late upswing. We now move on ten or twenty years, to those who grew up in the upswing. Those on the Left, who have roots in the working class, or close connections with it, will know of the Depression from bitter childhood experience or at least family experience much discussed; but those on the Right will mostly have suffered little more than inconvenience from the Depression, and by the time they were ready to take a wider view of it, it was gone. *This* generation's right wing learn from the upswing – *their* upswing – one big thing: that the capitalist system, with its market mechanism, is wonderful, and that interference with it is a nuisance. They may at first accept their elders' cautious compromise policies intellectually, but their hearts are not in them, and when in the peak and early downswing those policies appear to run into trouble, this new generation of -formers and -makers is easily persuaded that the fault was in the fact, not the form, of the compromises: away with them, and back to pure doctrine! They associate themselves with a new, or radical, Right: not conservative, but reactionary – wishing to put the clock back to old inequalities of wealth and power (and at least for a time largely succeeding); promising (and inevitably failing) to restore old bonds of loyalty and old structures of security. Thus Thatcher, Kohl, Chirac and Bush. Thus also the men of the 1920s, like Coolidge and Hoover in the USA and Montagu Norman and Baldwin in Britain, whose ambition was to get back to the prices, the industrial relations, and the capitalist freedoms of the period before 1914. The victories of the reactionary Right of the 1920s turned to dust and ashes a few years later, but they proved slow learners in the 1930s; they are slow learners now. Here is an insight into the long wave: upswings breed reactionaries, who help to beget depressions.

Looking back before the First World War, we must not expect to find the (almost) world-wide regularities of fluctuation described above, in crises, integration, and political colour; for we had no world-wide economic long wave then. The 'mixed crises' which arose in its absence were, as we saw in Chapter 1, variable both in their severity and their results. We can generalise about them in one respect: to the extent that they produced a better 'match' of the socio-institutional framework with the reigning, or incoming, style, they did so, as we shall see, largely through political and economic reintegration. The absence of any serious crisis in the main period of diffusion of the steel and science style (1880–1910) led to the development of extreme political disintegration in at least one key country, and can thus be blamed for the severity of the first 'crisis of the upswing', the First World War.

ECONOMIC INTEGRATION

The rate of interest, to be discussed in the next chapter, is important chiefly for its effects on investment. In this, however, it is only one aspect of a broad relationship, between the providers of financial capital and the users of it. Not all capital is provided at fixed interest, and even where fixed interest capital is concerned, there is much else that affects how much is borrowed and for what purpose, besides the precise numerical compensation paid to the lender. At least as important is the character of the relationship between borrower and lender: how close, trusting and well informed it is. The same applies (only more so) to the relationship between the providers of share capital and its users, that is the top management of the firm (who are, of course, the borrowers at interest). We may call such close, trusting and informed relationships, a high degree of integration of financial capital and management. With a high degree of such integration, more capital will be raised and invested, and to better effect.

There is a parallel relationship further down, between management and labour. There is of course more obvious potential for conflict here, and what is at stake is the extent to which conflict – essentially over the distribution of added value between the parties – can be prevented from interfering with joint efforts and co-operation to maximise the total added value, the net income of the firm. Success in this we may call, again, a high degree of integration of management and labour – which should not be taken to imply the subordination of the latter. High integration is compatible with vigorous union defence of workers' interests; conversely, an atomised work-force without any independent organisation may have a very low degree of integration with management. (See Freeman and Medoff, *What do Unions Do?* for an excellent discussion of possible efficiency gains from unions.) Integration, again, has a crucial effect on the level and nature of investment. If it is high, then other things being equal management will be prepared to put more capital into the hands of the labour force – most of all, it will be prepared to put more capital into their heads, that is to say, spend money on increasing their level of skill, their human capital. Such investment may be inhibited by the fear of giving employees increased power within the firm, which will be used against management, or increased power in the labour market, to get a well-paid job elsewhere, and walk away with the firm's investment – or it may be that the management does not know or respect them well enough to realise what they are capable of. These are all aspects of low integration.

I have suggested that integration at both levels is likely to be relatively high in the early upswing and low in the early downswing. We can see why if we take the early upswing's high integration as starting point. In the upswing, capital blossoms and spreads itself. Firms expand overseas, responding to freer trade, easier movement of capital, increased confidence. Later, more defensively, they come together, in great waves of mergers. Both of these movements make top management more remote from workers. At the same time the gap is widening between financial and industrial capital, for the same reason – the greater size and complexity of firms. In the most recent long wave, in the USA and UK, this occurred in two distinct phases: in the first phase, the increasing difficulty of exercising control gave management more independence of shareholders and more scope to form and follow their own objectives. In the second, shareholders (mainly financial institutions) became increasingly concerned with the income from their shares, and more and more impatient with managers who could not or would not make high profits – their main sanction being to reduce the market price of the firm's shares or to sell to a take-over bidder.[4] By the 1980s the use of financial controls and incentives (including profit-based bonuses) was putting heavy *short-term* pressure on management for increased profitability, which deterred it from investing at the rate which the firm's long-term prosperity demanded.[5] This short-term performance pressure particularly inhibited spending on training, and on the long-term development of radically new product ranges[6] – categories which had become increasingly important. Clearly, for management under such ignorant pressure from above, integration with workers was scarcely possible, particularly as its key feature, the development of their skills, their human capital, was being discouraged.

Let us now look at the opposite movement, which brings integration back to its high point of the recovery. The traumas of the depression crisis drive the three parties of industry – financial capital, management and labour – back into closer partnership with one another. In the last depression, of the 1930s, and early 1940s, this was assisted by the closing of geographical frontiers, through tariffs, restrictions on capital movements, and war; capital, become so footloose in the boom, now had little choice but to go into domestic industry, and had to get to know it better. Likewise, after the long conflicts of the downswing, management learned to reach a new *modus vivendi* with the workers. We shall see in Chapter 6 how this was associated with a less unequal relationship with them, and how in fact every reintegration within the firm, as within society in general, involves such a reduction in inequality.

This new *modus vivendi* was associated, in almost every western country, with an upsurge in the membership and strength of trade unions, and it accordingly involved recognition of the unions' rights to represent the workers. At this stage the unions and their leaders had their members' full confidence, and a powerful and respected position socially and politically. In most countries and industries, there followed gradual disintegration during the upswing, not so much initially, in the relationship between management and unions, as in that between unions and their members, as the leadership became *too* co-operative with management and ineffective in representing workers' interests. This growing gap found expression in the widespread upsurge of shop-floor militancy in the late 1960s and early 1970s, which formed an important part of the 'crisis of the upswing'. The union leaders responded by paying more attention to their members' wishes, but this did little to reverse the process of disintegration, rather to change its form: it moved back towards the old gap between management on the one side (under more pressure from shareholders now) and workers and their organisations, on the other side.

Economic integration is not unchanging in its relevance to economic growth. Variations in the management-worker relationship, in particular, are more important now than previously – in the small firms of the last century there were neither the same problems nor the same possibilities. Nor are its fluctuations neatly symmetrical in each country over the course of the Wave. A country may reintegrate much more in and after the depression than it disintegrates in the periods before and just after – that is the Japanese case, for the depression of the 1930s–1940s, as I shall argue later. Conversely, another may disintegrate much more in and after the boom than it reintegrates later – which appears to be the case for the United States and Britain over the last long wave. So much the better for our theory, for it can help to explain the shifts in countries' relative position in the world economy, while at the same time, if you take all the countries together, aggregated or averaged, you find something of the symmetry you need.

Disintegration between taxpayer and state

Another 'vertical' economic relationship is that between the State and those who provide it with its revenue. Here too conflict is inevitable, in the sense that it is in each individual taxpayer's interest to pay as little as possible. We can talk of serious disintegration in this relationship where the effect of taxation, and the efforts that are made to avoid and evade it, is to cause serious distortion of the economy. Methods of production may be adopted, for example, which are not the most efficient, because they facilitate tax evasion or avoidance. Clearly the potential for such disintegration has increased as the incidence of taxation has risen; but it would be wrong to suppose that actual disintegration must be in direct proportion with the level of taxation. There is more to it than that: taxes when new are likely to cause less distortion than they do later on, for it takes time to find ways round them. It takes time, indeed, to *make* ways round them: taxes, typically, are simple when introduced, and then in response to lobbying by interested groups, allowances are quietly introduced which much reduce their bills without attracting the public outcry which would follow any attempt to abolish the whole tax. The incentive to do what is necessary to qualify for such allowances tends to cause more distortion than would the wish to avoid a simple tax altogether. It appears that new taxes are generally introduced, or the system at any rate tidied up, in the reforming period around the end of the depression crisis. The gradual degradation of the system follows, continuing until the next reform. One development which currently facilitates distorting evasion or avoidance is the liberalisation of trade and capital flows which began in the last upswing and will continue until the depression crisis forces governments to bring it under control: multinational firms in particular find enormous scope for reducing taxation through ploys like transfer pricing and getting governments to bid against one another for their investments.[7,8]

SOCIAL INTEGRATION

In the chapters to come the social leg of the integration tripod has a rather minor role; which is just as well, since the concept itself has, frankly, not been so well thought out as the other two. The tentative argument which follows is offered because the concept does seem to offer interesting insights into the current situation.

It is not entirely fanciful to liken the three-way relationship between men, women and children to that between the owners of capital, management, and labour force. Traditionally men (fathers), like owners of capital, have had ultimate power – through their wallets – but most have chosen to exercise it with a degree of remoteness. Women, like management, have usually occupied a central position of full-time responsibility. And the success of both enterprises – the production of goods and the production of future adults – rests on the resources (of all kinds) invested in the workforce and the children, respectively.

We must not press the analogy too far. Children (young ones, anyway) are more passive participants in their 'production process' than workers are, and consequently the key relationship in social integration is that between parents. This varies, of course, among countries, and changes over time, and it seems reasonable to suppose that it may be linked to the other changes in the 'socio-institutional framework' which we have been discussing. Each technological style, after all, offers new roles in production and consumption which have implications for the relationship of the sexes. Political changes, too, affect the legal framework within which the family operates and the material support it receives. I think one can argue plausibly that there has been, over the last long wave, a fluctuation in family relationships – an ebb and flow of social integration – which closely parallels the other fluctuations we have been examining. (I doubt whether one can find such a fluctuation further back; on the other hand, in the modern west political integration appears to remain quite high, reflecting the strength of parliamentary democracy. Thus if one conflates social and political integration into one category, one can find a continuing fluctuation which has changed its character.)

Let us start, as usual, with the upswing of the last long wave and assume – for the sake of argument – a high degree of social integration. That is, there is a *modus vivendi* between men and women (backed by the State) such that the family *works*: children are brought up in a way adequate to make most of them (in due course) reasonably good citizens and productive workers. Such a situation can plausibly be discerned in the early 1950s, associated perhaps with the early welfare state. But the fast diffusion of the new style and the expansion of the economy produced new rivalries here, as elsewhere in society. In the last upswing, in the 1950s and 1960s, this took the form of women asserting their rights as workers – their rights to 'have a career'. Undoubtedly, in a long perspective, this formed part of the general social drift towards equality (see Chapter 6). But in the short run it rather distracted attention from the fact that women retained primary responsibility for child care, and that so long as they had this, they needed a great deal of support from *somewhere* in discharging it. If they now expected – or were expected – to work outside the home, then they might need rather less material support, but more support of other kinds. (Moreover, whatever strides they made towards 'equal opportunities', they were bound to remain at a great disadvantage in earning power so long as it was *their* careers which were interrupted by children.) At the same time as they began to demand equality of opportunity outside the home, they became less tolerant of inequalities and injustices within the home; they became more ready to end an unsatisfactory marriage.

The response of men in the USA has been well described by Barbara Ehrenreich in *The Hearts of Men*.[9] They too became more ready to break up marriages, for *their* reasons.

> So when a successful middle-aged man ... feels that he wants a livelier and new young wife, he may see no reason why he should not go out and get one. At the other end of the scale are the numbers of unemployed and low paid men who rather than face their failure as breadwinners ... simply opt out.[10]

At this point it falls to the State to protect the children at risk, by enforcing the system of alimony and child support, and/or providing support itself. In the USA at least, it fails abysmally to do so.

> Only 15 per cent of America's 19.2 million divorced and separated women were awarded [alimony] payments last year and only three quarters of the 15 per cent actually received any money ... 60 per cent of absent fathers in the US pay nothing at all towards the support of their children. ... A study in California showed that, a year after divorce, women and children's standard of living had dropped by 73 per cent, while men experienced a 42 per cent rise in standards.[11]

And why? Perhaps because the State is, in effect, male:

> I suspect that the real motivation behind the lack of enforcement of child support is an emotional response to the massive social and economic changes that our nation and the world has undergone and is still undergoing. ... The old order has been upset. The seemingly contradictory views about child support may well be a public manifestation of private fears, of control issues within the family. Absent, delinquent fathers are protected by their male peers, in a kind of team play or male bonding in a public playing field.[12]

While the explanation of this breakdown of the family must be somewhat speculative, one can be confidently gloomy about its effects:

Children lose their father, their home, their self-esteem and ... financial well-being ... Finally, they often lose their mother's time too, as she struggles to make ends meet doing two jobs or a job and part-time studying, in an attempt to fight her way to a decent place in the job market.[13]

We now have firm statistical evidence of the effects of this in adult life. In Britain the children of divorced parents, by their mid-thirties, were less well-educated and more likely to be in low status jobs, than others of their social class. Men were more than twice as likely to be unemployed. Women showed significantly more symptoms of emotional stress and depression, and had a higher alcohol intake. Women from non-manual backgrounds were three times more likely to have no educational qualifications. Results from the United States were similar.[14]

The ebb tide of social disintegration is running fast now, and it is contributing to the development and misery of the underclass (see Chapter 6 below).[15] What is needed is that men, and the State, should accommodate themselves to the change in women's attitudes and behaviour, and work out a new *modus vivendi* to replace the old one which has broken down. Little progress seems to have been made as yet in this direction, particularly in the USA and UK. The reactionary Right is in the ascendant now, and women in unsatisfactory family situations are just another underprivileged group, to be ignored. The affluent have their rights: if a woman can neither attach herself firmly to an affluent male, or get her own affluence, hard luck.[16]

Chapter 4

Monetary feedback

As was argued in the last chapter, the relationship between the owners and the users of capital is a complex one; and that is true even where the connection between them is the relatively straightforward one of lending money at interest. In some places and periods there may be little capital raised for investment even though its price, the rate of interest, is low; in others, although that rate is high, much may be raised and spent. Nonetheless, it is clear that a low interest rate does *tend* to raise the rate of investment, and thus the rate of economic growth. Interest rates may be defined and measured in two ways: nominal and real. The former are those which meet the eye; the latter are those which really count. The real interest rate is, the nominal interest rate *less* the rate of price increase (or *plus* the rate of price decrease). Thus if the nominal rate of interest is 10 per cent per annum but the rate of inflation is also 10 per cent, the real rate of interest is nil; on the other hand, if the nominal rate is 10 per cent but prices are *falling* at 10 per cent a year, the real rate is 20 per cent. Clearly a prospective borrower would be much encouraged by the former situation, deterred by the latter. Unfortunately, unlike the nominal rate of interest, which is usually fixed over the period of the loan, the rate of price increase is not at all certain. The rate of price inflation or disinflation which counts, when calculating the real interest rate, is that *expected by the borrower*, over the period of the loan. Expectations start from experience, so we shall begin by looking at price movements over the long wave, in the industrialised, Northern countries where the key interest rates are determined.

THE LONG WAVE AS A PRICE CYCLE

As we have already seen, it is the apparently regular fluctuation of prices (until the 1930s) which gave rise to the long wave concept in the first place. Solomou (1987) argued, like many others, that much of these movements could be accounted for by the major wars.

Certainly major wars, particularly the Revolutionary and Napoleonic Wars near the beginning of the period, and the two World Wars in this century, have been accompanied by quite rapid inflation (that is to say, fast-rising prices), and the same can be said for the immediate aftermaths of the wars, when and where there was disorder. This is hardly surprising, as wars cause shortages of supply, which virtually any economic theory would regard as inflationary, and they reduce competition, as seas are blockaded and frontiers closed. With order restored, after the wars, the next decade tended to see falling prices; again scarcely surprising, since the supply shortages and trade obstructions disappeared.[1]

Wartime inflation and post-war dis-inflation account for most of the first apparent long wave in prices (1790–1849) (see Figures 4.1, 4.2 and 4.3). On the continent of Europe, indeed, the downswing ended (according to Rostow, 1978) in the early 1820s: from then on the steady increase in population led to an upward tendency in the price of grain[2] and other foodstuffs, which in turn appears to have led to a slight upward trend in retail prices until the mid-1840s. For France, however, Solomou[3] finds prices falling until 1831; the downward trend resumed in the 1840s. In Britain the Corn Laws were used to protect domestic farmers from imports after 1815, but since the country was still self-sufficient in an average year prices still fluctuated greatly, as elsewhere, with the weather. From the mid-1830s expanding population put increasing strain on domestic supplies, and average prices of grain moved up towards the Corn Law ceiling; but this trend was soon checked by the dismantling of the Corn Laws, beginning in 1842.[4] It was this shift to free trade and the consequent fall in food prices which brought the overall price index to a low point around 1850 (see Figure 4.4). The prices of industrial products, which had been falling steadily from

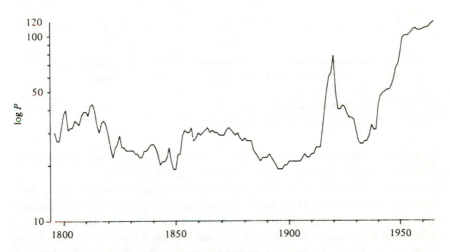

Figure 4.1 British wholesale prices, 1796–1965
Source: Solomou (1987), Fig. 4.1

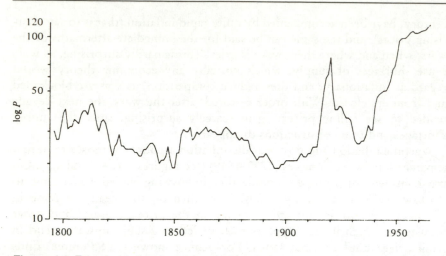

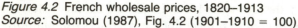

Figure 4.2 French wholesale prices, 1820–1913
Source: Solomou (1987), Fig. 4.2 (1901–1910 = 100)

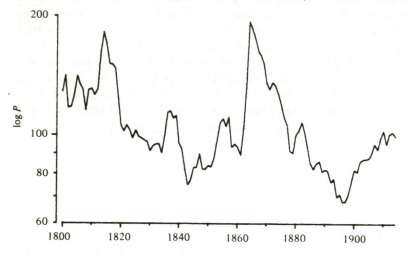

Figure 4.3 US wholesale prices, 1800–1914
Source: Solomou (1987) Fig. 4.4(a) (1910–1914 = 100)

the end of the war till an upward 'blip' in the shortage years of the late 1830s, were fairly steady from the early 1840s to the early 1850s.[5]

Up to this point, then, there seems no clear-cut 'peacetime' trend, or long wave, in prices overall. This may be largely accounted for by the dominance up to this point of agricultural prices, for which climatic factors and the pressure of population are crucial. Only for Britain do we have a separate set of industrial prices. In relation to agricultural prices, as Figure 4.4 shows, they tend to fall from around 1810 until they reach a trough in the early

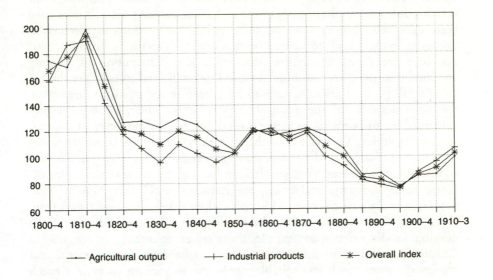

Average of 1865 and 1885 = 100.

Figure 4.4 (a) UK prices, 1800–1913, agriculture and industry
Source: Mathias (1969) Table 7

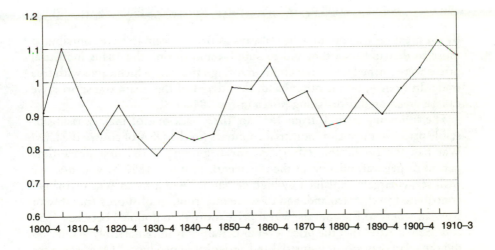

Average of 1865 and 1885 = 1.

Figure 4.4 (b) UK prices, 1800–1913, industrial/agricultural price ratio
Source: Mathias (1969) Table 7

1830s, then returning nearly to their 1810 position by 1850. This behaviour seems a little odd, in the context of the technological long wave. As we have seen, each new style is based on some radical innovations in production processes which lead to drastic reductions in certain industrial costs. As these are taken up, in the production and distribution of existing commodities, the prices of those commodities will tend to fall. Yet the big relative fall in these prices appears to have been in the twenty years before the crystallisation of the steam transport style. The puzzle is largely explained by Britain's status as the leader, and by the character of the two succeeding styles. The main breakthrough embodied in the steam transport style was a reduction in the cost of *transport*; and even that depended on the country and its existing situation. Britain having already invested in waterways, horse tramways and roads, the railways could only offer a small reduction in the variable cost of transport; their main advantage (apart from speed) was that they got rid of the bottlenecks which were beginning to develop in the existing system. In most other countries, as we saw in Chapter 2, a transport infrastructure had to be built from scratch, and waterways were much less suitable; there the impact on costs was much greater. Not that the reduction in costs was (in any direct sense) only on transport: we saw that steam transport freed industry to use the least cost energy source, whether steam or water, so that much of the gain came from lower manufacturing costs. But in this sense British industry was already free, long before 1830. So its cost reductions came with the improvement of the steam engine and water power, and their progressive application to more and more manufacturing operations – which took place particularly rapidly, before 1830. After 1830 the overall price level was buoyed up considerably by the great railway boom – the railways in Britain seem to have contributed more to demand than they did to supply; and during the 1840s industrial prices were pushed up by the boom in foreign markets which came with free trade. In France, on the other hand, the advent of the steam transport style can be given credit for falling prices in the 1840s.[6]

The following period, from 1850 to 1873, was one of mainly rising or stable prices in the major industrial countries (in the USA of course the Civil War had the predictable effect). At the beginning is the first peace-time period of general inflation in the nineteenth century, 1850–6, which as we shall see, is largely explained by high demand. The Crimean War of 1854–5 contributed to that demand, and to some interruption of supply (notably of Russian wheat to Europe: the wheat price more than doubled between 1851 and 1855[7]). After that the price level in Britain stayed remarkably stable,[8] as did the relative prices of industrial and agricultural products.[9] Once again we see a steady, evolutionary process of economic development. In France, on the other hand, there is a definite downward trend in prices from 1857 to the outbreak of the Franco-Prussian war in 1870. Initially this may again reflect the effect of the diffusion of the steam transport style in a technological follower; latterly the country's adoption of free trade may have contributed.

The rhythm of innovation certainly helps to explain the very sharp fall in prices in the 1873–82 period. As I showed in Chapter 2, it was at just this period that the benefits of cheap steel were being generally felt: besides reducing manufacturing costs, it was sharply cutting transport costs, through the use of steel rails, steel ships, and steel steam engines[10] on land and sea. The great US railway boom of 1866–73, based on the Bessemer rail, led to the opening up of huge areas of the Midwest for wheat cultivation, which affected world markets in 1873–82.[11] Cheaper transport reduced prices, not only through lower costs, but also through increased competition. Prices were also depressed by low demand world-wide (see Chapter 9). After 1885, depending on the country, the falling price trend slowed down, or ceased altogether. A number of factors may have contributed to this stabilisation. Demand, in general, recovered during the 1880s. By 1880 a new upsurge of tariff protection had begun, in which only Britain and a few small nations did not join. It may be also that the technological long wave had reached a stage where process innovations like those in steel were no longer bringing about such rapid cost reductions as before.

After 1896 the world returned, for the first time since the brief boom of 1850–6, to a more-or-less general upswing in prices, which continued until 1914. During this period – at least until 1907 – there was a definite movement of the terms of trade in favour of the primary producers: food and raw materials prices were rising relative to those of manufactures (see Chapter 7). The reason for this seems to be that industrial growth was faster during the period – Solomou puts the turning point at 1890[12] – and agricultural growth was slower than before.[13] This deceleration seems to have been mainly due to the closing of the American frontier after 1880:[14] the USA rapidly lost its previous position as the world's greatest agricultural exporter. We can thus explain rising prices partly by the relative shortage of agricultural products in the 1896–1913 period. Another factor may have been the rapidly increasing strength of trade unions in industrial Europe[15] which could have turned once-for-all price increases into something of a wage-price spiral. This can be related to another part of the argument: it was the diffusion of the steel-and-electricity style which spawned large factories with a high concentration of skilled workers – excellent conditions for unionisation.

The Great War and its aftermath of course turned gentle inflation into a very rapid rise in prices – hyperinflation in some countries – which was largely reversed in the following period, up till 1933. This last period of falling prices coincided again with the early diffusion of a new technological style and with a weakening of trade unions which, as argued in Chapter 2, can be partly blamed on the new technological style. Another factor which helps to explain it, latterly, is of course the Slump (see Figure 1.3).

After 1933 the behaviour of prices, in historical perspective, became a little odd: prices recovered somewhat, in most of the North, even while the depression continued. We might put this down to the drastic increase in protectionism (reducing competition) at the beginning of the 1930s. Price increases in the 1940s and 1950s were very much as one might have expected in war and upswing. It was from the mid-1960s onwards – from the peak of the boom – that the behaviour of prices became extremely odd, Northern inflation accelerating into the downswing. To some extent this could be explained by the unusual movement of primary product prices, particularly that of oil, which rose sharply in the early 1970s; but by the early 1980s the relative prices of primary products and low technology manufactures were falling rapidly, and yet – in deep depression – Northern inflation was still continuing (Figure 1.3).

It was clear by this time that the rules of the game had changed. They had been changing already in the previous downswing, in the 1920s and 1930s: what had happened, in essence, was that the Fordist technological style, with the economies of scale it brought with it, had made manufacturing firms large and their markets oligopolistic, not competitive. The (growing) service sector was oligopolistic too, and there was even government intervention in the Northern primary product industries to reduce their sensitivity to market forces; the primary sector was, in any case, of declining importance in the Northern economies, even when imports were taken into account. In the upswing, oligopoly had no more tendency to raise prices than more competitive markets did. In the downswing, however, it could resist price falls as competitive markets could not; indeed, where the economic failures and social tensions of the downswing increased pressure for wage rises, it could actually produce rapid inflation in the teeth of low demand and mass unemployment.[16] The incoming technological style looked likely, in due course, to take market structures some way back towards the status quo ante Ford, but for the time being the elegant symmetry of the 'price long wave' was spoilt.

REAL AND NOMINAL INTEREST RATES BEFORE 1914

The nominal rate of interest before 1914

Alongside price changes, the other component of the real interest rate is, as we have seen, the nominal interest rate. Following Keynes, I take it that the nominal rate of interest is in effect the price of money, and is determined by the supply of, and demand for, that much misunderstood commodity. To understand what has happened to the interest rate we have, then, simply to understand the evolution of the demand and supply of money. Simply? I think it can be made reasonably simple, if we stick to the broad view and cut a scholarly Gordian knot here and there.

To begin with we can dispose quickly of the demand for money. For our purposes it depends on the money national income, that is the real national income times the price level, so demand for money rises with increases in real income and increases in prices. The supply of money, on the other hand, demands more than a sentence. First we have to recognise that the supply of money, as broadly understood, consists mainly of deposits in banks and similar financial institutions, and is created, for their profit, by a complex network of these organisations and others. They create it not out of thin air, but by the stretching, or multiplication, of the *monetary base*, the money issued by the central bank. The size of the monetary base depends on the circumstances, and policy, of the central bank; the extent to which it is multiplied depends partly on central bank policy, and more importantly on the way financial markets are organised and the degree of confidence which exists in them.[17]

Let us look first at the monetary base, which I take to have been the key determinant of money supply during the nineteenth century. Money was, of course, originally made of precious metals, and the link with them has only gradually loosened over time. At the beginning of our period paper money was still an innovation, regarded with considerable suspicion and only issued in any quantity during wartime. During peacetime, until 1914, the 'note issue' of central banks was closely tied to their holdings of bullion – *gold* bullion increasingly after mid-century, as other central banks came into line with the gold-standard system of the Bank of England, and abandoned silver. The higher the output of gold, the faster it was accumulated by the central banks, and the faster their note issue (and for that matter, their issue of gold coin) increased. The importance of the great gold rushes was first recognised by Kondratiev: they flooded the world's central banks with gold and so increased the monetary base, which for a given 'bank multiplier' meant a proportionate increase in the overall money supply and a reduction, other things being equal, in the rate of interest. At the same time, the payments by the central banks for the gold worked like an increase in government expenditure to stimulate the economy: the gold miners and merchants were in effect working for the central banks, and being paid by them, just as (say) road builders were being paid by governments. (In the language of the modern economist, this implies a fiscal as well as a monetary stimulus.)

Now it happened, as Kondratiev (1935) pointed out, that the great gold discoveries of the nineteenth century were rather neatly bunched, in a long wave pattern – in the late 1840s, and then in the 1880s and 1890s: 1881 in Alaska, 1884 in the Transvaal, 1887 in West Australia, 1890 in Colorado, 1894 in Mexico and 1896 in the Klondike. This is not hard to explain. First, prices of other commodities were lowest during these periods – prices in terms of gold; which is as much as to say that the price of gold, in real terms, was at its highest at these times, and it was thus most worth looking for. At the same time, as we shall see in the next chapter, these were times of 'migration push', when surplus labour from the old lands spilled into the new – what more natural than that some of that surplus should go prospecting, in territories where (unlike most of Europe) gold deposits were still to be found? The migrants ensured that once the gold was found, there would be no shortage of labour to dig it. Thus falling prices after 1815 were followed by increasing gold output from 1820, and – as migration surged – by a more rapid increase from 1848, with the Californian and Australian gold rushes (see Figure 4.5). But already from 1853 onwards, gold output had reached a plateau. After 1872 – following a long period of roughly steady prices – it actually turned down; but the steeply falling prices of the decade after 1872 were followed around 1883 by an upturn in gold output, which trebled in the 1890s and was still rising until 1914.[18] Why was the acceleration of the 1890s so much more sustained than that after 1848? One difference was the slower inflation in the later period; but probably at least as important was the change in the location of gold-mining. It can be argued that the continuing rise in gold output after 1900, contrasting with the levelling off in the mid-1850s, was due largely to the forcing down of the real wages of black mineworkers in South Africa.[19] The earlier gold rush areas depended on a limited Northern labour force which dwindled as prosperity increased, most of the later ones on effectively unlimited Southern labour whose price could even be depressed as required.

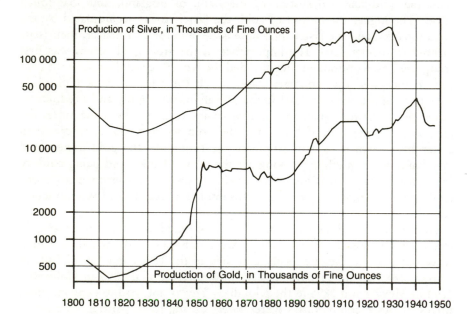

Figure 4.5 World output of gold and silver, 1800–1950
Source: Vilar (1976) Fig. 18, p. 352

Variations in gold output certainly go a long way to explain changes in money supply and interest rates in the latter half of the nineteenth century. Thus the stock of money in the UK rose considerably faster in the 'gold rush' period between 1846–50 and 1856–60 than in the following decade. The problem was that (until 1856) the demand for money must have been increasing very much faster still, given rising incomes and more quickly-rising prices: thus it is not surprising that UK rates of interest turned up after 1852 (see Figure 4.6). The fall in gold output after 1873 came at a time when the demand for gold was high, from countries joining the gold standard.[20] The UK stock of money seems to have grown unusually slowly over this period.[21] However, interest rates did not rise – on the contrary (Figures 4.6 and 4.7) – for the rapid falls in prices were reducing the demand for money. Nominal interest rates fell to their lowest-ever levels during the late 1890s, and rose only slowly thereafter, the flow of gold being enough at first to keep pace with rising prices and output after 1896.

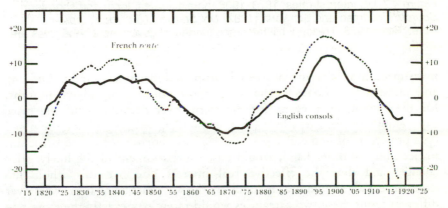

Figure 4.6 British and French bond prices, 1820–1920
Source: Kondratiev (1935 [1979]) chart 2
Note: The chart shows deviations from the secular trend smoothed with a nine-year moving average. Bond prices show the inverse of long-term interest rates.

Real interest rates and effects on economic growth before 1914

The main difficulty in assessing the effects of interest rate changes in this and other periods is that we do not know how prospective borrowers would have calculated the real interest rates they implicitly faced. How far, for example, in a period of rising prices, would they have projected such inflation forward into the period of the loan? That would presumably have depended on how long was the period of the loan, and how long was their experience of price movements. In Chapter 1 I set out three categories of

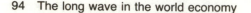

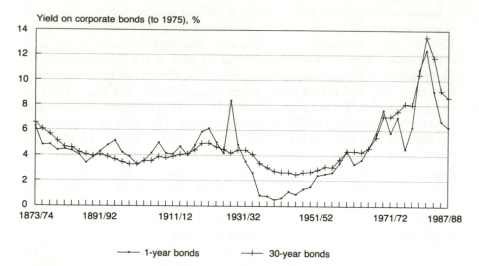

Figure 4.7 US interest rates, 1873–1988, nominal rates, long- and short-term
Source: Friedman and Schwartz (1982) *UN Statistical Yearbook, passim*
Note: From 1976, Treasury bill rates and long-term government bond rates are used.

investment, in stocks (inventories), in plant and machinery, and in building and infrastructure. Loans for the first purpose would be repaid over months, for the second, over years, for the third, over decades. Thus the price expectations relevant to a loan for stockbuilding would probably be based on a projection of immediate past experience; a borrower for a construction project, on the other hand, would base his assessment of the likely price changes and thus the effective real interest rate over his whole life experience. (We should bear in mind, by the way, that being borrowers over different *terms* these two categories would rarely pay exactly the same rate of interest: the short-term rate fluctuates much more than the long-term rate.) It was this which made stockbuilding so cyclical in the nineteenth century: any brief downswing would set off a decline in prices which would make short-term real interest rates look very high; once the price cycle seemed to have turned, on the other hand, money for stockbuilding suddenly seemed very cheap. Any one borrowing 'long', however, at any time after 1815 would have been well aware that the long-term tendency was for stable or slowly falling prices, and would have made allowance accordingly.

Thus the brief though brisk inflation of 1850–6 would have had little influence on the behaviour of investors even in plant and machinery, let alone those in building, and as soon as interest rates rose, as they did in the second half of the decade, such investors would have been deterred. The price deflation after 1873 was a good deal more prolonged, and it is easy to imagine that by the end of that decade it was having an influence on investors in plant and machinery as well as stocks. (On the other hand, assuming that investors in infrastructure were *not* influenced by it, they would have been encouraged already by the pronounced fall in nominal interest rates since the beginning of the decade.) Likewise, at some point in the long inflationary period after 1896 one would have expected investors in plant to have changed their expectations.

There is another effect of price changes which has to be added to that through real interest rates. As Fisher argued in 1933 about the effects of the Slump, anyone who has borrowed heavily before the price downturn comes, now finds his debt burden becoming steadily heavier: perhaps to the point of bankruptcy, certainly to the point of reducing his 'credit rating' and limiting his capacity to undertake new investment.[22] In the 1870s, this effect would probably have bitten deeper and earlier than the change in expectations on investment in plant. Whether this effect is symmetrical, and encourages investment equally when prices are rising, is doubtful: but it must have had *some* beneficial effect in 1850–6 and 1896–1914. The Fisher effect is particularly apparent for international debtors: the fall in prices in the 1870s is presumably largely to blame, for example, for the bankruptcy of the Egyptian and Ottoman governments, and the poor credit rating of many governments after such periods must have inhibited their expansion and their contribution to international trade.[23]

Conclusion: monetary feedback before 1914

If we could ignore fluctuations in gold output, we would certainly find that monetary feedback before 1914 was fast and negative, through the following mechanism. Starting with an upswing, we have a rapid rise in prices (the effect of output on prices being particularly strong in this period). Rising output and prices together push demand for money up faster than supply can possibly rise: so nominal interest rates rise. This discourages investors the less, the more they have been influenced by the inflation: thus stock-building is least affected. But once a downturn begins, the stockbuilding investors are discouraged too. It would be hard therefore to sustain any general upswing for long; and by the same token, any general downswing would be to a large extent self-limiting.

Now let us bring in gold. Again we have a negative feedback process, but this time more complex, and longer. A downswing leads to falling prices, and thus gradually raises the real price of gold (and silver, so long as it formed part of the 'monetary base'), making it more attractive to prospect for, and to mine once found. Moreover we may expect a downswing to be associated with a 'migration push' of people from Europe overseas, providing more prospectors and miners. Thus gold output rises, which leads to a rise in the money supply (and also, as we saw, to some 'fiscal' stimulus). In time, of course, the upswing causes the whole process to go into reverse;

but the lags here are longer. How important, then, was negative feedback through gold, and how long were the lags? The answer changes through the period. At the beginning, at the end of the eighteenth century, Britain was 'off gold' during the Wars, and so the stocks of gold and other precious metals were probably of less monetary importance than later. In any case, there is no evidence of any clear-cut long wave fluctuations of world, or Western, economic growth. After 1815 gold (at first alongside silver) certainly counted, and continued to do so. What seems to have changed after that – to have steadily increased – was the responsiveness of gold output to economic conditions. Presumably this was because the span of European control, and the ease of European movement, was increasing. What is more, each response was sustained for longer – due perhaps, as I suggested, to the greater availability of Southern labour. We see, then, a fall in prices which extended from the early 1870s to the mid-1890s and mainly took place in the first half of that period, having an impact on the real money supply which was concentrated in the 1890–1913 period. It is from the 1890s, then, that we can begin to see monetary feedback as having a significant pro-cyclical effect – tending to generate an economic long wave.

REAL AND NOMINAL INTEREST RATES AFTER 1914

The money supply and interest rates after 1914

Even before 1914, the relationship between the gold stock and the money stock was becoming looser, due to the greater sophistication of the financial system.[24] After the outbreak of war the determination of interest rates, like many other things, was never the same again. First, the gold standard was abandoned, and never returned to – even when countries claimed to go back to it, like the British in 1925, they were only really returning to their old parity with the US dollar, not to the old relationship between the gold holdings of the central bank and its issue of money. The creation of money henceforward depended much more than before on the policies of the main central banks – the US Federal Reserve Bank above all – and much less on the output of gold. But before we discuss those policies, let us consider a third factor: the extent to which the financial institutions, particularly the commercial banks, *multiply* the monetary base created by the central bank. I bring it in at this point because some writers, including Minsky (1964, 1982), have claimed to find a long wave in the money multiplier in this century.

The money multiplier

What happens is that A, who has money, hands it over to B, a bank, which chalks it up to A as a deposit (so A still has the money, 'in the bank') and then lends it to C, perhaps to pay D; who can then put it into a bank, so that

D too has 'money in the bank' – and the bank can lend it to someone else. . . . This process of multiplication is governed by rules laid down by the central bank, which limit it – so that in practice, the 'relending' is of a proportion, not all, of a bank deposit. But central bank policy is not the only factor to be reckoned with. When they are so inclined, the financial markets can always come up with innovative means of multiplying money which are not, at the time, fully controlled by the central bank. When are they so inclined? When companies and households are keen to borrow; and when financial institutions are *confident* that borrowers will repay.

The borrower may pay the interest, and repay the principal, out of the flow of income from an investment – the profits of a business, for example – or out of the resale, at a higher price, of the assets purchased with the help of the loan. It will only make sense to lend, and to borrow, in the first case if sufficient income is expected, and in the second, if a sufficient rise in price is expected. Now even in the downswing a very large proportion of businesses continue to make profit, rather than loss, and the profit may well be sufficient to meet their commitments so long as they have not 'over-borrowed'. It is the second type of borrowing – to buy assets for resale – which will probably be disastrous in the downswing, for as we have seen it is at this period that prices usually fall. It is only in the upswing – and not the early upswing, when memories of burnt fingers are still fresh – that borrowers and lenders will have enough confidence in rising prices for these speculative loans to be made; and even the first, less risky, kind will seem safer in the upswing. The longer the upswing goes on, the more the monetary base will be multiplied, and the more this multiplication will be linked to loans which would be risky in a downswing. Thus the financial structure becomes more and more *fragile*. In other words, as Minsky puts it:

> The hypothesis is that the financial panic which is present during deep depressions and absent during mild depressions is not a random exogenous affair; rather it is endogenous to the economy. The financial panic is made possible by the changes in the financial structure which take place during the long swing expansion.[25]

Banks and other financial institutions will generally have created deposits for their clients whose total money value is much greater than the reserves of 'cash' held by the institutions. Once clients suspect that the deposits are fragile – as they do in a downturn – many will try to encash their deposits; and the more they do so, the less the institutions can meet those new demands. The resulting crash makes some financial institutions bankrupt, while others become much more cautious; by the end of the downswing, the money multiplier is much lower than it was at the beginning.[26]

One problem with such a model of a monetary long wave is that there is no obvious reason why the fluctuations should be of the long wave length:

they could just as well, for example, form part of a Kuznets long swing, and indeed in the nineteenth century, as we shall see, they seem to have done so, particularly in the United States. On the other hand, if one can take some sort of long wave in economic growth as given, one may expect to find a monetary long wave which reflects it, and acccentuates it. This is particularly likely where prices have moved with economic growth, for a key part of Minsky's story is that rising prices in the upswing encourage individuals and institutions to 'overextend themselves', and that their obligations are made more onerous by the fall of prices in the downswing. It is in the 1900–45 period, then, that we would expect the best 'fit' for Minsky's model, particularly in the United States, where the upswing over the first half of the period was not 'dented' by the First World War. His evidence is indeed impressive: in the seven years before the Crash of 1929 US households' liabilities-to-income ratio, and the market value of the shares they owned, increased much more rapidly than their income.[27] In the following ten years they came, painfully, down to earth. It appears, too, that in the inter-war period as a whole (1920–41) the supply of money responded quite sensitively to the demand for it, as Minsky predicts.[28] Another indicator of financial fragility is the ratio of private to public debt: the lower the better, since public debt is a liability of government and thus a relatively safe sheet-anchor for the financial system. This ratio was higher in 1929 than at any other time between 1920 and 1980.[29]

Unfortunately, outside the inter-war USA, Minsky's model performs rather poorly. The German debt-to-income ratio *fell* between 1913 and 1929 – from 2.15 to 1.09 – and yet the German banking crisis of 1931 was quite as bad as the American one. Over the same period the British ratio rose from 1.55 to 2.76, but the British banking system went through the horrors of 1929–33 unscathed.[30] Nor does the post-war period fit very well. It began, at least in Britain and the United States, with the financial system in a very safe condition, largely due to the enormous expansion of public debt during the war; it is not the Depression that should be given the credit. Since then, as Minsky has shown,[31] the system has become more fragile. That fragility was reflected in the crises of 1974; but there was no crash. The process of increasing debt-to-income ratios and overextension of the financial system resumed, and continued through the downswing. If there is a crash to come – which, in the USA in particular, is perfectly possible – it will have to come much later in this downswing than in the last. Clearly one factor which has made the financial system less fragile, post-1945, is the continuation of inflation through the downswing; another advantage is the much greater ability and inclination of central banks to step in to prop up the system, and maintain confidence. Modelski may be more relevant here than Kondratiev: one root of the problem in the inter-war period was that the American banking system, like the country as a whole, had suddenly acquired a status for which it was not yet ready.

Much more now depends on the conscious and deliberate policies of central banks, and the politicians whom, with more or less independence, they serve. It may be, then, that we should seek a link between fluctuations in interest rates and changes in the attitudes and policies of these people, the monetary 'policy-makers'. Such a link does seem to exist: as I argued in the last chapter, there has been, for whatever reason, something of a political pendulum, swinging out to the Right in the 1920s and again in the 1980s, and to the Left in the 1940s. When the pendulum is furthest Right real interest rates reach their peak (see Figure 7.6); when it is at the other extreme, they reach their trough. The cause-and-effect connection may not be straight-forward, and other factors surely play a part. International disintegration can be seen at work in the 1920s: there was no well-ordered world financial system and the 'dollar standard' by which parities were fixed did make, as Friedman and Schwartz (1963) argued, for 'tight' monetary policies. The same disintegration is apparent in the 1970s and 1980s, with similar results (see Chapter 11). Does gold still play a part? Its role in the international monetary system has continued to decline, and in national systems has disappeared altogether. It is just possible that it has continued to have some influence through the international system, and what it has would have followed the old rhythm: thus after declining prices in the 1920s raised gold's real value, it went up further when the USA devalued the dollar to $35 per ounce. Output responded. From 1940 inflation steadily reduced the real price of gold since the money price stayed fixed at $35 per ounce, and output was checked; the US decision in 1971 to free the gold price, and its consequent meteoric rise, led to a big rise in output.[32] But it is very hard to see how the effect could have been significant in this half-century.

The long waves in ideology and the money multiplier together go far to explain interest rate fluctuations during the twentieth century. Interest rates in the US and UK first rose significantly, but not steeply, during the First World War; which was nothing to be wondered at, given rising prices and overheated economies. What was odd was that they were kept high throughout the 1920s – which, since prices were falling, meant very high real rates indeed (Figure 7.6). This must be ascribed to a definitely deflationary monetary policy, partly owing, as Friedman and Schwartz (1963) argue, to the exchange rate policies pursued. In the Slump, the fall in money income, and thus in demand for money, might have been expected to bring about a sharp reduction in interest rates. However, the fall in the money multiplier, as explained above, prevented this: in Britain, for example, it was not until 1932 that long-term interest rates fell below 4 per cent, and short-term, below 2 per cent. (Note also that where confidence was severely damaged, as in the United States, the rates at which businesses could borrow fell nowhere near so far and fast as the rates paid by governments).[33] Really low interest rates, from the mid-1930s, accompanied the shift away from the ideology and doctrines of deflation towards more moderate, 'Keynesian' views. They were maintained through the inflation of the 1940s – implying negative real rates – and began to creep up during the 1950s and 1960s: a rise which can be seen as a belated recognition that rising prices were here to stay, rather than as a change of policy. Low real interest rates persisted into the 1970s, and even briefly became negative during the high inflation of the mid-1970s – though the effect of this depended on whether borrowers expected the inflation to continue at the same rate. At all events, nominal rates went up during the late 1970s, and inflation rates, a little later, came down; the real rate of interest, from 1979–80, settled down, in the West in general, at the highest level since the 1920s (see Figure 7.6).

Conclusion: monetary feedback since 1914

What is odd is the degree of continuity beyond 1914. Although the explanation offered is quite different, we seem to have found much the same result since that time as in the decades before it: slow negative feedback at work. The only change is that it has become even slower. To judge by interest rates (nominal and real), monetary factors were definitely reflationary by the mid-1930s at the latest – which, by most people's dating, was at least a decade before the end of the downswing. More than fifty years later, at what would seem to be a later point in the wave, they are still, by the same criteria, decidedly deflationary.

Chapter 5

Population feedback

The very length of the long wave – just two generations – hints, as I have already suggested, at a link with population. I shall argue in this chapter that population feedback works, in the circumstances of the twentieth century, to accentuate the long wave – pro-cyclically. In the different circumstances of the nineteenth century it had, by contrast, a 'spoiling', counter-cyclical effect. This change in effect arose, as we shall see, from changes in economic and social arrangements, and in international relationships.

Let us begin by looking at the first link in the chain of causation: the effect of an upswing on population.

THE EFFECT OF AN UPSWING ON POPULATION

Two hundred years ago it was taken for granted – by Adam Smith, for example – that an upswing in economic growth would lead to a corresponding upswing in the growth of population. Birth-rates would rise, death-rates fall, and there would be an inflow rather than an outflow of migrants. But since that time we have seen, in the countries which have grown richer, that the birth-rate has fallen to an extraordinarily low level – so low that in spite of the similar fall in the death-rate, and at least some net immigration, these richer countries' populations have been virtually stagnant, while poorer peoples multiplied at an unprecedented rate. Does this not cast doubt on the relation between income and population?

Certainly the long-term effect of economic growth on population is a complex one. Once it has had time to affect women's status in society, and people's attitudes to children, then the way is open for the 'perverse' effect of prosperity on fertility. But such shifts are not the immediate and automatic response to a few years' fast growth. When we look at the statistics, the old simplicities turn out to be not a bad guide to population growth over the long wave. It is, and has been, generally true that *in the short run* an increase in the rate of economic growth makes for an increase in the birth-rate and a decline in the death rate, while a fall in the growth-rate

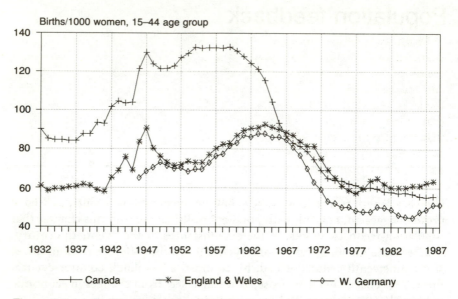

Figure 5.1 (a) Fertility fluctuations, 1932–89, Canada, England and Wales, and West Germany
Source: Munnell (1982) Table A-1, *UN Statistical Yearbooks, passim*
Note: Before 1940 the figures are estimated from crude births data assuming 1940 number of 'child-bearing women'; from 1985 (Australia, 1983) they are estimated from 'births per 1,000 inhabitants.

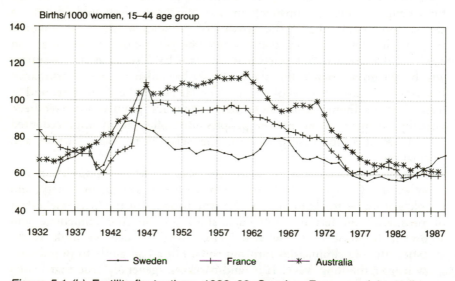

Figure 5.1 (b) Fertility fluctuations, 1932–89, Sweden, France and Australia
Source: Munnell (1982) Table A-1, *UN Statistical Yearbooks, passim*

has the opposite tendency (not that the death-rate need rise, just that it would fall more slowly than otherwise).[1]

In the twentieth century, the 'core' countries have enjoyed too high a standard of living for their death-rates to be very sensitive to economic conditions. But birth rates are another matter; right across the continents and across the social structure an upswing brings a 'baby boom', like that of the late 1940s–60s in the North, and a downswing brings a 'baby slump' like that of the 1930s and the 1970s–80s[2] (see Figures 5.1 and 5.2). It seems clear that the prospective parents of each generation set standards for themselves and their children according to the circumstances in which they have grown up. If, when their child-bearing age arrives, it looks as though it will be difficult to reach those standards, they 'economise' on the number of their children in one way or another (perhaps by postponing marriage). If their economic situation seems unexpectedly favourable, on the other hand, they 'treat themselves' to an extra child or two. This would explain, for example, the findings of D'Souza (1985) in a study of rural Indian families, that it was above all the 'downwardly mobile' who restricted their families.[3]

The response of fertility to prosperity has particular implications for the twentieth century, with upswings and downswings in successive generations. It accounts for the way the 'children of the downswing' have large families in the upswing, while the children of the upswing cut back their families, in the downswing. As Richard Easterlin, who gave his name to these long cycles in fertility, pointed out,[4] these fluctuations are the more remarkable because the children of the downswing are relatively few in number; for them to produce a 'baby boom' the increase in births per parent must more than compensate for the drop in numbers of possible parents. It does, comfortably – the number of parents in the USA in the 1950s was around 10 per cent under trend, while birth-rates were 20 per cent over trend.[5] As Keyfitz argues, this overcompensation is encouraged precisely by the small numbers in the child-bearing age bands:

> Not only would their promotion be relatively rapid, but in any one position, in so far as there is age-complementarity in production, they would frequently have the advantage of meeting situations in which they were too few to do the necessary work, with resulting appreciation of their services. This would often be expressed in material terms and would result in high wages and good prospects relative to what people of their age would be paid in a different age configuration, and they would have a sense of security and well-being. Their confidence is well-founded, for they will spend their whole working lives in the same advantageous position. They translate their advantage into child-bearing, perhaps projecting their security into the next generation and feeling that their children will be in demand just as they are.[6]

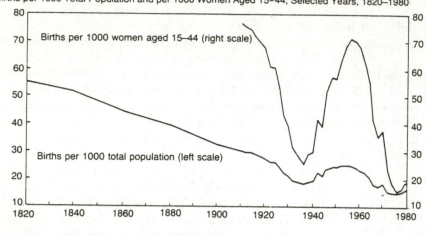

Births per 1000 Total Population and per 1000 Women Aged 15–44, Selected Years, 1820–1980

Figure 5.2 Fertility in the USA, 1820–1980
Source: Munnell (1982) Fig. 2–1

Their unfortunate children, of course, are not: not only do they have to rear *their* families in the downswing, but they have to compete with a crowd of rivals of their own age for whatever job opportunities there are.

The downswing in population growth need not wait for the depressing effect of the economic downswing, or for the arrival in the child-bearing ages of a large 'cohort' of 'baby-boomers'. There are two reasons for expecting it to come earlier, as in fact it did in most of the developed countries during the 1960s. First, in 'good times' women are likely to decide not only to have more children, but also to have them sooner: 'Part of the baby boom was thus due to a timing overlap'.[7] Once that overlap is over, there will be some decline. (In the same way, in 'bad times' women delay having children, with the opposite, also transient, effect.) Second, and more important in the 1960s, the long wave upswing is long enough for the long run effects of economic growth, and the accompanying changes, to show through. As we shall see, the reforms which launch the upswing include an improvement in education. Now a rise in educational attainment, particularly of women, appears to have a strong tendency to reduce the birth-rate,[8] as does almost any improvement in women's status and position in society.[9] Moreover the years of the upswing provide good opportunities for women to take employment; their attitudes to employment gradually respond to this, and as they warm to paid work they cool towards the alternative, child-rearing.[10]

The effect of economic growth on migration since the 1920s

So far we have discussed only the 'natural' growth of population – that is, fertility and mortality. For the population of the world as a whole, this is all that matters; but it may be important for the world economy just how the world's population is distributed among different countries; and that may be very much affected by *migration*. Every international migration is, of course, an emigration and an immigration, and its causes can be grouped into those relating to circumstances in the country of emigration as well as in the country of immigration; in other words, migration *push* and migration *pull*.

For our purposes the relative strength of migration push and migration pull is of great importance. In any downswing shared both by sending and receiving countries, we may take it that push tends generally to increase, but pull declines; in any general upswing it will be the other way about. Now it is generally known that pull has predominated since the 1920s: for people in poorer countries have generally been quite glad to move to richer ones, even during the upswing, but the richer countries have mostly been prepared to let them in, in large numbers, only when they were short of labour, that is, in the upswing – particularly the latter part of it. So in the upswing migration has risen; in the downswing it has fallen, coming to a virtual halt in the 1930s, as Figure 5.3 shows, and again nearly ceasing after 1973 (except for the USA – see below).[11]

The general effect of this pattern of migration on population in the richer countries has been to quicken growth when it was relatively quick already. However, most migrants are young adults whose numbers in the native populations were, as we have seen, reduced in the upswing and increased in the downswing; and so the effect has been rather to even out swings in the population in this age group. (Whether this has had much effect on the 'life

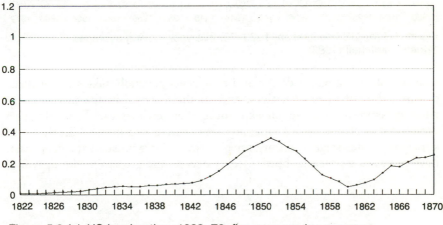

Figure 5.3 (a) US immigration, 1822–70, five-year moving averages
Source: Mitchell (1983)

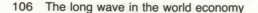

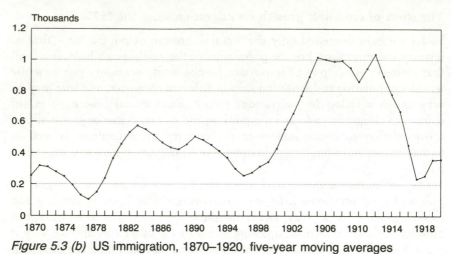

Figure 5.3 (b) US immigration, 1870–1920, five-year moving averages
Source: Mitchell (1983)

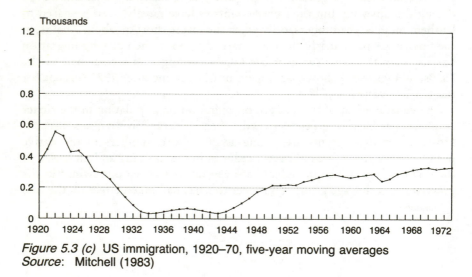

Figure 5.3 (c) US immigration, 1920–70, five-year moving averages
Source: Mitchell (1983)

chances' of the natives is doubtful. Immigrants generally take a lower place
on the ladder than most natives, and so their arrival in the upswing, by
allowing employers to go on expanding their businesses, allows them to
create more senior/skilled openings for native workers.) Clearly – to
anticipate a later stage in the argument – these flows must, at the very least,
have removed a potential bottle-neck to economic growth in the upswing.

Effects of economic growth on migration before the 1920s

Before the 1920s – certainly between the early 1840s and the end of the century – the nature, timing and effects of migration were quite different. During that period, migration was not so much from poor countries to rich, as from over-populated to under-populated, from the Old World to the New: mainly, from Europe to the Americas. Until the US immigration laws of the early 1920s the door to the Americas stood open – restrictions on immigration were insignificant, for the healthy at least,[12] and there was usually a fair chance of finding work somewhere, although clearly it was much better during times of boom (which were by no means necessarily the same as in Europe). All the would-be migrant needed was the fare; the importance of the early 1840s as the beginning of this period, was that they saw a very sharp fall in fares, with the development of the railways, and the improvement of the efficiency of ships, as we saw in Chapter 2.[13]

During this period, then, it was possible *in principle* for the 'push' effect to be as important as the 'pull', or more so. What their relative importance actually was, has been hotly debated. We can start from the established fact that there were four great waves of emigration from Europe during the period: 1844–54, 1863–73, 1878–88 and 1898–1907 (Figure 5.4). Most of the emigration, and most of the fluctuations in it, was to the United States; the debate has centred around 'pull versus push' in emigration to that country, in the context of Kuznets long swings. As we saw in Chapter 1, it has been shown that the United States economy has had such 15–20-year cycles, particularly during the second half of the nineteenth century; that other countries in the 'Atlantic economy' had them too, to a lesser extent, during that period; and that the European swings were, roughly, *inverse* with those

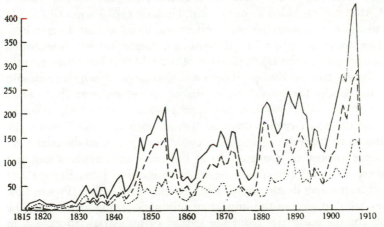

Figure 5.4 Emigration from Europe per 100,000 population to all overseas countries, to the USA, and to countries other than the USA, 1815–1908. ——— To all countries,----To the USA, ... To all countries except the USA.
Source: Thomas (1973) Fig. 34

of the USA: upswings on one side of the Atlantic tended to coincide with downswings on the other. Naturally the US discoverers of their long swing assumed that theirs was cause and the European swings, such as they were, were effect. Their upswings drew in not only migrants but also investment from Europe (the latter particularly from Britain), and the resulting shortage of labour and capital was then thought to have caused downswings.

This explanation of European swings would have been convincing if only the Americans had been able to explain their own satisfactorily; but they could not.[14] It occurred to Europeans like Brinley Thomas (1973) that if there were a strong *push* element in migration, the boot might be on the other foot: the cause and effect relationship might be, at least partly, from Europe to America. One way of gauging the relative strength of pull and push is through the analysis of lags: do upturns and downturns in migration start before turns in economic activity (e.g. railway building) in the USA, or after? If before, that is a point scored for 'push', with the US economy apparently responding to immigration as a supply of needed labour (and an extra source of consumer and housing demand). If the changes in migration come *after*, then that is consistent with the theory that they are all, or mostly, due to 'pull' factors. Thomas's findings are clear up to 1867: it was until then definitely migration which led economic activity in the USA; this (as he argues) was only to be expected since the USA was then an under-populated agricultural country which in its progress towards industrialisation was heavily dependent on immigrant labour. After 1867 the lags are mixed, and best summarised by dividing the migrants into two categories, 'industrial' and 'agricultural', according to their occupations in Europe: the former's movements seem to lag behind US activity, the latter to precede it.

Some of the detail of Thomas's account of migration has been disputed,[15] and his general verdict on the causes of Kuznets swings looks implausible now that Currie has provided a convincing, climatic explanation of the US cycle. But that does not mean the 'push' effect was unimportant. Even where the precise timing of an upturn or a downturn in migration was determined mainly by conditions in the USA, the *size* of it could still have been mainly decided by the situation in Europe. There was also scope, when there was no pull from the USA, for 'push' emigrants to go elsewhere: thus when immigration to the USA was low between 1860 and 1863, migration to Canada, Australia and Argentina soared, falling back in 1863–7 when the USA became more attractive again. What could have provided the push? An unusually large 'cohort' of young adults is Thomas's main explanation; and certainly there is a clear correlation between emigration from Europe and the excess of births over deaths some twenty-eight years earlier (Figure 5.5). If one takes account also of the impact of innovations and calamities (the pressure on cottage industries from the spread of industrialisation, e.g. in Southern and Eastern Europe at the turn of the century; the potato blight in the 1840s), then the association between migration waves and the various 'push factors' is striking.

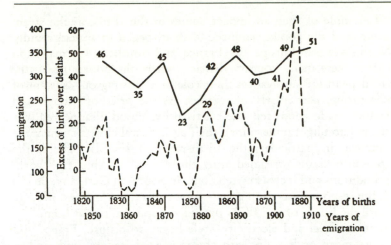

Figure 5.5 European natural increase and emigration, 1820–1910. ———
Quinquennial excess of births over deaths per 1,000 population. – – – Annual
emigration from Europe per 100,000 population.
Source: Thomas (1973) Fig. 35

There has been a strange echo of this period in the last decade and a half
within the Americas. Although rules on immigration into the United States
have been quite restrictive, they have not been effectively enforced: it has
been easy to get into the United States (and stay there) not only by the
overland route from Mexico, but also by air, on tourist visas;[16] once there,
jobs, of a sort, have been available, with no questions asked. In consequence
the flow has responded to the migrants' need, to migration push, which has
of course increased as the situation among potential immigrants – notably in
Latin America – grew more and more desperate; by the early 1980s the
inflow was running, according to some estimates, at over one million a
year.[17] Whether this immigration could be expected to have the same
economic effects as that during the nineteenth century, we discuss below.

The technological long wave and population

We would expect a new 'style's' effects on social structures to be mildest in
the countries which pioneer it, for it is there that such structures are best
matched to it to start with, and there that it evolves gradually, rather than
being copied in a hurry from a foreign model. This has implications for
many aspects of our argument, including population. Whenever a new style
begins to diffuse rapidly through an economy (or to affect that economy
from outside through imports) it displaces traditional forms of production,
and forces their labour force to find other employment, or go without. Such
disruption will certainly tend to reduce the birth-rate for a time, and it
will also lead to migration, internal and international. One early, well-

documented example of such an impact comes in the 1840s, as the steam transport style, and the goods produced with it, began to spread rapidly through North-Western Europe. In France and Southern Germany, in particular, there were many country districts where the poorer peasantry had come to depend for survival on their role in a 'putting out' system of rural manufacturing, particularly of textiles. As the price of foreign and domestic factory-made goods fell, their artisan livelihood disappeared (the spread of the potato blight undermined their agricultural efforts at the same time). In France, in particular, the birth-rate fell sharply. There, the displaced peasant/artisans streamed into the towns, looking for work, worsening conditions and increasing tensions. In Southern Germany, on the other hand, the response was to migrate overseas, to the Americas, in large numbers, until the boom of the 1850s provided opportunities at home.[18]

By the time the steel and electricity style began to diffuse, France and Germany were more or less up with the industrial leaders, and so less disturbed by industrial change; although rural artisans were displaced, the opportunities for them in their own country's factories were quite good. It was when, in the 1890s, the new style began to have an impact on countries further south and east – Italy, Austria, Hungary, Russia – that the events of the 1840s were repeated (apart from the potato blight): displaced peasant/artisans again went to seek their fortune in the Americas.

THE EFFECT OF POPULATION ON ECONOMIC GROWTH

We are now half-way to an understanding of population feedback at various periods. Having outlined the effect of economic growth on population, we now have to assess the effect of population on economic growth.

Ester Boserup (1981) shows how high density of population makes it practicable to develop sophisticated forms of production which require a large market. From that point of view the more people the better, and one would expect any acceleration in population growth to stimulate economic growth. On the other hand, there are resources which are in fixed supply, like land, and others, like minerals, which are exhaustible: as such resources become scarce, high density of population becomes a liability rather than an asset. The balance of advantage will depend on the place and the period: clearly an almost-empty area like the US Midwest in the early nineteenth century could only benefit, economically, from an increase in population, while a densely populated area (like the Netherlands throughout the period) could scarcely hope to gain as much as it lost. In general one could expect population growth to become less beneficial, on balance, as time passed (at least since 1780): first, and obviously, the density of population has greatly increased in most countries; second, as we saw in Chapter 2, dramatic improvements in transport technology have brought more and more consumers within range of a producer at a given site, even without increases in population.

By the nineteenth century, in Europe and Asia, usable land was decidedly scarce in most areas, and so any rise in the birth-rate or fall in infant mortality would lead, in fifteen or twenty years, to an increased surplus of labour; after some further delay, some of that surplus would emigrate. (As we have just seen, Thomas found an average lag of twenty-eight years between an upturn in fertility and the consequent upsurge in emigration overseas.) This, as it meant filling up near-empty land, certainly led to increased economic growth in the countries of immigration.

The 'vent' of migration was not perfect: although, as I said above, the gates of the United States stood open, still the uprooting would be cruel, and of course the journey there would cost more than many could afford – particularly those who most needed to go. So a surplus of labour would be reflected in poverty and hidden unemployment in the countryside, and open unemployment in the cities, with the driving down of wages in the occupations easiest to enter. Those years or decades, then, in which the labour force grew more than usual, would be marked, in the 'old' lands, by more social distress; but the total national output would not be depressed. On the contrary: there is always *some* use for an extra hand on a farm – land can be worked more intensively, a hillside can be terraced, a marshy patch drained. In other areas of the economy too, there would be more investment – more housing, and more capital being laid out by the more prosperous fathers to set their sons up in business. And if that was so in Europe, how much more true was it in labour-hungry North America, with its abundant natural resources? With more workers, whether native or immigrant, there would assuredly be more output, and roughly in proportion.

Population feedback before the 1920s

We have now discovered a crucial element of our 'evolutionary' theory: a counter-cyclical feedback loop for just that part of our period where the absence of an economic long wave would otherwise be odd. Let us explain it one step at a time, starting when mass migration first became feasible, around 1840. The arrival of a new steam transport style, and 'mixed crisis' which it helped to provoke, was largely responsible for the 1844–54 wave of migration. (The other cause was the high birth-rates after the Napoleonic Wars.) Thus population provided fast negative feedback in the late 1840s and early 1850s – first improving the growth rate of the world economy in what would otherwise have been a period of deceleration before the crisis reforms and monetary feedback unleashed expansionary forces; then, briefly, adding to those expansionary forces. From the late 1850s to the late 1870s its fast negative feedback would have worked in the opposite direction: European prosperity inhibited emigration and this reduced the rate of expansion in the world overall. From the late 1860s to the late 1870s there would also have been slow positive feedback at work, with a similar effect: the low birth-rate of the crisis years produced an echo in a small cohort of adults of 'emigration age'. These deflationary effects would have exacerbated the Kuznets downswing after 1873, but by the end of the decade they were played out. By 1880, when monetary factors and the newness of the steel-and-science style would have been deflationary, population feedback once again would have had an expansionary effect: the European baby boom generation of the 1850s was now old enough to take ship (slow positive feedback) and the recession helped to persuade them to do so (fast negative feedback).

From about 1890 it is once more possible to speak of European prosperity, which continued (with the exceptions of Britain and Germany) until 1914; accordingly, we would expect fast negative feedback from population soon to begin to damp down world expansion. The same deflationary effect could have been expected from slow positive feedback, rather later: that is, we would have expected a small cohort of babies from the 'bad years' in Europe in the late 1870s and 1880s, to produce a small cohort of emigrants from about 1905 onwards. In fact matters at this point become more complicated, mainly because of the widening area of Europe involved in the 'Atlantic' economy. Before 1890 it had been only the countries of Western Europe which had provided large numbers of emigrants, and so far as *they* were concerned, the feedback was as just described.[19] After 1890 the migration from the relatively backward countries of Eastern and Southern Europe rose rapidly, to become the main stream after 1900. In 1873–90 these countries were just being brought into the 'world economy', and beginning to benefit from better transport for their agricultural products; so they were not depressed and had something of a baby boom then (see Table 5.1). This large cohort, reaching adulthood in rural areas, found artisan employment squeezed by the belated development of steam-powered industry in the towns. Thus what had been only a brief pro-cyclical effect after 1850, and again after 1873, appears to have been sustained to some extent right through the 1890–1914 period.

Table 5.1   Eastern Europe: natural increase and emigration, 1861–1915

Period	Eastern Europe. Average annual rate of natural increase (per thousand)	Average annual oversea emigration from Eastern Europe	
		Period	Thousands
1861–80	10.6	1891–95	400.9
		1896–1900	405.7
1881–90	13.5	1901–5	785.9
		1906–10	1,114.3
1891–1900	13.8	1911–15	1,039.5

Source Thomas, 1973, Table 46

Population feedback since the 1920s

As we have already seen, the 'vent' of unhindered immigration to the United States was closed, rather abruptly, in the 1920s (and to the rest of the Americas virtually closed in the Slump) and only opened again when it was less needed, after the Depression was over. Migration push could then do nothing to mitigate the downswing of the late 1920s and 1930s, while migration pull accentuated the upswing of the 1950s and 1960s. But in any case, by the 1920s it was beginning to be doubtful whether high immigration was likely to have much effect on the American economies. The Prairies and the Pampas and the other good land available for European settlement had been settled: the 'frontier' had now been 'closed', and the amount of new labour the Americas could absorb depended – much as in other countries – on the rate of expansion of their industry.

There was a more gradual change to be reckoned with, which has continued to this day, and still has a long way to go in the periphery and semi-periphery: the divorce between the factors which affect the supply of labour and those which affect the demand for it. The peasant farmer, if he has another son or daughter (supply of labour), will find some use for him or her (demand for labour). This is particularly easy when he is producing, at least partly, for the family's own consumption – for that, with an extra mouth to feed, will presumably increase. But even when he is producing for the market, he can count on selling the extra output, since agricultural markets are competitive – you sell what you choose at a price you cannot choose, and cannot affect. For the nineteenth century artisan or entrepreneur, the situation was not dissimilar. The employee on the other hand cannot call work into existence for any extra children he may have – and we are, in the developed countries, most of us employees now. Even those who *are* self-employed are rarely now producing for competitive markets on which they could unload whatever extra output a larger family enabled them to produce; they are certainly not producing for their own subsistence.

The neo-classical economist would say that nonetheless the extra children can call the extra work into existence for themselves by bidding down the price of labour. Along with other post-Keynesian economists I reject that supposition. This is no place to rake over such a well-debated controversy, except to make one post-Keynesian point which fits well into my reasoning here: in so far as excess labour *does* drive down real wages it increases inequality, and that, as I shall be arguing, tends nowadays to depress the economy decidedly.[20]

We are left, then, with only one counter-cyclical effect of 'population feedback': that in the downswing the total output of peasant farmers in the underdeveloped world is higher than otherwise because their labour force is larger. This is hardly likely to have a noticeable positive effect on the world economy. Indeed if they put more output on to world markets and depress primary producer prices thereby, that will increase international inequality and (as I shall be arguing below) thus tend to *depress* the world economy. It seems clear, on the other hand, that the change in the rhythm of migration has put a pro-cyclical factor in place of a mainly counter-cyclical one. What has happened since the 1920s is that during the upswing (particularly the later part of it) poor countries' problems are alleviated by the emigration of part of their surplus labour force, in particular by the remittances of foreign exchange they send home to their families. In the downswing, when most emigration stops, those already abroad begin to divide into two categories: those who return, increasing the surplus of labour at home, and those who have established themselves in the rich countries, and bring their families to join them.[21] Either way, the remittances of foreign exchange stop, increasing international imbalances. What of the current 'echo' of nineteenth century migration push, in immigration to the USA? Following the argument above, it seems unlikely that the USA can benefit greatly nowadays from an increase in its labour force when it is not short of labour to start with. At least, on the other hand, the countries of emigration must benefit from the remittances? Yes; but as I show in Chapter 7, their emigrants in the downswing *now* include an unusually large proportion of well-educated and qualified people, escaping from crisis at home, who are by no means surplus to their country's requirements; losing them is highly damaging to Southern economies.

APPENDIX TO CHAPTER 5

Demographic effects on saving

While one counter-cyclical effect of demographic rhythms has turned pro-cyclical, another pro-cyclical effect has appeared from nowhere during the current long wave. Here I must acknowledge my debt to neo-classical economics; it is decent, I suppose, having just rejected one neo-classical idea on the effects of surplus labour, to make amends by borrowing another, albeit for a use for which it was not intended.

The life-cycle theory of saving explains differences in the proportion of income saved among different groups of the population, by pointing to the effects of age differences (thus helping to undercut the unfashionable Keynesian notion that wealth and poverty are largely responsible). Put very simply, the point is that people of working age run up savings for their retirement, then (having retired) run them down – *dissave*. Now this may seem an odd idea to borrow, because it has come under strong attack from empirical economists. If it is valid now – *if* – it certainly has become so only recently. In the last century, most working people were able to save very little, and if they happened to outlive their capacity to work, they fell back on the charity of their children, other relatives, or (God help them) the workhouse. Those few who owned most of the wealth did so as landowners or entrepreneurs, and as such might well continue to accumulate till their death, even if they passed the responsibility for day-to-day management to their children or others. Even the 'old' middle class of small entrepreneurs were mostly in a similar situation.

Nowadays the poor, and the not so poor, can rely on the State, through the social security system, to provide them with pensions in their retirement, financed generally on a Pay As You Go basis – that is, today's pension payments are made out of today's taxes, or contributions, levied on the working population (Rosa, ed., 1982).

So why should people's saving, or dissaving, be affected by their age? Before answering this question, we have to be clear about what we mean by saving and dissaving. What I propose to show is that the 'age profile' of the population can affect the level of demand in the economy; from this point of view, saving means spending less on consumption than one receives in income (thus depressing demand). Dissaving means spending more than one's income (thus boosting demand). Further, we should, in this context, be interested in any *investment* spending people undertake, or cause to be undertaken – not in pieces of paper, but in real assets. Let me make this clearer by following the hypothetical careers of two people, John Lifecycle, Junior (from the age of 20 to 45) and his father, John Lifecycle, Senior, from age 45 to age 70. At the outset, John L., Junior is at college, and although he receives much support from his parents, and some from the State, he is obliged to run up increasing debts in order to complete his studies. In this period, then, he (and his fellows) are making a considerable net contribution to aggregate demand, both through their own dissaving, and through their impact on their parents, who will during this period either save less, or even dissave, in order to meet the strain of their children's education. (Thus a US study reported by Russell, 1982, pp. 100–1, shows that those under 25 were dissaving at the rate of some 7 per cent of income, in 1972–3).

By the age of 25, however, we can be fairly sure that John L., Junior is earning, and self-supporting. He will be improving his 'net asset position' – in other words, what he owns, relative to what he owes, and he will, taking one year with another, go on doing so until his retirement (according to the study reported by Russell, at a fairly steady rate of about 9 per cent, for 25- to 54-year-olds). But do not suppose that this involves a steady subtraction from demand from the beginning. John L. gets married, at 25, and has children some time during the next ten years. This means he has to find somewhere fairly spacious to live. We do not know whether he and his wife buy that dwelling, or rent it; but either way, they cause a net increase in housing demand during that period (25–35): an extra house is built, to make room for them and their family. From 35 onwards, on the other hand, their 'net accumulation of assets' is almost entirely on paper (except if they make their first house purchase later – in which case this would simply mean exchanging their paper for a house, not extra housing demand) and so involves a net reduction in demand. Indeed, they are reducing demand by more than meets the eye, for John L., Junior, since (say) the age of 30, has had a job with an 'occupational pension' attached. Henceforth, besides his contributions to the government's PAYG scheme (which are paid straight over to a retired person, and thus mostly spent) he and his employer are contributing a substantial proportion of his salary to a private pension scheme which is funded, that is, contributions go to buy paper assets of one sort or another. Both employer and employee contributions to a funded scheme are subtractions from aggregate demand.

Meanwhile, John L., Senior has been growing old. In his late 40s and early 50s his saving rate was held down for a while by the expense of keeping John L., Junior and younger sister in college; but from 55 onwards he (and the population in general, according to Russell) was saving at a faster rate than 25- to 54-year-olds, having fewer responsibilities and seeing retirement looming. He stops work, let us say, on his 65th birthday, and settles down to enjoy his retirement, with the help of his PAYG pension (paid in effect by John L., Junior and his fellows) and his occupational pension. The latter is unfortunately rather modest, for his company only introduced the scheme twenty years ago, so John L., Senior has accumulated much less in the fund than his son will have done before *his* retirement. Still, the two together are more than enough for the modest needs of John L., Senior and his wife, and they continue to save, albeit at a more modest rate than before. (The study cited by Russell found those of 65 and older saving about 6 per cent of income, in 1972–3.) They have, after all, to bear in mind that the occupational pension is not fully indexed for inflation, and that the longer they live the more likely they are to face high bills for nursing care, etc. Their real rate of saving, however, will be less than it appears, and may even be negative, for although they are increasing their own personal assets, they are draining assets, invisibly, from the occupational pension scheme.

The John Lifecycle example shows us three factors which will interact to affect aggregate demand: first, the age structure of the population, second, the importance of *funded* pensions as a source of retirement income, and third, the degree of *maturity* of any system of funded pensions. (If the funded system is not long established, it will be *immature*; that is a larger proportion of workers of any given age is covered by it, and are therefore busy building assets up in it, than the proportion of retired people who were covered at that age, and have assets from that time to run down.) Thus, if there is an exceptionally high proportion of 35- to 64-year-olds; if they are for the most part covered by an expensive system of funded pensions; and if this system is immature, so that over-65-year-olds are not yet benefiting much from it; then we have a powerful deflationary force at work.

Countries vary a great deal in the importance of funding. Munnell (1982) shows how the 'funded' private pension system has developed in the United

States, from next to nothing half a century ago (her Tables 2.1, 3.4, 3.5). Although the 'coverage' seems to have levelled off now at just under half the private sector work-force, the proportion of the private sector *wage bill* affected is a great deal higher, for 'In most industries the employees who are not covered are heavily concentrated in small companies that tend to be at the lower end of the wage scale' (Munnell, p. 54). The higher the income level, the higher the proportion of wage-earners covered by a pension plan (Munnell, Table 3.6). (Munnell shows, citing her own and others' studies, how workers reduce their own private saving to allow for the saving being done for them: she estimates, by 65 cents for each dollar of saving through pension plans (Munnell, 1982 pp. 73–7).)

In Italy, on the other hand, the state system of retirement provision is now so generous that there is little need or inclination to save for retirement (Castellino, in Rosa, ed., 1982; Greenough and King, 1976, Chapter 10). In France, although private occupational pensions provide an important supplement to the state system, they too are financed, I think uniquely, on a Pay As you Go basis (Rosa in Rosa, ed., 1982; Greenough and King, *op.cit.*).

It turns out, as we look further, that the US case is the more typical. Japan, the next largest economy after the USA, has a rather inadequate state pension system (and one which, uniquely, is mostly funded) and an equally inadequate private pension system, mostly funded; so individuals are obliged to save, in addition, for their own retirement (Greenough and King, 1976, Chapter 10; Takayama, in Rosa, ed., 1982). After Japan, in size, comes West Germany. In spite of a quite generous PAYG system, individual life insurance and private pension plans are important in West Germany. In 1970 private plans covered about 60 per cent of non-agricultural employees, and as in the US, they tended to be the higher-paid. Only about 20 per cent of these employees are covered by conventionally-funded plans, but 70 per cent are covered by the *Pensionsruckstellung* or 'book reserve' system, whereby employers build up reserves against future pension commitments, which they are, in the meantime, entitled to put to their own use. If such reserves were used to increase real investment spending, they need not decrease demand; but as Welzk (1986) has shown, this is not the practice: they have been used to accumulate existing assets, as a pensions fund might, and because of the tax advantages to the firm they have been built up well in excess of future requirements. (See also Greenough and King, 1976; and Juttemeier and Petersen in Rosa, ed., 1982). Next (leaving aside France and Italy) comes Britain, which has, next to a PAYG system less generous than Germany's, a funded occupational system which, in its coverage, generosity and rate of growth is very similar to that of the USA (Hemming and Kay, in Rosa, ed., 1982; Greenough and King, 1976; Hannah, 1986; see particularly Hannah's Tables 9.1 and A.1). The situation in Canada is much like that in the USA and UK (Greenough and King, 1976); there is a similar private pensions system in the Netherlands, which has grown up mostly since the last war and has been, by law, funded since 1954 (Greenough and King, 1976). Switzerland has an important funded private pension system, and individual life assurance (Janssen and Muller, in Rosa, ed., 1982) . . . I do not think I need go on as far as Luxembourg and Lichtenstein to establish that the French and Italians are, in this matter, heavily outnumbered.

Such differences are not, as they may seem, mere technicalities; far from it. To show why, let us suppose we have a country where, for some reason, the proportion of the population which is retired, is very small, and the proportion at work is correspondingly large. If pensions are financed by a Pay As you Go system, the contributions made by the working population will be low, in absolute terms – because there are few pensioners to support, and per worker even lower – because there are many workers to share the burden. The reduction in workers' disposable income, moreover, will be exactly matched by the increase in that of pensioners. But if this country instead had a pensions system which, like that of the USA, was largely *funded*, the picture would be very different. The working population would have subtracted from their disposable incomes much larger sums than the Pay As You Go system would have required, for these sums (or a large part of them) are to be put aside for the many pensioners of the future, not handed straight to the few pensioners of the present.

What of the maturity of the funded systems? As Munnell says of the US system, 'Much of the net annual increase in pension assets can be attributed to the immaturity of the private pension system'. The ratio of benefits to contributions in 1980 was only 0.51 (Munnell, 1982, p. 203, and Table 8.4). Since the age of the other systems is similar to that of the US (or younger) they will be at least as immature.

We can easily see the relevance of the last point for the long wave. Immature funded systems are deflationary, always; and most countries, over the last two decades, have had immature funded systems. The effects of demographic changes are unfortunately not so easily understood. It is clear that to the extent that countries have funded pension systems, or inadequate PAYG systems which individuals have to supplement with old-fashioned private savings, the ratio of the population working, to those retired, will help to determine the rate of consumption and saving. It does not follow, however, that the long-term trend to greater longevity, which is pushing down the worker/retiree ratio, is steadily increasing the propensity to consume; for it seems reasonable to suppose that people of working age know about the trend to greater longevity, and anticipate its results in their own case by saving more; so do people in the early years of retirement – which explains the positive rate of saving recorded among retired people. What we should be concerned with, particularly in the 'funded' countries, is the fluctuation *around* the long-term fall in the ratio, due to past baby booms and slumps, and the wartime slaughter of young men. In the USA Table A5.1 shows the fall slowing down after 1965, with the arrival of the baby boomers on the labour market, and quickening from the early 1980s (in fact the high and largely unrecorded immigration, mainly of 'workers', is probably delaying this), then decelerating again from the late 1990s until the baby-boomers start retiring around 2005. For West Germany, Table A5.2 shows a pronounced *rise* in the worker/retiree ratio from the mid-1970s to the early 1980s (reflecting not only the baby boom but the arrival at retirement age of the generation decimated by the last war) and a pronounced fall only from the middle 1990s, petering out soon after 2000, with the really fast fall coming, again, with the retirement of the baby-boomers – beginning here later, around 2015. Britain had a rapid fall until the 1970s, a slower fall during that decade (mostly due to the baby boom: Britain's wartime losses were much less than those of Germany), and is now experiencing a rise, with a fast-falling ratio to be expected only after 2010 (Table A5.3). These three countries seem fairly representative of Western countries in being, during the 1980s, well above what appears to be the long-term trend in the worker/ retiree ratio, and having to wait till the retirement of the baby-boomers to fall below that trend. They do, then, seem to confirm the impression of a demographic tendency to push up savings rates during this downswing, although (depressingly) the opposite tendency is not to be counted on until well after the upswing should, on past form, have begun. Japan, on the face of it, is an exception: as a recently-developed country it was going through a rather sharp 'demographic transition' from high to low birth-rates, and to much increased longevity, when other countries were in the middle of their baby booms. As a result, on the one hand the worker/retiree ratio is still

Table A5.1 Actual and predicted ratio[a] of workers to retirees in the US population, 1960–2055

Actual			Projections				
			Ratio alternative[b]			Ratio alternative[b]	
Year	Ratio	Year	I	II	Year	I	II
1960	5.75	1985	4.95	4.90	2025	2.89	2.39
1965	5.49	1990	4.65	4.52	2030	2.65	2.10
1970	5.44	1995	4.44	4.22	2035	2.59	1.98
1975	5.29	2000	4.42	4.10	2040	2.63	1.91
1976	5.24	2005	4.44	4.02	2045	2.69	1.85
1977	5.24	2010	4.24	3.75	2050	2.67	1.75
1978	5.18	2015	3.77	3.27	2055	2.65	1.67
1979	5.15	2020	3.30	2.80			
1980	5.13						

Source: Rosen, Table 1, in Rosa (ed.) 1982
[a] This ratio is defined as the number of people aged 20–64 divided by the number of people in the population 65 years of age or older.
[b] Alternative I assumes an average fertility rate of 2.1 over the forecast period, while alternative II assumes an average fertility rate of 1.7. The recent average is 1.8. Alternative II also assumes an improvement in age-specific mortality experience over the forecast period that is twice as large as assumed for alternative I.

Table A5.2   Ratio of workers to retirees[a] in the West German population,
             1975–2030

Year	Workers (millions)	Retirees (millions)	Ratio of workers to retirees
1975	24.5	10.2	2.40
1980	24.7	11.3	2.19
1985	25.2	11.7	2.15
1990	25.5	12.1	2.11
1995	24.9	12.6	1.98
2000	24.1	13.2	1.83
2005	23.3	14.0	1.66
2010	22.5	14.4	1.56
2015	21.4	14.5	1.48
2020	20.0	14.6	1.37
2025	18.3	14.7	1.24
2030	16.7	14.9	1.12

Source: Juttemeier and Petersen, Table 1, in Rosa (ed.) 1982
[a] Excluding public pensions for *Beamte*.

very high by international standards. Combined with the immaturity of its
funded pensions systems, this has produced a very high ratio of contributors
to beneficiaries (see Table A5.4). Since all three components of its pensions
system are funded, this may help to account for its notoriously high savings
ratio, now no longer balanced by a high investment rate. On the other hand
(the good news) the contributor/beneficiary ratio has been falling particularly
fast during the 1980s, if Takayama's data can be taken at face value, and will
continue to fall until about 2015; since large funded reserves have already
been accumulated there should be little temptation to increase contribution
rates.

Table A5.3   Ratio of working population to pensioners in Great Britain,
             1951–2032

Year	Low fertility (= 1.8)	Actual	High fertility (= 2.1)
1951	–	3.37	–
1961	–	3.13	–
1971	–	2.84	–
1981	2.76	–	2.76
1991	2.87	–	2.87
2001	2.99	–	3.03
2011	2.84	–	2.99
2023	2.41	–	2.66
2028	2.19	–	2.49
2032	2.04	–	2.40

Source: Hemming and Kay, Table 3, in Rosa (ed.), 1982
Note: Projections assume stable mortality rates among pensioners.

Table A5.4   Japan: Population ageing in the KNH,* 1976–2025[a]

Fiscal year	Contributors[b] (1)	Beneficiaries[b] (2)	(1)/(2) (3)
1976	24.6	2.1	11.5
1980	25.4	3.1	8.2
1990	29.4	6.7	4.4
2000	31.4	11.5	2.7
2015	31.4	18.2	1.7
2025	31.4	20.1	1.6

Source: Takayama, Table 1, in Rosa (ed.), 1982
[a]   Figures assume that the total fertility rate will remain unchanged at 2.1 in the projected future – which is above the current rate.
[b]   Contributors and beneficiaries are in millions.
*   KNH = Kosei-Nenkin-Hoken, the public pension system for private sector employees – taken as the largest, and most representative, system.

> If the KNH had had a pay-as-you-go system, with current workers paying taxes to finance pensions for current retirees, the tax rate for male employees in 1976 could have been reduced to only 3.9 per cent instead of the actual rate of 9.1 per cent (or 9.8 per cent, taking the government subsidy into account), which supports a partially funded system. (Takayama)

The fluctuation of the worker/retiree ratio are not the only demographic factor which should concern us. The share of under-35-year-olds in the population is also important, and important everywhere, not only in 'funded' countries: they, like the over-65s, have a reflationary tendency, first mainly through their effect on consumption, then through investment. But not every age group among the young is equally reflationary. The very young – say under 5 – have a strong tendency to keep their parents' saving down, because they prevent their mothers working (and those who work nonetheless usually have to pay for child care); they also tend to induce new investment in housing. Then, until about 15, comes something of a pause: since most schooling is free, the burden tends to shift somewhat from the parents to the State; and many parents will be saving up for the child's higher education. From the late teens onwards, the strong reflationary effect returns, first through 'dissaving' for higher education, then through investment in housing.[1]

This gives us a striking insight into the effect of the baby boom and its ending. While the baby boom was in progress, 'junior demography' was reflationary – and all the more so where, as in Germany in the late 1950s and early 1960s, it was associated with a large 'cohort' of people in their twenties. In the early years after its ending – that is, very roughly, in the 1970s – there was a deflationary effect, given the large 5- to 15-year-old cohort and the small cohorts in front and behind (this was more pronounced in countries like Germany where the 'boom' began late). Then by the 1980s, even where the baby slump continued, 'junior demography' was becoming reflationary again, as the large cohort moved into the 15- to 35-year-old age group; alas, by the 1990s they would be moving on, towards thrifty middle age[2] (see Table A5.1).

Chapter 6

Inequality feedback (1) In the North

The concept of inequality

Since the concept of inequality is going to play a central role in the argument, I had better explain very carefully what I mean by it. We are concerned with an economic issue, so our primary interest is in economic inequality, of income and wealth, but of course such inequalities are interlinked with inequalities of power of various kinds, and with differences in expertise and organisational skills; power and knowledge lead to wealth, wealth leads to power and knowledge. (Indeed economically-useful training is nowadays often called 'human capital formation'.) Economic inequality (like other kinds) can be seen along different planes and dimensions. It can be seen, as it were, 'vertically', in terms of classes and occupational levels in one society, and 'horizontally' or 'spatially', in terms of differences among regions and countries.

This distinction would be quite straightforward if the different levels in one society lived close together (as servants used to live upstairs, in their masters' garrets, and work in their basements), while each society was quite separate from the others. That used to be not far from the truth, but as the mobility of people and goods increased the distinction became more and more blurred. Are inequalities between different classes spatial rather than vertical because (though working in the same place) they live in different dormitory suburbs? Surely not. Then what about the inequalities between migrant workers (who return to their families abroad in the holidays) and the rest of the population? More difficult to say ... Another example: a rich Englishwoman in the last century would have had her clothes made for her by a poor dressmaker who lived probably no more than a few streets away. The rich Englishwoman today may get some of her dresses from India. The first inequality between the rich lady and her dressmaker we would call a vertical difference within one society, the second we regard as part of the inequality between societies; but one could argue that the relationship between rich and poor is essentially the same in both cases – what has changed is the distance over which it can conveniently be conducted.

In the end we have to draw the line somewhere, and I shall follow normal practice by taking inequalities within countries – *intra*-national – to indicate the vertical dimension, and inequalities among them – *inter*national – for the spatial one.[1] But we must not lose sight of the 'dressmaker' point: as the world economy becomes more and more unified, international inequality becomes more and more important because it affects economic relationships which used to be purely *internal, intra*-national.

With that reservation, we can look at each dimension of inequality separately. We shall find that they have shown strikingly different trends over time. International inequality has grown enormously over the last two centuries, particularly the gap between the two main groups of countries, 'developed' and 'less developed', 'North' and 'South'. So has inequality within most Southern countries. We shall see that this is no coincidence: the situation within the South has been profoundly influenced by the increasingly close relationship with the North. In the North, however, there has been a very strong trend, at least over the last century, towards increasing equality. Clearly the fluctuations which directly concern us have to be seen in the context of these different trends, and I shall divide the discussion accordingly: the next chapter will deal with international, and Southern, inequality, this one with internal inequality in the North.

Sources of inequality

For most purposes the inequalities which matter are differences in income (and wealth) among households, allowing for the numbers of people in each ('standardised for household size').[2] The sources of inequality of household incomes are always changing. In nineteenth century Britain it was safe to say that the main inequality was between the few owners of wealth, landowners, capitalists, and rentiers with their rents and profits and interest, and the many who had to work for their living. Now, in Britain and other Northern countries, wealth, though still highly concentrated, is much wider spread than it was, and the division between profits, etc. on the one hand, and wages and salaries on the other, is thus a less useful indicator of house-hold inequality. Differences among 'earned' incomes, which were always relevant, are therefore now more important. Taxation, of course, affects the 'after-tax' distribution of income, although in fact in most countries it is not 'progressive' enough to have a substantial effect: it is government expenditure which, when its 'imputed' value is shared out, really makes a difference. Inequality is also affected by differences in numbers of earners per household, particularly by the existence of households without even one earner. One reason for this is of course unemployment, which clearly pushes up inequality in each downswing.

Another factor to be taken into account is the effectiveness of the household as a device for pooling and sharing individual incomes. Such pooling and sharing – assuming it takes place – can do much to mitigate inequalities among individuals. If Mr X earns much more than his wife, teenage son, or old mother, that makes no contribution to household inequality so long as they all live together. The larger is the average household size, the more scope there is for pooling to mitigate inequalities – which is worrying, since the average Northern household has for some decades been growing smaller. There are three main causes of this:

(i) Ageing of the population, combined with the increasing tendency of old people to live apart from their children.
(ii) The reduction in numbers of children per family.
(iii) The increasing rate of breakdown of marriages – and increasing willingness to be a single parent in the first place (see the discussion of 'social disintegration' in Chapter 3).

The first in fact does little to increase effective inequality since, although the old have lower incomes they have more assets than the average, and the provision of old age pensions is one area in which the State has become, in most countries, increasingly efficient. Nor is the decline in numbers of children a problem. It is the fission of the 'nuclear family' which has a serious impact on inequality: the children normally stay with the parent who has the lower (or no) earnings, and the transfer of income ('maintenance') from the other parent in most countries is very poorly organised by custom and law, nor is the state generous in making up the shortfall. (Most of us who are not old expect to be so, one day. Few of us who are not single parents expect to be so. The State reflects our concerns.) The effect is the greater because not only is family breakdown more and more common, but it is increasing most quickly among the poor. This has now reversed a trend which was working against inequality until mid-century: with declining mortality fewer and fewer families were broken up by death.[3]

THE EFFECT OF THE LONG WAVE ON INEQUALITY

Trends and cycles in inequality

In the North, there is no doubt that over the course of the last 100 years the inequality of distribution of income and wealth has fallen a great deal (see Table 6.1 and Figures 6.1 and 6.2). We have to account, then, not only for cyclical movements but for a strong trend of decline in the long run. The decreasing trend in inequality can be ascribed to two other trends: technological advance, and increasing specialisation in high technology activities, within the world division of labour.[4] Together, these meant that a larger and larger proportion of the population of the core became, first, users of expensive physical capital, and second, owners of expensive human capital, that is, of the training and skills needed to fit them for their high technology tasks. It is inevitably difficult to exclude such people from

Table 6.1   Changes in income distribution in Europe to the late 1950s

Income shares, per cent	1880	1913	1928/9	1938/9	1948/9	1957
TOP 5 per cent						
United Kingdom	48	43	33	29	23.5	18
UK AFTER TAX				24	17	14
Prussia	26[2]	30				
Germany/W. Germany		31	21	28[6]	24	18
Netherlands				19	17	13[7]
Denmark	36.5[1]	30[3]	26[4]	24.5	19	17.5[7]
Sweden			30[5]	28[6]	20	17[7]
SWEDEN AFTER TAX				25.5[6]	17	
TOP 20 per cent						
United Kingdom	58	59	51	50	47.5	41.5
UK AFTER TAX				46	42	38
Prussia	48[2]	50	49			
Germany/W.Germany		50	45	53[6]	48	43
Netherlands				49	45.5	38.5[7]
Denmark		55[3]	53[4]	51	45	44[7]
Sweden				56[6]	46	43[7]
SWEDEN AFTER TAX				54[6]	43	
LOWEST 60 per cent						
Prussia	34[2]	33	31			
Germany/W.Germany		32	34	26.5[6]	29	34
Netherlands				31	34	40[7]
Denmark		31[3]	25[4]	27	32	32[7]
Sweden				23[6]	30.5	34[7]
SWEDEN AFTER TAX				23[6]	28	32

Source: Kuznets, 1963, Table 16. Kuznets's sources are heterogeneous and comparability over time is not perfect. (Inequality in Germany in the 1930s and 1940s is almost certainly overstated relative to other periods.)
Notes: 1. 1870. 2. 1875. 3. 1908. 4. 1925. 5. 1930. 6. 1935/6. 7. 1954/5.

some role in both the political process and the control of the workplace (participation in either is a useful lever to help get more participation in the other) – and the power thus gained will inevitably be used to exert pressure, in the long term irresistible, for great reductions in inequality.[5]

However, there are two tendencies which for a time can work in the opposite direction. The first of these 'counter-tendencies' involves the supply and demand for different types of labour – for high technology jobs, and low technology jobs. Although in the long term the supply of workers

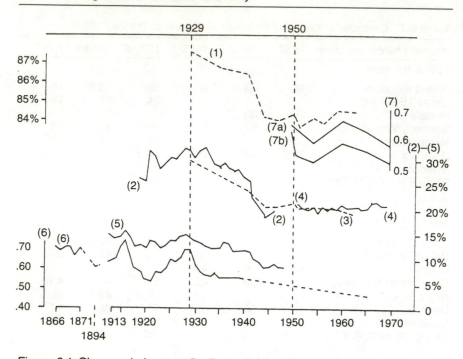

Figure 6.1 Changes in income distribution in the USA, 1866–1970
Source: Williamson and Lindert (1980) Fig. 4.3
Note: (1) = share of income received by top 60 per cent of households (OBE-Goldsmith); (2) share of income received by top 5 per cent of recipient units (Kuznets, economic variant); (3) = share of income received by top 5 per cent of recipient units (OBE-Goldsmith); (4) = share of income received by top 5 per cent of recipient units, social security population (Britain); (5) = share of income received by top 1 per cent (Kuznets, basic variant); (6) = coefficient of inequality among richest taxpayers (Tucker-Solrow); (7a) = variance in the log of personal income, males 25–64 (Chiswick and Mincer); (7b) = variance in the log of personal income, males 35–44 (Chiswick and Mincer).

only fit for low technology jobs dwindles along with the demand for them, this trend may be blocked for a time. There may be inertia in the educational system in the face of needs for rapid change; the system may be hampered by inadequate government support, due to political disintegration and reactionary policies; or it may be working with difficult 'material', due to social disintegration and/or increased poverty. (As we have seen, social disintegration also increases household inequality through the effects of family breakdown.) There may be impediments to training and upward mobility within firms – those, whether they can be 'blamed' on employers or unions, could be ascribed to 'economic disintegration'. Finally, there may be mass immigration of low-skilled workers from 'below' in the world economy.

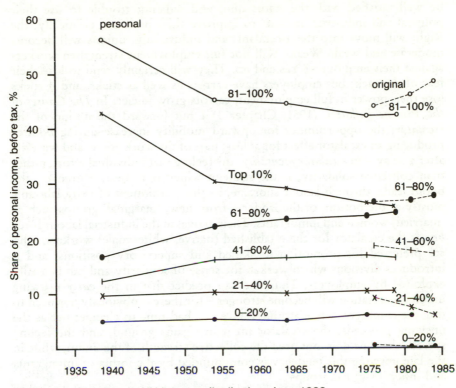

Figure 6.2 Changes in UK income distribution since 1938
Source: Phelps Brown (1988) Tables 11.4, 11.5 and 11.6

Disintegration and reaction, I have argued, increase during the downswing, until the depression crisis or after it. And (as we saw earlier) in this century, with the one exception of the present-day USA, immigration is higher in the (late) upswing and early downswing. So it is at some point in the downswing that we can expect an abundance of under-qualified, and a shortage of highly-qualified, labour. Unfortunately this coincides, more or less, with the opposite movement in demand for labour: it is during the downswing that the new technological style begins its diffusion, increasing the demand for new skills, and reducing that for old skills, and the unskilled. There will then be a severe excess supply of 'low technology' workers (those with old skills, or none) together with some excess demand for 'high technology' workers: 'structural' unemployment is thus added to that due to low demand, and market forces work to increase income inequalities.

The second 'counter-tendency' is also caused by prosperity. When their real incomes are rising steadily, and *a fortiori* when fast economic growth opens good prospects for upward mobility, the mass of the population will be well satisfied with the status quo, and will not trouble to use their political and industrial 'muscle' to improve their position; politically, the Right will move into the ascendant, and industrially, unions will become moderate and weak. Weak? Will not full employment strengthen workers against their employers? Yes and no. They will certainly tend to lose their fear of the sack; but employers have carrots as well as sticks, and if sticks lose their power in full employment, carrots grow juicier. In *The Causes of the Present Inflation* (1981, Chapter 3) I put forward the notion of the *escalator*: the opportunities for upward mobility increase during booms, producing an escalator effect for at least part of the work-force, and with it – after a delay – an *escalator mentality*: the feeling that individual effort, rather than collective solidarity, is the strategy which pays best. Moreover, the boom leads, through labour shortage, to the recruitment of extra labour – mostly at the bottom of the ladder – from new, 'marginal' groups such as (married) women and immigrants. Their arrival in the industrial labour force *boosts* the escalator for the established (native, white, male) workers, who are preferred for promotion to skilled and supervisory positions; and it introduces divisions which weaken the sense of solidarity and can be easily exploited by employers. Thus one can predict that in the *early* upswing union organisation will become stronger – for there is obviously less need to fear the employer, while attitudes have not had time to change; but as the upswing proceeds, the escalator mentality gains ground, and the feeling spreads that one does not need the collective strength of the union, while in the late upswing this tendency is compounded by the influx of immigrants and other 'marginal groups'.

The consequences of the slow undermining of the Left and the unions take time to show. It is partly a matter of generations, as I argued in Chapter 3: the generation in power in the upswing, even at the beginning of the downswing, have been deeply influenced by the previous downswing and depression crisis. In most 'Northern' countries that period, in the last long wave, taught employers and politicians – even of the Right – to accept unions as 'social partners'. In some countries, like the UK, they were thus able to increase their membership in the late upswing and early downswing (largely among state employees) even while their members' attachment to them was weakening.[6] In others, like the United States, where employers' and politicians' acceptance had always been more grudging, the decline began relatively early, although it accelerated in the downswing (which, exceptionally, was a period of high and largely illegal immigration in the USA)[7] (see below). A similar 'inertia' in politics led to the further extension of the welfare state and progressive taxation in the late 1960s and early 1970s in many countries. Inertia in fact makes the ebb tide stronger when it finally comes: unions and Left go on offering the same services and policies, using the same structures, while the world changes around them. This leads the working class, already doubtful whether they need unions and the Left, to conclude that 'they don't do much for us anyway'.

The results of this 'second counter-tendency' will be apparent in some places and times in the late upswing, otherwise in the early downswing of the long wave. They will be decisively reversed in the depression crisis, once the mass of the population have come to see the status quo as intolerable and have been mobilised for radical change; the reforming surge that results will continue into the early upswing.

There is nothing automatic about equalising reforms as a response to depression – on the contrary, as we saw earlier, the generation in power at the beginning of the depression has quite different inclinations. But the more reactionary their policies, the deeper they dig themselves into the mire, and failure discredits them. The depression crisis is a period of learning: a painful one, with trial and error the main method employed at government level. Lower down, people slowly learn by bitter experience the lesson that market forces do not always give those who trust to them all they deserve; that collective action may be the only chance for individual betterment; and that the State should do more for the unfortunate. If, as happened last time, the crisis culminates in war, these lessons are learnt much more quickly and thoroughly; and in the defeated countries, the rich will lose assets through physical destruction and the wrath either of their victorious opponents, who hold them responsible for waging war, or of the people, who blame them for losing it.

The 'levelling' or equalising elements of this surge will vary, between waves and countries, but they are bound to include the State playing Robin Hood – taking from the rich to give to the poor, through taxation and expenditure, and perhaps even through once-and-for all measures like land reforms. In the last levelling surge (in and around the 1940s) there was also a great expansion of trade union membership and strength. In practice the contributions of governments and unions will not be unconnected. Governments do not make U-turns in their basic policies without powerful pressures from below, pressures which are likely to be reflected in growing union strength. Unions, in turn, are profoundly affected by government policies and legislation.[8] Levelling may also result from an increase in competition among firms, reducing their rate of profit. This may happen without specific State action, because more and more firms manage to jump on the bandwagon of the new technological style; but it may also result from new laws and policies, like the dissolution of the Zaibatsu in Japan in the late 1940s.[9] The thorough reintegration I have already spoken of will then, inevitably, take place in a context of increased equality.

There may be some movement towards equality later in the wave. If the upswing is interrupted by a considerable period of slow growth, this may have a similar impact to the depression, though weaker (thus slow growth in the USA in the middle and late 1950s seems to have contributed to the Civil Rights-Great Society move to the left in the 1960s). More generally, for the reforming generation bred by the previous downswing, a further move towards equality may seem a natural response to any difficulties in which the moderate conservatives of the upswing may find themselves. (See the discussion later of the industrial relations crisis around 1970.) There is also the possibility that a crisis of the upswing may lead to war, as in 1914, with the pressures for equality that this will bring. But at some point a reorganised, reactionary Right gets the upper hand, and holds it until far into the downswing.

The cyclical effect of the long wave will not, then, produce a simple movement from higher to lower inequality and back again. The reduction in inequality, which takes place mostly in a short period in the late downswing and early upswing, will be much greater than the increase, which will also be concentrated in the early downswing (although the preconditions for it were accumulating in the upswing). Nor will the regressive movement simply take back some of the gains of all the strata which were 'levelled up' earlier. At least in the UK and USA, currently, the political and economic forces at work are such as to *concentrate* the losses much more than the gains. Thus in the late 1940s the whole of the working class – that is, about the bottom two-thirds of the income distribution – appear to have gained fairly evenly, at the expense, mostly, of the rich. The losses of the late 1970s and 1980s, on the other hand, have fallen, in the UK and USA, mostly on what is now being called the *underclass*, disadvantaged by position in the labour force (in 'secondary', low technology jobs, or none), often by 'ethnic' affiliation, and increasingly by family situation (single parenthood, etc.).[10] An ominous aspect of the new inequality in these countries is the shift of poverty from the old to the young: as Martha Hill (1985) shows for the USA, the old are much better protected, by pensions, than they used to be, while children are now suffering increasingly from the break-up of families and the ineffectiveness of the alimony system.[11] The suffering may be no worse for the young than for the old, but the long-term social and economic consequences of child poverty are clearly likely to be much more grave.[12]

This account of long wave fluctuations in inequality is in sharp contrast to that of Mandel, outlined already in Chapter 1. Mandel is concerned mainly with one element of inequality, the 'functional' distribution of income between profits and wages, and he argues strongly that there is a shift from wages to profits at some stage of the downswing, which prepares the way for the upswing, and ultimately a shift back which helps to bring about a new downswing. There is much in Mandel's long wave theory to take issue with; we begin with his explanation of the shifts between wages and profits.

Profits and wages in the long wave: the origins of the long boom

How does the capitalist economy escape from the downswing? According to Mandel, as we saw in Chapter 1, the working class has to suffer 'climactic historical defeats after decisive episodes of the class struggle', in order for 'a sudden and sharp rise in the rate of surplus-value' to come about; which can in turn, 'if it gets and maintains momentum, reverse radically the tendency of the average rate of profit to decline, thereby initiating ... a long term upsurge of ... economic growth'.[13] How was the working class defeated, then? Mandel mentions 'Fascism, World War 2 and the Cold War' as bringing about 'a radical change in the overall sociopolitical environment in which the system operates (destruction of trade unions, elimination of bourgeois democracy, atomisation of the working class ...)'.[14]

This is very odd indeed. The destruction of trade unions, etc., did, of course, take place under the Nazi, Fascist and Japanese militarist regimes, wherever they ruled and conquered. But these regimes were beaten – smashed – and from their ruins, and in the countries they had conquered, arose the most vigorous trade union movements and 'bourgeois democracies', ever seen in those countries. (On the unions, see Figure 6.3.) Just the same tendency, though less sudden, was observed in the undefeated countries. The working class of the North was as far from 'atomisation' in the late 1940s as ever before or since; this is as our theory would predict at the end of a depression-crisis. At that point the Cold War began. Mandel's reference to that has some sense, for it is clear that it had the effect (it may even have had the aim) of dividing and weakening labour movements, particularly those of countries like France and Italy with strong Communist parties. It also helped to stop the advance of the US unions into the South.[15] But at the end of the day, it would be absurd, except perhaps in France and Italy, to speak of an atomised working class.[16] The Cold War had given capitalists not that, but an organised working class which had stopped getting stronger, and had leaders now who were more inclined to do deals. No, what happened in the 1940s was not Mandel's atomisation, but my reintegration.

Why should booms reduce profits? The case of the 1960s

We now move on some twenty years, to what for Mandel was the next decisive phase of the class struggle, the late 1960s. There is a Marxist tradition, not at all at odds with the thinking of the Right, which regards the existence of an 'industrial reserve army of labour' as an effective discipline on workers. Once full employment is achieved in the upswing, the capitalists are deprived of their stick, and the workers start to get out of hand. This may lead directly to lower profits, as higher wages are exacted from the helpless capitalists; or it may lead to inflation, as higher wages are conceded but passed on in prices – and then the government is forced to step in with deflationary measures which reduce demand and profits; or the rampant workers may burst forth in 'proletarian insurgencies' – waves of strikes, mostly – and shake capitalists' confidence profoundly. All three such effects are embraced by Mandel's concept of upturns in the class struggle; just such an upturn, he claims, took place in the late 1960s.

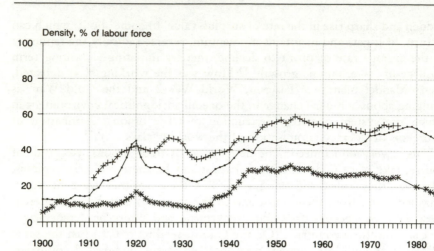

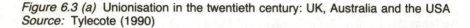

Figure 6.3 (a) Unionisation in the twentieth century: UK, Australia and the USA
Source: Tylecote (1990)

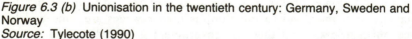

Figure 6.3 (b) Unionisation in the twentieth century: Germany, Sweden and Norway
Source: Tylecote (1990)

After these horrors (we are told), the consequent downswing is almost a relief to the capitalist. At least he gets his stick back. But Mandel does not think this enough: capitalists need not simply unemployment, but a 'decisive victory in the class struggle' before they are able and willing to embark on a

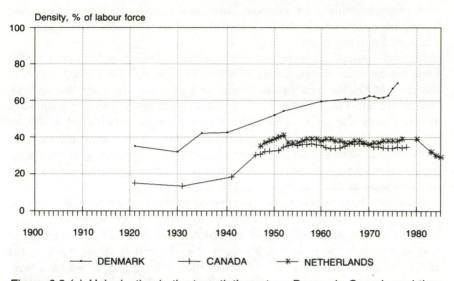

Figure 6.3 (c) Unionisation in the twentieth century, Denmark, Canada and the Netherlands
Source: Tylecote (1990)

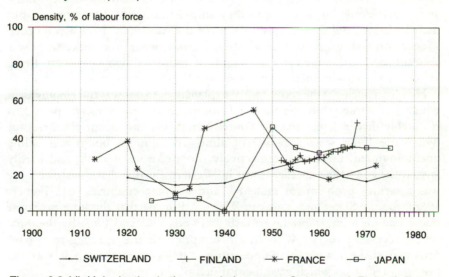

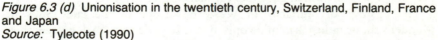

Figure 6.3 (d) Unionisation in the twentieth century, Switzerland, Finland, France and Japan
Source: Tylecote (1990)

new programme of rapid accumulation using new technology. Here there is clearly some similarity to the idea that the depression crisis finishes with, and is resolved by, 'reintegration'. But what reintegration! If integration implies some kind of constructive partnership between groups, this is the sort of partnership seen between rider and (reluctant) horse: the rider, having been thrown, climbs back into the saddle with better reins, a larger whip, and sharper spurs.

Mandel's assertions were not made without evidence. Screpanti (1984) finds major strike waves, across Western Europe and the United States, in the early 1870s, the periods just before and just after the First World War, and in the late 1960s–early 1970s. These periods correspond to long wave peaks, except the early 1870s, which is a peak nonetheless of a shorter 'wave'. He distinguishes these specifically *proletarian* movements from more broadly-based ones at other times; in the 'proletarian insurgencies' industrial workers had the confidence to take on capitalists on their own and for their own ends.[17]

How can these upheavals be interpreted in our framework? We seem in each case to be dealing with a crisis of the upswing, or one aspect of it. There is every reason to expect rapid expansion and technological change to heighten tensions in industry. Moreover, in the earlier strike waves – the 1870s and around the First World War – the upswing was, as we have seen, accompanied by an upswing in prices which tended to reduce the real wages of industrial workers (while of course benefiting the peasantry – and capitalists' profits). No wonder the industrial workers struck at such times, and struck alone; but in doing so they showed not only their strength, but their isolation, and their disadvantages. In the late 1960s there was no such squeeze on real wages; still, in Western Europe, where the strike wave was concentrated, the after-tax real wages of industrial workers were being affected by a rapidly increasing *tax wedge*.[18]

How convincing is the conventional explanation, that it was full employment which let workers 'off the leash'? Looking at the most recent period, it is notable that in Japan and the United States, the two major countries for which the 1960s were a decade of almost continuous boom and falling unemployment, there was, respectively, no strike wave at all, and hardly any, at the end of the decade. It was in Western Europe that the strike wave was a serious problem for industry, and in some countries (e.g. France, 1968), for the State; and it was in Western Europe that the long post-war boom had been interrupted, variously between 1965 and 1967, by the most severe recession so far. While the resumption of the upswing may have provided strikers with their opportunity, it looks as though it was the previous recession which gave them much of their motive.

The upsurge of militancy in Western Europe in the late 1960s fits Mandel's thesis rather than mine only if it is regarded as a major strengthening of worker solidarity. It was in my view no such thing. What had happened was that the boom-induced quiescence of the rank and file union members had encouraged their leaders in most countries to take an exceptionally conciliatory position. They had let management do much as it pleased in the rapid introduction of Fordism (the British unions were uniquely resistant); and some co-operated in incomes policies which led to a shift from wages to profits, as in West Germany in 1966–8. In countries like France where the unions were weak to start with, worker quiescence had fed an attitude of arrogance among government and business leaders. Once the escalator mentality had been shaken by the sharpest recession since the war, rank and file workers were inclined to take the first opportunity to assert themselves. When that arrived, in the next upturn, the decentralised character of their militancy caught the employers off guard; success then made militancy infectious.[19] The wave of militancy thus made more impression on observers, and had more inflationary impact, than the underlying social changes warranted.

Some indication of the real underlying changes is provided by the figures for union membership. During the late 1960s and 1970s, union density (membership as a proportion of the employed labour force) fell in the USA and Japan (see Figure 6.3). In some Western European countries it fell, in others it rose; however, in some of the latter (the UK for example), the increase in membership was concentrated in the (growing) public sector – where membership was encouraged or even compulsory – and among women, a natural response to their increasing identification with the paid labour force. Male workers in the private sector continued to drift away slowly from the union movement. Once employers had reorganised and recovered their nerve, the underlying weakness of the unions became apparent.

What actually happened to profitability?

It is hard, then, to accept Mandel's explanation of the alleged shifts from wages to profits and back. Did such shifts, in any case, take place? Before we consider the evidence, we have to come to terms with the terminology: the various concepts of *profit* and *profitability* need careful definition. Once wages and salaries have been deducted from a firm's 'added value', what is left is gross profit. After making a guess at the depreciation of capital, and subtracting that, we have net profit, before tax; subtract the relevant taxes, and we have net profit, after tax. Sum these quantities across an economy or sector, and we have gross or net profits, before or after tax; we might be concerned with profits *on domestic operations* – whether or not they accrue ultimately to a domestic firm or to a foreign-based multinational; or we might wish to measure profits from whatever source, home or abroad, *accruing to domestic firms*. All these are still only quantities: most interest is shown in two percentages:

1 The *share of profit* in national or sectoral income – for which we may, of course, take profits gross or net, pre-tax or post, etc., and add rent to them, or not, as we choose.

2 The *rate of profit*, or *return on capital*, that is the absolute quantity of
profit (however defined) divided by the value of capital (a very difficult
concept to measure, for both theoretical and practical reasons).

The data on profitability for the last thirty or forty years are not very
trustworthy, but for what they are worth, Poletayev (1987) finds that, for
the major Northern countries, they register a trough in share and rate of
profit in the late 1870s, a peak in the early 1900s, another trough in the early
1930s, and a peak in the mid-1950s. These movements are unremarkable,
being easily explained by peaks and troughs in the rate of investment and
capacity utilisation.[20] We certainly do not need to put a Mandelian interpretation on the fact that rises in the rate and share of profit came some time
before the upswing. Firms adjust their capacity to downswings by scrapping
and low investment; once they have done so, 'distress selling' ceases and
prices and profits recover.[21]

What is more striking, and better documented, is the fall in profitability
(share and rate) in most of the North during the latter part of the last
upswing. In some countries this began in the late 1960s, in others only in the
early 1970s – but in all except France and Japan it preceded the clear end of
the upswing after 1973,[22] and cannot therefore simply be put down to falling
demand and capacity utilisation. It could be taken as bearing out the 'low
unemployment profit squeeze' hypothesis. Weisskopf, however, has suggested (1987) that it might have been increasing import penetration which
accounted for declining profits.

The mention of import penetration reminds us of the interconnections
among capitalist economies, and these must make us wary. A large part of
the increase in international trade has taken place within multinational
companies. Such companies are notorious for *transfer pricing* – setting prices
charged by one subsidiary for goods and services supplied to another, in
such a way that it is the subsidiaries located where profits taxes are low
which make most of the profits. It is therefore possible that a large part of
the recorded decline in profits is a figment of the company accountants'
imaginations. But I suspect that the effect of such deceits was modest, so far
as *changes* in recorded profits are concerned. More likely that multinationals'
profits increasingly *were* being made where they said – in those Southern
countries which (as we see in the next chapter) were at this period building
up their manufacturing industries at an extremely rapid pace – Brazil,
Mexico, Taiwan, South Korea, Hong Kong. In some cases multinationals
were straightforwardly substituting capacity in the South for that which
would have been, or actually had been, located in the North. In other cases
the same effect was achieved indirectly: multinationals were building up
their Southern production to supply new Southern markets – as in the case
of the Brazilian vehicle industry; which did not hurt Northern vehicle
manufacturing at all.[23] The new subsidiaries sent back their profits, and their

Table 6.2 Profit movements in Western industry, 1955–72

	Canada	Germany	Netherlands	Sweden	UK	USA	France	Japan	Australia	Italy
1A										
1955–67	28.4	31.2	34.0	24.1	26.0	21.6	–	39.9	25.0	27.5
1968–72	24.5	24.9	29.0	22.6	20.1	19.7	–	39.4	25.6	22.5
1B										
1955–67	20.0	23.2	–	12.6	15.5	31.9	–	25.2	–	12.4
1968–72	15.6	17.8	–	11.6	10.4	27.1	–	26.8	–	11.0
2A(I+T)										
1955–67	29.5	40.1	32.7	25.6	22.4	26.7	–	35.0	27.8	36.3
1968–72	27.0	36.7	29.4	21.9	20.8	23.4	–	35.2	34.7	30.1
(NFC)										
1955–67	–	–	–	–	22.4	21.9	21.0 (1960–7)	–	–	–
1968–72	–	–	–	–	19.8	19.0	22.8	–	–	–
2B(I+T)										
1955–67	12.4	30.4	–	9.6	10.4	23.0	–	17.1	–	21.5
1968–72	10.1	23.8	–	7.7	8.4	18.5	–	19.0	–	18.4
(NFC)										
1955–67	–	–	–	–	11.2	19.3	11.6 (1960–7)	–	–	–
1968–72	–	–	–	–	7.8	17.2	14.6	–	–	–

Source: Tylecote, 1986 b

Definition: 1 A narrow coverage – 'manufacturing'.
2 A broad coverage – 'industry plus transport' (I + T) (i.e. manufacturing, mining, construction, public utilities, and transport and communications industries); or 'non-financial corporations' (NFC) (non-financial corporate and quasi-corporate enterprises, including public corporations).

A In terms of net profit shares (net operating surplus as per cent of net value added);
B In terms of net rate of return on capital (net operating surplus as per cent of the net capital stock of fixed assets, excluding land).

cost to the Southern balance of payments was balanced by the increasing export of low-technology manufactures (for example, footwear, in the Brazilian case) which reduced profits, capacity, wages and employment in the corresponding low-technology industries in the North. We would not expect to find this process at work in Northern countries like Japan and France which were late industrialisers with (at the time) relatively low wages in manufacturing, and only a small stake in multinational enterprise; and we would not then expect so much, if any, decline in profitability there. It turns out (see Table 6.2) that precisely these two countries were exceptions to the declining trend. If the 'international' explanation is correct, we would expect to find that the fall in profitability *on operations in the North* (which is what we have been discussing) was not matched by any fall in profitability, from whatever source, of Northern firms.

Was there then such a fall in profitability 'from whatever source'? Pitelis (1986) has provided figures for the share of after-tax gross profits in gross private disposable income in the UK and USA in each peacetime quinquennium between 1920 and 1984 – subtracting profits due abroad, but including rent and income from abroad. A miracle: the decline in profits has vanished!

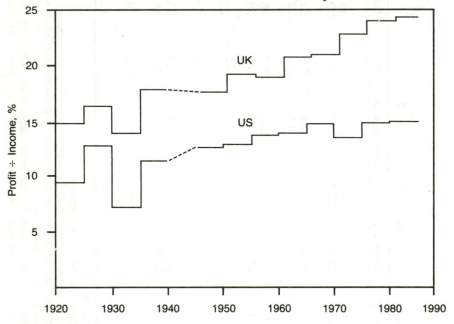

Figure 6.4 Profit shares in the USA and UK, 1920–84
Source: Pitetis (1986) Tables 1 and 2
Note: Profit is Gross Trading Profits after taxation of companies and financial
institutions before providing for depreciation and stock appreciation; it
includes rent and income from abroad but excludes profits due abroad (net
of UK tax) and taxes due abroad. *Income* is Personal Sector Disposable
income plus Undistributed *Profit.*

In the UK they climb steadily, from the early 1930s trough, except for small dips just after the war and in the late 1950s. In the USA the steady climb after the Depression has no dips until 1970–7 (which was certainly a bad time for US business) and ends, as in the UK, at an all-time high (Figure 6.4). Pitelis's figures may even somewhat understate the rise since the 1950s, if Cowling (1982) is to be believed. For Cowling, recorded profits are thoroughly misleading: as firms grew larger, and the majority of shareholders had less and less say over their control, as their profits and management's salaries were subjected to tax at higher and higher marginal rates,[24] managers increasingly *appropriated* corporate income as 'perks' of one kind or another. The true profit position of firms, so far as their relations with customers and workers are concerned, is, for Cowling, better gauged from the share of profits *plus overheads* in total income; and this share, he finds, has risen steadily.

Are the findings for the USA and UK likely to hold for the other countries with an apparent decline in profits? Not necessarily, for Anglo-American firms were much quicker than most others to internationalise their operations. Perhaps the others – excluding France and Japan – did suffer some decline; but then they had had, in the aftermath of wartime devastation, exceptionally high rates of profit. A return to peacetime normality is not ominous and needs no explanation beyond the passage of time.

Three conclusions seem reasonable, from the evidence considered. First (allowing for transfer pricing and Cowling's arguments), profits on operations in the North did not fall so far or so soon as has been claimed, during the late upswing (late 1960s – early 1970s). Second, what falls there were cannot be blamed on an increase in worker bargaining power, brought about by low unemployment, nor could they have been expected to depress investment *world-wide*, although they might have tended to push it Southwards to some extent. Third, there is no evidence that the share of profit in disposable income in the North fell – it *rose* in the UK and USA.

This is enough, I think, to show that Mandel's explanation of the downswing is implausible – but not enough to turn it on its head. As I am just about to explain, what is relevant to the argument here is not the distribution of income between profits and wages, but income inequality more generally, and there is no evidence of any general increase in this in the North between the 1950s and the 1970s. In Europe, on the contrary, the statistics suggest some levelling, particularly in after-tax income. There are three counter-arguments: first, Cowling's, on 'perks'; second, that illegal immigration into the United States produced an 'underclass' whose incomes would be largely unrecorded; third, that the shift from low incomes in old age to low incomes in single-parent families meant an increase in *real* inequality in some sense (e.g. many old people had assets they could run down – few single parents had; old people have more modest requirements for consumption than young, and in any case if *they* go without, little economic damage is done). Nonetheless it is clear that we shall not be able to blame the downswing, initially, on increased inequality in the North. We would, on the other hand, be on much firmer ground if we were to point to its *persistence* through the 1980s as due to some extent to the marked increase in inequality which undoubtedly took place in most Northern countries in the decade after 1975.

THE EFFECT OF INEQUALITY ON GROWTH

Having argued through one half of the feedback loop, we turn to the other. It appears that fast growth, in the long run, makes for high inequality (even if that effect may wait until other factors have brought a downswing); likewise slow growth leads rather more quickly, through a depression crisis, to lower inequality. Can we also conclude that high inequality makes for low growth? We begin this section, as we ended the last, with Mandel, for he argues that at least one contributor to inequality – the rate of profit – must rise sharply, as a precondition of recovery from a long wave downswing.

Must profitability rise to launch an upswing?

In fact Mandel's arguments imply that what is most important is the *expected* rate of profit – it is for future profits that capitalists invest. It is not even clear, however, that a rise in the *expected* rate of profit is a precondition of the upswing. All we really must concede is that at any given time there will be some expected rate of profit which a particular firm will treat as a minimum: if an investment project is not expected to make at least that, then the firm will not go ahead with it. But investment may rise without a general rise in expectations of profit. For example, we may move from the early stages of diffusion of a new style, when only a few firms have what it takes to make a success of new technology, to the later stages, when markets become more competitive, and barriers to entry are lower. In the early stages there may be a few investment projects expected to make huge profits, while the majority are not worth going ahead with; in the later stages distribution is much more even, with more projects expected to make above the minimum rate. Or it may be that the cut-off point is lowered, because, for example, the interest rate falls, so that the cost of capital is lower. Both these assumptions are plausible for the long wave upswings on record.

Another assumption which it would be unwise to make is that the upswing requires a prior rise in private investment. There are other components of aggregate demand which may rise instead: government expenditure of various kinds, or private consumption.[25] It is certainly hard to imagine that the upswing could be *sustained* without a rise in investment, because there would otherwise soon be a shortage of capacity; but that only requires that investment rise in the wake of rising demand. Such a rise is almost inevitable whatever the previous situation, since a rise in demand increases both actual profits and (a fortiori) expected profits on new investment. The observation that profits and investment are higher during an upswing than in the previous period thus tells us nothing at all about the causes of the upswing.

It may still be argued that, other things being equal, a rise in the existing rate of profit is bound to *help* bring about an upswing. Will it not make businessmen more optimistic? And is it not true that the more profit is made, the more can be ploughed back into new investment? Yes, though there are other sources of finance than profits (borrowing, for example), and other uses for profits than investment – dividends, for example, and the accumulation of financial capital. The real difficulty with this line of argument is the other things assumed to be equal. They should not include consumer expenditure, for an increase in the share of profits tends to decrease private consumption, as Kalecki (1954) showed long ago. It does this for two distinct reasons: first, profits ultimately accrue to people who on the whole are wealthier than the average, and such people consume relatively little of any increase in income.[26] Second, it is usually a long time before these people actually receive the extra income in visible, disposable form, for

(a) much or most will be *retained* by the firm for physical or financial investment, and
(b) even what *is* distributed as dividends will be for the most part held by financial institutions – pensions funds and insurance companies – for reinvestment, not dished out to the ultimate beneficiaries for immediate consumption.[27]

Kalecki (1954) argued, in fact, that far from a shift from wages to profits paving the way to the recovery from the Depression, it had paved the way into it: he showed that there had been such a shift in the USA during the 1920s, which had undermined consumer spending so that, once the investment boom of those years was over, aggregate demand was insufficient (see Figure 6.4).

The closer we look, then, the less plausible Mandel's thesis seems: it is in general neither necessary nor even desirable for the relaunching of rapid economic growth that capitalist profits should increase at the expense of workers' earnings; nor is a reverse movement, from profits to wages, likely to contribute to the downswing. One exception must be conceded – an exception which may have misled Mandel. In countries devastated by war, there is no need to worry about inadequate consumption or demand. It is the supply of goods which is the problem, and the need is to hold down consumption as far as possible so as to leave resources free for rebuilding the country's stock of capital. In such circumstances a high rate of profit is all to the good. Just such a rate was, as we have seen, achieved in continental Europe in the late 1940s, though more through agreed restraint by unions than by Mandel's 'atomisation of the labour force'. (The *share* of profit was not so much above normal as the rate, for the stock of capital was low; and rents and interest were exceptionally low. The share of wages in national income was thus reduced much less than the rate of profit was raised.)

The effects of inequalities of income

We can generalise Kalecki's warning about the effects of a rise in the rate of profit. Whether total consumption is adequate to sustain demand will depend to a large extent on the distribution of income and wealth. If this becomes more unequal, the poor lose, and they have to reduce their consumption in much the same proportion, or fall deep into debt. The rich gain; and they are not obliged to make an equal increase in their own spending, nor will they: instead, they will choose to use some of their gains to increase their stock of paper assets, particularly if those gains have not even been distributed to them, but kept by firms as retained profits. Thus total consumption spending will fall. (Government spending and transfers must of course be taken into account: to the extent that it taxes the rich to give to the poor, or to direct its own spending to their needs, it reduces the inequality of (after-tax) income in a way which will stimulate aggregate demand.)

Under-consumption will not be the only ill-effect of an unequal distribution of income and wealth. The existence of poverty cheek by jowl with affluence causes all kinds of social tensions and demoralisations, which will damage the economy. The education (even the physique) of the next generation of workers may be the worse for it, particularly when, as recently, children make up a large proportion of the poor. And it may set back the development of mass production industries, since there will be a wide range of goods required for the different income levels, rather than a narrow band of more or less standard products. (This appears to have told against Britain in its nineteenth century rivalry with the United States.[28])

Differences in pay

As we have seen, differences in pay are of growing importance as a source of inequality. They are most likely to be damaging if they are horizontal – between groups of workers at broadly the same level in different industries, or even in different firms in the same industry. If such differences are large, then low-wage firms and industries may be able to survive and prosper in spite of techniques which are less advanced or even in every way less efficient than those of higher-wage rivals. What is more, if horizontal differences seem for some reason reasonably secure and permanent, firms presently employing high-wage labour will have an incentive to move to the low-wage labour: to spend effort and money on a change which will do nothing in itself to improve efficiency. Likewise, a firm already enjoying relatively low wages may well prefer a strategy which will help to keep them low – say by making the workers as ignorant and divided as possible – to one which would increase efficiency by tapping workers' potential for initiative and participation and would thus at the same time make them more formidable opponents in any dispute over wages. (In the terms of Chapter 3, such inequalities make for *disintegration* between management and labour, and thus for low productivity.) Now we have no reason to think that there has been any marked increase in horizontal differences in Northern industry, at least until the 1980s. However, there has been an equivalent change – the growing unity of the world economy, referred to at the beginning of this chapter. Where forty years ago a labour-intensive US firm might look for some reduction in wages by shifting production from (say) Massachusetts to the Carolinas, now it can as readily move to Mexico or Haiti, and cut its pay to a small fraction of previous rates. This change was already apparent in the 1960s. (We shall see in the next chapter how much manufacturing exports from South to North have grown.)

Horizontal differences are important, but they are never so entrenched as *vertical differentials* between different levels in the occupational hierarchy: top management and lower management, skilled, semi-skilled and unskilled workers. To explore the effects of differentials, let us lump management and skilled workers together as 'skilled', and all the rest together as 'unskilled'; and let us suppose this skilled/unskilled differential is large, in the economy as a whole. We shall find that this leads to a rather wide difference in pay levels between capital goods and consumer goods producers, in favour of the former, for they have a relatively large proportion of skilled workers. (See the argument of Chapter 2 on the limited scope to mass-produce capital goods.) So capital goods – machinery etc. – will be relatively expensive (by comparison with a state of affairs where the skilled/unskilled differential was small), and it will be less profitable to re-equip with new capital goods with a view to saving labour. Habakkuk (1962) cites a lower skilled/unskilled differential as one reason for the greater willingness in the USA, as compared with the UK, to adopt labour-saving inventions in the early nineteenth century. He points out that it is not simply the relative pay in capital goods *vis-à-vis* consumer goods industries which is important. A decision to adopt the most labour-saving technique available needs more expenditure not simply on capital goods, but on the *most advanced* capital goods, which, as such, are built by particularly skilled people, since (being most recently developed) their manufacture has been least exposed to routinisation. Moreover the workers in the consumer goods industries most readily replaced by machines are those performing relatively simple tasks – presumably the less skilled. The lower the pay differential between these less-skilled consumer goods workers, and the most-skilled capital goods workers, the greater the incentive to mechanise further.[29]

It may be that the greatest significance of wage inequalities is as a *reflection* of the broader social situation. Where the difference in pay between top management and the lowest grade of workers is very large (and where there are large differences in pay among industries and firms) we can take it that those near the bottom are more or less powerless, and more or less despised. Not only will those in control of the firm have little financial incentive to economise on their labour by making them more productive, they will probably also have little *inclination* to raise up their status and improve their comfort, which would normally be a side-effect of greater productivity. In fact, since there will be little real contact and communication between top and bottom in such a situation, the boss will be in a very poor position to appreciate what changes might improve productivity. When the worm turns, and the low-paid organise, they win not simply more money in their pocket, they win respect, consideration and consultation.

CONCLUSION: THE EFFECTS OF INEQUALITY ON GROWTH IN THE TWENTIETH CENTURY

Growth and inequality before 1900

We have, then, made the case that inequality provided slow negative feedback in the twentieth century long wave. How far do these arguments apply to the earlier period? None of the paths through which twentieth century growth affected inequality could have been of much importance earlier: the role of the government, and thus its potential for redistributing income, was far smaller; the trade unions were far weaker; and since international inequality was much less pronounced, free trade, assuming it was induced by a boom, would not have had the same effect of increasing internal inequality. What actually happened to the distribution of income and wealth in the main Northern countries during the 1780–1914 period is not at all clear: it largely depended, we can assume, on whether the expanding industrial sector had more or less inequality than the (relatively) contracting agricultural sector.[30]

Where an agricultural society with a decidedly equal distribution of land evolved, as the USA did after 1840, into an industrial society with a highly unequal ownership of capital (and a stratification of wage earners between native and immigrant, North and South, to boot) then inequality was bound to increase considerably – and Williamson and Lindert have shown it did, in the USA, though not to a high level by comparison with Europe. Where the original agricultural society had highly unequal ownership of land, as in most of Europe, then industrialisation would have no such effect, more likely the reverse; and Kuznets has shown for some European countries that by 1900 there was, in general, a trend towards equality. We can surmise from this that any period of fast growth in Europe would, by bringing on industrialisation, have made for less inequality, and in the United States, has made for more.

Changes in the effects of inequality

Many of my arguments on the ill-effects of inequality clearly had less force before this century. At the beginning of the Industrial Revolution, less was lost if those at the bottom were low-paid, ill-regarded and unorganised – first, because firms were relatively small, and so the 'boss' could see with his own eyes what the situation was on the shop floor; second, attitudes were different in society at large. When the watchword was

God bless the squire and his relations
And keep us in our proper stations

even those at the bottom might take great inequality as a fact of life; modern society, on the other hand, preaches equality of opportunity, so that great inequality of achievement leads to either resentment or self-contempt or both, which is liable to lower productivity.

Keynesian or Kaleckian arguments about 'underconsumption' also had little relevance when there was no dense network of financial intermediaries standing between income and the spending of it. What income the poor got, they pretty soon spent; but what the rich got, they spent too, either in the traditional style of conspicuous consumption, or in the newer 'bourgeois' manner of investment in the expansion of their businesses or the 'improvement' of their lands. There was very much less scope than now for Keynes's paradox of thrift, in which extra saving begets not productive investment but simply a shortfall of effective demand, and thus less income and investment. On the contrary, however miserable it might make the poor to be squeezed for the benefit of the rich, so long as the rich did put that extra income into productive investment, it raised the growth rate and came back, in the end, as extra income for the poor. It was easier, too, for rich landowners and capitalists to put the necessary finance together for large projects.

To make this sort of concession is not to go to the opposite extreme and treat extreme inequality as necessary for growth before the rise of industrial capitalism. As we shall see, one of the advantages of the British economy over the French and other continental economies in the eighteenth century appears to have been its relatively equal distribution of income, which among other things provided a mass market for the new factory-made goods. At the same period the northern states of the United States had an even more equal society, through narrow pay differentials and easy access to land, and yet they more or less kept pace with Britain as it accelerated away from the rest. That might be put down to the United States' abundance of natural resources; but some of the credit might go to the superior health, education and ambition of the American poor, thanks to that lesser inequality. We shall look later at other cases which make the same point. It was, after all, not impossible for more equal societies to match the advantages of inequality. Agricultural co-operatives, pioneered in Scandinavia around mid-century, could mobilise the same resources of land and labour as could the large landowner; the 'universal bank', pioneered in France at much the same time, could draw together from small savers more finance than any rich individual could deploy. And given the right pressures from below, the modern state could be induced to carry through projects beyond the reach of private capital. Once the necessary innovations in institutions were made, the advantages lay wholly on the side of equality; and as I have argued, they grew more and more telling.

INEQUALITY FEEDBACK: CONCLUSION

The general drift of the discussion so far has been to suggest that within Northern countries, low inequality makes for rapid economic growth. But the effect has not been constant over the last two centuries: it was modest at best at the beginning of the period, and by now, I have argued, it is large. Nor is it immediate or mechanical. For example, if during a boom there were an increase in income inequality via an increase in the share of profit, as might well happen, this would not bring the boom to an end at once. In the short run the effect of the profit increase might well be to increase the growth rate further, as business confidence improved, and high profit encouraged high saving, which released resources for high investment. But once the investment boom is no longer sufficient to maintain demand without high consumption, any increase in inequality will undermine the boom, as happened in the 1920s. If the increase in inequality arrives later (as in most Northern countries in the late 1970s) then it will not help to cause the downswing – we must seek other reasons for that – but it will certainly exacerbate and prolong it.

In the effects of growth on inequality we have also to distinguish between the short run and the long. Certain sources of inequality, like unemployment, decline in the upswing, and to that extent there is a fast feedback from rapid growth to lower inequality; on the other hand, the long run effect of fast growth is to strengthen those forces within the economy and polity which will, in the end, work to increase inequality. Confusingly, this effect only becomes apparent in the downswing, and is thus hard to disentangle from the fast feedback from that – or from the initial effects of the new technological style, which are also to increase inequality.

Chapter 7

Inequality feedback (2) International and in the South

To set the scene we begin with a brief essay on the evolution of international inequality during our period.

INTERNATIONAL INEQUALITY IN THE WORLD ECONOMY SINCE 1780

By 1780 the West Europeans had been masters of the seas for more than two centuries. They had conquered, they had plundered, and increasingly they had traded, through their control of the sea.[1] As the world economy developed it would be a world economy *of* the West Europeans, in which the vast bulk of trade involved them, their colonies, and ex-colonies, as seller, buyer, or both. But for the moment, their trade was held back by a number of limitations, which would ease as the years went by. First, even their ships could not carry freight cheaply over long distances, and so trade across the oceans was restricted to cargoes of very high value per unit of weight or volume. Where there was a land journey of any length at either end, the restriction was severe indeed.[2] Second, their general level of technology was not far above that of South and West Asia and only marginally superior to East Asia.[3] That meant a military inhibition – they could not (yet) simply impose themselves upon Asia as they had upon the Americas, and rearrange the economy of the most populous continent, for their convenience; they had to find genuinely willing trading partners.[4] And while their civil technology was so little better than that of the East, such partners would be hard to find.[5] So, for the time being, most of their trade, by volume, was with each other, and with Eastern Europe, particularly on the trade routes which crossed the Baltic and North Sea,[6] and the trade which was expanding most quickly was that on the shortest ocean route, across the North Atlantic, with the West Indies and the British colonies in North America.

The curb by transport costs was pushed back rapidly and continuously over two centuries. At sea, improvements in sailing ships did most to reduce costs until the late nineteenth century, when they were gradually superseded by coal-, then oil-powered ships: in these, the cheapening came first mainly from improved engines, latterly the diesel, then from increases in size, and most recently from the drastic reduction in handling costs achieved by 'containerisation'. On land, the reductions were first gradual, via the improvement of road surfaces and the extension of the canal network where practicable; then from the mid-nineteenth century they were rapid, with the onward march of the railway; after 1900 scarcely less rapid, as the improvement of road haulage and, again, containerisation, made the main contributions. There are now few products which would not be moved half-way round the world, by sea and land, in response to a 30 per cent difference in manufacturing costs.

The fall in transport cost – backed by a parallel improvement in communications (telegraph, telephone, radio) – was an indispensable element in the development of any true world economy. In the development of the particular world economy we have got, the other indispensable element was the widening of the technological gap. The narrow West European lead I spoke of, was in fact held by the *North*-West Europeans – by Britain and her North American colonies, Holland, Belgium and France, with their neighbours to the east and north, not far behind. These early leaders have since enjoyed two centuries of continuous technological advance, with a definite tendency to accelerate, which has brought them (and their later offshoots, like Australia) further and further ahead of the world average, let alone the backmarkers. The only other countries to get into the leading 'advanced technology' group have been those eastern and northern neighbours like Germany and Scandinavia, and Japan, one of the East Asian countries which was not far behind at the beginning.[7]

In other words, the long-term trend has been towards *increasing international inequality*.

The character of international inequality has not greatly changed: it involves the possession (or lack) of advanced, or 'high', technology. High technology means the capacity first to produce sophisticated goods and services – high-technology *products* – and second to do this and other economic activities efficiently, particularly in terms of labour productivity – high-technology *processes*. The *possession* of high technology does not simply mean the *location* of high-technology production on one's territory, though in 1780 and even 1880 the two in practice came to much the same: it means the ownership and effective control of such production wherever it is located, and by now, with the growth of multinational firms, that is a very different thing. There is another important distinction, between technical expertise, narrowly defined, and the broader organisational capacity which is in practice required to reap the fruits of that expertise. Possession of high technology requires both. As Japan and the other East Asian countries have shown, those with the latter need not take long to acquire the former. In order to do so, however, they need to keep control of their own affairs, and whether they succeeded in that depended not only on organisational skills but on technical expertise in the military area. At the outset of our period it was in military technology that the North-West European advantage was most marked.

The military factor in the evolution of international inequality

At every stage in their rise to world domination the North-West Europeans made telling use of their military strength, tested and improved in a hundred neighbourly wars.[8] Their military relationship with each overseas territory tended to go through two stages: first, the direct use of force, either for outright conquest or (as in the Chinese case) something less, which made settlement possible (North America, Australia, etc.) and/or trade (China, India, etc.). Where North-West European settlement was sufficiently thorough, as in North America and Australia, the territory became effectively an extension of North-West Europe (NWE). Otherwise, the second stage followed: power passed, sooner or later, to some group within the territory, settlers or native, who used North-West European military technology to help maintain and extend their control. Even in this stage there was an advantage to be gained by the North-West Europeans, through the sale of arms and the likelihood that the new rulers would be inclined to maintain the trading relationship with them, little changed.[9]

The relationship with most of Asia and North America followed the two-stage pattern quite faithfully, the first stage beginning with the British and Dutch conquests in India and Indonesia before 1780, and culminating in the British and French seizure of Palestine, Lebanon, Syria and Iraq in 1919; the second stage began around that high point of empire and was completed in the 1950s. Matters proceeded rather differently in Central and South America, because these lands had already been conquered by the Spaniards and Portuguese in their heyday, before they fell under the shadow of their Northern rivals. There were settler elites already in place, and it was possible to move directly to the second stage – their 'liberation' of the continent, during the nineteenth century, mostly with British help and encouragement. The settler elites then used NWE arms to conquer the lands still under native control. Sub-Saharan Africa was another slightly deviant case: at the beginning of our period it was being milked of people, for use as slaves in the Americas, which proved to be most conveniently done using a sort of bastard second stage, in which local chiefs unscrupulous enough to co-operate in the trade were supplied with NWE arms with which they built up their power and seized their 'exports'. After 1809 the British turned against the slave trade and slowly squeezed it out, leaving the degraded African States to rot. The more usual first stage then began, late, most of Sub-Saharan Africa being conquered in the 'scramble for Africa' after 1870; so did the second stage, with the independence of Ghana in 1956.[10]

Whatever NWE owed to its military technology in the development of *its* world economy, its civil technology was, in the long run, more important. Led by the British until the late nineteenth century, NWE rapidly built up its capacity to supply goods – manufactures – which the rest of the world wanted; it introduced crops where necessary, and helped to provide ports and railways, so that the would-be buyers could be sellers too, of products which it wanted. Initially the trade was quite simply of NWE's manufactures for the rest of the world's 'primary products', i.e. the products of agriculture and mining. But there is no rule which lays down that high-technology countries must only sell manufactures and that low-technology countries must only sell primary products. In the first place, what once counted as a high-technology product, too difficult for low-technology countries to make or at least to make cheaply, may now count as relatively low-technology, the necessary techniques having diffused through most of the world. We saw that long ago with the simpler textiles; we are seeing it now with steel. Second, although low-technology countries may not actually *possess* all the know-how required for a product, multinationals may be producing it on their territory, with imported equipment and components – radios and other electronic goods are a current example. Third, it may be profitable for a high-technology country to make a low-technology *product* with high-technology processes. Anyone with the right climate and soil can grow wheat, for example, but the cheapest way to grow it nowadays involves very high technology – marvellous feats of mechanical and chemical engineering – and countries like Canada and Australia are not the less 'advanced' for relying largely on the export of such goods.

The pattern of trade is always changing, then, with the development of new techniques and the diffusion of old ones, but its basis remains the unequal relationship between a small number of advanced countries with a monopoly of the latest products and techniques, and a larger number of more backward countries, always adopting established techniques from the advanced countries and yet (as a group, on average, and in the long run) falling further and further behind. The small advanced nucleus now extends beyond North-West Europe, to Central Europe, Scandinavia, Italy, North America, Australasia and (last that shall be first) Japan; so we can now drop the ugly abbreviation NWE and call it either the core, or the North. (The latter term is more current, though it ignores the Australasians). The more backward trading partners of the core have been called the periphery, and that name seems to be a good one too, but the world is not so simple as to fit well into two categories; what shall we call those countries intermediate between the clearly backward and the most advanced? Semi-periphery?[11]

The term semi-periphery is now familiar in the literature,[12] but I propose to use it in my own, precise sense. First let us clarify what a *peripheral* country is. It is one which possesses only low technology in terms of both products and processes. (Any high-technology operations on its territory will be under foreign, 'multinational' control.) It plays a low technology role in world trade, being dependent on the core for high-tech. goods or (at best) for the high technology which multinationals use on its territory. A semi-peripheral country, for me, is just one step up: it *participates in world trade* as though it was peripheral but on the other hand it does possess certain high-technology sectors, or *proto*-high-technology sectors, which use advanced techniques and make advanced products, but cannot (yet) hold their own in competition on the world market, so that they have to be protected and nurtured by tariffs and subsidies. These 'proto-high technology' sectors can be described, together, as an 'internal core', and the rest of the economy as an 'internal periphery'; the internal core *exploits* the internal periphery in the sense that it trades with it on less favourable terms than could be had on the world market. (The simplest, crudest way of doing this is to protect the internal core, and not the internal periphery, with tariffs or other forms of import controls. There is, however, the alternative of keeping at least the appearance of free trade, while providing the internal core with support of various kinds paid for by the internal periphery, through a land tax, for example.) This arrangement can be described as *high technology bias*: any country with a significant degree of high technology bias, of exploitation of an internal periphery by an internal core, and trading with the rest of the world as a peripheral country, is semi-peripheral. High technology bias (HTB) is likely to be particularly attractive to a large peripheral country seeking to catch up with the core, particularly if it is trying to build up its military strength. The classic example is Russia, the spur being the humiliation of the Crimean War of 1854, although its policy only took clear shape in the last quarter of the nineteenth century. In this century, HTB has become the norm among the stronger of the 'developing' countries – Mexico, Brazil, Argentina, Venezuela, South Africa, India, Turkey and Egypt.[13]

The other intermediate category is simpler but rarer: it consists of those countries with an overall level of technology intermediate between core and periphery which trade accordingly – selling medium-technology goods, or goods produced with medium-technology processes, to countries both above and below them in the world economy. Germany in the first half of the nineteenth century fitted quite well into this category; so did Japan in the first half of this century, and Taiwan and Korea now. (In 1850 it was the simpler types of textiles that Germany sold; in the 1980s the Taiwanese specialised in simple machinery and metal goods.) Such countries, because their trading position is higher than that of the semi-periphery, belong to the *semi-core* (a term of my own coinage). The semi-core includes countries with a more-or-less open, free-trading policy (like Taiwan now), and protectionist, 'closed' countries, (e.g. present-day USSR, Czechoslovakia, Poland, Hungary and East Germany). One would expect some high technology bias even in the relatively open ones, as they seek to move up further; but they do not depend upon HTB to the same extent as the semi-periphery, which cannot drop it without returning to the periphery.[14]

Armed with our four categories – and ready to assign countries to higher or lower positions in each – we can now make a brief sketch of the evolution of the world economic system since 1780. The emerging core consisted of Britain (rapidly going into the lead), Belgium, Switzerland and France, with the erstwhile leader, the Netherlands, falling back for want of coal or water power into the semi-core – a category which also contained Sweden, the German and Czech lands, and North Italy; it is too soon to speak of a semi-periphery because the appropriate policy measures had not yet been adopted by backward states. The periphery consisted of every other territory which had strong trading links with North-West Europe: the rest of Europe and the Americas, much of the African littoral, Eastern India and the East Indies.[15]

By 1850 Britain was beginning to lose the long lead she had opened up over the rest of the original core: Belgium, Switzerland and the (expanding) Northern USA were catching up fast, with only France merely holding its own. The German and Czech lands, led by Prussia, were rapidly moving into the core. To match the expansion of the core, the periphery was expanding and being drawn into a tighter trading relationship with the core – all of India, for example, with the completion of the British conquest, was now within the peripheral category, and British force had 'opened up' China, in the opium wars.[16]

By 1900 Russia had, as mentioned, already taken its place as semi-peripheral country no. 1, with its western territories – Finland, the Baltic States and Poland – taking a big share in the role of internal core. Brazil had begun to edge into the semi-periphery, with some protection of its industries. Japan, constrained by treaties with the Western powers, was practising high technology bias without tariff protection. Ahead of these countries in the race to catch up the core were Austria-Hungary (its western territories, at least), Italy, and the Scandinavian countries; these were semi-core countries, or in the Scandinavian case, on the edge of the core. United Germany was now very much in the core, Canada, Australia and New Zealand belonged there too by their virtue of their use of high technology processes, for all that their exports were of primary products. And the United States had taken over the lead from Britain at the top of the core, and like Britain a century earlier, was increasing its lead with every year that passed.[17]

Half a century later, after two great wars, the map of boundaries had altered greatly, but that of the world economy had changed only in directions already charted. Russia, after terrible sacrifices in war and peace, had reached the semi-core under a Communist regime which installed itself preaching equality and proceeded to practise extreme exploitation of its peasant internal periphery.[18] Its vassal states in Eastern Europe were also in the semi-core (East Germany, Czechoslovakia, Poland and Hungary) or in the semi-periphery (Bulgaria, Romania, Albania). The other European states were all in the core now, except for Greece, which by virtue of its shipping might just count as semi-core, Spain and Portugal (semi-periphery) and Yugoslavia (semi-periphery). The depression and second war (as we shall see) had persuaded the main Latin American states, with Turkey, Egypt, South Africa, and India, to move into the semi-periphery, determined to industrialise. China had arrived at the same conclusion, by way of near-disintegration, and near-conquest by Japan, under a new Communist regime. And Japan, which had first pursued ascent to the core by mostly peaceful means, then switched in the Depression to a military strategy, was now following a peaceful path under the Pax Americana.[19]

By 1985, after forty years of the Pax Americana and Pax Russica, almost all the countries which had been forcibly incorporated into the periphery had long been free, in principle, to do what they could to move out of it. Many of them had indeed made great strides in increasing industrial production, and the figures for gross domestic product suggested that they had been closing the gap between them and the core. Unfortunately a closer look suggested otherwise. Population growth in the periphery and semi-periphery had been much faster than in the core, so that the figures of economic growth *per head* compared much less favourably.[20] Moreover, much of the extra production capacity was owned by core multinationals, or had been financed by borrowing from the core. Much of the extra output had, therefore, to be subtracted to provide the multinationals with their profits, and to 'service' the debts.[21] Finally, as I pointed out in Chapter 1, the growth statistics ignored the loss of natural resources, and the division of those remaining among larger numbers. After all these allowances had been made, very few peripheral or semi-peripheral states were catching up at all. Fewer still could be said to have crossed the boundary between periphery/semi-periphery, and semi-core, and the only ones of those which had climbed any great distance were ex-Japanese colonies or city states of emigrant Chinese (South Korea, Taiwan, Hong Kong, Singapore; see below). For the rest, the core/semi-core and periphery/semi-periphery seemed like two neighbouring galaxies, each moving fast with some internal circulation, but moving ever further apart from one another. This was only a new expression of the long-term trend which I mentioned at the beginning of this chapter, towards greater and greater inequality among countries in the world economy.

Southern dependence and Southern inequality

To sum up the argument so far: the widening gap between core and semi-core (together to be called, simply, 'North') and periphery and semi-periphery ('South') is the most important element in international inequality. It is the difference in *technological capability* which is the key determinant of the relationship between North and South; further, the key *characteristic* of this relationship is the *dependence* of the South on the high technology of the North – whether in the physical form of goods imported from it, or in the (increasingly important) form of imports of the methods themselves, as through multinational operations within the South. In return the South supplies low technology goods and services of various kinds; these Southern exports used to be overwhelmingly composed of primary products but are now, to an increasing extent, manufactures (see Figure 7.1).

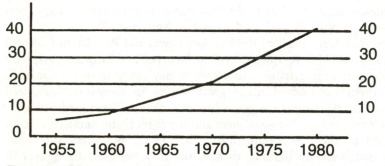

Figure 7.1 Share of manufactures in developing countries' exports to the North
Source: Calculated from UNCTAD (1983) *Trade and Development Report*, New
York: UN
Note: Developing countries' exports of manufactures to developed countries as a
proportion of their total exports to developed countries (excluding
petroleum).

We have seen that politically, the relationship between North and South tended to involve either

1 colonial or semi-colonial control of a Southern country by a Northern one, or
2 control of a Southern country by a local 'elite' using Northern military technology.

In either case the technological disparity between North and South is bound to lead to a severe distortion of political relationships within the country: those in power depend heavily on their link with the North and so less than they otherwise would on support within their own country. The extreme political inequality of the top-heavy State structure is bound to make for economic inequality: those in power redistribute income and wealth to themselves and their friends from the rest of the population. There is extreme regional inequality, to the advantage of the capital (and sometimes, too, the 'home base' of a dominant group).

Another, slightly more subtle source of inequality is the economic, as opposed to the military/political, link with the North. Traditional methods of production and distribution coexist with the latest Northern technology: those few Southerners who have the capital, skills or connnections to own or operate the latter, will be very well rewarded. The gap will be the wider to the extent that the State decides on High Technology Bias in favour of a protected and subsidised 'internal core' using more or less advanced technology.

These factors make for ever-increasing inequality,[22] but there are counter-currents. Colonial or semi-colonial rule of course creates nationalist resent-ment: the longer it continues in the face of such resentment the more the nationalist leaders – initially an elite themselves – feel forced to mobilise popular support and accordingly to espouse egalitarian ideology and policies; communism, at the extreme. The further left they have gone the longer it takes after they win power to abandon these pretensions – and the more precarious their position once they do. Even local elites with obvious links with the North cause nationalist resentment, which will combine with that of the have-nots; the Iranian Revolution is a recent case in point. From the argument in Chapter 3 we can see that there are two sets of circumstances (besides defeat in war) which make the existing regime particularly vulner-able. The first arise from rapid economic growth and consequent political disintegration: in this category we can put the Mexican Revolution of 1912, the Cuban Revolution of 1958 and the Iranian Revolution of 1978–9; the second arises from economic difficulties. To understand how and when these will become acute we have to look more closely at the relationship with the North.

CYCLES IN THE NORTH-SOUTH RELATIONSHIP

The obvious gauge of the state of the relationship is the terms of trade.

The best known measure of the terms of trade, is the Net Barter Terms of Trade (NBTT) which measures against a base year value of 100 the ratio of the prices of the South's exports to the North, to those of its imports from the North. There are objections of principle to the use of NBTT because it ignores changes in productivity on either side (Spraos, 1983), and there are many practical difficulties of measurement (Solomou, 1987). For our purposes, then, NBTT figures are only worth using if they show such marked fluctuations over the long wave that these problems seem un-important. Over the last century, the period of the economic long wave, they have done so: as we see from Figure 7.2, there has been a 'wave' in NBTT similar to those in economic growth – favourable to the South in upswings, unfavourable during downswings.

This conclusion is supported by Spraos's (1983) employment-corrected double factorial terms of trade (ECDFTT) data for the 1960–78 period,

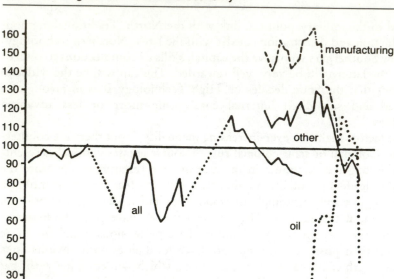

Figure 7.2 Net barter terms of trade of developing countries, 1897–1986
Source: UNCTAD (1987) Table 2.5; except for 1986, which I have calculated from
          Ray (1987)
Note: 1897–1970 series is for primary products against manufactures, 1913 =
        100; *source*: Spraos (1983). 1960–86 series show NBTT of various
        categories of 'developing countries and territories'. The dotted line shows
        those for 'major petroleum exporters', and the continuous line those for all
        other countries, among which are included 'major exporters of
        manufactures' whose NBTT are shown by the dashed line. Here, 1980 =
        100.

summarised in Figure 7.3: these provide a better indicator of what was
happening in terms of real purchasing power per head.

However, this regular pattern is only sustained for the entire period if we
exclude *petroleum* from the series. If we include it, we find a marked
irregularity in the long wave: in the early 1970s, just as, or just before, the
downswing should be producing a deterioration in the Southern terms of
trade, there is a marked improvement, and relatively favourable NBTT
persist, to some extent, until the collapse of the oil price in 1985–6.

Causes of terms of trade fluctuations

The explanation is made simpler if we leave petroleum out of account for the
moment. It is inherent in technological backwardness and dependence that
the economic structure lacks diversity and flexibility. Southern countries

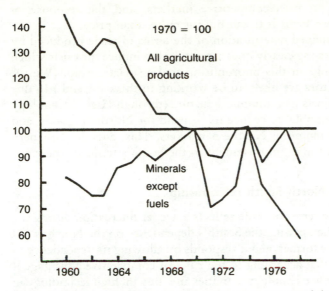

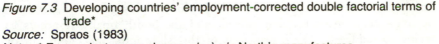

Figure 7.3 Developing countries' employment-corrected double factorial terms of
trade*
Source: Spraos (1983)
Note: * For product group shown, *vis-à-vis* North's manufactures.

find a very limited range of products which they are able, at least during the
upswing, to sell profitably in the North. These exports form the bulk of
their total exports (which is far from being true of any Northern country's
trade with the South) and a central part of their economy; not only their
economic, but their political and social structures become set in the shape
which fits this export trade and the complementary imports. Economic
growth then comes to imply continuous increases in the exports of these
products, for which the Northern market is inevitably limited. The prospect,
and even the reality, of falling real prices for these exports does not lead to an
early change of course, because of the lack of diversity and flexibility; it is
easier, for each Southern country individually, to seek to go on expanding its
revenues by *increasing* its traditional exports. (For the South as a whole this
is of course self-defeating.) Only deep economic, political and social crisis is
likely to be enough to shake the Southern country out of this economic cul-
de-sac.

Thus the terms of trade could be expected to move against the South even
if there had not been a downswing in the North. When there *is* a downswing
in the North, of course, the adverse movement goes much further: while
Northern demand falls, and puts severe pressure on prices in the competitive
markets on which most Southern products are sold, there is little compensation for the South from the fall in demand for Northern goods, for these are

generally not sold on price-competitive markets, and the response of oligopolistic Northern firms is to cut output rather than price.

The sharp and sustained deterioration of the terms of trade produced by the long wave downswing clearly does a great deal to induce the crisis which is necessary for change in this unpromising trading relationship. (We see below that other factors are likely to be working to the same end.) In due course, the South adjusts its economic structure (through High Technology Bias, where this is possible) to reduce its demand for Northern goods, and its supply of goods requiring Northern markets. This, and the Northern upswing, both make for an improvement in the South's terms of trade.

Other facets of the North-South relationship

The movement of the terms of trade reflects a deeper fluctuation during the long wave. During the upswing the South's dependence on the North is not uncomfortable for the former, and it responds by allowing its dependence to increase – accepting that according to the rules of comparative advantage it should specialise in low technology activities and 'buy in' high technology in one form or another from the North. In the downswing dependence becomes very uncomfortable indeed, and the South finally responds by trying to reduce it. The expressions of this slide into, and climb out of, dependence change over time. In 'The South in the long wave' (1989), I set out six other facets of it, besides the terms of trade:

(i) *The demand in the South for useless or inappropriate goods supplied by the North*: for example, baby milk[23] (inappropriate intermediate and capital goods may also be important).
(ii) *The South's demand for Northern weapons* of war and repression.
(iii) *The movement of Southern capital to the North.*
(iv) *The movement of Southern 'human capital' to the North.*
(v) *The South's 'net asset position' vis-à-vis the North* (the value of assets in the South owned by Northerners, *plus* Southern debt to the North, *less* assets in the North owned by Southerners).[24]
(vi) *The rate of interest* charged by the North on Southern debt.

The first four of these facets are of little importance until after the Second World War: the demand for useless Northern goods, and the flight of human and financial capital, could only become really important once improvements in communications, and Northern cultural penetration, had passed a certain point, while the South's demand for Northern weapons was insignificant until it had achieved political independence. Now all are important, and all have moved to the South's disadvantage during the current long wave. Any Southern elite, while it remains in power, becomes increasingly besotted with things Northern – thus (i) has increased. The more it loses touch with its own people the more it needs Northern weapons

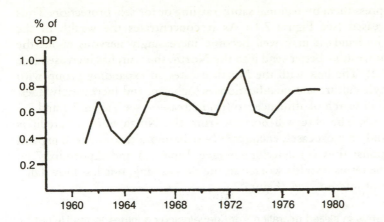

Figure 7.4 Developing countries' net arms imports, as % of GNP
Source: Calculated from figures in Sivard, R. L. (1982) *World Military and Social Expenditures, 1982*, Washington DC: World Priorities. See also Deger (1986)

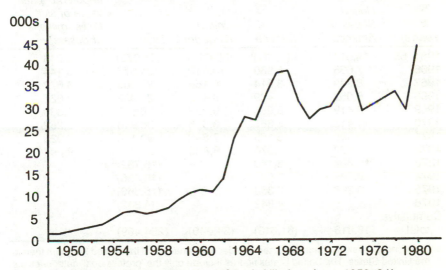

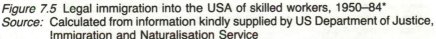

Figure 7.5 Legal immigration into the USA of skilled workers, 1950–84*
Source: Calculated from information kindly supplied by US Department of Justice, Immigration and Naturalisation Service
Notes: * Professional and technical workers from Asia (less Japan), North America (less Canada), South America, and Africa. (1) A similar series for 1934–49 shows immigration never exceeding 1,000 per year. (Same source). (2) This figure must seriously understate the recent rate of skilled Southern immigration into the USA, for according to Crewdson (1983) the illegal immigration, which by the early 1980s was of the order of 1 million per year, consisted, besides the 'wetbacks' wading the Rio Grande, largely of relatively educated 'tourists' arriving by air and quietly overstaying their visas.

either to impress them by regional sabre-rattling or for self-protection. Thus (ii) has increased (see Figure 7.4). As it concentrates the wealth of the country in its hands it may well become increasingly nervous about the safety of that wealth – better send it to the North; thus (iii) has increased (see Appendix 7.2). The link with the North creates an expanding group with Northern-style culture and qualifications which can, and increasingly does, move North in search of affluence; so (iv) increases – see Tables 7.1 and 7.2 and Figure 7.5. The elite will borrow from the North until its credit is exhausted, and, in most cases, encourage Northern multinationals to expand their operations; thus (v) deteriorates (see Table 7.3 and Appendix 7.1). Finally, as the terms of trade worsen in the downswing, one last blow falls: the real rate of interest rises (Figure 7.6).

Table 7.1 Trends in skilled migration from developing countries to the United States of America, Canada and the United Kingdom, 1961–76

	Number of skilled migrants from developing countries[a]				Imputed capital value of skill flows (millions of dollars)
Year(s)	United States of America	Canada	United Kingdom	Total	
1961–65	14,514	(6,147)[b]	(20,411)[c]	(41,072)	5,048
1966	7,635	5,930	10,812	24,377	3,144
1967	8,239	8,614	8,156	25,009	3,672
1968	8,052	7,489	9,418	24,959	3,821
1969	8,419	8,286	9,932	26,637	4,333
1970	11,412	6,867	8,635	26,914	5,252
1971	16,098	6,195	7,843	30,136	8,028
1972	15,822	7,070	8,833	31,725	9,094
1973	10,602	6,180		(16,782)[d]	
1974	8,725	7,631		(16,356)[d]	
1975	9,298	6,362		(15,660)[d]	
1976		4,842		(4,842)[e]	
Cumulative total	118,816	(81,613)	(84,040)	(284,469)	

a The concept of skilled migration used is wider for Canada and the United Kingdom than for the United States. The United States figures include only the 'professional' categories (i.e. engineers, natural and social scientists and doctors) whereas figures for the United Kingdom and Canada include 'professional, technical and kindred workers'.
b Total for 1963–5 only.
c Total for 1964–5 only.
d Total for the United States and Canada only.
e Total for Canada only.
Source: UNCTAD, 1979, *The Reverse Transfer of Technology* (Geneva: UN)
Note: Over the period covered, the US, UK and Canada received some 75 per cent of the skilled migration from developing countries to developed ones (same source).

Table 7.2: Skill flows in relation to domestic stock of skilled manpower: sample estimates for a selected number of developing and developed countries

Skilled migrants as a percentage of domestic stock or annual output

Country	Physicians Surgeons	Scientists	Engineers others
Developing countries of emigration			
Pakistan[a] (1970s)	50–70		
Syrian Arab Republic[b] (1971)	40		
Iran[b] (1971)	30		
India[a] (1966–7)	30	25	
Philippines[c] (1975–6)	21	11	10
Sri Lanka[d] (1971–4)	20	19	36

a Outflow as a percentage of annual output.
b Outflow as a percentage of stock in that year.
c Average annual flow of skilled emigrants as a percentage of average annual increase in domestic stock. The figure for 'others' dates to 1968–70.
d Outflow for the years 1971–4 as a percentage of stock in 1971.
Source: As for Table 7.1

Table 7.3 Debt indicators for developing countries in selected years, 1970–84

	1970	1974	1978	1981	1984
Ratio of debt to GNP	14.1	15.4	21.0	22.4	33.8
Ratio of debt to exports	108.9	80.0	113.0	96.8	135.4
Debt service ratio	14.7	11.8	18.4	17.6	19.7
Ratio of interest service to GNP	0.5	0.8	1.1	1.9	2.8
Total debt outstanding and disbursed ($ bn)	69.0	141.0	313.0	488.0	686.0
Private debt as per cent of total	50.9	56.5	61.5	64.1	65.0

Source: World Bank, 1985 p. 24
Note: The very large increase (more than five-fold) in the ratio of interest service to GNP is clearly only partly explained by the shift to private, non-concessional debt; more important is a factor not shown in the table – changes in interest rates; see Figure 7.6, below.

The depression crisis which thus develops in most of the South is thus far worse than that of the North – which has, among other consolations, a most favourable turn in its terms of trade. How does the South respond? We do not yet know, because the only crisis brewed from all the ingredients listed is that which is in progress now. In the 1930s, many Southern countries were in an extremely difficult situation, due to the terms of trade and (in many cases) debt; but most of the other difficulties were missing then, and besides, they were to some extent prepared. The First World War had provided something of a rehearsal for the slump, cutting the South off to a large extent

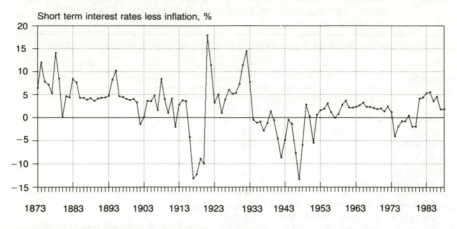

Figure 7.6 US real interest rates, 1873–1989
Source: UN Statistical Yearbook; Friedman *et al.*, 1982; OECD *Economic Outlook*, June 1990; Mitchell, 1983
Note: 'Interest rates' are one-year corporate bond yields to 1974, Treasury bill
rates from 1975. 'Inflation' is % change in consumer prices, throughout.

from Northern markets and sources of supply: the manufacturing industries developed then in the more advanced countries provided an invaluable base from which to begin the adjustment to the slump (see Galvao and Tylecote, 1990, on Brazil). The response to the slump, in many countries, was therefore quicker than any we have seen to the current depression crisis – for example, Vargas's Estado Novo in Brazil (1931) and Cardenas's reforming administration in Mexico (from 1934). A greater upheaval is required this time, before economy, society and politics can be reintegrated – for what I have been describing here is of course a long process of disintegration, in the terms of Chapter 3.

This is not the place to speculate on the form reintegration may take after the current depression crisis; better to look back on what happened after the last one. In a country like Brazil which was quite well prepared for the crisis, there were relatively superficial changes: the 'coffeecrats' of Sao Paulo moved much of their assets out of coffee into manufacturing, and the State – their State – became more favourable to industry, and (for a time) to industrial workers (Cardoso, 1979). In some other Southern countries, Northern powers intervened to help prevent any significant change: as Franklin D. Roosevelt is alleged to have said of the Nicaraguan dictator Somoza, 'I know he's a sonofabitch, but at least he's *our* sonofabitch'. (Northern colonial or semi-colonial power was not used obstructively everywhere; thus for example in India the British permitted a marked shift to import-substituting industrialisation (Tomlinson, 1979)). In both these categories inequality appears to have gone on rising steadily, or only paused during the depression. In many other countries, however, there were political upheavals which brought to power groups with a much broader constituency of support than the *anciens regimes*. The extreme example was of course the Communist revolution in China, completed in 1949. This quickly and drastically reduced inequality by dispossessing landlords and capitalists – including foreign ones. Other successful revolutionaries – Nasser in Egypt, Sukarno in Indonesia, Peron in Argentina, Cardenas in Mexico – carried less ideological baggage. Their levelling was more limited – in Egypt a modest land reform, in Argentina redistributive taxation and government expenditure, in Mexico land reform and expropriation of some foreign assets. What followed, too, depended on the character of the revolutionaries. A communist regime, for all that its officials may use their power to enhance their own living standards, is committed to an egalitarian creed: it can scarcely survive, let alone prosper, if it lets the gap between words and deeds grow to the point where apparatchiks live as far above the peasantry as the landowners and capitalists they dispossessed. Communist levelling is thus not only far-reaching, but not easily reversible. (This conclusion, as I write, is being pondered, painfully, in Beijing.) After non-communist revolutions the ebb comes sooner and easier. Since the right to own private property, in whatever amounts, has not been removed, new sources of inequality can quickly replace the old. Moreover, such regimes are less durable than Communist ones: Sukarno and Peron were over-thrown, and Cardenas's and Nasser's successors had none of their pre-decessors' egalitarian inclinations (see Lane, 1971; Lardy, 1978; Voslensky, 1981).

Inequality has, then, followed different courses in different Southern countries, but if we take the whole South, averaged, it is clear that there is a long wave fluctuation – a steady tendency to rise is reversed in and just after the depression crisis. We have now to consider how this fluctuation may affect economic growth.

INEQUALITY AND GROWTH IN THE SOUTH

Southern expansion inevitably depends to a large extent on the North. Almost any fool in power can show a respectable record of growth if a Northern boom is providing buoyant export markets and Northern lenders are providing cheap and plentiful credit. It is, moreover, those countries most prepared to accept dependence on the North which will benefit most from such conditions – and be hardest hit when a downswing comes. Nonetheless, it is possible to analyse the effects of the changes provoked by the depression crisis. The South as a whole is bound to gain collectively from the changes made in the stances of its members *vis-à-vis* the North: every increase in High Technology Bias means some decrease in its demand for high technology products from the North, and in its supply of low technology products, which will tend to improve its terms of trade.[25] Even in peripheral countries which cannot yet aspire to advanced technology, there will be some move towards self-sufficiency, as people give up work on now-unprofitable mines and plantations, and return to the subsistence occupations of their forebears.

Beyond the gain on the terms of trade, other facets of the relationship also change in the South's favour. The net asset position improves. Thus in the 1930s and 1940s, in some Southern countries – particularly those which moved sharply to the Left – debts to Northern banks and governments were repudiated, and Northern property taken over with little if any compensation. Prudent Northern governments rewarded or conciliated other, more friendly Southern regimes by writing off part of their debts. Even where property remained in Northern hands, it lost value as a result of the depression crisis and/or new economic developments (see Tables 7.4 and 7.5).

There are gains, however, which do reflect the internal effects of internal changes in Southern countries. Some can be put down to reintegration rather than increased equality as such – although as we shall see, the two are not always easily distinguished. Thus the more-or-less revolutionary states of the 1930s and 1940s took over foreign and native firms, and set up new ones.

Table 7.4 United Kingdom investments in Latin America, 1913, 1930, 1938 and 1951. (Nominal value, in millions of pounds sterling)

Country	All securities				Government and municipal loans		
	1913	*1930*	*1938*	*1951*	*1930*	*1938*	*1951*
Argentina	320	360	368	38	33	40	3
Brazil	148	151	164	46	73	83	15
Chile	61	49	63	37	21	25	17
Uruguay	36		23	5			
Peru	34	84	25	22	7	13	8
Rest of South America	26		37	29			
Cuba	33		28	24			
Mexico	99	50	66	38		12	1
Central America			8	5			
Total	757	694	782	244		173	44

Source United Nations Department of Economic and Social Affairs, 1955, *Foreign Capital in Latin America* (New York: UN), which sets out at length the limitations of the data (p. 156) but still makes it clear that most UK assets in Latin America were covered

Now it might seem that there is no control more remote than State control; but that depends on the State. Any revolution worth the name – as Konrad and Szelenyi (1979) have brilliantly demonstrated for Eastern Europe – brings a large chunk of the *intelligentsia* into power (i.e. people, mostly

Table 7.5 United States private long-term investments abroad, 1914–50 (millions of dollars)

End of year	Direct[a]	Latin America Portfolio[b]	Total	World total
1914	1,281	368	1,649	3,514
1919	1,988	418	2,406	6,456
1924	2,819	854	3,673	9,954
1930	3,634	1,610	5,244	15,170
1937	2,918	1,183	4,101	11,074
1940	2,771	1,003	3,774	10,591
1950	4,735	610	5,345	19,435[c]

[a] Book values of controlled enterprises.
[b] Nominal values, consisting mainly of foreign bonds publicly offered in the United States, but also including share of foreign corporations owned in the United States by non-controlling interests. Nominal values of foreign bonds considerably exceeded market values of the securities in 1951. Dollar securities held outside the United States are excluded, except in the figures for Latin America in 1930. The figures for 1914, 1919 and 1924 include all Mexican obligations ($266 million, $265 million and $27 million, respectively), though a large portion of such obligations was in default. Defaulted Mexican obligations are excluded in later years, but other defaulted Latin American dollar bonds are included in data for 1937, 1940 and 1950.
[c] No allowance is made in this figure for the value of direct investments damaged during the war, written off, or expropriated without compensation.
Source United Nations, 1955. These figures are considerably more inclusive than those for Britain above

young, with few assets besides their wits and education). Such people will certainly man the top management positions in industry, and in the institutions supervising and financing it. They will initially be very close in background and attitudes to the lower managers, and have a fairly good understanding of, and with, the shop floor workers. They are reintegration personified. But the revolutionary tide ebbs, after a time. The first post-revolutionary *technocrats* act as befits their origins and their ideology, but the time comes when the same men, grown old, or their successors, let themselves be influenced by their positions and their interests. (It may come soon, after perhaps twenty years, with a 'superficial' revolution like those in Poland or Romania, and not for forty or fifty years when the revolution had broad support, as in Russia and China.) 'First they were Jacobins pursuing their programmes; now they are mandarins defending their privileges'.[26] Within a paper-pushing bureaucracy the gaps between managers of enterprises, and those above and below them in the hierarchy, grow wide.

Is increasing inequality inevitable?

It has been argued that economic development in a Southern country is bound initially to involve an increase in inequality, since the high-technology nucleus will grow at the expense of the rest. This will increase inequality, as measured by the Gini coefficient,[27] until the 'nucleus' accounts for more than about half the work-force; after that, the shift between sectors will make for less and less inequality, until with the complete disappearance of the low-technology sector this source of inequality disappears too. However, there is no reason why economic development *should* take this path; it might involve the gradual raising of the technological level of the low technology sectors, which would make for lower inequality from the beginning. And where we do observe increasing inequality, the explanation may be a good deal less encouraging than the growth of a high-technology sector. It may be that what is growing is not the high-technology sector, in its share of the work-force, but the gap between it and the rest of the economy – in technological level, and in income, under the influence of the core.[28] At the same time, there are important, and perhaps growing, sources of income inequality within sectors.[29] Nor is the income of sectors always tied closely to their technological level. Whether through deliberate exploitation of the 'internal periphery', or in a more haphazard way, the peasantry and others may find themselves selling at lower prices and buying at higher. Likewise, the position of 'informal' workers may worsen because there are just too many people looking for jobs washing cars, or trying to sell matches on street corners.

I propose to argue, on the contrary, that high inequality in the South is not quite inevitable, and is highly unfavourable to long-term growth. Let us consider the evidence. We have already seen that the economic record and prospects of the South in general are rather poor. The exceptions are few, and fall into three categories. The first are oil-rich countries like Kuwait and Saudi Arabia, whose success needs no explanation. The second are 'Southern socialist' countries like China. In spite of Party privileges, etc., and the difficulty of measuring the distribution of income,[30] it is clear that these have been, compared with most of their non-socialist 'peers', unusually equal in their distribution of income. Their Party dictatorship, on the other hand, makes them exceptionally unequal in the distribution of political and economic power; and that is now proving their undoing. The third group of 'fast growers' (whose record is much better than the second) contains only four countries: Taiwan, South Korea, Hong Kong, and Singapore. Their obvious common feature is that they are inhabited by people of Chinese extraction or with close cultural affinity with China; they also have in common, exceptionally low Gini coefficients of household income; i.e. very low inequality. For Singapore and Hong Kong this is unremarkable: both are tiny city states with very little land, which spares them regional differences and the differentiation between town and country, or rich landowner and poor agricultural labourer. And both (if we want an explanation of their high growth) have a very high concentration of Chinese entrepreneurs and would-be entrepreneurs. But South Korea and Taiwan are more striking. They are large enough to have been mainly agricultural, at least at the beginning of the period, so their low inequality (which goes right back to the 1950s) demands explanation – and so does their growth.

I propose to explain Taiwanese and Korean growth *via* their equality – and to start by explaining that. The foundation was a very thorough land reform. In both cases this was pushed through by regimes which, although right-wing, were unusually independent of any landowning element, and had the support of the Americans (who wanted a loyal anti-communist peasantry). Land reform is essential in 'levelling up' the rural poor, but it is not in itself sufficient, as the Mexican example, and many others, have shown. The rural poor (who were almost all the poor in Taiwan and Korea, at the beginning) need three more things: education; co-operatives with proper government support and encouragement; and decent local roads. The Japanese, who ruled both Korea and Taiwan until 1945, had done something in all these directions, and the post-war governments, particularly that of Taiwan, did a great deal more (Mason, 1980; Ranis, 1977).

Under such circumstances the smallholding peasantry, maligned by a host of 'experts' from the eighteenth century writer Arthur Young to the German Social Democrats[31] and Stalin, reveal themselves as marvellously efficient producers, in terms of output per acre.[32] They supply the towns well and cheaply and spare the balance of payments the burden of food imports. That is not all; they perform other wonders. For one thing, they stay put: the towns are not burdened with an economically useless lumpenproletariat. For another, they control their fertility – they are determined not to subdivide their farms, and they get the education – not only the men, the *women* get the education – to know how to do it, and not be hidebound by tradition. But the wonder of wonders is their direct contribution to industrialisation. They have just enough income to be able to afford simple, cheap consumer goods (and capital equipment) and they make up most of the population: so they provide a mass market for manufactured goods which can be made locally with the sort of technology which native entrepreneurs, with little capital or expertise, can master. But those goods would have to be made very cheaply, for the peasantry to be able to afford them – and they themselves provide the very cheap labour that is required to keep costs down, in spite of technology that is, to begin with, rather inefficient. Those families with less land per head – for even a thorough land reform leaves *some* differences – can gain a great deal by supplementing their farm income with even very low wages. The factories spring up in the small rural towns, and their work-force streams in, on bicycles and buses, along the same bountiful dirt roads that take their crops to market. So it was in Taiwan.

Rural industrialisation completes what land reform began – the levelling up of the rural poor. It also provides a good base for the next stage of development: a large pool of workers with some basic technical training, and a network of small, flexible firms suitable as subcontractors to the larger urban enterprises which alone can tackle higher technology and foreign markets. The latter may need to be nurtured for a while in the hothouse atmosphere of acute high technology bias: both Taiwan and S. Korea had high tariff protection of manufacturing industry during the 1950s (Mason, 1980). However, if high technology bias continues for long, particularly if it relies on its crudest form, protection, it has, I have argued, serious consequences both for growth and for inequality – and all the worse for small countries where the home market can support very few enterprises in each high technology sector.[33] Far better to seek an overseas market for what the country is now capable of producing competitively: cheap manufactures produced with its own, independent, medium technology. The cosseting tariff protection is reduced (as it was in both countries in the 1960s) and its industry looks outwards. What is done in the name of that idol of the Right, the free market, has an egalitarian effect, for it increases the demand for the labour of the poor; and as their skills increase, and the capital and expertise of their employers, they move from working for a pittance in a sweatshop towards what a Western worker would recognise as a living wage. Without minimum wage laws, unions worth the name, or redistributive taxation, Taiwan achieved and held a Gini coefficient for household income of around 0.3[34] – a figure that counts as success for a Western European social democracy and is far superior to the normal 'developing country' figure of 0.5 – simply because an intelligent government determined to rise in the world economy chose the only strategy of ascent that would really work. (South Korea did nearly as well; see Table 7.6.)

Some of the morals to be drawn from the Taiwanese and South Korean cases have been drawn already for the North, and throughout our period: low inequality encourages large-scale production for the home market; and it makes the poor more productive *today*, because they are better fed and clothed and housed, and *tomorrow*, because they are better educated.[35] Others are more specific: when low inequality is achieved mainly by land reform, it brings with it

1 a large increase in agricultural output per hectare;
2 the possibility of reconciling a very cheap labour supply, particularly for rural industry, (a) with the high levels of nutrition, morale, education etc., which make for high productivity and are not normally associated with cheap labour, and (b) with the pattern of income distribution required for a mass home market.

This latter benefit has now become crucial in the South, for it makes it possible to break out of a vicious circle in which most Southern countries are now trapped: Northern products and Northern technology are fatally attractive, and all the more so when a Southern society is polarised into a privileged nucleus which can (just about) afford 'Northern' products, and an unregarded poverty-stricken 'rest'. 'Northern' products must either be imported or made locally with imported technology, components, etc.

Table 7.6 Distribution of income among households in Africa, Asia and Latin America (Gini co-efficients)

Africa

Country	Year	Gini co-efficient[1]
Benin[2]	1959	0.414
Congo[2]	1958	0.447
Gabon[3]	1968	0.584
Ivory Coast[3]	1970	0.487
Kenya[3]	1969	0.574
Malawi[2]	1969	0.452
Senegal	1970	0.513
South Africa	1965	0.563
Swaziland[2]	1974	0.637
Tanzania	1968	0.509
Chad[2]	1958	0.347
Togo[2]	1957	0.338
Tunisia[3]	1970	0.455
Zambia[2]	1970	0.618
Zimbabwe (formerly Rhodesia)	1969	0.629

Asia

Country (territory)	Year	Gini co-efficient[1]
Hong Kong	1971	0.434
India	1964–65	0.428
Iran	1971	0.561
Rep. of Korea	1970	0.351
Lebanon[2]	1960	0.521
Malaysia	1970	0.520
Philippines	1971	0.490
Sri Lanka	1963	0.486
	1973	0.375
Thailand	1969	0.504
Turkey	1968	0.549

Latin America

Country (territory)	Year	Gini co-efficient[1]
Argentina	1961	0.425
Brazil	1960	0.500
	1970	0.540
Chile	1968	0.503
Colombia	1974	0.520
Costa Rica	1971	0.466
Ecuador[3]	1970	0.595
El Salvador[3]	1961	0.502
Honduras	1967–68	0.612
Mexico	1969	0.567
Panama[3]	1970	0.528
Peru[3]	1961	0.561
Puerto Rico	1963	0.463
Uruguay	1967	0.449
Venezuela	1962	0.531
	1976	0.510

Source: Lecaillon et al., 1984, Table 3

Notes: 1 Assumptions: Similar ratios for the distribution by households and for the distribution by individuals. Ratio lower by 0.03 for the distribution by households than for the distribution by individuals.
2 According to the distribution by individuals.
3 According to the distribution by economically active persons.

Either way, the Southern country becomes more dependent on the North, and in the latter case, more polarised.[36] Where however it has low inequality of income distribution, and a certain minimum of technological capacity, it has another option: to produce basic goods for mass consumption, for which labour-intensive low- to medium-technology exists (or can easily be created) and will, with productive cheap labour, be the most productive method of manufacture. In due course it can adapt both products and technology to exploit the appropriate niches on the world market.[37]

The cases of Taiwan and Korea conform well to the inequality feedback pattern, in that their 'equalising reforms' came in the early 1950s, at the end of the depression crisis – just after, and largely because of, the Chinese Revolution, a rather better-known example of equalising reform. In another sense, however, they were somewhat anomalous: they only came into existence as separate (let alone independent) countries at that time, due to the upheavals of 1945–50. It would be still more instructive to look at the effects of a similar fall in inequality in a country which showed some continuity as a state over a period of a long wave or more. There is such a country – Japan; a country which now belongs squarely to the North (as Taiwan and South Korea soon will) but in 1939 was still, in terms of income, a Southern country.

EQUALITY AND THE RISE OF JAPAN

We have no Gini coefficients for pre-war Japan, but its distribution of income and wealth then seems to have been unremarkable for a country at its income level and stage of development. The Japanese countryside was treated as an internal periphery in the classic manner – squeezed by heavy land taxes from the outset of industrialisation in the late nineteenth century, and later by tariff protection of domestic manufacturing.[38] The resulting inequality between rural and urban population was accompanied by decided inequality of land ownership in the countryside, and a greater gulf in the towns between the modern sector, dominated by the Zaibatsu groups, and a low-technology competitive small business sector. The pattern of inequality was completed by the ownership of the Zaibatsu by a small number of rich families. Until the Second World War, inequality seems to have been increasing, for the Zaibatsu were strengthening their grip on industry, and poverty and over-population were an increasing problem among the small farmers. (The latter problem was of great political importance, since the Japanese army was recruited overwhelmingly from the countryside, and with its right wing allies was inclined to use conquest and colonisation as a solution to social tensions.)

The defeat of 1945 changed the political situation utterly. The colonists returned, and the land problem had to be solved another way; the American occupiers were determined to break the power of the Zaibatsu, whom they

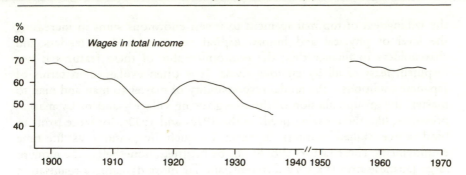

Figure 7.7 Relative income shares in non-primary industries in Japan, 1900–70
Source: Minami and Onio (1981)

blamed (with the Army) for Japanese aggression; the collapse of the Japanese empire and economy disgraced the old hierarchy and created tremendous pressure for egalitarian reform.[39] The outcome was a land reform as thorough as the Taiwanese and South Korean, which were modelled on it; the confiscation of the property of the Zaibatsu families and the break up of the Zaibatsu groups (they reformed later, but never regained their old grip on the economy); and a permanent shift in attitudes which made it necessary drastically to reduce pay differentials within firms – though the gap between small firms and large remained.[40] One result of the urban changes was an extraodinary drop in the share of profit between the late 1930s and the mid-1950s (see Figure 7.7). In the countryside, the land reform sharply reduced inequality of income (with the help, as in Taiwan, of the necessary government spending on infrastructure, support of co-operatives, etc.).[41] It also created a new, homogeneous class of smallholding farmers who became the backbone of the (ruling) Liberal Democratic party, and were rewarded for their allegiance by agricultural and regional policies which discriminated in favour of the countryside and thus tended to 'level it up'. Thus in the course of a decade or so, Japan went from the (rather high) inequality of income and wealth typical of less developed countries, to a distribution equal even by the standards of the post-war North.[42]

The effects were equally extraordinary. The rate of growth of the Japanese economy during the 1950s and (even more) the 1960s has never been matched except by Taiwan and South Korea in the 1960s and 1970s. There is no reason to overstate the case by ascribing this only to the changes just described; what does seem clear, at all events, is that the land reform had effects much like those in Taiwan, on agriculture and the small business sector, and that the urban changes brought about a dramatic rise in integration in the large firms which have been the spearhead of the Japanese rise towards economic leadership in the world. This extraordinarily high integration is expressed in the participative structure of the large Japanese firm, the commitment to its objectives of employees from the shop floor up, the willingness of top management to invest enormous sums in increasing the level of physical and human capital per man, and of lenders and shareholders to finance this; the economic value of these features is not disputed, least of all by envious rivals. It is often explained in terms of Japanese traditions – the feudal responsibility of master to man and man to master; the group cohesion of the rice-growing village – and/or by market pressures, like the growing need, in the 1920s and 1930s, for large firms to bind scarce skilled workers to them by such innovations as life-time employment. These factors should not be belittled; nonetheless the modern large Japanese firm is a very different, and far more dynamic, organisation than its predecessor of the 1930s. The latter was dominated by the absolute power of the owner: the servile deference required even from managers, let alone shop floor workers, was an obstacle to effective participation in decision-making, and no inducement, even in a deferential country, to enthusiastic loyalty. The modern Japanese ideal of the large firm as a quasi-family community, growing organically, was scarcely realisable in the 1930s, when corporate empires could be freely extended, as in America and Britain now, by take-over. No, the critical period was in the aftermath of the war, when the top managers of large Japanese firms struggled to retain, or regain, control in the face of a revolutionary ferment led by left-wing unions. They succeeded only by making their control more attractive to the shop floor than the alternative. This was achieved by extending the principle of life-time employment to all the permanent labour force, and combining it with assured, gradual promotion by seniority; by drastically reducing pay differentials except those linked to seniority (which do not cause inequality of life-time earnings); by giving unions a recognised, if carefully circum-scribed, voice and role within the firm. (At the same time the large firms attached to themselves, in a stable relationship, a penumbra of small ones.) The coat was made from old cloth, but it was new for all that.[43]

THE CONTRIBUTION OF THE SOUTH TO THE NORTHERN LONG WAVE

We saw in Chapter 6 that increased inequality, though it benefited the rich directly, might damage their interests in the long run by undermining economic growth. That was argued in the context of one society; might it not also be true where the rich and poor in question are whole countries within the world economy? The simplest way to make this case is to argue that the improvement of the Southern terms of trade contributes to the upswing in the North by leading to increased demand for its export industries; conversely when they deteriorate, Northern exports fall. This can only be right, however, if there is *asymmetry* in the responses of North and South to a shift of income from one to the other. An increase of £x in the South's income, due to an improvement in its terms of trade, leads it to spend some fraction of that, £bx, on extra imports from the North. Thus there is an increase in demand of £bx for the North's exporting industries. The income of the North will have fallen by £x, and so home demand in the North will fall by some fraction of that, £cx. For aggregate demand in the North to rise, b must exceed c. In plain English, the South's spending on Northern goods must be more sensitive to its income, than the North's own spending on those goods is to its own income.

Why should we expect the response to be asymmetric? First because the South, and not the North, is 'balance of payments constrained', i.e. it will spend whatever its balance of payments will allow, on imports. Then $b = 1$. But c is less than 1, since some of any change in Northern income will 'leak' into a change in savings, and thus be subtracted from the change in demand. Second, the South's imports can exceed its exports, to the extent that it receives a net inflow of capital from the North. This flow is affected by the terms of trade: when they favour the South, the outlook for investment there seems favourable, and there is a net inflow – in effect, the North lends to the South to finance increased demand for its own industry; a deterioration causes it to cut the financing off. (The outlook for investment in the South will of course be influenced by other considerations than the terms of trade – export volumes, for example, which were rising fast in the late 1950s when the terms of trade were worsening – and by the general economic, social and political outlook in the South.)

It is not only Southern demand that may be regarded as having a powerful influence on the North: Southern supply too may play an important role. For the South's products are not only inputs for Northern industries; they also compete with the outputs of some of them. When the price of Southern goods falls, the price of (or demand for) these Northern goods falls too, unless tariffs are used to compensate. Latham (1981) and Kindleberger (1973) have both argued that falling prices for US wheat and cotton, determined by movements on the world markets for these commodities, preceded the 1929 crash, and contributed to the Slump by impoverishing the (US) Midwest and South. (Solomou, 1987, disputes this; but his NBTT data would look less favourable if converted to Spraos-type ECDFTT. The effect of price falls *after* 1929 is indisputable.) Here again, in order to give force to the argument, we have to assume some asymmetry. The loss to the wheat or cotton farmer was a gain to someone else in the North, to consumers mostly, who might spend more, as the farmers spent less. Why should not the effects cancel out? The answer is the same as before, in essence: the farmers were relatively poor, and had to reduce their consumption by much the same amount as their income fell, while part of the benefit to consumers went into savings; the farmers were also producers, who borrowed to invest (in machinery, etc.) and now had little inclination or opportunity to do so.

In the current downswing the effect of Southern supply on Northern industries should not be sought in primary products. The traditional low-technology producers – the farmers – suffered little if at all during the 1970s, since prices of their products were at first rather favourable, and they had since 1930 acquired a good deal of government protection and support. They must now, anyway, be reclassified, as largely high-technology in their production methods. Accordingly we cannot take their present difficulties, due to low world prices and diminished protection, as deflationary. Where Southern competition has really bitten is in manufactures. It was in the 1970s, as we saw in Figure 7.1, that the South built up most rapidly its role as an exporter of low-technology manufactures. These are of two main kinds: traditional manufactures, mostly produced independently, that is with Southern inputs, management and ownership (for example clothing, footwear and now steel); and the low-technology *operations* (like assembly) within newer manufacturing industries, like electronics, in this case under the control of Northern multinationals. In the former case Southern exporters came into direct competition with unrelated Northern firms; in the latter, it was the Southern labour force which was competing with Northern workers for effectively the same jobs in the same multinationals. The results in the two cases were not dissimilar: in both, some Northern workers lost their jobs, and those who kept them had to accept lower pay relative to Northern workers in safer, high-technology jobs; this, since most of them had relatively low pay to start with, made for increased inequality – as too, of course, did the loss of jobs.

The effect is to change the distribution of income within the North: multinationals' shareholders gain, along with employees of high-technology industries (who get their low-technology goods more cheaply) while low-technology workers lose: this redistribution from have-nots to haves must (according to simple Keynesian logic, assuming different marginal propensities to consume) reduce consumer demand.

The oil price: effects of its recent fluctuations

It may have seemed misleading to look at the South's terms of trade *excluding* petroleum, and then describe them as worsening from the beginning of the current downswing. *Including* petroleum they held up well, right into the 1980s. There is, however, good reason to look separately at oil. In the early 1970s, oil production in the South was concentrated in a few countries with mostly small populations. The income from it went mostly to these countries, or to the shareholders of the major oil companies. Thus one initial effect of the first two 'oil shocks' – the price rises of 1973–4 and 1979–80 – was, paradoxically, the same as that of the price falls for other primary products: they increased international inequality (in this case, *within* both the South and North, rather than between South and North). Now as we have seen, if the effect of a change is to increase inequality it will elicit an asymmetric response. The richer oil-exporting countries (Saudi Arabia,

Kuwait, the Emirates) chose to increase their demand for foreign goods by much less, for every dollar gained, than the oil-importing countries were forced to reduce theirs, for every dollar lost; the oil companies' shareholders spent less for each dollar gained, than oil consumers cut for each one lost. Further, the extent of the price rises caused damaging uncertainty in investment decision-making. A wide range of oil-using investment plans were now unprofitable at the new price of oil, and were accordingly dropped.

In the medium term – within three or four years after each shock – the effects were much less bad. The oil exporters increased their expenditure relative to their revenues – the poorer ones indeed were spending themselves into debt. More Southern oil exporters appeared – Egypt and China, for example – who were ready to spend every extra penny; and the lowest spender originally, Saudi Arabia, cut back output to the point where (by 1985) it too was spending more foreign exchange than it earned. Meanwhile, investors had adapted to the high price, and were now spending heavily on the production and conservation of oil and other energy sources.[44] By this time it was no longer fair to say that high oil prices were contributing significantly to the downswing.

By the same token, the oil price plunge of 1986 should not have been expected to have the same effect on demand as if it had taken place a decade earlier. The hopes for a stimulus to the world economy from this third oil shock rested on the inevitable reduction in inflation, and the expectation that this would improve consumer and business confidence, and free Northern governments to reflate their economies. This was not wrong, but it was not all: there were other effects. The South's gains from the high oil price, now spread much more evenly than at the beginning, were suddenly removed. Most of the gains went to Japan, the United States, Germany, France and Italy, although of course Southern oil importers (a smaller category than in 1973) gained something too. There was thus the usual depressing effect of a worsening of the Southern terms of trade. Moreover the sudden plunge of energy prices made nonsense of many energy production and conservation investments. Inevitably the result would be the rapid cancelling of many such investment programmes, but only a slow and cautious build-up of energy-using investments – the converse of what happened after 1974. Finally, the financial predicament of some oil producing governments and companies threatened the stability of the world banking system.[45]

The effects on inequality and growth of the oil price fluctuations after 1972 were thus surprisingly similar to those in other Southern exports. So indeed were their causes. As we shall see in Chapter 12, they could be explained, like the other changes, by the general move towards international specialisation according to comparative advantage. (The perverse result was due to oil's special position as an exhaustible resource supplied in huge quantities with a high degree of seller concentration.)[46]

THE NORTH – SOUTH RELATIONSHIP IN THE LONG WAVE: CONCLUSION

This chapter has traced a clear fluctuation in the economic relationship between North and South over the twentieth century long wave, and a similar fluctuation within the South. The upswing encourages the countries of the South to commit themselves increasingly to the role of suppliers of low-technology products in exchange for high-technology products, and for high technology *tout court*; and in the downswing they suffer for having made this commitment. One index of this 'suffering' is the terms of trade, which turn against them in the downswing (sharply, if measured in NBTT; drastically, if in ECDFTT), but other aspects of the relationship, enumerated above, turn against them too. At the same time, and not by coincidence, most of them move far into increased internal inequality. The crisis thus engendered inclines them, ultimately, to change course towards self-sufficiency and reduced inequality, and these shifts, together with the effects of higher world demand, work in their favour during the next upswing.

It was argued that the oil price rises of the 1970s, which seemed anomalous, in fact conformed at a deeper level with the general pattern of increasing international inequality. It was this increase in international inequality which partly accounted for the downswing in the North and in the world economy as a whole, since it reduced the demand of the losers more than it increased that of the gainers. Another contribution to the downswing was made by the surge of Southern exports of low-technology goods – primary products in the 1920s, mainly manufactures in the 1970s – which competed with low-technology Northern production. This tended to force down Northern incomes which were on the low side already, increasing internal inequality in the North, and reducing demand there. Here we see the link, foreshadowed at the beginning of the last chapter, between international and internal inequality.

So far, the entire discussion of the North-South relationship as a factor in the long wave has been limited to the twentieth century. What was so different about the nineteenth century that it has to be treated separately?

The obvious reason is that there was no economic long wave, which deprives us of the starting point for the twentieth century analysis. But there was another important difference: the world economy, as we have seen, was far less *polarised* than it has since become. This was not simply because much of the 'South' had yet to be 'opened up'. Southern and Eastern Europe – even Scandinavia at the beginning of the century – and Japan had a distinctly peripheral role, since they sold low-technology products produced with low technology methods. Even the United States, though not peripheral by my definition since (outside the South) its *methods* were high-tech., was, like Canada and Australia now, a seller of almost exclusively low-technology products, which meant that its terms of trade moved in the same way as the periphery's. But these countries were far less *dependent* than the South now (or then): we can see that first from the much narrower gap in income levels, and second from the fact that they are all now members of the core or semi-core. They were, accordingly, much better able than the South to cope with the effects of poor terms of trade. They were ready, like only the Four Asian Tigers now, to react quickly to such adversity by finding more lucrative products for the domestic or foreign market, as the Danes switched to bacon and butter after the grain price collapsed in the 1870s. Berend and Ranki put it well:

> the losses or gains sustained in the course of trade did not simply follow from a country's core or peripheral position, but were ... to a very considerable extent determined by a country's ability – or inability – to adapt to the demands of the market.[47]

There have also been changes in the North, in the effect of fluctuations in the terms of trade. The large majority of its population in the nineteenth century were too close to bare subsistence to save significantly even in good times. When a fall in primary product prices raised their incomes – and the effect was considerable, because the main imports, like grain and cotton, went mostly to them – consumer spending, and housebuilding, went up proportionately more than it does in the same circumstances today.

So the relationship between Northern primary product exporters and manufactures exporters in the nineteenth century was far less *asymmetric* than that between North and South in the twentieth; that is a flaw in Rostow's long wave theory, which conflates the two.

APPENDIX TO CHAPTER 7

Appendix 7.1   Northern assets in the South, and Southern debts to the North

Between 1870 and 1914 there was a higher rate of investment by Western European countries (principally Britain) in primary producing countries than ever before or since; the main receiving countries were mostly those now regarded as 'Northern' but also included Latin American countries, notably Argentina which received an inflow of capital between 12 and 15 per cent of GNP during the first two decades of the twentieth century. There were debt crises due to difficulties in making servicing payments, mostly in the 'Great Depression' period (1873–96) (World Bank, *World Development Report*, 1985).

Although by 1929 the total volume of foreign-owned assets in what we would now call the South was considerably higher than in 1913, the rate of increase had been much slower than before 1913; the heaviest investment had been by the USA in Latin America during the 1923–9 period (Aldcroft,

1977; World Bank, 1985). The figures in Tables 7.4 and 7.5 relate to UK and UK investments only, but this is not enough to make them misleading, given the dominance of Britain in foreign investment before 1914 and that of the USA afterwards. (The main recipient of French investment was Russia, which in 1914 accounted for 7.1 per cent of the total stock of accumulated direct investment abroad; after 1917 all was lost. Similarly China accounted for 7.8 per cent in 1914 and 5.8 per cent in 1938, and all was lost after 1949 (Dunning, 1983).)

The fall in value of assets after 1930 is largely due to the large proportion of investments made in government fixed interest debt; for example, about 80 per cent of US investment in Latin America had been in fixed interest bonds, and by the end of 1935 85 per cent of Latin America dollar bonds were in default (Aldcroft, 1977). Since the holders of these assets were mostly individuals, whose losses had no effect on the stability of the financial system, Western governments perhaps tried less hard on their behalf than when (as in the present crisis) those threatened are major banks. Until the late 1960s, not surprisingly, private lending at fixed interest was small; most external capital for developing countries came in the form of official aid, private supplier credits and direct investment. From 1970 onwards, however, there was a huge increase in fixed interest lending, partly in the form of export credits but mostly from commercial banks (World Bank, 1985). Table 7.5 shows the results.

Appendix 7.2:   Capital flight

Since capital flight is mostly secret, all statistics on it are guesses. One plausible assumption is that it approximates to the figure for errors and omissions in the IMF balance of payments statistics. This would, for example, yield a figure for capital flight in 1982 of $92 billion, according to Alex Brummer (*Guardian*, p. 21, 10 March 1986, quoting John T. Cuddington of the World Bank). There is, at all events, a general impression that capital flight was unimportant before 1960. In the last decade it has become huge. The *Guardian Weekly*, 13 April 1986, quoted *World Financial Markets'* current issue as reckoning the increase in debt of eighteen countries in Latin America, Asia and Africa at $451 billion, of which $198 billion represented capital flight, broadly defined, since 1975. Some analysts treat it as caused mainly by market distortions – over-valuation of the local currency, normally. While this clearly has played a role, for example in capital flight from Mexico, we may still ask why the currency was over-valued – was it partly in order to facilitate flight? – and we may point to the evidence, now clear for the Philippines and Haiti after the departure of their respective dictators, of capital flights being used as a way of putting beyond the reach of all rebellions, the spoils of abuse of power.

(See 'Dictatorships and their ill-gotten gains', *Guardian Weekly*, 16 March 1986, p. 11, and D. R. Lessard and John Williamson, *Capital Flight and Third World Debt* (Washington DC: Institute for International Economics, 1987).)

Part II
History

Introduction

A *résumé* of the theoretical argument

I have argued that long fluctuations in rates of growth in the world economy in the industrial era since 1780 need to be studied in the framework of an evolutionary model. Such a model starts from a recognition that economic dynamics are mainly determined by economic, political and social institutions and that these, and their interactions, change over time. The only factor in long fluctuations which does not appear to have changed greatly over the last two centuries is the succession, approximately every half century, of technological styles. These, which were defined and described in Chapter 2, are new paradigms or intellectual patterns of the broadest possible relevance, influencing the direction of technological change, which develop in response to the drastic reduction in cost of one or a few key factors of production.

Another fluctuation which changes relatively little over the period is the 'Modelskian' long cycle in international relations, of some 100 to 120 years. This begins with a long 'global war' out of which emerges a world power, a largely maritime nation, in a leading position technologically, which dominates international trade and is initially beyond challenge. (The link between technological leadership and world power is not clear-cut in Modelski's first cycle, nor in his third, but during our period it is indisputable.) As time passes a political challenge arises, from a continental power whose strength is mostly on land; the challenge culminates in another global war in which the continental challenger is finally defeated on land by an alliance including the old world power and its successor. The long cycle has changed somewhat over our period: at the beginning there was the oddity of an exceptionally long, more or less continuous global war of some twenty-two to twenty-three years largely due to the fact that (uniquely) the new world power was the same as the old, Britain. The last global war was divided into two acts with an interval longer than both of them together – the First and Second World Wars. This was associated with the reluctance of the new world power (the USA) to take over from the old (Britain) and a consequent power vacuum from 1918 to 1945.

The timing and length of global wars, and the character of the peace settlements, have a strong influence on long economic fluctuations, but they can scarcely account for them: specifically, they cannot account for the 'long waves' of approximately fifty years in duration allegedly identified by Kondratiev and others. The succession of technological styles, on the other hand, might well be able to do so, given a suitable model of the interaction of technology and economy. Such a model is proposed by Carlota Perez, who argues that to diffuse rapidly – and thus stimulate rapid economic expansion – a new 'style' requires a 'socio-institutional framework' which is well *matched* to it. To begin with, the existing 'framework' is decidedly *mismatched* to the new 'style', this inhibits diffusion and causes an economic downswing, and a crisis. The crisis breaks up the log-jam, and leads to a new, reformed, socio-institutional 'framework' well matched to the now-established 'styles': fast diffusion and expansion ensues, with the genesis of a new 'style' . . .

I have argued that this model, though elegant, fails to explain the absence of any identifiable economic long wave in the first half of our period, and needs a great deal of modification. Most important is the recognition that a new 'style' can lead to not one but three types of crisis, depending on the extent and nature of the 'mismatch' with the socio-institutional framework. A serious *economic* mismatch leads to a *depression crisis*, which is roughly what Perez has in mind. However there may be no serious economic mismatch, and we may therefore see an upswing; and yet (or as a result) a *political* mismatch may develop to the point of causing a *crisis of the upswing*. I argued that the alternation of these two types of crisis was to be expected once an economic long wave was established. Before that point, no such crises could be expected, at least in the world economy as a whole; instead one should look for a third type, of *mixed* crisis, following neither a long upswing nor a prolonged depression but produced by a degree of both political and economic mismatch to a new style, and set off by a bad harvest or two. Linked to the delineation of two types of mismatch and associated crises, were the concepts of economic and political *integration* and *disintegration*. These were based on the assumption that the key relationships among institutions were essentially vertical ones; in the economy, between shareholders, managers and workers (with the State also playing a role), and in politics, between different social classes. Integration in each sphere meant a degree of harmony among these strata, and tended to produce, respectively, economic expansion and political stability. (A less important category, *social* integration, was also mentioned).

I then went on, in Chapters 4–7, to set out a number of *feedback processes* which together could account for the change from a long run growth path without a long wave to one in which, after 1930, a clear long wave pattern appeared to have developed.

A feedback process (or loop) is necessary for any *endogenous* cycle. (The Perez model as described and modified is not strictly endogenous unless the appearance of new styles is taken to be a function of the economic cycle –

which I have not assumed.) A negative feedback loop in a growth cycle is one where (say) fast growth tends to cause X which tends to cause slow growth. Positive feedback has fast growth tending to cause Y which tends to cause fast growth. Where we have (or would otherwise have had) a cycle of fifty years, the most perfectly pro-cyclical feedback loop is a positive one with lags adding up to fifty years, or no lags at all; or a negative one with lags adding up to just twenty-five years. A perfectly counter-cyclical loop involves the converse – e.g. positive feedback with lags of twenty-five years. For brevity I speak of a feedback process as *fast* if it is complete within ten years, as *slow* if it is complete within twenty to thirty years.

The *monetary feedback* process was the first to be examined. In its simplest form (approximated in the late nineteenth century) this works as follows: an upswing leads to higher prices and higher real demand for money, and together these mean very much higher *nominal* demand for money. On the other hand, the higher prices (of goods) are tantamount to lower real prices for gold, whose money price is fixed. So gold output levels off; this limits the expansion of the money supply (tied to gold). In sum, there is rising demand versus limited supply of money and this leads to higher interest rates. Thus after a certain point in the upswing monetary feedback is *counter-cyclical*. Conversely, once a downswing starts, with falling prices, a sequence of events begins which ends with low interest rates and (once again) counter-cyclical effects; early in upswing and downswing monetary factors are pro-cyclical. Before the late nineteenth century we lack evidence on monetary feedback; afterwards it changes in its mechanism first because the link between money and gold loosens and later because the effect of growth rates on prices becomes less clear. Instead the effect of the long wave on interest rates appears to work through changes in economic doctrine and policy. A long upswing tends – with a lag of some twenty or twenty-five years – to produce a generation of opinion-formers and policy-makers with 'deflationary inclinations'; a downswing has the opposite effect. (The changes in doctrines and policies may also be in part responses to changes in circumstances. The deflationary ones may be a rational response to economic disintegration at national and international levels. Reflationary doctrines and policies may be taking advantage of more favourable circumstances of economic reintegration.)

The end result is that the feedback process has become gradually more pro-cyclical: monetary policy has become expansionary until near the end of the upswing, and deflationary through most of the current downswing (so far).

Next was population feedback. This is remarkable for its change in direction about half way through our period. At first it was counter-cyclical in tendency: fast expansion made for a 'baby boom' with a lag of perhaps five years, and when the babies grew up, after a further twenty or so, that increased both the available labour supply and the demand for goods for new households, etc. So positive feedback came just soon enough after an upswing (or downswing) to inhibit any tendency to a long wave downswing (or upswing). After the 1840s, when mass transatlantic migration became feasible, the counter-cyclical tendency became a great deal stronger, because the extra (European) labour could migrate to the Americas where it would have a much greater impact. Moreover migration added a fast negative feedback to the slow positive feedback: a crisis or downswing in Europe made (more) labour surplus in Europe and drove it to the Americas to stimulate expansion there. (Both these lags were a little too long to be perfectly counter-cyclical: at the beginning of a upswing or a downswing they would be pro-cyclical.)

Around the end of the century the feedback through migration began to change: the migrants now came mainly from Eastern and Southern European countries which released labour as they industrialised – the faster the industrialisation the faster the migration. After the First World War there was a decisive shift in US policy to migration control, which was operated there (and in other countries of immigration) to allow large scale immigration only during upswings. Given that these were henceforth quite well synchronised in Europe and the Americas, the effect was to create a fast positive feedback and suppress the other feedback effects. Moreover the effect of extra labour at home – the original slow positive feedback – diminished as the scope for self- and family- employment dwindled; in fact resulting unemployment could even have deflationary effects through lower wages. It thus appears that population feedback became, and remains, decidedly pro-cyclical.

The third and last feedback process involves *inequality*: it can be split into three, involving:

(i) internal inequality in the North,
(ii) internal inequality in the South, and
(iii) international inequality, particularly that between South and North.

With these feedback processes it has to be borne in mind that the fluctuations are around a very marked trend: in the first case, clearly declining, in the second and third, clearly increasing. With that in mind, the essential interactions are similar in form: fast growth tends to lead to higher inequality which makes for slow growth ..., the lags being such as to make this negative feedback pro-cyclical. Population feedback plays a role here: the arrival of a baby boom on the labour market makes for increased inequality, particularly when it migrates. So does the cycle of disintegration – depression-crisis – integration, for the reintegration, with opinion-formers and policy-makers moulded by the downswing, involves various moves towards reduced inequality. (In the North, these include 'welfare state' reforms and stronger unions, in the South there are revolutions in a number of countries; between South and North, there is a shift of the South (with or without revolution) to decreased dependence on the North and (largely in consequence) improved terms of trade.

The strength of inequality feedback, in all three forms, has increased enormously, particularly since the beginning of this century. This is mainly because the link from higher inequality to slow growth, debatable at best at the beginning of our period, is now very strong.

The overall argument is summed up graphically in Figure 8.1.

It is fairly straightforward to think of a feedback loop as pro-cyclical (or counter-cyclical) if it contributes to (detracts from) a long wave which can be seen to exist historically. Where on the other hand (as in the earlier part of our period) there is no such identifiable fluctuation, the sense of this approach is harder to see. It still has meaning and value, however, if we can find a period of general fast growth in the world economy which – with the appropriate feedbacks – would have tended to produce a long wave. If then we find that it did not do so, we can infer *either* that the feedbacks were, on balance, counter-cyclical, *or* that any pro-cyclical effect was outweighed by some 'shock' from outside the system. Early this century we must look for a shock, since the 1892–1913 period had all the makings of a long wave upswing, and feedback was on balance pro-cyclical. Modelski's long cycle obligingly produces and explains the shock of global war, which turned the period 1914–20, which would otherwise have seen a mild crisis of the upswing, into a savage recession, and transformed the 1920s from the beginning of a downswing, to a period of recovery. The long cycle also helps to explain why the early nineteenth century saw no general upturn at all – for it meant that what would otherwise have been a brief and quite fruitful mixed crisis, followed by the fast diffusion of the new style, became a prolonged global war, after which the style was, in Britain at least, no longer new. (Moreover the nature and outcome of the global war was, as we shall see, unfavourable to the new style.) The only mixed crisis which was permitted, by its place in the long cycle, to be brief and fruitful, was that of the late 1840s in Europe. A general upturn duly followed – but at this period counter-cyclical feedback processes predominated, and largely as a result it did not lead to a long wave.

We have begun, I fear, to anticipate and trespass upon the historical account, so without further introduction let us begin it.

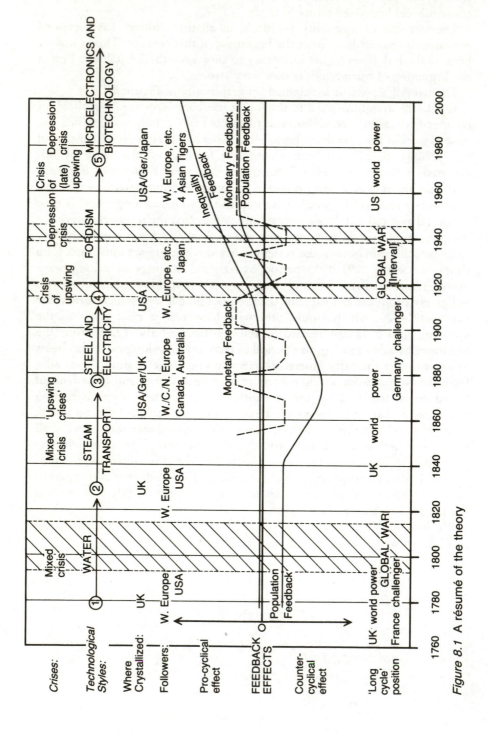

Figure 8.1 A résumé of the theory

Chapter 8

A historical account, 1780–1850

In a sense, modern economic history only begins in about 1850. Before then, we only have reasonably reliable data on economic growth for Britain, the United States and (to a lesser extent) France. These three countries, important as they were, did not dominate the 'world economy' of the day to such an extent that we can judge its performance from theirs. Nor was there, much before 1850, a 'world economy' with any close linkage through trade, communications and flows of capital and labour: it was, as we have seen, only during the 1840s that the steamship, the telegraph and the railway established such links among the 'Atlantic Economies' of Europe and North America. Before 1850, then, we have a sort of economic prehistory, a prehistory which extends to the long wave: for we have just enough information on economic growth in the early nineteenth century to say with some confidence that it did *not* follow a long wave pattern. Let us for example look at the only more or less complete series for national income, that for the USA (Figure 8.2 and Table 8.1). If we take Kondratiev's dates for price peaks (1814) and troughs (1790 and 1849) as the basis for long wave upswings and downswings, the 'upswing' of 1790–1814 has a lower growth rate (3.3 per cent p.a.) than the 'downswing' of 1814–49 (5.4 per cent p.a.). If we look instead for Kuznets swings of 18/19 years, based in the manner of Currie (1988) on rainfall fluctuations, the result is much more satisfactory: 'rainfall upswing' periods have markedly higher growth rates than 'rainfall downswings', except for the 1806–25 period. (The 'upswing' of 1806–15 was marred first by the blockade and counter-blockade of Britain and Napoleonic France, and then actual war between the USA and Britain; the 'downswing' of 1815–24/5 was blessed by the ending of hostilities.) Nor do the series on industrial production, which we have for Britain from 1782 and for France from 1815 (Table 8.2), suggest a long wave pattern. What leaps to the eye from the British data is the damage done by the 'global war' from 1792 to 1815; the only other apparent feature is a slight tendency for growth to decelerate – a deceleration which disappears in the more accurate series in Table 8.3. If we take it that French industry in 1815–25 benefited from the end of the war, the main impression from the French data is a marked *acceleration* over forty years.

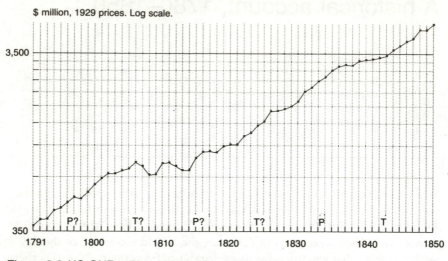

$ million, 1929 prices. Log scale.

Figure 8.2 US GNP, 1791–1850, with rainfall peaks and troughs
Source: Mitchell (1983); Currie (1988)
Note: Rainfall swings before 1830 are derived by extrapolation.

Table 8.1 Growth of US GNP, 1789–1852, in rainfall upswings and downswings

Rainfall upswings	per cent p.a.	Rainfall downswings	per cent p.a.
1789–1796/7	7.3		
		1796/7–1806	5.2
1806–1815 [WAR]	0.6		
		1815–1824/5 [PEACE]	4.8
1824/5–33/4	6.7		
		1833/4–1843	3.3
1843–52	6.3		

Note: before 1830 rainfall peaks and troughs have been estimated by extrapolation from Currie's series, 1988, which is the direct source for data after 1830. Growth rates are calculated from Mitchell, 1983.

Table 8.2 Juglar growth rates of industrial production, Great Britain and France, 1782–1857 (per cent per annum)

Juglar period	Britain	Juglar period	France
1782–1792	4.8		
1792–1802	2.4		
1802–1815	2.1		
1815–1825	3.9	1815–1824	1.4
1825–1836	3.7	1824–1836	0.5
1836–1845	3.3	1836–1847	2.3
1845–1857	3.3	1847–1856	2.8

Source: Mitchell, 1978

Table 8.3 British industrial output growth, 1700–1831 (per cent per annum)

1700–1760	0.71
1760–1770	1.23
1770–1780	1.79
1780–1790	2.40
1790–1801	1.83
1801–1811	2.72
1811–1821	2.63
1821–1831	3.65

Source: Crafts, 1983, Table 3

On the other hand, it has become equally clear that there was a technological long wave at this period. Accordingly, it seems sensible to begin the historical discussion at roughly the point when the technological long wave began, with the crystallization in Britain of the first technological style, and to ask four broad questions:

1 Why did the 'water style' crystallize in Britain? (We have already seen how it did so, in Chapter 2.)
2 What effects did it have on the 'socio-institutional framework'; in particular, how far was it responsible for the French Revolution, and what changes in the 'framework' did that bring about, in France and elsewhere?
3 How was it that the appearance of a new technological style and the reactions it provoked, failed to lead to the upswing of an economic long wave?
4 How did the 'socio-institutional framework' respond to the appearance of the second technological style?

INTEGRATION AND EQUALITY IN THE BRITISH TAKE-OFF

It is now clear that impressive technical and economic progress was being made in many parts of North-West Europe, and the northern English colonies across the Atlantic, early in the eighteenth century. Newcomen's steam engine for pumping, and Darby's use of coke for iron-smelting, were only two of the important innovations of the first two decades of the century – and if we thought the rest of the continent was sunk in torpor, we now learn that Newcomen's engine, introduced in a English coal-mine in 1712, was being used only eight years later in a Belgian coal mine, near Liège.[1] A steady increase in the share of manufacturing in French output has been traced back as far as 1715–20.[2] On the other hand, it has now been very plausibly argued that much of what we take for progress in technology is little more than reluctant adaptation to the pressure for increasing population on natural resources (Wilkinson, 1973). English ironmasters did not, even after Darby's success, actually prefer coke to charcoal – but they were forced to resort to coking coal as the country rapidly ran short of wood; miners would much rather have managed without Newcomen's expensive steam-pump – but as they were forced deeper and deeper by the exhaustion of reserves near the surface, they faced more and more serious problems of drainage.[3] Even the increase in the share of manufacturing can be seen in this light: it was well known by contemporaries that it was extremely difficult to get labour for manufacturing industries in any area until serious shortages of land developed, since the poor preferred to farm; even those who found themselves without enough land to sustain themselves ('cottagers') chose to take in work within the 'putting out' system while remaining on the land, rather than make themselves dependent on an employer.[4]

There is, however, a positive side to population increase, as we saw in Chapter 5. Progress in manufacturing is limited by the size of the market: there may be all manner of efficient methods available which it does not pay to use unless they can be operated at a certain minimum output without paying high transport costs in order to reach the consumer. The more consumers there are within easy reach, the more attractive such methods will be. The size of the market does not, however, depend simply on the density of population within a given area. It depends also on transport costs and the pattern of consumer demand in that population. We have seen already in Chapter 2, how the British, taking advantage of their geography, had by 1780 constructed a network of waterways, supplemented by roads, which drastically reduced transport costs and so greatly enlarged the area which a given factory, mine, or farm could supply. But how many people, within even an enlarged market area, could or would buy the products of a given factory? The very poor would not be able to spend much on anything besides food; the rich had a great deal to spend, but would spend most of it on luxuries which were made to order by specialised craftsmen. It was the middle-income category who provided the market for the new machine-made manufactures and it was in Britain that there was (except perhaps for Holland) by far the largest proportion of middle-income consumers (not only larger tenant farmers, but many wage-earners, since English wages were about twice the level in France, Britain's main rival).[5]

These high English wages, as we might expect, played a role on the supply side. As we have already seen, the rate of introduction and diffusion of technical progress depends on first, how great an increase in profit the improvement offers, and second, how far the producer can afford to forego a given improvement in profits. With high wages, the labour-saving technical progress of the eighteenth century made much more difference in Britain than in France.[6] Lower transport costs also meant more competition from producers elsewhere, and that forced firms to keep up, technically, with their competitors. French firms in compartmentalised local markets had less need to find out what producers in other places were doing, and match it.

We thus already find low inequality (by current standards) playing a decisive role in economic growth.[7] With it, closely linked as usual, was high integration. As Habakkuk (1955) showed, British landowners, even the aristocracy, were accustomed to mixing with their 'inferiors'. Their younger sons were often obliged to take up middle-class occupations – and if they made a success at them might buy land and return to their fathers' class. The fathers themselves might well go into a business venture with a middle-class partner, while the sons might take artisans as partners for their technical expertise. This social fluidity and intimacy made possible a degree of what I have called economic integration: vertical relationships of such a character as to allow concentration on the enlargement, rather than the distribution, of output. Inequality and the social gap between rich and poor was greater in the (declining) regions of cloth manufacturing in the growth of England than in the West Riding.[8] By contrast, France in the late eighteenth century presents, in Landes's comparative account,[9] a picture of considerable economic disintegration: of institutional structures, formal and informal, decidedly obstructive to economic growth.

To accept such an adverse verdict on the *ancien régime* is a very dangerous thing to do, for it involves taking sides in one of the most bitter and long-lasting conflicts known to academe: the argument between the 'orthodox' and 'revisionist' schools of French historians over the Revolution of 1789–93. The orthodox treat the Revolution as essentially progressive, the revisionists see it as an unfortunate and damaging interruption of what would otherwise have been a smooth and relatively successful evolutionary process. While I propose later to exercise a foreigner's right – denied to the French – to take a distance from both schools, I must side rather with the orthodox on their point of departure, the obstacles to progress existing up to 1789. The economic disintegration of the *ancien régime* was symbolised by the judicial concept of *dérogeance*. Business – activity purely for the making of money – was not proper for a gentleman. Such was the traditional prejudice, and *dérogeance* gave it teeth, for it meant the loss of noble status for any 'gentleman' found guilty of such degrading activities.

That was bound to hurt, for with noble status went very real tax privileges. Successive governments limited the scope of *dérogeance*, exempting sea-borne commerce (1669), large-scale commerce (1701), mining, glass-making and metallurgy (1722), and as the eighteenth century went on a number of nobles began increasingly to ignore it. The revisionists, accordingly, have been able to point to a great deal of activity on the part of nobles, particularly in the 'exempted sectors' of manufacturing, where they predominated, taking advantage of their tax privileges and using their contacts in the administration to get subsidies and orders, and exemptions from regulations. But what of the bourgeoisie? They lacked the nobles' tax privileges; and if, in spite of that, they succeeded in making money, their chance of using it to acquire and keep noble status – which everyone aspired to – depended on being more gentlemanly than the gentlemen. The Dukes of Orleans and of Deux-ponts could get away with setting up textile factories; and even if anyone had dared to take away their noble status, their sons would have got it back when they died; but a rich bourgeois landowner who had just acquired noble status, or hoped to, would by doing likewise have been risking his children's position as well as his own. Certainly there is evidence that such people held back even more than the nobles from such investments.[10] More generally, middle class enterprise was inhibited in the towns by guild regulations and in the countryside by the medieval rules on the use of land. The tangle of national and local regulations was, during the eighteenth century, gradually diminished by government and bypassed by entrepreneurs, until (in Price's judgement) it was no longer a 'very significant cause of economic backwardness';[11] but all the same, it was an obstacle, as was the system of internal customs dues. It is perhaps on attitudes, however, that we should lay most emphasis, the attitudes which underlay *dérogeance*. As the British traveller Arthur Young recalled,[12] he had sat in England at the tables of great noblemen and listened to them talk earnestly with their tenants, of far inferior social status, about how crop yields might be increased by rotation, drainage and so forth; in France, only in deference to a foreigner's whim would his noble hosts even invite a ... *peasant*, let alone talk to him in such a way.[13] As the two countries differed at dinner, so they did in economic integration, in general.

THE FIRST CRISIS AND ITS CAUSES

The effects of the water style

The new 'water' style has left two sorts of traces in the records: the first, positive, mostly in Britain: a quickening of the growth of production and exports in the key sectors, particularly cotton textiles (see Table 8.1) – also in canal-building; the second, negative, most visibly in France. The effects on France must be seen in the context of French industrial development up to 1780. Throughout the century, France had been in fierce competition with its old northern enemy in every sphere, and at mid-century could certainly be numbered among the technological leaders (Crouzet, 1967). Its industrial production continued to expand steadily thereafter – but its progress in technology slowed down: 'Cette expansion se developpe dans une curieuse et relative stabilite des techniques' (Labrousse *et al.*, 1970, *Histoire Economique de la France*, II, p. 162).

The results of French stagnation in technology can be gauged from the growth of the exports of the two countries:

France,   1716–49,   4.1 per cent per annum;
            1747–78,   1.0 per cent per annum;
            1778–89,   1.4 per cent per annum

(This flatters French performance in the last period, 1778 exports being depressed by war.)

Britain, 1716–45, 0.5 per cent per annum;
1745–79, 2.8 per cent per annum;
1779–1802, 4.2 per cent per annum.

(Labrousse *et al.*, 1970, *Histoire Economique de la France*, II, p. 503)

By the early 1780s the advantage of British exporters in third markets was becoming painfully evident to the French – for example through the sharp decline in exports of cloth from the Languedoc to the Levant in the early 1780s.[14] At the same time, Franco-British trade was increasing by leaps and bounds. Taking 1716 levels as 100, the value of foreign trade with Britain was at 300 by 1775, and 1080 by 1789.[15] It appears that the British had broken through in methods of producing (for example) cotton textiles, which the French then bought, selling in exchange goods like silks where the British had not yet made such a breakthrough, and were therefore uncompetitive by virtue of their higher wages.

Just as by 1760 France had clearly lost the military struggle for overseas empire, so by 1785 it had decisively lost the struggle for technological leadership. From that point on, discontent with the *ancien régime* increased dangerously among two groups: those, like many in Languedoc, who were suffering through Britain's success, and those (some of them the same people) who saw the gain to themselves and their country to be made by imitating it. French artisans and industrial workers were certainly suffering: while their numbers grew, their employers, with the support of the State, made great efforts to keep wages down and thus maintain their only advantage over their British competitors. 'Compagnonnage', a sort of trade unionism, expanded rapidly after 1770 and became increasingly militant from 1779–80; by 1786–7 all the industrial centres were seething.[16] At the same time, not surprisingly, there was fierce resistance to those French producers who were attempting to introduce British methods – there was a Luddite movement from 1780 onwards which reached a peak in 1788–9.[17] Meanwhile, the bourgeoisie, with much to gain, were frustrated by the landowners' tax privileges, entrenched social and political position, and rising share of national income as agricultural prices rose.

By the late 1780s (so it seems with hindsight) all that was required to light the match of revolution was a bad harvest. That came in 1787–89.[18] While the grain price in the North of France doubled, the nominal wages of town workers fell by 20–50 per cent in the industries where demand was sensitive to falling incomes.[19]

The French Revolution was then, in its origin, the first of our *mixed crises*: a crisis triggered by the arrival of the water style, and its effects on France from within and without. The course and consequences of the Revolution were much affected, however, by its repercussions on international politics, and the resulting 'global war'. Other European governments felt threatened by the new regime in France and the example it might set to their more discontented subjects. Some of the contenders in the struggle for power in

Paris saw gain to France, or to themselves, from foreign war.[20] From April 1792 the revolution was fighting for survival against the armies of the *anciens régimes*, first of Austria, then of Prussia, and the others. As it got the upper hand, the alarm bells rang in London. Those in power there, already nervous of the Jacobin example, could not tolerate the renewal of the 'continental challenge' from a Greater France controlling the Low Countries and dominating Western Europe. From 1793 onwards every development in France was taking place in the shadow of the enmity of the old world power and new technological leader.

The effects of the French revolution

> When France in wrath her giant-limbs upreared,
> And with that oath, which smote air, earth and sea,
> Stamped her strong foot and said she would be free,
> Bear witness for me, how I hoped and feared!
> (Samuel Taylor Coleridge, *France: An Ode*)

As a 'mixed crisis', the French Revolution might be expected to have removed some, but not all, of the institutional obstacles to the rapid diffusion of the new style. Many such obstacles, in France, it did remove. It '"cut down the dense growth of feudal, manorial, patrician and burgher influences", the sources of local power that were the obstacles to economic change'. It

> eradicated the guild. In consequence the field of enterprise was widened ... and innovation released from the disapproving restraint of traditional craft practice. Similarly, as provincial tariffs and tolls yielded to the centralising revolutionaries, new national and international markets outside the guild's parochial span became available to French manufacturers.
> (Trebilcock, 1981: 126)

> The revolutionary governments of the 1790s and Napoleon had given France institutions and laws which secured property and profit, safeguarded inventors against infringement, protected employers against organised labour, and provided a flow of trained engineers and technicians.
> (Pinkney, 1986: 25)

The new French broom swept, moreover, far beyond the frontiers of 1789. At one time or another, under the revolutionary regimes or Napoleon, the French armies controlled most of Europe. The Low Countries, Switzerland, Western Germany and Northern Italy were under French control for a long period, and in particular Belgium and the North Rhineland of Germany were treated as a part of France. The changes made in the institutions of these countries were thus similar to those just described in France.[21]

Why then has the Revolution had a bad press from many economic historians, as tending to retard rather than to accelerate economic development, at least in France? And why is it universally agreed that no acceleration followed it? One element of the explanation may derive from the character of the Revolution as a mixed crisis, and thus partly a reaction *against* economic development. One result of it was the strengthening of the peasantry, economically and politically. Some have blamed subsequent slow growth largely on this, regarding the peasantry as reactionary and held back by the small scale of their farms.[22] We have already seen in the last chapter that such a judgement was wrong elsewhere; O'Brien and Keyder (1978) have rebutted it in the French case. All the French peasant really needed to become progressive and enterprising – as he was to prove when he got it – was good access to markets and suppliers: that is to say, a good transport network. As we saw in Chapter 2, French topography is not at all suited to water transport, and the canals already built, lacking pound locks and adequate water, were worth less than they seemed. On average only 10 km a year were added to the canal system under the revolutionary and Napoleonic regimes.[23] The *ancien régime* had on the other hand bequeathed a good network of roads; alas, this had been built and maintained mainly through the forced peasant labour of the *corvée*, which was abandoned in 1787 as the monarchy tottered, and was neither restored nor effectively replaced until 1836.[24] Agricultural and industrial development were alike inhibited.

The failure of the Revolutionary and Napoleonic regimes to improve the transport system can be, to a large extent, explained by war, which preempted the resources required (see below). There were other ways in which the global war inhibited expansion and the diffusion of the new style in France and its neighbours. One was the British blockade. Since early in the century, the French had been seeking to catch up technologically with the British by copying their methods, and by importing machinery and skilled workers from them, and for almost as long, the British had been seeking, by legal prohibitions, to prevent them from doing so. Henderson (1972) shows that before the Revolution, British efforts were generally unsuccessful; but after war broke out in 1793, movement of all kinds between Britain and France was naturally a great deal more difficult. Moreover, the pressure on French manufacturers to adopt British technology eased, as British exports to France, and the Continent generally, fell away. Thus, for example, the diffusion of power-spinning, in spite of shortages of skilled engineers and imported British machinery, had begun in France and Catalonia in the 1780s, and in the Rhine Valley, Silesia and Saxony in the 1790s; but it was halted by the war.[25]

The global war was also extremely costly in a direct sense. The eighteenth century had somewhat tamed and civilised war. Royal armies marched and manoeuvred but inflicted relatively few casualties on one another, nor – being fairly well supplied and disciplined – did they inflict much death or

destruction on civilians. The main strain was on treasuries and taxpayers –
and indeed the financial aftermath of its participation in the War of
American Independence did much to bring down the *ancien régime*. All this
was lost in the revolutionary wars. The French, without financial reserves or
credit, were bound to lose, under the existing rules; so they changed them.
They innovated in military tactics, attacking (for example) in column rather
than in line.[26] Time after time the French column broke the opposing line,
but at terrible cost in casualties. They innovated (or rather regressed) in the
matter of supply: their armies took what was needed from the local
population, by summary taxation or straightforward pillage, and if that gave
them an incentive to get into enemy territory and keep moving forward, *tant
mieux*. (The classic case of this was Napoleon's invasion of Italy in 1796.[27])
Neither innovation in fact proved ultimately successful, in the face of the
British campaign in the Iberian Peninsula after 1809.[28] But they meant that
the physical damage, loss of life, and economic disruption inflicted on all the
main countries of continental Europe over more than two decades, were
huge. Britain, of course, protected by the 'wooden walls' of its fleet, was
physically unscathed, and its war casualties were modest; the economic
burdens of the war, on the other hand, were heavy. It can be argued that the
war benefited the British economy nonetheless, since it eliminated European
competition, overseas; but it also cut British trade with the Continent. In
any case, from a world perspective, it was a negative-sum game: if Britain
gained anything, others lost much more.[29]

The length of the war did institutional damage, too, which was less
striking but longer-lasting than that just described. Within France it gave
military aims priority in government policy, and tended gradually to reduce
the influence of those who were really interested in economic expansion.
'Napoleonic protectionism had gradually ceased to be a spur to industry and
become an instrument of war, and this was the cause of its failure'.[30]
Similarly, Napoleon's great innovations in education and finance, the
grandes écoles and the Banque de France, provided human and financial
capital, then and afterwards, not for industry, but for the State. Where
Napoleon did set out to help industry, it was very much in the restrictive
spirit of the autocrat. Thus in his new *statut de l'ouvrier* of 1803 he re-
established the *livret*, in effect an internal passport for industrial workers,
which had been abolished during the Revolution.[31] The French capitalist
was to be spared as far as possible the annoyance of labour shortage and the
need to show a minimum of consideration to his employees, which
stimulated his British rivals. In France's neighbouring countries French
conquest did indeed bring reforms; but these probably would have come
anyway, a little later, through domestic pressures, plus 'Jacobin contagion'. As
it was they were tainted by association with rapacious French troops and in-
sensitive French officials[32] and what was gained in speed was lost in acceptance
by the population. Further afield the results were mixed. The rout of Prussia's

army by Napoleon at Jena in 1809 drove its administration to carry out far-reaching reforms.[33] In Britain, on the other hand, war allowed Pitt and the Tories to tar the reformist Whigs under Fox with the Jacobin brush, and to initiate a long period of reactionary and repressive government.

The peace of 1815 naturally did much for the continental economies and something for the British. The peace *settlement*, however, had grave deficiencies from the economic point of view, deficiencies which reflected the nature of the global war which had just ended. As we saw when introducing Modelski's model in Chapter 1, this global war was exceptional in that the new world power which emerged at the end of it was none other than the old world power, which had seemed fatally weakened by the War of American Independence shortly before. This explains the unusual length of the global war (twenty-two years): there was no new world power to help the old to a quick victory against the continental challenger. It was twelve years before the British finally won the war at sea and sixteen before they produced an army which could even hold its own against the French. It also explains the reactionary nature of the peace settlement, epitomised by the chief negotiator on the British side, the Duke of Wellington. Wellington, an Irishman educated at a French military academy, was an incomparable general who did much to compensate for the deficiencies of the English aristocracy[34] but – as he was to show when Prime Minister of Britain – he was at the same time a bitter opponent of any sort of progressive reform. Since the other main figures at the Congress of Vienna represented the monarchies which had resisted the Jacobins from the beginning, Wellington was among friends, who shared his aim of ending the threat not only of France but of revolution, once and for all. Accordingly, the Bourbons were reinstalled in Paris, and the Princes of Orange in the Hague. Most of the advanced and reformed north of Italy was handed over to the Hapsburg Emperors; the part of Germany with the greatest industrial potential, the North Rhineland, was assigned to its most conservative state, Prussia. Finally, and fatally, Belgium was taken from France and made over to the Netherlands.

The damage done at Vienna was twofold. First, it put almost all the territories which had benefited from French reforms under more or less reactionary regimes. Second, it broke up the large economic unit which had been created during the wars in Western Europe. It was the latter effect which was, at least in the short term, the more disastrous. As we have seen, France with her frontiers of 1789 – and 1815 – was thoroughly ill-suited to the requirements of the water style. She needed the lands of the Rhine basin, combined with her original northern and north-eastern provinces to form a regional unit which could have fully matched North Britain for resources and transport network. Belgium above all was vital to the French economy, offering it an endowment of resources equal to Britain's in suitability for the water style: the great River Meuse and its tributaries reached into the

Ardennes Hills, and by the waterways were thick seams of coal.[35] With the Rhine-Meuse basin joined to France, she would have had a home market, and productive potential, which could have quickly surpassed Britain's. But while she had the Rhine and Meuse lands, the strains of war prevented her from making full use of them; before peace returned, she had lost them. Given peace, reform and unity these lands would have provided a large area of rapid diffusion for the water style while it was still diffusing rapidly in Britain (and had begun to do so in the northern USA). That might well have created an economic long wave upswing responding to the first technological style in the same way that the upswing after the Second World War did to the Fordist fourth. The political and economic breakup of the Rhine Basin in 1814–15 thus completed one of the great missed opportunities of world economic development.

Economic growth after the peace of Vienna

The progress which actually followed the peace was uneven. Two fragments of the Rhine Basin did indeed progress. Belgium emerged as second only to Britain, industrially, during the two decades after 1815, in spite of her exclusion from the French market for which she had produced in the two decades before.[36] Switzerland, at the south of the Rhine basin, also showed her ability to go it alone with the water style in the years after 1815, albeit on a more specialised basis than Belgium. The other economic treasure, the North Rhineland, on the other hand, grew only slowly. Its good access to the sea, water power in the Eiffel, and coal (as yet undiscovered) in the Ruhr counted for little in the face of Dutch obstruction of access to the Rhine, and a dull Prussian administration.

The French economy, too, performed at much below its potential until the 1830s. Peace, which reopened the flow of British technology, also reopened the flow of British goods. Many French producers in the key sectors of the water style – coal, iron and cotton – were quite unable to stand up to British competition. Had France kept Belgium – which *was* competitive in these sectors – it might have accepted the principle of comparative advantage, and let these industries go under *within* the old French frontiers. As it was, the French government was naturally unwilling to see whole industrial sectors virtually wiped out, and protected them with high tariffs: wartime protection was restored in 1816, and the rates raised further in 1820.[37] (The US government followed a similar policy, with the average tariff on manufactures rising from 8 per cent in 1789 to 25–30 per cent in 1816 and a peak of 45 per cent in 1828.)[38] The result was to burden those (light) industries which could have been competitive internationally with the high costs of the (heavy) industries which could not. All industries were under less pressure to advance technologically than if they had been exposed to international competition and faced (lower) international prices for capital

Table 8.4 Railway building in the early industrialisers, 1830–50

Kms of line opened by end	Britain	France	Germany	USA	Belgium
1830	157	31	–	37	–
1831	225	31	–	153	–
1832	267	52	–	369	–
1833	335	73	–	612	–
1834	480	141	–	1,019	–
1835	544	141	6	1,767	20
1836	649	141	6	2,049	44
1837	870	159	21	2,410	142
1838	1,196	159	140	3,079	258
1839	1,562	224	240	3,705	312
1840	2,390	410	469	4,535	334
1841	2,858	548	683	5,689	379
1842	3,122	645	931	6,479	439
1843	3,291	743	1,311	6,735	558
1844	3,600	822	1,752	7,044	577
1845	3,931	875	2,143	7,456	577
1846	4,889	1,049	3,281	7,934	594
1847	6,352	1,511	4,306	9,009	691
1848	8,022	2,004	4,989	9,650	780
1849	8,918	2,467	5,443	11,853	796
1850	9,797	2,915	5,856	14,518	854

Source: Mitchell, 1978, 1983
Note: Ireland is included in the British figures for 1831–9 and 1841–7.

goods and fuel. As if these handicaps were not enough, the French economy was burdened with a heavy war indemnity.[39]

There was no general and protracted upsurge in growth, then, after 1815. The British, with the Belgians at their heels, went on progressing steadily within the water style, 'stretching' it by a gradual increase in emphasis on the steam-engine as a power source and the horse tramway as a cheap extension to the waterway system. The Americans did likewise, linking their two great waterway systems in 1826 with the Erie Canal and developing the paddle-steamer, after 1829, for use on waterways where neither sail nor horse was suitable. The Swiss put their skills and water power to good use. The rest progressed only slowly, until after 1830. The acceleration had to wait for the arrival of a style which could accommodate itself better to the lines which the statesmen of the Congress of Vienna had drawn on the map.

THE SECOND CRISIS: EFFECTS OF THE STEAM TRANSPORT STYLE

By about 1830 the steam transport style had crystallized – it was there, it was available to anyone who had the financial resources, the skilled manpower, the organisational capacity and the freedom from legal restraint, to use it.

Which is to say, to very few people outside Britain, Belgium and the Northern USA.[40] There was, therefore, no great economic leap forward in the 1830s, outside those favoured areas. In them, the new style soon began to diffuse quite quickly, but their success with the old style meant that its effects on growth rates were modest, particularly in Britain. (Thus of the European countries, Britain built railroads the most quickly, as Table 8.4 shows, although it had the best waterway and road system. Not that the railways were not needed: they arrived, as I argued in Chapter 2, in response to developing bottlenecks and shortages.) The effects of the change are apparent rather in the structure of the economy; for example, the railway boom had major effects on the engineering and construction industries.[41]

As the new style spread, there were inevitably social repercussions. It facilitated the growth of the new industrial conurbations, and increased the pressure of competition from factory production on artisans like the handloom weavers. It can scarcely be coincidence, therefore, that it was during the early diffusion of the new style that there arose – among artisans and industrial workers – the most serious challenge to the established structures of British society in the nineteenth century, the Chartist movement. From 1838 to the late 1840s the Chartists agitated for far-reaching parliamentary reform and a range of social and economic changes.[42] They failed in their central aims, but other pressure groups with more limited objectives succeeded in theirs. Thus the Anti-Corn Law League induced the government between 1842 and 1846 to reduce and then abolish the protective tariffs on wheat.[43] The public health movement which grew up during the 1830s achieved major legislative successes during the late 1840s, notably the passing of the Public Health Bill in 1846.[44] The factory movement gained equal success in regulating hours of labour, culminating in the passage of the Ten Hours Bill in 1848. Together, these reforms eased the diffusion of the new style – respectively ensuring improved supplies of food and cleaner water for the new conurbations, and increasing the incentive to mechanisation.[45]

The new style put relentless pressure on those countries near the leaders – near them geographically, and in technological capacity – to come to terms with it. Those who would not jump on the bandwagon would be run down by it – put out of business by competition from the new style's products. Tariff protection for obsolete methods was not to be relied upon. French artisan weavers found themselves undercut by steam-powered mills springing up inside the country; those mills then lobbied for free trade in coal, and for railways. The railway companies soon became a powerful force opposing the tariff protection of iron and steel.[46]

The governments of these countries made piecemeal responses to the pressures of and for the new style. In France, the *Loi Guizot* of 1833 required every commune to maintain a school, and slowly the illiteracy of the majority of the population – a formidable handicap economically – receded; in 1836, for the first time since the *corvée* was abolished in 1787, there was a law assuring resources to construct and maintain local roads. After a slow start to railway-building, the Railway Law of 1842 cleared the way for railways to be built quickly and rationally.[47] The high levels of tariffs on industrial goods were reduced, most markedly in 1847.[48] These reforms were enough to make possible a sharp acceleration in economic growth which Crouzet[49] reckons as beginning about 1835 and reaching a peak in the mid-1840s. There was a similar response to the pressures of the new style in most of the German states; reforms there, for example, relaxed guild restrictions on who could manufacture what, and how.

The economic acceleration of the 1840s (matched in the USA) bears out the argument in Chapter 1 that, in the nineteenth century at least, a new style could quicken economic growth without a crisis being required, to break the inertia of the socio-institutional framework. But it was argued there also that a social and political crisis would be brought about by the early diffusion of the new style. So it was in the 1840s. In the west and centre of continental Europe, and in a slightly different way in Ireland, the old social and economic structures crumbled under the pressure of the advancing steam transport style. Until then, industrialisation had gone hand in hand with increasing population in the countryside, for those with too little land to support them turned to working within the 'putting out' system of manufacturing to earn enough for subsistence. Now, as Pinkney writes of France:

> The industrial base of the rural economy was undermined and eventually destroyed by the new factory industry ... Rural industry was a casualty of forces, clearly emerging in the early and middle forties, which were brought to bear on it by the economic depression of 1847–50. With it went the means of support of a considerable part of the rural population.[50]

For many, particularly in Ireland, the last hope was the potato – the only crop, then and now, capable of yielding enough, in a temperate climate, to sustain a family on an acre.[51] When the potato blight struck in 1845, that last hope was gone, and many cottagers who had not fled the land already, left it now, or starved.[52] The towns were no haven; they lacked the housing and sanitation needed to cope with the influx, and although employment there was expanding, it was not expanding fast enough. Money wages were held down, but there was a sharp rise in the price of staple foods – for while demand for them was rising fast in the towns, output was held back by the departure of the cottagers (even with an overpopulated countryside, in the days before mechanised agriculture you could never have too many hands at harvest time). This rise in food prices helped to spread the crisis to Britain, where the exodus of the cottagers had been largely completed earlier; so did the arrival of many of the displaced Irish. Others from Ireland, and from the harder-hit parts of Germany, began the first great wave of transatlantic migration; but even with the drop in fares, few of the poorest could afford to to so far, and the emigration was nowhere near enough, at the beginning, to take the pressure off.

In 1848, following a bad harvest,[53] the lid blew off the kettle. The lethal combination of discontent in the countryside and hunger in the cities led to riot and revolution starting in Paris and spreading eastwards in a speeded-up replay of the Revolutionary years. By the end of the year the Orleanist monarchy in France had gone for good and the German princes, great and small, had temporarily lost control.

No doubt the harvest failures were the immediate causes of the 1848 revolutions; and it can be seen that the spread of the 'steam transport style' contributed to them, through the dislocation of agriculture. But industrial and technological change had undermined the old order already. Kitchen sums it up well:

> There can be no doubt whatever that the disastrous effects of the rise in food prices from 1846 were a major causal factor in the revolution of 1848 [in Germany]. . . . But as Rudolf Stadelmann has shown, it is a mistake to see the revolution of 1848 purely in terms of economic hardship, either in the long or the short term. It was the result of a widespread feeling that the day of reckoning had come, that the old order had failed and lost its legitimacy. Life had become too complex and too hectic, menacing changes loomed on the horizon, the old certainties were lost. The world of the railways, the factory, the steam engine and applied science could not be mastered by the autocratic state, however enlightened its servants, and in its underworld were menacing forces that threatened to break loose and disrupt the ordered certainties of the familiar social world. *These dire prophecies of doom were symptoms of the fact that the political and constitutional structure of society was contradictory to the social and economic reality and needs of a rapidly modernising society.* (Emphasis added.)
>
> (Kitchen, 1978: 80–1)

At first sight it might appear that the 1848 revolutions were quickly reversed. In France, the liberal capitalists, allied with the prosperous peasantry, turned their guns on the city artisans who had helped bring down the monarchy. By the end of the following year even parliamentary democracy had been replaced by the new autocracy of Louis Napoleon, soon to become Napoleon III. In Germany the eclipse of the princes left the liberal nationalists in what passed for control; but they had nothing to offer the urban poor, and little organised support in the countryside, and were easily swept aside, once the landowning conservatives had pulled themselves together. The Hapsburg Emperors quickly restored order in Vienna, and with the help of a Russian army put down the Hungarian insurrection. Yet there was, economically, something to show for the upheavals. The gains were clearest in France. 'In return for their support in the difficult months of 1848 and 1849, [the liberal capitalists] received a regime more disposed to encourage industrialism than any other French administration between 1789 and 1914'.[54] 'The 1848 revolution was the point of departure for a monetary revolution: the value of the notes that had beeen issued by the Banque de France rose from F250m. to F650m. between 1848 and 53'.[55] The new government set up the Credit Agricole and the Comptoir d'Agriculture to deal, at last, with the shortage of credit for the peasantry.[56] Thus encouraged, the private sector was equally innovative, developing a new sort of bank, of which the archetype was the Credit Mobilier (1851), designed to attract small savers, channelling their cash into industrial investment.[57] Railway construction, given coherence by intelligent state direction, surged ahead. Tariffs were steadily reduced.[58]

It is in Germany that the advantages of the post-1848 regimes are least obvious. There was certainly no burst of progressive legislation. Indeed, trying not unsuccessfully to win popular support, the princes' new conservative ministers actually put the clock back, and reintroduced some guild restrictions. Still, many of the gains of 1848 were kept. In many of the German states remaining feudal rights were abolished in 1848, completing the process begun in 1806 of the liberation of the peasantry from restrictions on their movement. Other gains which were more transitory – such as the increases in wages won by journeymen and workers – helped to pull the economy out of the depression caused by the harvest failures (soon an investment boom was to provide ample demand).[59] The great change for the better, however, was that the liberal bourgeoisie henceforward had a working partnership with the state, even though it had fallen back into the hands of the conservative aristocrats. In the 1850s capitalists knew where they were. In Germany their big push for political power, alongside the rest of the middle class, had failed, and they knew they were excluded from political power for the foreseeable future; they channelled their energies into their own sphere, where legislative changes now allowed them more scope.[60] For example, they were quick to copy the Credit Mobilier; indeed, with the relaunch of the Schaffhausen Bank in 1848 as a joint-stock company, they could be said to have anticipated it. The bank, in its own words, was intended:

> to induce the capitalists of the country, by recommendations based on exhaustive investigations, to turn idle capital towards such enterprises, which, when properly launched, in response to existing requirements, and offering the guarantee of expert management, bid fair to yield reasonable profits.
>
> (Kitchen, 1978: 84)

In other words, it aimed to promote the integration of finance and industry; and with later foundations, it seems largely to have achieved it.

(The French and German banks of this kind took different, complementary paths: the Germans financed their own industry, the French, other people's, mostly in Central and Eastern Europe.)

In general, then, the revolutions of 1848 seem to fit well into the category of a mixed crisis, leading to only partial reform in both economic and political spheres. In Germany in particular, it was in the political sphere that the deficiencies of the settlement were most marked. As we shall see in the chapters which follow, those political deficiencies had grave consequences, which spread out to affect the whole world economy.

Chapter 9

A historical account, 1850–1896

THE FIRST WORLD BOOM AND ITS FADING

It is clear that there was in the early and middle 1850s the first truly international boom. As we see in Table 9.1, world industrial production grew at a rate of 7.6 per cent per annum from 1850 to 1856.[1] All the major economies shared in this rapid expansion. Here at last – it would seem – is a long wave upswing *à la Perez*: a boom produced by a new style freed to diffuse fast by reforms which were provoked by its own early impact. The trouble was, it did not last. The first truly international boom was ended in 1857 by the first truly international crash, and the next decade, 1856–66, showed growth rates for world industrial production of only 2.8 per cent per annum, before a brief return to rapid growth (4.5 per cent per annum) in 1866–72. Certainly the 1850–72 period as a whole shows a faster growth rate than the next twenty years – but the contrast between what van Duijn calls the 'second Kondratiev upswing',[2] and the alleged 'second Kondratiev downswing' of 1872–92 is dangerously dependent on the choice of beginnings and ends for the periods compared. It is obviously misleading to start a period in the trough of a Juglar cycle (which 1850 is) and end it at the peak of such a cycle – this makes the growth rate artificially high. For world industrial production this is unavoidable because the data for many countries only go back to 1850. The two major countries for which earlier data is available are Britain and France; if we start our 'Kondratiev upswings' at the last Juglar peak before 1850 (Britain, 1845; France, 1847) and finish our 'Kondratiev downswings' at the Juglar peak before 1896 (Britain and France, both 1890) the result should be less misleading (see Table 9.2).

Again, the earlier period does show the faster growth – 3.1 against 2.1 per cent p.a. for Britain, 1.7 against 1.2 per cent p.a. for France. On the other hand, the difference for France is not large, and the apparent 'downswing' for Britain during 1873–90 continues into the following 'upswing period' – suggesting a 'climacteric' or longer-term shift to slower growth. What is more, it may not be enough to use Juglar peaks for dating. There is, as we saw in Chapter 1, another cycle intermediate between the Juglar and the Kondratiev; the Kuznets or long swing. Solomou (1987) argues that one

Table 9.1 Growth rates of world industrial production, 1850–1913

Juglar period	% per annum	Long period	% per annum
(1850–56)	7.6	1850–72	4.6
1856–66	2.8	1872–92	3.0
1866–72	4.5		
1872–83	2.7	Long swing	% per annum
1883–92	3.4		
1892–1903	4.3	1856–72	3.4
1903–13	4.1	1872–92	3.0

Source: van Duijn, 1983, Table 9.5

Table 9.2 Growth rates of British and French industrial production, per annum, 1845–1913

Juglar period	Britain	France	Juglar period
1845–57	3.3	2.8	1847–56
1857–66	3.2	0.6	1856–66
1866–73	2.3	2.1	1866–72
1873–83	2.2	1.9	1872–82
1883–90	1.6	0.4	1882–90
1890–1903	1.8	1.6	1890–1903
1903–13	2.3	3.5	1903–13
Long period			Long period
1845–72	3.1	1.7	1847–72
1873–90	2.0	1.2	1872–90

Source: van Duijn, 1983, Tables 9.2 and 9.4

must date from Kuznets peaks to Kuznets peaks to avoid 'cheating'. That means comparing the 1856–72 period with that from 1872 to 1892. World industrial production then shows a deceleration from 3.4 per cent p.a. to 3.0 per cent p.a.; in the 'right' direction but scarcely significant.

Once again, it seems that the technological long wave failed to produce a corresponding economic long wave – if there was one, at all events, it was faint. The explanation of the first failure was that a geographically 'fussy' new style was obstructed by war and then political fragmentation in its natural field of diffusion; and that the mixed crisis it provoked turned into a global war which both prolonged the crisis and made it less productive of reform. As a result an economic long wave upswing never got started. The steam transport style was *not* 'fussy', the mixed crisis of the late 1840s was brief and quite productive of economic reform, and a general upswing did seem in the early 1850s to have started. Why then did the upswing peter out, resuming only when the impetus of the steam transport style was almost exhausted?

Let us work towards an answer by looking first at the causes of the 1850s boom. First, in the USA there was a Kuznets boom (due perhaps to climatic causes). As to Europe, in the last chapter we reviewed the changes in 'socio-institutional framework' which enabled Germany and France to join fully in the rapid diffusion of the steam transport style, and Britain to keep up its steady progress in the lead. There were also more general 'stimulants'. Chapter 4 discussed the upsurge in gold output from California and Australia, from 1849 onwards, which injected extra purchasing power, increased liquidity, and reduced interest rates throughout the world economy. Chapter 5 mentioned the mass immigration of the late 1840s and early 1850s, which boosted growth in, and demand from, the United States. If that immigration is to be put down simply to 'pull' from a US Kuznets boom, it is of no great significance for us here. What went up would soon come down, then go up again in the next Kuznets boom. But (as argued already in Chapter 5) there was 'push' as well from Europe, due to the size of the 'young adult' cohort, and the 'mixed crisis'. Migration then was rather larger than would have resulted from a Kuznets boom alone.

How different, then, were these factors after 1856? Most of the following decade counts as a Kuznets downswing, but that was balanced in due course by an upswing, to 1872–3. The improvements in 'socio-institutional frame-work' can be taken to have remained valuable well after 1856. That leaves us with the gold rushes and migration push as possible clues to the mystery of the missing upswing. Let us take them in turn.

We saw in Chapter 4 that 'monetary feedback' was not expansionary for nearly so long a period after the gold discoveries of the late 1840s as it was to be after those of the 1880s. From about 1856 the expansion of gold output virtually stopped. Interest rates in the late 1850s and 1860s were decidedly higher than in any ten-year period between 1890 and the war. Both these developments may be ascribed in large part to the extraordinarily rapid rise in prices in the 1850–6 period, which reduced both the real price of gold and the real value of the money supply: the increase in demand which drove up prices was due in turn partly to Britain and France's brief but expensive war against Russia in 1854–5.[3]

Expansionary population feedback faded as quickly as the boost from money. The 'post-war baby boom' of the 1820s was too old by the 1860s for much further migration, and Europe felt more prosperous than in the late 1840s, even if its growth rate was once again modest. In consequence, as we saw in Chapter 5, the US Kuznets boom from the mid-1860s to the early 1870s drew a smaller surge of migrants out of Europe than any other of the 1840–1914 period.

It was, however, another factor which probably did most to hold back growth in the 1856–72 period – the most damaging of the modern wars but for those called global, the American Civil War. The economic effects of the Civil War within the country have been much discussed and debated; as Patrick O'Brien (1988) showed in his recent survey of the literature, there is little dispute that the economic damage to the USA (mostly to the South) was substantial, and that post-war recovery was far from complete by 1873. So its effect was significantly to depress the US growth rate over the 1850–73 'upswing' period, and somewhat to increase it over the 1873–96 'downswing' period, in which the recovery was, more or less, completed. That was not all: the trading partners of the United States were also seriously affected. US exports of cotton were drastically reduced during the Civil War and for years afterwards; other sources of supply were developed in due course, in Egypt, India and Brazil, but the effect of the War was for several years to cause serious depression in the British cotton industry, and those of the other European countries (the French was by far the largest).

> The impact of the American Civil War (1861–5) on the industry ... was of course pronounced ... throughout 1862, 1863 and 1864 an intense cotton famine had prevailed the world over ... [there was] a tremendous cutback in output enforced by the sheer lack of raw material ... By the end of 1865 [the British industry] was probably getting as much cotton as it could use, [but] given that it was a higher cost material with which it was then being supplied ... the consequently higher price of the finished article had a dulling effect on demand ... It was not until 1871 that American supplies regained their prewar level.
>
> (Murphy, 1973: 576).

While British output of cotton goods had grown from 1850–5 at 6 per cent per year, and from 1855–60 at 4.25 per cent per year, over the 1860–73 period taken together its growth rate was a mere 1.5 per cent.[4] The growth of British gross domestic product slowed from 2.5 per cent a year in 1845–56 to 1.8 per cent in 1856–65 before recovering to 2.8 per cent in 1865–73 (see Table 9.3). The growth rate of world industrial production fell to 2.8 per cent per year in 1856–66 before recovering to 4.5 per cent in 1866–72 (see Table 9.1).[5]

The Civil War does much, then, to explain the non-existence of a long boom in the 1850–73 period, and thus to account for the second failure of

Table 9.3 Growth rates of British gross domestic product, 1845–1913, % per annum

Juglar periods		Long periods	
1845–56	2.5	1856–1913	2.0
1856–65	1.8	1856–73	2.3
1865–73	2.8	1873–1913	1.8
1873–82	1.6	1882–99	2.5
1882–89	2.7	1899–1913	1.1
1889–99	2.3		
1899–1907	1.0		
1907–13	1.8		

Source: Solomou, 1987, Tables 3.1 and 3.2
Note: The 'income' estimate of GDP is used throughout except for 1845–56 for which only the less reliable 'compromise' estimate is available.

the technological long wave to induce an economic long wave. So far so good; but we can do better. We can set the *causes* of the Civil War in the framework of our theory – which will enable us to understand, in due course, why there was a major war which 'interfered' with this long wave upswing, and the next, but not the most recent.

The steam transport style and the Civil War

We have seen already how the appearance and early diffusion of the steam transport style after 1830 contributed to the European crisis of the 1840s and its catharsis in the revolutions of 1848; and how the reforms then and afterwards helped to launch the international boom of the early 1850s. There was, however, no such impact on the United States. The North was already more English than England in the suppleness of its structures and its ability to cope with economic change. Geographically, too, railways were the answer to its prayers. The new style, together with the influx of European labour (for which it was largely responsible), provided the North with an opportunity for industrial take-off, which it took, quickly. The same breeze brought good news for the South, of quite a different kind: the growth of industry elsewhere, specifically cotton textiles, meant a long boom in demand for just that southern product best suited to the slave economy. So long as King Cotton ruled, there would be no voluntary transformation of Southern society. But the railway-led industrialisation of the North brought the prospect of involuntary change closer.[6] Mass Irish and German immigration rapidly increased the numerical preponderance of 'free' states over 'slave', though that would be little threat to the South, by itself, so long as its alliance with the West held – based on the interests of both agricultural regions in free trade and the western states' use of New Orleans as their port.

However, the advance of the railways across the Appalachians unlocked the industrial potential of the northern Mississippi basin, and soon gave the western states not only the means for close contact with the North-East, but also the basis for political alliance with it. The free-trading Democratic party which had represented both South and West for decades, steadily lost ground in the West to the Republican party, which represented both industrialists and abolitionists. With the victory of the Republicans in the 1860 elections under the westerner Lincoln, the South saw the writing on the wall; as McPherson argues in *Battle Cry of Freedom*,[7] Southern secession can be seen as a 'pre-emptive counter-revolution' intended to preserve a status quo under threat.[8] Thus the *ante bellum* USA satisfied three preconditions of an acute 'crisis of the upswing': it originated in a country which:

(a) had not had radical reforms before the upswing;
(b) had groups entrenched in power who were 'out of date' to start with;

(c) had experienced a long period of rapid economic growth which made the threat to these groups from the preponderant character of the society quite intolerable.

We may add that the Civil War had results typical of a crisis of the upswing: it left the social fabric of the country little changed. As O'Brien shows, the conservative Northern Republicans who won the war had no inclination to follow up the abolition of slavery with a levelling of Southern society even as far as the limited degree of equality prevailing in the North. The sharecropping system which they allowed to emerge left the blacks thoroughly dependent on their ex-owners, and their economic weakness was soon compounded by their increasing numbers. This entrenched inequality within the South, and between it and the North – a feature of US society which was to have grave consequences in the 1920s, but not before. For the next fifty years the dynamism of the North was quite enough; and as Freeman has shown,[9] Northern institutions turned out to be very well adapted, or adaptable, to the requirements of the next technological style.

European crises

The US Civil War was not, of course, the only war of importance in the 1850–73 period. It deserves emphasis because it was the only one long enough to have serious economic effects at the time; but there were European wars – that of France and Piedmont against Austria in 1864, and Prussia's wars against Denmark (1864), Austria (1866) and France (1870–1) – which are worth examining to see what their long-term effects might have been. Can we treat these wars too as part of some sort of European 'crisis of the upswing', akin to that which erupted in 1914? In continental Europe, unlike the United States, there *had* been the crisis of the late 1840s, which had ended with reforms of varying degrees of thoroughness. Those in the German-speaking lands were, in the political sphere, the least far reaching. Prussia in particular had emerged with the anachronism of a landowning caste holding all the levers of political power while its role in the economy was already modest. During the 1850s, with moderate representatives like Manteuffel in control, this caste sought to maintain its power by not using it too much to its own advantage. The favourable economic situation made a 'balanced' policy painless for the Junkers. High grain prices and the improving transport network gave them a lucrative export trade to England; they insisted on encouraging this, and keeping the price of consumer goods down, by a low-tariff policy on manufactures, while they remained exempt from land taxes. The urban bourgeoisie, who would mostly have preferred high tariffs, were consoled by the opportunities open to them with the coming of the steam transport style, the improved financial structure, and the flood of labour coming off the land. And the peasantry (who did have to pay land taxes) were at last enabled to buy their freedom from feudal obligations on reasonable terms, by the state-owned mortgage banks set up after the 1848 revolution – the price providing welcome cash for the Junkers with which to develop and extend their estates.[10] As economic growth proceeded, however, the Junkers' political position became increasingly precarious: the Conservatives who represented their interests were a minority in the Diet and a shrinking one at that. During 1861 the Junkers lost their exemption from the land tax, and the 'Old Liberal' majority in the Diet blocked a proposal to expand the (Junker-officered) army. The political crisis which ensued led to the emergence in December of that year of a new, decidedly liberal, 'Progressive Party' which comfortably outnumbered the Conservatives.

Like their counterparts in the American South earlier in the year, the Junkers saw themselves beleaguered, and chose not to go quietly, but to strike back; and unlike the Southern aristocracy, they still controlled the State – through that arch-Junker, King William I. The following autumn William accepted the Junker nominee for Prime Minister, Otto von Bismarck – of whom the previous King had said, in 1848, that he was to be used only once the bayonet freely reigned.[11] Much like the English kings in the early seventeenth century, the Prussian king could rule in the teeth of parliamentary opposition if he was prepared to do without new taxes, but the position was at best precarious. The conservative newspaper *Die Kreuzzeitung* prophesied when Bismarck took office, that he would 'overcome domestic difficulties by a bold foreign policy'; and that was precisely what he did. Victory in the war against Denmark 'undermined liberal opposition to absolutism on the home front';[12] but only for a time. A new and bigger victory was needed, and duly won, against Austria, in 1866. 'This second successful war brought about the moral collapse of the progressive liberals in North Germany'.[13] The Progressive Party split, and the 'moderates' in it became the National Liberals, potential allies of the Junkers thereafter. Even that was not enough. The legislation which had been pushed through after the victory of 1864, to expand the army and place it outside Parliamentary control, had to be renewed every seven years, and a majority for its renewal was still in doubt; moreover, it was necessary to complete the unfinished business of German reunification, on the Junkers' terms. Bismarck managed to provoke the French Emperor – whose position was also precarious – into war. Again he won a quick and crushing victory. Having been

> prepared to risk three wars as an almost desperate therapy for stabilising the monarchical system ... from then on [the Junkers] were able to feed on the massively prestigious success of Bismarck's diplomacy and the Prussian military ... the National Liberals succumbed, as desired.[14]

Thus the German case, like the American, satisfies the three preconditions set out above for an acute 'crisis of the upswing'. The economic dynamism which helped to bring about the crisis also provided the opportunity for successful aggression.

The results of the European wars were not unimportant in the long term. Defeat is bound to have some effects on the socio-institutional framework, at all events when it is as crushing as those suffered by Austria and France. The Austrian response was to make the great compromise with Hungary of 1867, and to give both halves of the new Austro-Hungarian empire parliamentary government of sorts. This increased the stability and flexibility of the Hapsburg monarchy, and was the basis of its impressive economic growth until 1914.[15] The French went one better, and acquired a parliamentary republic with universal (male) suffrage; that too, it can be argued, had beneficial effects on their economy. Victory, by contrast, is likely only to confirm the status quo; but in this case the Piedmontese and Prussian victors achieved the reunification of their countries, and that naturally called for some measure of institutional change. Bismarck, who did nothing by halves, set up the new German parliament on the basis of one man, one vote; he was, according to Taylor[16], seeking to swamp the middle-class urban Liberals with the votes of conservative peasants. (The reform meant less than it seemed, since the new Reichstag had even less power than the Prussian parliament, and that remained entirely unreformed.) Then, to be on the safe side, he gave the Liberals most of the reforms they wanted:

> All his effort ... went into reconciling the liberals to the continuance of Junker rule. Between 1867 and 1879 the German liberals ... were given at a stroke uniform legal procedure, uniform coinage, uniformity of administration; all restrictions on freedom of enterprise and freedom of movement were removed, limited companies and trade combinations allowed.[17]

These reforms only accentuated the contrast between Germany's economic dynamism and its lack of political integration.

We shall see that these changes were of great significance in the way they shaped European responses to the next technological style.

THE 'GREAT DEPRESSION', 1873–96

The causes of the downswing after 1873

> This, by despair, bred hangdog dull; by Rage,
> Manwolf, worse; and their packs infest the age

> Gerard Manley Hopkins, from *Tom's Garland: upon the Unemployed*, 1887.

If the 1873–92 period was not a 'great depression' in terms of economic growth, nonetheless it did begin with an unusually severe recession, and even if we go on to the next cyclical peak, in 1883, the average growth rate of world industrial production was as low in 1873–83 as in the 1856–66 period (2.7 per cent – see Table 9.1). We can find a number of reasons for the severity of the 1870s recession. One factor must have been climate.

We are already familiar with the regular fluctuations in rainfall in the USA which seem to have been the underlying cause of the Kuznets cycle there. Since US rainfall peaked in 1871, with a trough in 1880, the climate there was deflationary for most of the 1872–83 period. Now, no regular fluctuation has been found in the European climate to match that in the USA. As Solomou has shown for Britain[18], not only were fluctuations in Europe irregular, their impact on output was also not straightforward. In the USA, clearly, the more rain the better: drought was and is always the main worry. Europeans are less easily satisfied: they also complain (with reason) when it is too wet. The appallingly wet weather of 1875–81 in Britain depressed agricultural production.[19] Over the same period, French agricultural production was also depressed, though this may owe as much to the effect of *phylloxera* on wine output and *pebrine* on silk production, as to bad weather.[20] The weather presumably played some part, too in the poor performance of German agriculture in the late 1870s.[21] Thus a random fluctuation in the European climate (plus pests) worked in the same direction as a regular fluctuation in the American.

Lower agricultural output in Europe in the late 1840s had caused a huge increase in food prices and thus thrown most of the burden on to the towns. The rise in prices in the late 1870s was, however, very modest, and for this the town dwellers had to thank the rapid growth of American agricultural output during the same period – 5.2 per cent per year, from 1873–80.[22] (The causes of this surge, in the teeth of the weather, are discussed below.) The effects of low agricultural output in Europe were felt most directly, then, in the agricultural sector, and indirectly – through the drop in rural purchasing power – in industry.

Another factor, which in this context is not 'accidental', was demography. As Thomas shows, migration from Europe in the 1873–8 period was extremely low, due (alongside the downswing in the USA) to the low birth-rates in the late 1840s and early 1850s (see Chapter 5, Figures 5.4 and 5.5): this must have accentuated, though it did not initiate, the slump in American railway construction over the same period.

It seems likely also that in two countries the recession after 1873 was a reaction to previous euphoria: the United States after the Civil War, and Germany after its victories, were seized by a degree of irrational optimism which led to over-investment, and it was these two countries which suffered a real financial crash in 1873.[23] But there may have been something more to that euphoria than the effects of victory. We saw earlier that the Bessemer rail (the first use of the new cheap steel) had drastically improved the economics of railway transport: although at first steel rails required a greater outlay, they lasted much longer and permitted much higher speeds. It was the Bessemer rail which led the railway expansion into the Great Plains in the 1866–72 railway boom, and it was the railways built then which made possible the surge in grain production which followed.

Just as the revolution in iron and steel technology probably accentuated the 1866–73 boom, so it may well have exacerbated the recession which followed. For the most obvious problem in industry during the middle and late 1870s, and in agriculture a little later, was the steep fall in prices, which greatly increased the burden of debts already contracted, and (to the extent that it was expected to continue) made real interest rates look discouragingly high (see Figures 4.1 to 4.4). One might have expected some fall in prices in a recession, of course; the particular problem here was that this was very much an *international* recession. Since the long boom in international trade had encouraged tariff reductions (outside the USA) and cheap steel in various ways had cut transport costs, international recession meant an international price war. At first, in the steel industry, it was a very unequal contest, for until the Gilchrist/Thomas process was perfected in 1879, the new steel-making processes required low-phosphorus ore, which was much more freely available to the British than to their main competitors. The German iron and steel industry, represented by the National Liberals, clamoured for tariff protection at much the same time as the Conservatives, representing the Junkers, realised the implications of cheap Russian and American grain for themselves. The 'alliance of iron and rye' duly forced through tariffs on these commodities in 1879 – the same year as Gilchrist and Thomas freed the German steelmakers from any real need for protection.

The causes of the recovery

Having explained the severity of the 1870s recession, we have now to explain also why it was followed not by a continuing long wave downswing, but by generally quite rapid growth which made the 1873–96 period far from the 'great depression' it has been called. The first country to show a strong recovery was the United States: the trigger was an upturn in railway building,[24] due no doubt largely to the strength of agricultural exports. But what sustained the US recovery was the flood of immigration which followed, reaching a clear record for the century in 1882[25] (see Figure 5.3). European emigration remained high until the early 1890s, and here we see two stabilising, counter-cyclical feedback processes at work: first, the 'slow population feedback' from the 'good years', by which the 'baby boom' in western Europe in the late 1850s and early 1860s produced a labour surplus ready to migrate some twenty-eight years later; second, the rapid feedback from the bad years of the late 1870s, which drove young men west at the first opportunity thereafter. There was another rapid counter-cyclical feedback: the fall in prices (as we saw) increased the value of the stock of money (with the help, later, of rising gold output) and this helped to reduce interest rates[26]; where manufacturing investment stayed low (as in Britain) the low interest rates and free availability of finance encouraged construction investment to take up the slack.[27] As we saw in Chapter 4, the rise in gold output after 1880 gave a sort of fiscal, as well as monetary, stimulus to demand.

Until after 1890, nonetheless, the European economies were, in general, rather depressed: it was the US economy, powered by immigration, which was the locomotive of the world economy, with a higher-than-average growth rate (see Figure 9.1 and Table 9.4). In the 1890s it was continental Europe which took over that role. The European boom of the 1890s is an example of both adaptation *to*, and adaptation *of*, a new technological style. Even after the problem of phosphorus was solved in 1879, the new steel technology, unlike steam transport half a century earlier, was a much greater blessing for some countries than others. Germany was well placed (it suffered in the 1880s largely from falling demand from steel, due to the completion of its rail network).[28] Most other continental countries fell into one or both of two disadvantaged categories:

1 They lacked the coking coal and iron ore required for a strong iron and steel industry. (This applied to all but Belgium, Austria, Russia and Spain; Sweden made high quality steel from its own iron ore plus charcoal.) Most were also short of the ordinary coal required for steam power (though the Netherlands and Denmark could easily import it from Britain).
2 They were at too low a level of technology generally to join in industrial competition on equal terms (this applied to Eastern and Southern Europe generally).

Table 9.4 Growth rates of US gross domestic product, % per annum, 1873–1912

Juglar period		Long period	
1873–84	4.0	1873–92	4.6
1884–92	5.3	1892–1906	4.1
1892–99	3.1		
1899–1906	5.1	1884–99	4.2
1906–12	2.2	1899–1912	3.8

Source: Solomou, 1987, Table 3.24

During the 1880s most of these countries began to tackle their problems in one or both of two ways:

(a) by tariff protection – which made a great deal more sense for countries like Austria-Hungary and Russia than for its American and German pioneers, giving 'infant' heavy industries the necessary security;

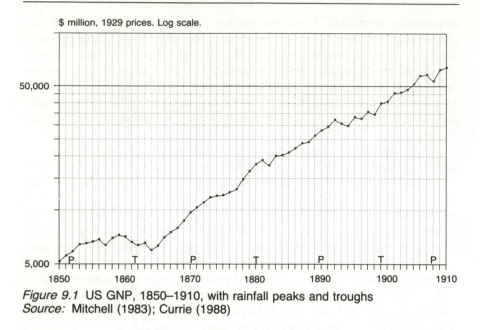

$ million, 1929 prices. Log scale.

Figure 9.1 US GNP, 1850–1910, with rainfall peaks and troughs
Source: Mitchell (1983); Currie (1988)

(b) by the development of new science-based technologies which were not inhibited by their shortages of raw materials.

As Rondo Cameron (1985) shows, the Netherlands, Switzerland, Denmark and Norway developed sophisticated metal-*working* industries using imported iron and steel, mostly from Britain and Germany.[29] France and Italy, having saddled themselves with expensive steel through protection, also developed strong engineering industries; so did Sweden. The key resource these industries depended on in international competition was simply *know-how*. Likewise, most of the coal-poor countries were rich in water-power. Having to use that instead of steam was a disadvantage, but from about 1880 a declining one, as hydro-electricity spread; and countries with cheap hydro-electricity could use it for other purposes besides powering machinery, as the French showed in building up their aluminium industry. Germany, of course, was at the forefront of technological progress in many of the new industries, notably organic chemicals and electrical engineering, and so shared fully in the prosperity after 1890 (see Tables 9.5 and 9.6).

There is something missing from this account of the diffusion of a new style based on steel, electricity and science – a process of crisis-and-reform to ease its progress. If the early diffusion of the water style set off the French Revolution, and that of the steam transport style led to major institutional changes in the late 1840s, where is the corresponding crisis in the history of the steel-and-electricity style? There is none, except perhaps for the 1905

Table 9.5 Growth rates of German net domestic product, 1857–1913, % per annum

Juglar period		Long period	
1857–64	2.6	1857–74	2.5
1864–74	2.3	1874–84	1.3
1874–84	1.3	1884–1900	3.2
1884–1890	2.8	1900–13	2.9
1890–1900	3.4	1884–1913	3.1
1900–07	2.7		
1907–13	3.2		

Source: Solomou, 1987, Table 3.11

Revolution in Russia (rather late, as diffusion there was late). The reason may already be clear: the crises of 1864–71 in Europe, and 1861–5 in the USA, had brought about sufficient institutional change to ensure that later social tremors did not become earthquakes. That is not to say that there were no periods of severe strain. In Germany the unnatural maintenance of Junker rule made a degree of strain inevitable, and the bleak economic situation from the late 1870s to the mid-1880s brought it to a peak. Bismarck's main answer to any threat was to distract the German people with enemies: having fought all the wars he could reasonably pick, his bogeys now had to be internal (though if possible connected to external

Table 9.6 Economic growth rates of 'old' and 'new' industrialisers, 1870s–1913

	TOTAL OUTPUT		Gross domestic product	
	1870s–1890s[a]	1890s–1913[a]	1890s	
'Old'				
Britain	1.9	1.8	2.4	(1889–99)
USA	4.2	4.0	3.1	(1892–99)
Belgium	2.0	1.9	1.9	(1989–1900)
'New'				
Austria[b]	2.3	2.5	2.6	(1891–1900)
Denmark	2.8	3.5	3.0	(1890–1901)
France	0.8	1.8	2.0	(1892–99)
Germany	2.3	3.2	3.4	(1890–1900)
Italy	0.7	2.2	1.7	(1890–1901)
Netherlands	1.4	2.3	–	
Norway	1.4	2.5	2.0	(1890–1901)
Sweden	1.8	3.3	3.0	(1891–1900)

Source: For 'total output' van Duijn, 1983, Table 9.8; for GDP own calculations from Solomou, 1987 and Maddison, 1982
Notes: a: '1870s' date is 1873 except for Belgium, France and Germany (1872) and 1874 (Austria, Denmark, Norway and Sweden). '1890s' date is 1890 except for USA (1895), and Austria, Denmark, Norway and Sweden (1891).
  b: GDP throughout.

threats). The Marxist Social Democratic Party was declared a threat, and (with its newspapers) made illegal in 1878. As the recession continued, Bismarck took advantage of the development of anti-Semitism, and fostered it himself, for his own electoral purposes, before the Reichstag elections of 1884.[30] A climate of militaristic nationalism was also encouraged.[31] Yet, at the same time, he made some strikingly progressive moves: between 1883 and 1889 he set up compulsory insurance for workers against sickness, accident, incapacity and old age – a welfare state *avant la lettre* but for the fact that it was financed almost entirely by the workers and their employers rather than by the State.[32]

It is normal for a serious crisis to elicit both regressive and progressive responses. Bismarck's peculiar genius was that one politician made both at the same time. Elsewhere, with less dictatorial governments, a more usual sequence was observed: the triumph of conservatism first, the ascendancy of moderate reform later. Thus in Britain Gladstone's Liberals split disastrously in 1886 after their leader had committed them to radical reform, and reforming elements in the United States and France also remained weak and divided until the end of the century; in all three countries the reformers' turn was to come. The Conservatives diverted their peoples with imperial adventures like the scramble for Africa of the European powers in the 1880s or the American war against Spain in 1898. As has been shown for Britain,[33] imperialism was not profitable for the imperial country, but nor was it significantly damaging to the growth of the world economy.

For the time being, social, political and economic institutions were adequate: the diffusion of the new style was not blocked, nor did it lead to internal upheaval or major war. Thus was a Great Depression averted.

Chapter 10

A historical account, 1896–1945

UPSWING AND CRISIS, 1896–1921

We too had many pretty toys when young:
A law indifferent to blame or praise,
To bribe or threat; habits that made old wrong
Melt down, as it were wax in the sun's rays;
Public opinion ripening for so long
We thought it would outlive all future days.
O what fine thought we had because we thought
That the worst rogues and rascals had died out.
All teeth were drawn, all ancient tricks unlearned,
And a great army but a showy thing;
What matter that no cannon had been turned
Into a ploughshare? Parliament and king
Thought that unless a little powder burned
The trumpeters might burst with trumpeting
And yet it lack all glory; and perchance
The guardsmen's drowsy chargers would not prance.

W. B. Yeats, *Nineteen Hundred and Nineteen*

Are not Yeats's words a fitting elegy for the last upswing before a global war? And it is clear that the period to which his nostalgia refers is, near enough, that between 1896 and 1914. He is not the only one, of course, to speak favourably of that time; it is known in French history and reminiscence as *l'Âge d'Or*, the Golden Age. Peaceful it clearly was (bar a little imperial slaughter), but was it prosperous enough also to be clearly identifiable as a long wave upswing? It would be unfair to measure from 1896, for that is a trough of a short, Juglar cycle; but even if we go from the Juglar peak of 1892 to the peak of 1913, we can see, from Table 10.1, that there does seem to have been an upswing, by comparison with 1872–92: the growth of world industrial production quickened from 2.95 per cent to 4.1 per cent. These average figures conceal some large variations among countries: France follows the long wave impeccably – *L'Âge d'Or* was not

$ million, 1958 prices. Log scale.

Figure 10.1 US GNP 1890–1950, with rainfall peaks and troughs
Source: Mitchell (1983); Currie (1988)

called that for nothing (Table 10.2) – but the British economy moved in the wrong direction, its growth slowing in the last two decades before the First World War to a baffling crawl (Tables 9.3 and 10.5). The general pattern, so far as there is one, resembles neither of these cases. Agricultural production continued to grow at much the same rate as it had since mid-century, not slackening in the great depression and not quickening now. Industrial production grew rather quickly in a number of countries in 1892–1913; but in most of those the acceleration had come quite early in the 'great depression'. US growth actually slowed down somewhat, comparing 1873–92 with 1892–1906 – and if the latter period is extended to 1912 the slowdown is quite marked (Figure 10.1, Table 10.3). The fact that world industrial production grew more quickly after 1892 can be treated partly as a trick of the averaging process: in the later period the fast-growing countries, *through* their fast growth, had relatively large economies compared to the earlier period, and so have to be given a heavier weighting when working out the world average growth rate.[1]

I think nonetheless we should treat the long wave upswing after 1896, or 1892, as something more than a statistical artefact: for within a world economy, fast growth in one economy, or group of economies, may have some tendency to depress growth elsewhere; and the larger the fast growers become, the stronger this tendency. There are two ways in which this may have happened in the period after 1892. First, the faster the growth in one

Table 10.1 Growth rates of world industrial production, 1892–1951 (% per annum)

Short period (peak-to-peak)		Long period	
1892–99	4.6	(1872–92	3.0)
1899–1907	4.0	1892–1913	4.1
1907–13	3.7		
1913–24	0.8	1913–37	2.1
1924–29	5.8	1924–37	3.2
1929–37	1.5		
1937–51	3.0	1929–51	2.5

Source: Solomou, 1987, Tables 3.33 and 3.36

Table 10.2 Growth of French gross domestic product, 1892–1950 (% per annum)

Short period (peak-to-peak)		Long period	
1892–99	2.0	(1875–92	0.7)
1899–1904	1.3		
1904–12	2.2	1892–1912	1.9
1912–24	0.7		
1924–29	3.0	1912–37	0.8
1929–37	−0.5	1924–37	0.9
1937–50	1.4	1929–50	0.7

Source Solomou, 1987, Tables 3.18 and 3.23

Table 10.3 Growth of US gross domestic product, 1892–1951 (% per annum)

Short period (peak-to-peak)		Long period	
1892–99	3.1	(1873–92	4.6)
1899–1906	5.1	1892–1906	4.1
1906–12	2.2	1892–1912	3.5
1912–18	3.0		
1918–23	3.1	1912–37	2.1
1923–29	3.3		
1929–37	−0.2		
1937–51	4.4	1929–51	2.7

Source: Solomou, 1987, Tables 3.24 and 3.30

country the greater the shortage of *money* world wide, and thus the higher the level of interest rates; and indeed interest rates did rise, although not very much – for reasons to be explained in a moment. Second, most of the fast-growing countries of the time benefited from tariff protection of their industries, and from the higher prices for their primary products, due to industry's growth outpacing agriculture's, world wide. Their gain was to some extent the loss of the already-industrialised countries, above all Britain, whose real wages were held down by those high prices, and whose exporting industries tended to emigrate, to some extent, to get inside the tariff walls. So it remains impressive that – in spite of this tendency to a zero-sum game – the world economy did, overall, grow faster in this period.

The explanation of this upswing falls naturally into two parts. First, we ought to explain the performance of those countries whose overall growth did actually accelerate after 1892. To do this we have merely to continue the argument of the last chapter. Most of the faster growers were, in today's phrase, Newly Industrialising Countries (NICs) – Canada and Australia, plus most of Northern, Eastern and Southern Europe – which by this time had managed to establish reasonably competitive manufacturing industries, with the help, as we have seen, of the industrial use of science, as well as the mobility of financial and human capital. Their nascent industry had expanded fast in the 1872–92 period; now that it was more firmly established it was not difficult to keep up the pace, and the larger industry's share, the more it contributed to economic growth overall. France, no NIC, spurted only in the 1890s – which is easily explained in terms of her agricultural problems, and her difficulties with energy sources until hydro-electricity was available. Germany's growth was fairly smooth from 1884, after the very poor performance in the crisis decade just before (Tables 9.5 and 10.4).

We have next to explain why the acceleration did not call forth negative feedback effects such as those which slowed world growth after 1856. It will be recalled that there were three of these, in the earlier period: a decline in migration, a decline in the growth of the (real) money supply, and war. Let us take them in turn: migration first. In the NICs of Southern and Eastern

Table 10.4 Growth of German gross domestic product, 1884–1952 (% per annum)

Short period (peak-to-peak)		Long period	
1884–1890	2.8	(1874–84	1.3)
1890–1900	3.4	1884–1900	3.2
1900–07	2.7		
1907–13	3.2	1884–1913	3.1
1913–25	0.3	1913–28	0.4
1925–28	5.5	1913–38	2.1
1928–38	3.3	1925–38	3.8
1938–52	1.0	1928–52	2.0

Source: Solomou, 1987, Tables 3.11 and 3.16
(Note: the figures until 1913 are for net domestic product.)

Table 10.5 Growth of British gross domestic product, 1889–1951 (% per annum)

Short period (peak-to-peak)		Long period	
1889–99	2.4		
1899–1907	1.0		
1907–13	1.2	1899–1913	1.1
1913–25	0.3		
1925–29	2.0	1913–37	1.1
1929–37	2.0	1925–37	2.0
1937–51	1.7	1929–51	1.8

Source: Solomou, 1987, Tables 3.2 and 3.8

Europe the progress of manufacturing, with the spread of railways, under-mined cottage industries, as it had done in France and Germany some fifty years before, and the people displaced by this process accounted for much of the third great wave of migration across the Atlantic, starting in the late 1890s (see Figures 5.3 and 5.4). This migration gave a powerful impetus, in turn, to the industrial growth of the United States, as the first and second waves had done. Unlike those waves, however, it did not ebb as industrial expansion continued in the migrants' countries of origin. The gap between living standards in the United States, and those in Southern and Eastern Europe, was so great, and the pool of potential migrants so large, that once the first migrants from an area had established a 'bridgehead', there was no shortage of friends and relations eager to follow them. Immigration thus remained above trend from 1902 onwards, and the second largest number of immigrants ever recorded arrived in the USA in 1913.[2] Taken together, the two Juglar cycles from 1899 to 1912 thus showed nearly as fast growth in the USA as the two from 1884 to 1899 which had benefited from slow growth in Western Europe (Table 10.3).

Another source of fast negative feedback in the 1850s had come from the stagnation of gold output after 1852. The same might have been expected this time. As we have seen, there had been, in some sense, a shortage of gold in the 1870s, which was effectively over by the mid-1890s, as gold output responded to the rise in its real price in the 1870s recession, and the rise in its real price made a given quantity of gold go further. The upswing did not reverse the process which the 1870s recession had set off: prices rose, but only slowly, and gold output went on rising. As I argued in Chapter 4, the main difference between periods was that the earlier gold rush areas depended on a limited Northern labour force which dwindled as prosperity increased, the later ones on effectively unlimited Southern labour whose price could be depressed as required. The rate of interest, which had touched bottom in the mid-1890s, rose only very slightly in the following decade and a half (see Figure 4.7); the rising trend of prices made interest rates in real terms very low indeed.

The last negative feedback which was largely absent from the 1892–1913 period was war and revolution; the Boer War around 1900 and the Russian Revolution of 1905, following the war with Japan, did little economic damage. As we saw in the last chapter, the relative political stability of the early part of the period can be explained by the 'crises of the upswing' of 1861–71 and their outcome. By the end, there was not stability, but the lull before the storm.

The diffusion of the steel and electricity style

If an upswing is a time of fast diffusion of a newly-established style, we would expect the 1896–1913 period to have seen a great expansion in output

Table 10.6 Growth of output of 'old' and 'new' products in the major economies, c. 1878–1913

		USA	UK	Germany	France	Russia
Rate of growth % **per annum, 1878–96:**						
Steel		11.6	8.3	13.7	9.5	26.3
Sulphuric acid		—	0.6[1]	10.5	5.3[2]	5.8[3]
Level of Production:						
Steel	1896	5,366	4,198	4,697	1,181	1,022
(000 tonnes)	1913	31,803	7,787	17,609	4,687	4,918
Sulphuric acid	1896	1,068[4]	770[5]	553	625[6]	60[7]
(000 tonnes)	1913	2,809[8]	1,082	1,727	900	292
Electricity	1902	59.7	0.5	1.4	0.4	—
(giga watt hrs)	1913	247.5[9]	2.5	8.0	1.8	2.0
Motor vehicles	1896	4.1[6,10]	6.10	4.3[11]	14[12]	—
(thousands)	1913	485	—	17.9[9]	45	—
Rate of growth, % **per annum, 1896–1913**						
Steel		11.0	3.7	8.1	8.4	9.7
Sulphuric acid		6.7[13]	0.5[14]	6.9	2.8	10.4[15]
Electricity		15.3[16]	15.8[17]	17.2[17]	14.6[17]	—
Motor vehicles		43.5[14]	—	33.0[18]	27.1[14]	—

Source: Mitchell, 1978, 1983

Notes:
1. 1880–1900	10. Private cars only
2. 1878–1900	11. 1907
3. 1880–97	12. 1905
4. 1899	13. 1899–1914
5. 1895	14. 1900–13
6. 1900	15. 1897–1913
7. 1897	16. 1902–12
8. 1914	17. 1902–13
9. 1912	18. 1907–12

of the products associated with that style. Table 10.6 shows the rate of growth of output, in five major countries, of four such products: two relatively 'old' products, steel and sulphuric acid, and two decidedly new, electricity and motor vehicles. Growth rates were indeed high for all over the period, except for the British output of sulphuric acid – an indicator of the poor performance of its chemicals industry, and more generally of its science-based sectors. But where the figures are available, the same table shows that the rates of growth for the previous, 'depression' period, were for the most part even higher. This tends to support the view that the steel-and-electricity style did not meet any serious institutional obstacles to its early diffusion which required some kind of crisis to overcome them. On the other hand, in absolute terms all four products were starting, in the 1870s and 1880s, from such a low base that they could make at first only a modest contribution to economic growth: it was indeed their very fast growth in the 1878–96 period that put them in a position to contribute to the acceleration of the 1890s.

The fruits of the upswing: crisis and new style

While one style was diffusing fast, the next, as usual, was crystallising. Chapter 2 showed how the Fordist style developed in the United States. It was inevitable that the United States was the pioneer of the new style. By 1900 its income per head was considerably higher than that of the richest European state – Britain – and its wage level much higher. After so much immigration, its population was also much larger than any European state's except Russia's. It was thus uniquely well placed on the demand side: it had a far larger market than any other country for the new consumer durable industries – motor vehicles and 'white goods' – which were to be the main 'carrier branch' for the new style (see Table 10.6).

The American advantage was almost as great on the supply side. In its level of general education it was clearly superior to its main European rivals, although Germany had the edge in higher education in certain scientific fields.[3] Its large firms had by now reorganised themselves, taking advantage of the railway and the telephone, to operate on a continental scale; and with that educated manpower, plus immigrant Europeans, they had been responsible for a rapidly increasing share of the world's inventions and innovations – leaving even Germany far behind (see Table 10.7). As important as their strength in innovation was the direction of it: product innovation was directed almost exclusively – in a lightly-armed country with a large, prosperous and homogeneous middle class – to the satisfaction of the wants of the private consumer; and process innovation was used to save expensive labour by the lavish use of its abundant oil and coal and the electricity produced from them. That abundance was of course also useful on the consumer side. Not so much for 'white goods': refrigerators' and washing machines' consumption of electricity was modest. It was the electricity distribution network, to the home and inside it, which used huge amounts of labour and materials; it was an investment which a rich country like the United States was in a position to make before any others. The refined petroleum required by motor vehicles, on the other hand, was easy to distribute, but the quantities involved were very large: the huge quantities of oil cheaply available from underneath the United States, were most important here.

In terms of size and technical capacity, the United States's only real rival should have been Germany. Britain, clearly, was no longer in contention, having performed on almost every yardstick very badly since 1870. A number of other countries which had performed very well – like Switzerland and Sweden – were simply too small to do more than contribute a few

Table 10.7 Numbers of 'major' innovations by country and decade, 1810–1970

	UK	USA	France	Germany	Belgium	Netherlands	Scandinavia	Other
1810–19	2			2				
1820–29	2		1					
1830–39	4	1	1					
1840–49		3	1	1				
1850–59	1	3	1	1				1 (Sw.)
1860–69		1	1	2	1			1 (Sw.)
1870–79		4		3		1	1 (Dk)	
1880–89	5	9		3				
1890–99	1	3	2	2				
1900–09	1	5	1					
1910–19	1	6	2	1				
1920–29	1	5		1				1(Ca.)
1930–39	3	9		9				1(Sw.)
1940–49	2	12		2				1(Ar.)
1950–59	3	12	1	1				1(Au.)
1960–69	1	6		2		1		1(Ru.)

Source: Calculated from van Duijn, 1983, Table 10.1
Note: In 'Other' column Ca. = Canada, Sw. = Switzerland, Ar. = Argentina, Au. = Austria and Ru. = USSR.

innovations each; even France did little more, its fast growth during the Golden Age coming too late to make up for the loss of Alsace-Lorraine in 1870 and its near-stagnation in the 1860–90 period. Only Germany, among the European countries, had the combination of size and technological dynamism needed to make a really important contribution to a new style; and indeed, German innovations in the electrical and (above all) chemical field were important, as it turned out. But not only did the new style not crystallise in Germany, Germany lagged behind a number of its European rivals in the development of some of the crucial engineering industries. The reasons for this are worth exploring because they turn out to be closely connected to the country's exceptional lack of political integration.

Let us take up the story in 1879. Bismarck's successful aggression had in effect forged a military-industrial complex *avant la lettre* which dominated German politics. Both parts of this coalition – the officer-landowner Junkers and the heavy industrialists like Krupp and Thyssen – felt threatened by the recession of the 1870s and the increasing competition from foreign steel and grain which accompanied it; accordingly, they protected themselves with tariffs on these products, which were not only maintained, but increased, after 1879.[4] The protection of industry and agriculture was not general. In agriculture, it was on grain, particularly rye, produced mainly by the East Elbian Junkers – in 1900 approximately 24,000 people out of a total population of 56 million;[5] the potato growers got nothing out of the grain tariffs and the stock rearers lost by them, through higher feed prices. In industry, the protection was mainly on the products of heavy industry, particularly steel. This was a disadvantage to the downstream industries, particularly once after 1900 Germany produced ever-increasing surpluses of steel: the surplus had to be 'dumped' on foreign markets at low prices and the only way to maintain the producers' profits was a high domestic price level defended by tariffs and cartels. Trebilcock mentions a price differential between home and foreign prices of German sheet iron of 40 per cent – 100 marks a ton abroad, 140 at home;[6] it is not hard to connect this with the extraordinary failure of Germany in automobile production – which it had pioneered – in competition with France: by 1913 France, with about half the population, produced *two and a half times* as many motor vehicles as Germany! (Table 10.6). Foreign competitors in the wire-working industries (Holland and Belgium) and shipbuilding (Britain) were similarly favoured.[7]

The effect of protection, combined with cartels, was to distort the distribution of income as well as the pattern of industrial growth: real wages rose at only 1 per cent per annum between 1890 and 1914 while national income was rising much faster,[8] and Kuznets found that in Germany, alone of the European countries for which he had data, inequality of income was increasing during this period.[9] Nor did the State do much to mitigate this situation by its other tax and expenditure policies: income tax rates on the rich, according to Wehler, were 'lamentably low', and even those the Junkers evaded, with official connivance.[10] Seventy-five per cent of tax revenue was spent on the military budget, in 1913 as in 1875,[11] largely of course on the output of heavy industry – the development of the navy after 1898 was seen as an ideal outlet for surplus steel and a compensation for the shipbuilding industry's handicap of high input prices.[12] These were not policies calculated to encourage a market for consumer goods, or to encourage German scientists and engineers to turn their talents in that direction. Indeed, much of the thrust of invention and innovation in Germany, from the mid-nineteenth century to the mid-twentieth, was diverted away from the increase of labour productivity through machine power, and the development of new products to satisfy new wants, into a drive for self-sufficiency or at least reduced dependence on actual or potential enemies. The synthetic dyestuffs, after 1870, freed her from dependence on British-controlled indigo; synthetic ammonia, after 1910, reduced the need for British-controlled nitrates. There was a similar diversion of effort away from civil purposes in general, to the needs of the military-industrial complex.

If the distortion of prices and incomes in Germany inhibited the economy, nonetheless growth was respectable, and even real wages did increase steadily. There was in no sense an economic crisis in the years before 1914.[13] What did develop there, and was of crucial importance to our argument, was a political and social crisis: a typical crisis of the upswing. On the one hand, there were the Junkers and the heavy industrialists, the old alliance of iron and rye, still holding State power, and depending more and more on it for their *economic* position; on the other hand, there were all their opponents – the Radical Liberals, associated with light industry and the Protestant middle class, the Centre, representing Catholic peasant farmers and artisans from South Germany, and – last and most feared – the Social Democrats, representing the industrial workers. Every year their opponents' preponderance in numbers increased, and although the alliance of iron and rye was safe in the Prussian Diet, entrenched behind the three-class franchise, there was 'one man one vote' in the Reichstag; and besides, 1848 had shown it was unsafe to become *too* unpopular.

How could the Junkers and their new allies in heavy industry keep their privileges, and a measure of control? As we saw in Chapter 9, Bismarck, in his last years, in the 1880s, found a method which provided a pattern for his successors: to conjure up all manner of internal and external enemies – Catholics and Jews, Russians and French – link them in the public mind, and whip up alarm about the imaginary threat to a high pitch every seven years, as the time for the Army Law (for military funds) came round; in between times, steadily to inculcate a spirit of militarism as deeply and widely into German society as possible.

At the beginning, the game was kept within bounds and under control – the Junkers after all did not want a war, least of all the sort of war they eventually got, with a mass army in which they were swamped by commoner officers, and in alliance with the Catholic Hapsburgs of Austria whom they had thrashed in 1866. But after 1900, as the electoral strength of their opponents mounted inexorably, things got more and more out of hand. The various chauvinist and anti-socialist associations and pressure groups were more and more taken over by commoners who lacked the Junkers' sense of the limited aims of the exercise.[14] The Navy League's success in launching the battleship building programme (appreciated as it was by Krupps[15]) helped to make an enemy of Britain – indeed Britain had to be identified as a potential enemy to begin with, for the programme to have any sense. Worst of all, because it was necessary to get Centre votes in the Reichstag, the Centre's nationalism had to be appealed to; and the only sort of nationalism the South German Catholic could accept was Pan- (or Greater) German, including his Austrian neighbours and co-religionists. That meant binding the Reich hand and foot to the tottering Austro-Hungarian Empire, with its rebellious Slav subjects; it meant also making an enemy of the Tsar – who for similar reasons of insecurity was laying more and more stress on his mission as Saviour of the Slavs.

The last straw was the Social Democrats' unprecedented success in the elections of 1912, when they won more than a third of the votes. With their left-liberal allies they were now just forty-seven seats short of a majority in the Reichstag.[16] It had become necessary to bring together every possible opponent of the social democrats, and indeed to appeal even to social democrat voters. The Junkers, swallowing their pride, accepted the 'petty bourgeoisie' into 'the magic circle of conservative politics'; one consequence being 'the growing importance of the Pan-Germans in the counsels of the right'.[17]

War began to seem a less risky option than peace with an ever-increasing social-democratic vote; and short of war, the least that was required was war fever. Russia was the most attractive enemy, because it was the only one that the working class could really take seriously – with the blood of the St. Petersburg Soviet of 1905 still fresh on the Tsar's hands. But its disadvantage as a potential enemy was that merely preparing for war against it made no sense – since it was growing rapidly stronger, demographically and industrially, if it was to be fought, it had to be fought soon.[18]

The prospect, for the Junkers in office, was appalling: to pick a fight with one old friend, Russia, which would bring in France; since according to the Schlieffen Plan they had to attack France through Belgium, that would mean war with another old friend, Britain. Some certainly wanted war; the Duke of Ratibor for example, in spring 1914, argued that 'the commercial and bourgeois classes' were 'about to gain the upper hand at the expense of the military and land-owning classes. In view of this, a war was called for to restore order to existing relationships'.[19] Others, like the Chancellor, Bethmann Hollweg, certainly did not; but they could find no coherent alternative policy. When the Hapsburgs finally picked the fight for them, the General Staff said 'Go on', and the Chancellor said, 'Hold back'. 'What a joke – who does rule in Berlin, then?' cried the Austrian Foreign Minister in frustration.[20] The answer was, no one both able and willing to stop the drift to war.

The effects of political 'disintegration' in Germany continued throughout the war. Germany was not forced to fight the war to a finish: in 1916, through neutral intermediaries, the Allies let it be known that they would settle for a draw, for a peace on the basis of the status quo ante 1914. But that would have merely thrown Germany back into the crisis of peace, only worse than before; and besides, the ruling groups had by this time formalised their plans for a means to end that crisis for the time being, through annexations in both East and West. When you are playing for double or quits, a draw is no use. The following year, with Russia's revolution and the collapse of its army (after the defeats of Serbia, Romania and Italy), the gamble seemed about to come off. The German Army, victorious in the east, could now throw its whole weight against the western Allies and overrun France before the Americans had time to intervene *en masse*. What followed is well known: the German offensive of spring 1918 failed by a whisker to make the breakthrough which would have opened the road to Paris. What is less well known is a crucial reason for that failure. One million German soldiers were at that moment engaged elsewhere, in the occupation of the Ukraine.[21] Why? There was no military danger in the East, nor any *immediate* economic gains to be had there. But the monster of aggressive chauvinism had been created to divert internal tensions, and had become year by year stronger and more unruly: it had to be fed.[22] The annexation programme could not wait. The result, of course, was defeat.

We can conclude, therefore, that Germany's very low degree of political integration did much to cause, and to prolong, the First World War. It would be easy to show also that the similar or worse position of the Hapsburg Empire led its government, once German support was assured, into the aggression against Serbia which was the immediate *casus belli*.[23] Again, war might have been avoided, outside the Balkans, had Russia prudently left the Serbs to their fate; she did not because the lack of political integration in Russia had forced the Tsar into Pan-Slavism just as the Hohenzollerns had been driven to Pan-Germanism. As Arno Mayer, in *The Persistence of the Old Regime*, puts it, the War was intended as a 'pre-emptive counter-revolution' by the landed aristocrats.[24] To generalise this verdict, we can call the First World War the international expression of a crisis of the upswing of the most extreme kind. But there is another theoretical framework in which we can fit it. As we saw in Chapter 1, the theory of *long cycles* treats *global wars* as a regular phenomenon in which a hegemonic or world power is challenged by a 'continental' rival before (usually) being replaced in its position not by the challenger but by one of its 'maritime' allies. From that point of view, then, it is not the upswing nor the particular development of German society that we have to blame for the war, but the decline of Britain as a hegemonic power, and the rise of Germany, which gave the latter its chance to make a challenge. Blame too the United States' delay in taking on the political role which corresponded to its new economic power.

In fact I think both perspectives are fruitful. Long cycles help us to understand that there could have been no *global war* between 1815 and (say) 1890, because the world power, Britain, was too strong – thus Bismarck recognised that the victory of 1870–1 had taken German expansion about as far as was safe, and that any attempt to resolve the fresh domestic difficulties of the early 1880s by further aggression might doom Germany to Napoleon's fate. Equally, after 1890 the opportunity for the continental challenger began to open. What the broad brush of long cycle theory cannot explain, however, is the timing of the outbreak of global war within the long wave – the previous one had after all broken out in 1793, about a decade after the crystallisation of a new technological style, not more than thirty years after, as in 1914. It has, moreover, to treat the First and Second World Wars as different phases of one global war – the interval between phases being thus far longer than any in previous global wars. Finally, it does not really explain why the interval, the peace after the First World War, had a growth rate so much lower than the peace after the Second. That, however, is precisely what I propose to do.

The effects of the First World War

I have argued that a crisis of the upswing does little if anything to resolve the tensions, arising from 'disintegration', which produce it, although it tends to change their form. By not leading to thoroughgoing reform it fails to reduce – it may even increase – inequality among and within nations. How far is this true for the First World War? In our answer, we must take care to allow for the effects of the Fordist style, which crystallized at about the time of the war.

It seems appropriate to look first at Germany. When the war was lost, the Hohenzollern Reich fell, Kaiser Wilhelm retreated to Holland, and the Junkers' *bête noire*, the Social Democrats, took over power for a time. But there was no revolution worth the name, nor even radical reform. Capitalism was safe with the Social Democrats – industry remained in its owners' hands, and there was not even a land reform to dislodge the Junkers from their Eastern estates; even more extraordinary, the Junkers kept their grip on the senior positions in the Prussian Civil Service. Attempted revolution from the left was crushed, and as Wehler shows, the Social Democrats, who might have been expected to carry through reforms, and had the chance to do so in November 1918, drew back, because the opportunity had come too suddenly.[25] They had become accustomed to working within a system in which incremental reforms were all they could hope for – not revolution, nor even a burst of radical reform. Moreover the elites who would have suffered in such reforms were not in the least persuaded of the need for them. What else could have been expected at such a stage in the long wave? There was as yet no challenge to old attitudes and institutions such as is posed by the diffusion of a new technological style, nor the grim stimulus to reflection given by a depression. The opportunities missed in Germany were missed everywhere else in the 'core'; only Russia, semi-peripheral and totally defeated, made a new start after the First World War – and that, it can be argued, a false one.

During and just after the war, some elements of internal inequality did diminish. Shortages of labour and rising prices favoured the spread of unionisation, even, to some extent, in countries not directly involved, and that helped to reduce wage differentials, particularly between skilled and unskilled workers. Rising prices also sharply reduced rentiers' real incomes. On the other hand, the share of profits was very high during (if not just after) the war, and little was done (unlike, as we shall see, the Second World War) to restrain or tax this increase.[26]

But such gains as the poor made – and this is characteristic of a crisis of the upswing – were not maintained, because they had not been based on a permanent shift in the balance of power. In all the major countries of the core, once the smoke of battle had cleared, the political scene was dominated by the right. In the British House of Commons an acute observer noted that the Tory benches were full of 'hard-faced men who looked as though they had done well out of the war'.[27] These gentlemen and their counterparts in France and the USA were determined to do as well out of the peace: as legislators, they quickly abandoned the programme which had been devised to placate returning soldiers and militant workers at the end of the war; as employers they set out, generally with success, to break the newly-acquired power of the unions. Unionisation fell again, and differentials gradually widened. Falling prices ensured that the war-time profits invested in government securities would increase in value; high interest rates likewise helped to give a good income from them; and a tight fiscal policy produced budget surpluses enough to cover interest and repayments. Britain was rather exceptional in that unionisation, and the relative wages of the unskilled fell back less during the 1920s than they had advanced after 1914. In the USA and France the *status quo ante* 1914 was achieved, in these respects, before 1929.[28] (As we shall see, this owed at least as much to the new style as to any effects of the war.)

Further east, there were instances of radical reform: Russia of course, and also, to a lesser extent, Poland, where peasants gained through land reform. But all reforms among the defeated nations, that is, all of Central and Eastern Europe, were, for at least a decade, overshadowed by the terrible legacy of the war: visibly, destruction, and loss of young men's lives; less visibly, war debts and trade dislocation due to the breakup of the old empires. These were countries which had been, in 1914, ripe for the balanced diffusion of the established, steel/electricity style. They were now set back, in what amounted to a sharp aggravation of international inequality. What progress they now made, indeed their recovery even, was much more dependent than it would otherwise have been on imports of high technology goods from the West. To purchase those, they had either to accumulate debt, or to export what low-technology goods they could find a market for. Either option made for increased international inequality and instability.[29]

Outside Europe, in the countries untouched by the war, its interruption of existing patterns of trade brought some benefits, through a forced burst of industrialisation;[30] but at the end of the war, in 1919–20, a brief period of very favourable primary product prices encouraged a burst of over-expansion of agricultural acreage. In the following decades this may have done as much harm as the industrialisation did good.[31]

The simplest way of describing the changes in international inequality brought about by the war is to say that the United States gained a great deal relative to the rest of the world. It gained in two ways, creating a double imbalance. Setting its holdings of assets abroad (including foreign government securities) against others' holdings of assets in the USA, it began the war as a substantial net debtor, and ended it as a huge net creditor; the change was due partly to the selling-off of British assets in the USA, as well as to the lending of huge sums of money to Allied governments. But the relative advance of the United States was even greater in productive capacity: its own increased hugely, while that of most of its European rivals either stagnated, or declined – through the suspension of investment, the destruction of physical wealth, and the slaughter of a generation of the newly trained and educated. There was during the 1920s perhaps a slight diminution of the second imbalance, in production, through the reconstruction of the devastated areas of Central and Eastern Europe and investment in new industry there; but this was only made possible by the widening of the first imbalance, in finance – there was no Marshall Aid after the First World War.

The effects of the Fordist style

If the strictly technical aspects of the new 'Fordist' style were all in place by 1915, the same could not be said for the organisational side. The firms which used the new technology needed large plants, of course, organised on Taylorised lines. They also needed a considerable number of them, producing different products, if they were to spread their risks and make the most of economies of scale in marketing, and research and development (both of increasing importance). True, Henry Ford himself scorned risk-spreading and product differentiation – 'you can have any colour so long as it's black' – but he as the technological pioneer could afford to, at first; later his firm paid for that arrogance. Aptly, it was Ford's great rival, Alfred P. Sloan of General Motors, who along with the management of Du Pont (GM's largest shareholder) found an adequate answer to the problems of controlling such large and differentiated firms – what Oliver Williamson (1970) has named the M-form corporation. In the M-form, the day-to-day management is decentralised to divisional level, and each divisional boss is assessed mainly by the financial information on his performance which he passes up to Head Office.[32]

Only with Sloan's work, in the early 1920s, was the Fordist style complete, and ready for export, either by foreign imitation or by the multinational expansion of US manufacturers. (Such expansion had been begun long before by Westinghouse and Singer, but was made much easier by the advent of the M-form.) At first, then, the main effects of the new style, even outside the United States, were felt through its diffusion *inside* the US. The sharp increase in inequality in the United States up to 1929 must have been due in part to the increase in market power gained by big firms organised in the new manner – whose workers had still to make their own organisational responses to the new style.[33] The increase in international inequality, which as we have seen was largely a matter of the gap between the USA and the rest, was naturally accentuated by the US lead with the new style. In fact it was in some ways accentuated by the beginnings of diffusion abroad. Just as Ford had not waited for Sloan, neither did some foreign imitators of his technology wait now; the quickest imitation was, naturally enough, by the French automobile industry, which as we have seen was the largest and most dynamic in Europe. But the French capital goods industry was not by any means strong enough to provide the necessary equipment: so burgeoning French vehicle exports within Europe were at the price of increased dependence on American capital goods.[34]

THE DETERMINANTS OF THE DEPRESSION

The 1920s

Any explanation of the depression after 1929 must begin and end with the United States. By 1929 that country was so large a component of the world economy, and so dominated the rest of it, that most other countries' situations could be defined largely in terms of their relationship with the United States – their debts to it, their trade with it, their use of technology bought or copied from it. Only one element of their relationship with the USA was, in almost every case, of less importance than before: their emigration to it (see Chapter 5). That indeed, like Sherlock Holmes's dog that did *not* bark in the night, had its own importance. The tight controls imposed on immigration to the USA in the early 1920s helped to aggravate unemployment in Europe.[35] What was worse for the world economy, they must soon have led to a reduction in foreign exchange earnings from immigrants' remittances and thus further increased the transatlantic imbalance.[36] Thus it may not be too far off the mark to count the reduction of transatlantic migration, via its effect on remittances, as just one more element in the increase in international inequality. Indeed one might even count it as having much the same cause, the First World War, since it seems to have been the threat perceived from a mass of would-be migrants, eager to leave their war-shattered countries, which tipped the political balance in the USA decisively towards restriction.

Monetary policy in other countries now became, in an entirely new way, bound up with the relationship with the United States. It was not simply that New York replaced London as the financial centre of the world, the main source of credit, but that the pre-1914 gold standard, which had allowed each country a degree of independence in its monetary affairs, was replaced, with the dismantling of wartime exchange controls in the early 1920s, by what amounted to a dollar exchange standard. Each central bank committed itself to defending a certain fixed exchange rate *vis-à-vis* the dollar. This considerably reduced its freedom of action, particularly its freedom to operate an expansionary policy which might lead to a balance of payments deficit.[37] Given that wartime inflation had in effect devalued the stock of gold on which international liquidity was based – a stock most of which had now piled up in Fort Knox – their freedom of action was small indeed. That did not, of course, apply to the United States. The freedom of action of the 'Fed', the Federal Reserve Bank of New York, was complete, so far as foreign pressures were concerned; the constraints on the Fed were domestic. Nonetheless the international role of the United States may have influenced the Fed's policy – the world's greatest creditor must easily incline to the view that high interest rates are a good idea (just as its shift into massive debt in the mid-1980s seemed to nudge the Fed towards the opposite attitude). The New York bankers who powerfully influenced the Fed's policy would traditionally have lent to domestic business borrowers, to whose interests they would not have been indifferent (after all, they and their clients would have owned those borrowers' shares); now much – perhaps most – of their business was with foreign borrowers with whom they would be less inclined to sympathise. Whatever the reason, dollar interest rates were higher in the 1920s than they had been before the war. With falling prices, real interest rates were much higher than before (see Figure 7.6).

High as interest rates were, there was no shortage of borrowers, foreign borrowers at least. The Germans borrowed heavily, to pay the French their reparations and to finance a recovery boom; so did most of Central and Eastern Europe; so did most of Latin America. Those familiar with the Third World's credit spree of the 1970s may be mildly amused to find nothing in that period so daft that it had not been done before in the 1920s – take, for example, the Colombian provincial government which drove a railway tunnel *halfway* through a mountain range while the national government was building a road over the top (neither project having the faintest prospect of generating the foreign exchange to service the loans which paid for it).[38] What is it about the early downswing that leads to massive sums of money being lent to Southern governments which could not on any sober calculation be regarded as 'good risks'? On the borrowers' side (as I have already argued) there are, first, highly unrepresentative governments, second, disappointing foreign exchange earnings which (with wishful thinking) may seem about to rise. Thus an important use of funds in the 1920s was to finance the holding of agricultural stocks in order to keep up prices;[39] this was in the (short-term) interests of the owners of plantations and latifundia who dominated the politics of most Southern states. On the lenders' side, there are large profits without sufficient scope for investment in the North. In the 1920s, as in the 1970s, this reckless borrowing held up Southern (and 'Eastern') purchasing power, and thus demand in the North, when it would otherwise have turned down – but that was only storing up trouble, and deflation, for later.

I referred just now to 'disappointing foreign exchange earnings'. Some writers, like Timoshenko (1933),[40] argued that the depression was largely due to a worsening of primary producers' terms of trade in the 1920s. In terms of the conventional measure, of Net Barter Terms of Trade (NBTT), this seems to be going a little too far: as Solomou shows (1987), by 1929 the NBTT were much as in the 'good years' just before 1914. But we may recall from Chapter 7 that the NBTT are only part of the story. Spraos's Employment-Corrected Double Factorial Terms of Trade (ECDFTT) give a fairer picture of changes in Southern purchasing power, and although we have no ECDFTT figures for the 1920s, we can guess that they would look a good deal worse than the NBTT, just as they do for the 1960s and 1970s.[41] We see here the effects of the twentieth century relationship between North and South, so different, as I argued in Chapter 7, from that between industrialised and primary producing countries in the nineteenth century. The dependence of the South blocks the diffusion – the continuing fast and balanced diffusion – of the established, and the new, technological styles. India and Russia, for example, should not have been exporting wheat in the late 1920s, and thus depressing the price – they should have been eating more of the stuff themselves, and perhaps, producing less; and they would have been doing so, had their industrialisation been moving smoothly and rapidly forward, like that of (say) the USA in the 1880s and 1890s. Within the United States, its own South should have joined in the diffusion of the new style, in production and in consumption, with a new well-paid salariat and industrial working class growing up to join in the continuous extension of the market for the new consumer durables. It would then have been offering smaller quantities of primary products to the rest of the country. Why what 'should' have happened did not happen, in each of these cases, has already been explained, at one point or another, and in each case in terms of internal or international inequalities.

Whether or not we can talk of a deterioration in the primary producers' terms of trade, even before 1929, their balance of payments position was certainly precarious by then, because of their debts. In the second half of the 1920s the Latin American countries were paying out, in interest and repayments of principal, nearly three times their capital inflow; the situation in Central and Eastern Europe was similar.[42] The difficulties of the primary producing *countries* had not yet, by 1929, had a major effect on demand in the industrialised countries – only in Britain was such an effect even measurable.[43] But the primary producers within Northern countries were another matter, particularly in the United States, where they played a major role. Even if the terms of trade of US farmers, defined as NBTT, grew no worse during the 1920s, in terms of ECDFTT they probably did so.[44] Kindleberger (1973) found the crisis of the US financial system beginning with the banks of the Midwest and South even before 1929; and such financial strains must have been matched by a downturn in farm demand for industrial goods. German agriculture was in a worse plight: the price of farm products within Germany increased only 30 per cent between 1913 and 1929, against 57 per cent for manufactures, so even their NBTT deteriorated; with agricultural productivity virtually stagnant during the 1920s the trend of ECDFTT must have been bleak indeed. Since the farm population remained at the 1913 level of 35 per cent of the population until 1933, this must have contributed considerably to low, and unequal, consumer demand even before the Slump.[45] There can be little doubt, overall, that gains by industrial sectors, and industrial countries, at the expense of primary producers, depressed demand: in the short run at least the beneficiaries of lower farm prices tended to increase their savings rather than their consumption, while the losers had to cut consumption.[46] This was of great significance once primary prices tumbled, after 1929.

We come back at last to the heart of the machine, and the heart of the matter: United States industry. With the service and construction sectors closely linked to it, manufacturing industry accounted for the bulk of employment and income in the economy; an economy whose external trade, in turn, while important to its partners, was of relatively little importance to itself. This is not to detract from the external factors already cited as contributing causes to the depression, but rather to suggest that the collapse of US industry at this period must have had internal causes too.

The 'regulationists' sum these causes up by arguing that the new Fordist regime of accumulation had not yet been matched by an appropriate new mode of regulation.[47] I would agree with that, if it can be taken to mean that the new technology, with Taylor's work organisation, Sloan's M-form structure of corporate control, and oligopolies in control of product markets, had tipped the balance in favour of the (large) employers, so that wages increased yearly at a slower rate than productivity, and the share of profits increased. What was lacking was a set of social and political institutions (a mode of regulation) capable of restoring the balance, and levelling up the distribution of income; but the lack caused a deficiency of demand only as the investment boom of the mid-1920s faded.[48]

The Crash and the Slump

> Be careful what you pray for – you might get it
>
> (Old French proverb)

> When the rich grow too rich, and the poor, too poor ... something happens
>
> (Chinese proverb)

Perhaps it will be as well at this point to make it clearer what we are trying to explain: not why there was a downturn, even a sharp downturn, in 1929, for I am not trying to add to the literature on the short business cycle, which is really quite well understood; but why this downturn became a slump which lasted a decade. We should not, therefore, lose interest in a factor simply because it seems to have little bearing on the events of 1929, or even 1930. That said, the wage-and-price setting institutions of US industry can be seen at their most revealing, and damaging, after 1929. It is not so very odd, in a boom, for profits to gain at the expense of the share of wages (though the gain in this case was rather large) nor is it necessarily harmful to further growth, since it makes the more room for investment. But it is very odd, in a recession, for prices to fall by less than wages – not only does it not happen now, it did not happen in the nineteenth century either. It happened in the USA in manufacturing industry in 1929–33, and as a result, profits held up, and dividends actually increased, as investment was being drastically cut.[49] If real wages had increased, as one might have expected (and as took place in Britain and Germany, among other countries) this would have done a great deal to keep up consumption demand, and through that, investment. As it was, with the collapse of the consumption of farmers and the unemployed, consumer demand fell precipitously. Fordism was certainly showing itself as in need of a new mode of regulation.

Some other American institutions failed in a rather more literal way at this time: a large number of banks, particularly in the agricultural areas, went bankrupt. While due in an immediate sense to the Slump, this happened fundamentally because the system of regulation and support had lagged behind the actual role of banks in a sophisticated industrial economy. Given the role the banks play in 'stretching' the monetary base into a much larger money supply, these collapses obstructed the moves which the policy-makers made, as usual, to reduce interest rates and thus stimulate the economy. In fact the loss of confidence and the shortage of banks able to lend, made business borrowing for several years more difficult and expensive than before 1929, even when by the usual yardsticks (yields in US government securities, for example) interest rates had fallen.[50]

The events of 1929–33 in the United States revealed that its institutions were not only incapable of regulating its internal arrangements – they made a thorough mess of its external relationships too. The infamous Smoot-Hawley Act which swept through Congress in 1931 drastically increased tariffs on a wide range of imports – this in a country which was already running a large trade surplus with the rest of the world – and thus turned a disaster for world trade into a catastrophe. It took a long world depression, and worse, to educate the United States in its new responsibilities.

Meanwhile the outlook for the United States' trading partners was extremely bleak – particularly for those who had been borrowing heavily in the 1920s. For while Smoot-Hawley and the fall in primary product prices made it impossible for most Southern and Eastern countries to earn enough foreign exchange to pay for even their minimum import requirements, they were suddenly quite unable to borrow either: first, they were too far in debt already, and second, the American lenders wanted their funds back as soon as possible, to meet their domestic commitments. Every possible means of economising on foreign exchange was forced on them: import and exchange controls, and (for the debtors) default. As the measures taken were general, rather than specifically directed against the main cause of the problem – the United States – they had a domino effect: countries (like Britain for example) which could have coped reasonably well with the cut in their exports to the United States, were faced also with a cut in exports to everywhere else, the 'dumping' in their own markets of foreign goods (like German steel) and defaults of foreign governments on obligations to British lenders. The result was that even Britain resorted to devaluation, and (in spite of its long adherence to Free Trade) to tariff protection of its whole Imperial market.

The protectionism of the 1930s did not involve a complete change of policy for most countries which practised it – not since the 1870s had there been anything remotely approaching general free trade – but it was a radical shift nonetheless, which had far-reaching consequences. In the short run, most of these were negative. Although most of the reduction in economic growth can be explained by the deficiency in demand, some (particularly in the smaller countries) must certainly be put down to the effects of trade restrictions. An economy is likely to be the poorer if its buyers of a foreign-made good have to depend henceforth on an inefficient local supplier – or do without, altogether. It is still somewhat worse off if (like many Balkan and Latin American countries in the late 1930s) it concludes bilateral trading treaties which tie it to one foreign supplier. Even the larger European countries like Britain, Germany and France, which had their own domestic suppliers of most products to begin with, lost the benefits of international competition and the opportunity for firms to specialise – not a small loss, where Fordist technology as already practised in the United States involved great economies of scale.[51]

There was an obvious political effect, also: the more trade is confined within the boundaries of states, and dependent outside them on treaties made by governments, then the more favour will businessmen show to the extension of those boundaries, and the increase of the power of their governments. It is going too far to blame protectionism for the Second World War, but there is some connection to be made; the link with Japanese expansion is particularly plausible.

In the longer term, however, the balance sheet of gains and losses looks very different. Protection was used by many Latin American and Eastern European countries, and Japan, to foster industrialisation, and thus the balanced diffusion of the steel/electricity style.[52] It had the similar effect in the more advanced countries, outside the United States, of decreasing their dependence on US supplies, particularly of capital goods. Such self-sufficiency might have been inefficient in the short term, but in time – by the 1950s and 1960s – it was beneficial: it allowed fast growth without balance of payments deficits, it led to products and processes better suited to non-American needs (more economical of raw materials, for example) and it brought more players into the game of invention and innovation, which had been tending towards a US monopoly.

THE DEPRESSION-CRISIS AND THE SECOND WORLD WAR

> The best lack all conviction, while the worst
> Are full of passionate intensity...
>
> ...And what rough beast, its hour come round at last,
> Slouches towards Bethlehem to be born?
>
> (W. B. Yeats, *The Second Coming*)

It would be a much happier world than it is, if the reforms to which the depression crisis gives rise and which form the basis for the following upswing, came readily and quickly. In fact they come, for the most part, only reluctantly, even accidentally, at the end of a long grim process of trial and error. In the 1930s there was much trial and much error. The attempts at a solution can be classed in two categories: internal, involving some change in domestic policy, and external, changing foreign policy. On the external side, trade policy could be quickly changed, and was, as we have seen, towards protectionism. Beyond that, there was little but military aggression, and that could attract only the strong 'have-not' countries, Germany, Italy and Japan; the weak countries had little opportunity for external aggression, and the established imperial powers, little incentive. So (leaving the three countries mentioned on one side, for the moment) the policy issues were largely internal. Would increased government expenditure be helpful, or should it be reduced below its already low level? And should action be taken to improve the position, and the purchasing power, of the poor – or should they be called upon to make sacrifices so that the rich might be encouraged to invest? Increasing government expenditure did not necessarily mean also taking the 'option for the poor' (as Hitler showed). But in most countries those who questioned orthodoxy on one issue, questioned it on the other too; and government expenditure was most easily financed at the expense of the rich, most attractively spent for the benefit of the poor.

Neither Keynesianism nor progressive reform made rapid progress in most countries during the 1930s (Scandinavia, particularly Sweden, being the main exception). The United States began with a limitation of choice which can, paradoxically, be seen as a considerable advantage: as of 1933, it was scarcely possible to believe that making the poor (still) poorer, the unions (still) weaker, government (still) less interventionist, offered any hope of a solution. The country, under Roosevelt, began tentatively to explore the scope for moves in the opposite direction. Even so Congress was intensely conservative until 1937, and the Supreme Court remained so even after that.

The unions started to get stronger (with the help of the Wagner Act after 1934) but they were starting from a very low base. By the end of the decade there was a definite change in public opinion, but not much increase in government expenditure or shift in income distribution; and unemployment was little lower. Britain's record economically was a good deal better, largely because of the reversal in 1931–3 of the 1920s policies of overvaluation and free trade (it is much more likely to be beneficial for a large country to move from free trade to moderate protection, as Britain did, than to go from moderate to extreme protection, as most others did; small countries can hope for little gain from any protectionist moves). Her banking system was unscathed by the Slump, and moved quickly after 1931 to lower interest rates, which helped to stimulate a building boom. Of radical change, however, there was little sign. The split in the Labour Party in 1931, like that in 1980–1, gave the Conservatives power for the rest of the decade, and they had no time either for Keynesianism or for squeezing their own supporters for the benefit of Labour's. They certainly gave no assistance to the unions, who gained ground only very slowly after 1933.

The most visible progress was made in France after a very unpromising start. Having led Europe in industrial expansion until 1929, the right-wing governments thereafter did virtually nothing in the face of the Slump: they allowed the franc to become overvalued, did not increase protection, and certainly gave no help to the unions or the poor. In the face of this adamantine conservatism a coalition of Socialists, Communists and rural Radicals formed a Popular Front and swept to victory at the elections of 1936. The victory of the Popular Front was followed by an upsurge of worker militancy and unionisation, and some real progressive reforms, but (due to the intense opposition of the conservatives, and the ambiguous character of the Radicals) the gains made were shaky. Nor were they of much economic use while they lasted: what was needed for an upturn in France, as elsewhere, was a leftward shift of the whole political spectrum, not the polarisation of 1936. The capitalist cat, claws unclipped, was still spitting defiance. The Popular Front gave workers shorter hours and longer holidays, and they won higher wages for themselves; but their employers soon made up their losses through higher prices, and the workers' higher purchasing power, even while it lasted, was offset by something of an 'investment strike'.

Elsewhere, radical solutions of quite a different character were being tried, and with more determination. With American credits withdrawn, the German economy declined after 1929 about as fast and as far as its creditor's – but it lacked America's immense wealth and stability. The choice which faced the country was not very different from that before the First World War – either a sharp shift to the left, or an aggressive militarism which would redirect the country's energies away from reform into hostility to internal and external enemies. In this choice, the role played by the Junkers and their old allies, the heavy industrialists, is instructive. I mentioned earlier that (having in every possible way instigated and inspired the various chauvinist movements and associations) the conservative establishment lost control of them, more and more, after 1900. This process took a leap forward after the First World War, with the appearance of Hitler as leader of the strongest chauvinist party, the National Socialist German Workers' Party. Dr Frankenstein beheld his monster, and did not like him very much: the Junkers disdainfully referred to Hitler as the Bavarian corporal (the adjective conveyed as much distaste as the noun); there were neither Junkers nor industrialists among the Nazi leadership, which like the party's membership drew mainly on the 'small people' of old and new petty middle classes; and they gave him no support before 1929. (Recent research reveals that even Krupp and Thyssen, the steel magnates who cashed in after 1933, had hedged their bets before, giving more money to Hitler's conservative opponents than to the Nazis themselves.[53]) This was scarcely surprising if one looks at the Nazis' early programmes, which included nationalisation of industry, and land reform![54] The 'respectable right' was, through the 1920s, strong enough and obliging enough to give the Junkers and industrialists what they wanted. The Junkers, for example, received a great deal of government subsidy to help protect them from the adverse changes in prices. One tenth of the land in the East Elbian 'rye belt' was bought by the State, at favourable prices, for redistribution.[55] After the downturn became a crisis in 1931, however, the conservative equilibrium was upset. The two extremist parties, Communists and Nazis, grew, and the Nazis grew faster. Even at their peak in late 1932, however, they still fell short of a majority in the Reichstag; and economic recovery was beginning. Meanwhile, however, the Junker Conservatives had lost confidence in conservatism: in early 1932 the Chancellor, Bruning, the leader of the Centre, the largest party of the 'respectable right', searching hard for economies in expenditure, had decided to stop the 'rye belt' subsidy, and liquidate the Junkers' debt-ridden estates. He was promptly overthrown, with the help of the Junker President, von Hindenburg.[56] Early the following year, von Papen, the leader of the Conservatives, threw their votes to Hitler, and Hindenburg made Hitler Chancellor. No more was heard of nationalisation or land reform; the Junkers' subsidies were safe; and high tariffs on grain put the rye price up.[57]

The Nazis' jettisoning of their pretensions to domestic reform (made definitive in the night of the long knives in 1934, when the leaders of their reformist wing, the SA, were slaughtered) forced them to redouble their emphasis on militarism. On this it was now easier for chauvinists to reach a consensus with the Junkers than it had been before 1914. Then the main problem had been that the popular enthusiasm was for a war with Russia, the Junkers' old friend, in alliance with the Hapsburgs, their old Catholic enemy. Now the Hapsburgs were gone, and the Tsar had been replaced by the Bolsheviks, an excellent enemy for the Junkers. The *Drang nach Osten*, the drive eastwards, could resume with a vengeance; no one had much desire for annexations in the West, and there was some chance of persuading Britain and France to stay neutral while Germany – on behalf of 'Western Civilisation' – pursued its 'anti-Bolshevik crusade'.

The social equilibrium which Hitler created in the 1930s was in fact remarkably similar to that which Bismarck had contrived in the 1880s. The Junkers and the heavy industrialists received state support, in the form of tariffs, subsidies, cartels and military contracts. The unions were suppressed, along with the social democratic and communist parties, and income differentials widened, back towards pre-1914 levels.[58] Relations with the Catholic Church returned to Bismarckian acidity. Bismarck had made racist speeches against Jews and Slavs, as part of the creation of internal and external enemies; such racism was Hitler's stock-in-trade. But the whole structure was more precarious, because it was fifty years more out of date, and Hitler, unlike Bismarck, really believed in his enemies. Dr Frankenstein had retired; his monster ruled in Berlin.

As Germany showed the way backwards, into repressive militarism – and Sweden, the way forward, into progressive Keynesianism – the conservatives who ruled in London and Washington faced similar, and linked, dilemmas at home and abroad. At home, there was no question of retreating from liberal democracy, with its egalitarian overtones, but they were not in the least inclined to seek a way out of the Slump through progressive reform. Abroad, German, Italian, and Japanese militarism threatened everyone, and could hardly be encouraged; but they could scarcely fight it without allying themselves with its left-wing enemies, and thus making them stronger at home and abroad. The Spanish Civil War, which broke out in July 1936, summed up and exacerbated the problem, with liberal democrats there fighting side-by-side with Communists and anarchists against the reactionary right. The Popular Front government in Paris initially gave some, lukewarm, support to the democrats; London could hardly oppose them openly – but what if they won, with Communist influence strengthened by Russian support, next door to a France where the left was alarmingly strong already? The British government chose neutrality, but that position was only sustainable so long as it remained at peace with Germany: war against Germany would have effectively forced it to oppose Germany's allies in Spain.

Until the summer of 1938 peace with Germany was uneasily maintained, while Hitler remilitarised the Rhineland and took over Austria – war over such issues would have been hard to justify, and to win. The situation changed, however, when Hitler came up against the most formidable obstacle to his advance eastwards: Czechoslovakia. War for Czechoslovakia would have been easy to justify: the Czechoslovaks had impeccable democratic credentials, and they had a long-standing treaty of mutual defence with Britain and France. What was more – and this cannot be stressed too strongly – it could have been, would have been *won*. The Czechs had been preparing for it for nearly twenty years, adding strong fortifications to the excellent natural defences of Bohemia: even alone, they could muster thirty-two divisions, half as many tanks as the Germans, and several thousand aircraft.[59] The Russians were bound by treaty, and more importantly self-interest, to join in, once the French did, and the Romanians could have been persuaded, or obliged, to give them passage – and at the same time, to cut off vital oil supplies to Germany.[60] The German general staff glumly contemplated the prospect of breaking their army's teeth in a hopeless onslaught up Bohemian hillsides, while French forces advanced on the Ruhr.[61]

The corporal and his army were saved from disaster by the British government, who did not want such a victory, in such company. Chamberlain remarked to the American ambassador on 21 September 1938 that 'war is the end of this civilisation... Communism or something worse is liable to follow'.[62] On 27 September, when war briefly looked likely, the French Prime Minister commented that Hitler was risking a conflict he could not win, but from which revolutionaries and Communists alone would benefit.[63] Chamberlain and most of the rest of his party seem to have succeeded in persuading themselves, therefore, that war was (a) not winnable and (b) not necessary, because Herr Hitler would keep his promises (the ones just made to them, to go no further, and not the ones repeatedly made to the German people, to lead them against Bolshevism). Since the British would not fight, the French would not; since the French would not, the Russians would not – and the Czechs could not. Hitler then gobbled up their country in two bites, the second in February 1939; and having thus augmented his tank and air forces by 50 per cent, he began to plan his next move, against Poland.[64]

At that point, the British government did something which A. J. P. Taylor in his *Origins of the Second World War* finds quite inexplicable, at least in rational terms. In March/April 1939 they gave to Poland and Romania precisely those guarantees of support against (German) aggression which they had refused to Czechoslovakia the previous autumn – yet those countries were quite indefensible, except, at a pinch, through a Russian alliance, which neither they nor Britain could have counted on, even if they now wanted it. It may well be that the British had simply woken up, six months too late, to the fact that Hitler would have to be stopped by somebody, somewhere. One obvious reason, however, why they were able to overcome their stupidity at this point, was that although they had now much more reason to fear defeat, they had much less reason to fear victory, for the Left was much weaker now. The Spanish Republic was safely dead, the French Popular Front was moribund, and the Czech left had been crushed. As for the Russians, if they did respond to the lukewarm Allied overtures, they would have to do so in defence of their right-wing Polish enemies.

Things turned out badly. The Soviet Union, not being pressingly invited to join Germany's enemies, agreed to join hands with her instead. Not only Poland, but Norway, Denmark, the Low Countries and even France were overrun, then Yugoslavia and Greece. The British conservatives then found (like the Roman in the myth about the buying of the Sibylline books) that those who try to haggle with history end up having to pay more, for less. They paid this price in three instalments. First, in 1940, Churchill's new government handed over domestic policy, in effect, to Keynes and the radical Liberals, Labour, and the unions, who proceeded to practise a rather radical form of egalitarian interventionism which set a pattern for post-war social democracy. Second, in 1941, Hitler invaded Russia, presenting Britain with new allies whom Churchill wrily excused with the remark that if Hitler invaded Hell he would feel obliged to speak politely about the Devil in the House of Commons. Third, during the rest of the war, Britain's large investments in the United States had to be sold off, to pay for munitions.

The American conservatives got a rather better bargain.[65] As the Japanese advanced into China, US opposition to their expansion hardened, and Roosevelt's administration gradually stepped up its support for China, as for Britain. After it persuaded the British to induce the Dutch government to cut off oil supplies to Japan from Indonesia, the Japanese decided on war against the West. After Pearl Harbor, the Americans too found themselves with Russian allies; internally, the needs and conditions of wartime caused the tentative steps towards progressive interventionism to turn to more rapid movement. Unionisation increased fast, wage differentials shrank, profits were held down by price controls, progressive income taxation was introduced. An unprecedented levelling of the distribution of income resulted.[66] That, and the high level of military spending, did the trick: while the economies of Europe could at best mark time as investment was sacrificed to the needs of war, the economic capacity of the United States was such that it could send millions of men off to fight, supply them and others with munitions, increase output of consumer goods, and accumulate productive capital rapidly, all at the same time. A new Fordist upswing began there in the early 1940s. Within a decade the rest of the world would join in.

Chapter 11

A historical account, from 1945 to the present

THE LONG BOOM

It is by now a cliché to thank the Second World War for the long boom which followed it in Continental Europe and Japan. Having lost so much, the war-ravaged could start again afresh with the latest and best in methods and equipment – so goes the explanation. Maybe – but twenty-five years is a long time for a reconstruction boom, by the end of which much of the post-war 'latest and best' had been replaced several times. The boom lasted so long (it might be added) because that was the time it took to catch up, more or less, with the United States, which at the beginning in 1948, had had a huge technological lead.[1] Again, reasonable enough – but what made it possible *this time* for those countries to chase the USA so successfully, for so long, when they had failed before and others (like Britain and Latin America) were failing now? Did something happen to them, *socially*, in and just after the war, which made them economically more dynamic than ever before?

The answer will come as no surprise. The occupied and defeated countries of Western Europe and Japan went through a drastic process of levelling, and political and economic reintegration, which made them ideally suited to rapid economic growth. The process, and the results, were not the same in each country. Japan was the most levelled – first literally, by bombing, which destroyed much physical capital at home (the capital abroad, in the Japanese Empire, was taken over by its inheritors); then wartime and post-war inflation took away most 'rentier' capital. But there was a second stage of more deliberate levelling, described and explained in Chapter 7.[2] The decrease in inequality in Japan in the 1940s was most remarkable, and most valuable, in that it reflected, and helped to establish, a social consensus. The new egalitarian interpretation of the 'firm as community' was shared by managers and workers: acceptance of it was the price paid by managers for the restoration of their authority – which they achieved, not without difficulty, during the 1950s. In the countryside, in the same way, the land reform was soon a *fait accompli*: the right wing Liberal Democrats established themselves in the country areas by providing their peasant constituents with government support, not by aligning themselves with ex-landowners. The result was an economic and social structure which was not only highly equal, but highly integrated.[3]

Nothing in Europe can match this – neither the process, nor its results. But the levelling in Germany was impressive by any other standards. As the Russian armies overran their estates east of the Elbe, Junker ladies fled to the West, some pushing their remaining possessions in prams. Their husbands – those who survived the slaughter – were to find their names and titles little use to them in the new West Germany, in which (according to Bolte's survey of social status[4]) an army major ranked well below a doctor and only just above a garage proprietor. Industrialists lost a good deal too: much of their property was the wrong side of the Elbe, and much of what was not was bombed. Owners of property in bricks and mortar suffered severely and they were prevented from taking advantage of the scarcity of what was left by stringent rent controls. Rentiers, finally, lost absolutely everything, since in the currency reform of 1948 the old Reichsmark was made valueless. The levelling nearly went a good deal further: industry, for example, was marked for a reform on Japanese lines, but the Americans called a halt to the process as the Cold War intensified, and subsequently workers' pressure for the nationalisation and democratisation of heavy industry was resisted by the new Christian Democrat government, who conceded only *Mitbestimmung*, co-determination.[5] Even that was a great deal better than nothing.

Elsewhere in Western Europe the changes were rather less far-reaching than in Germany, but important for all that. Typically, the Nazi occupation had divided societies into a section of the Right, including many industrialists, who collaborated, and the rest, who by the end of the war all supported the Resistance in varying degrees. The left tended to resist more bravely and effectively, thereby gaining adherents – and even more important, respectability. At the end of the war, it had its reward. In France, for example, immediately after liberation, the great industrialist Louis Renault was executed for collaboration – not by revolutionary Jacobins or *communards*, but after due process, by the government of the conservative Charles de Gaulle, which then confiscated his factories.[6] A few of the rich were shot, more were shorn, all were taxed, in most Western European countries, while the poor flocked to join the resurgent unions.

There was one exception of some importance to the leftward shift at the end of the war. The Italian conservatives had nimbly leapt aboard the Allied bandwagon in 1943 without any coexistence with the left in a resistance movement. The left (mostly Communists) who did most of the resisting then and until the end of the war, only briefly shared power and had little influence on policy-making. Fascist institutions were left almost unchanged, merely adapted to the needs of the clerical Christian Democrats. Still, from the point of view of regional inequalities, the Christian Democrats (like the

Japanese Liberal Democrats) had the virtue of being represented most strongly in the poorer areas, particularly the South, and could therefore be counted on to carry out a measure of geographical levelling; they inherited from Mussolini a large state sector of banking and industry, which played a part in this process.[7]

Britain, which had started its levelling process in 1940, voted at the end of the war to formalise it and take it a little further, under a Labour Government which (unlike its predecessors of 1924 and 1929–31) knew very well how to enact reforms, because its members had been doing it for five years already. No agrarian land reform took place – nor was one really necessary in so urban a country – there were no collaborators to expropriate, and full compensation was paid to the owners of the industries nationalised; but the steeply progressive taxation system of wartime was continued, and the proceeds of it were used now to build a Welfare State which made for fairer (working-class) shares than before the war.[8] The unions grew even stronger in numbers and in public esteem.

It would be hard to overstress the reduction in inequality between the late 1920s and early 1950s (see Table 6.1) but it might be argued that I have overstated the role of political and institutional changes in causing it. If we look at the case of the United States, which has probably been the best researched, Williamson and Lindert (1980) show that changes in taxation and other transfers did rather less 'levelling' between 1929 and 1948 than changes in 'pre-fisc', before-tax, inequality. A large part of these 'pre-fisc' changes was due to reduced inequality in earnings, and this in turn (Williamson and Lindert argue) arose from technological and demographic forces working largely through the supply and demand for skills:

> Total factor productivity growth was more evenly balanced among sectors than in any other era since 1840.... This change seems to have accounted for about half of the observed leveling between 1929 and 1948. Another 30% ... is explained by demographic forces: By having fewer babies and by shutting out would-be immmigrants from the Old World, Americans helped themselves achieve more equal pay between 1929 and the postwar era. (p. 289)

There is no contradiction between such a 'market' approach and an 'institutional' one, as we saw in Chapter 6: both market forces and institutional forces may be working in the same direction, and their effects may be hard to disentangle, as (for example) where reduced immigration helps to explain both higher unionisation and a relative surplus of skills. In Western Europe market forces probably did not do much to supplement institutional forces in the 1930s and 1940s: the halt to migration would not have had the same effect in countries which had not been receiving a large inflow of unskilled workers, nor would they have had the same balanced growth of productivity as in the USA, since this is associated with the later stages of diffusion of a 'style', which they had not yet reached. (But market forces may well account for the levelling up of the countryside. Agricultural workers in Western Europe closed much of the gap between their pay and that in manufacturing industry, between 1938 and 1948.)[9] Market forces will in one way have been working against equality in the war-ravaged countries of Western Europe, by pushing up the rate of profit on scarce industrial capital – it certainly was high, in most countries (Hill, 1979); but that merely meant an element of levelling delayed, until 'normality' returned during the 1950s and 1960s. Meanwhile, the high net profits of industry were no more at the expense of the worker than of the rentier (nominal interest rates being very low, and capital badly eroded by inflation) and the landlord (with frozen rents on a war-ravaged stock).[10] And of course profits did not accrue to a homogeneous class of 'industrial capitalists', rich men with big cigars, grinding the faces of a homogeneous class of poor workers. In 1940 profits in Renault and Mitsubishi had gone almost in their entirety to very rich people – stereotypical capitalists; in 1950 they went respectively to the French state and an assortment of the Japanese middle class. The recipients of profits had changed. They were also more heavily taxed.

The end of the levelling period

It was in the United States that *Halt!* was first called to the surge of reform. In foreign policy, rivalry with the Soviet Union was already the dominant consideration in 1946, and at home, by the autumn of that year, there were clear signs of concern at the way that unionisation was spreading among returning soldiers – even among non-manual workers and in the South – and that post-war militancy was leading to high wage demands and frequent strikes. The employers organised a highly effective counter-offensive industrially – they crushed the Foremen's Union of America, for example, and checked the recruiting drive in the South – and politically, put the Republicans back into a majority in both houses of Congress; they then used their political strength to pass the Taft-Hartley Act, which reduced the legal protection enjoyed by the unions.[11] The campaign against Russia abroad meshed with a campaign against its friends at home (real and imaginary); anti-communism became an article of the American creed, and helped to divide the union movement.

The anti-communist crusade influenced American policy as occupiers in Japan and (as already mentioned) in Germany, but its main impact was in France and Italy, where the Americans in 1947 succeeded in engineering splits in the Communist-dominated union federations, with the secession of a large proportion of the non-communist workers, followed by a employer offensive against those who remained: unionisation fell sharply in the following years, and the employers regained undisputed control of the workplace.[12] The Communists were forced out of the government in both countries, and government policy became sharply anti-communist. Elsewhere in Europe, the domestic effect of the Cold War was relatively slight: outside France and Italy, the Communists were only a small minority among the left and in the unions, and their isolation made little difference. There was little interest even among employers in attacking the social-democratic majority either in their own right or as supposed crypto-communists.

By the late 1940s or early 1950s, depending on the country, the period of rapid social change was over. The North as a whole settled down into a long phase of industrial peace, and political conservatism.

International reintegration

So far we have been examining the internal settlement(s) on which the upswing in the North was based. There was also an external settlement, which was in equally striking contrast to the situation before the war (and, for most apt comparison, that just after the previous war, in the 1920s).[13]

All talk of reparations ended within two years of the victory, nor did the devastated countries need to go deep into debt to get the resources they needed for reconstruction; instead, these were provided on the most generous of terms, as Marshall Aid. The arrangements for the longer run were equally encouraging. Under the protection of the Pax Americana, and more or less under the authority of the United States, an international monetary and commercial system was set up which had the clear aim of steady progress towards free trade and movement of capital. New industries could be brought to maturity, convalescent ones nursed back to health, behind the shelter of a degree of protection, but at the same time the stronger industries could reinforce success with a view to expanding exports and exploiting economies of scale. This made it possible for policy-makers to allow heavy dependence on imports, most importantly of energy. The Japanese, French and Italians, for long handicapped by the lack of cheap domestic energy sources, could now turn this handicap to advantage, by buying their energy wherever it was cheapest. In the diffusion of an energy-intensive technological style, this change was crucial.

As the West flourished under the Pax Americana, the East – Eastern Europe and the USSR – benefited after a fashion from the Pax Russica. The Russian economy, ravaged by the war, could provide no help for the others – on the contrary, the Russians took reparations, in the form of equipment, from their zone of Germany and from German-owned enterprises elsewhere. But they did introduce a system of international trade which was some improvement on national self-sufficiency, and the internal settlements made in their part of Europe were not dissimilar, in crucial respects, to the changes in the West: they levelled the distribution of income and wealth, and they increased the degree of economic integration in industry (if not agriculture) by putting young 'technocrats' in charge. As for the differences, it is now clear that, for the operation of an advanced late-twentieth century economy, Russian-style central planning is much inferior to its 'mixed economy' capitalist rival; but for the tasks of post-war reconstruction, and of the basic development of rather backward economies, central planning had something to be said for it (see Van der Wee, 1986, Chapter II).

Besides Europe, the other region which emerged from the war and post-war years socially transformed was East Asia. Japan we have already discussed; there were changes at least as important in China and Korea. The victory of the Red Army in China in 1949 led, as in Eastern Europe, to levelling and integration; what was more, it gave China, for the first time since the middle years of the Ming dynasty in the fifteenth century, a strong central government under native control. Quite as impressive as the strength of the new government in Peking, was to be the rejuvenation of its beaten Kuomintang predecessors, in exile in Taiwan (previously a colony of Japan); the economic miracle which followed was described in Chapter 7. In Korea, once its ruinous war was over, a similar arrangement could be seen: a Communist North, and a capitalist South with a social structure levelled by land reform, destruction, and flight. East Asia now had internal arrangements even more dynamic than those of its tutors, in the rival blocs. It also had help from them – some Russian aid to China (abruptly cut off after the split in 1958) and North Korea, and much American aid to Japan, Taiwan and South Korea. In East Asia, indeed, the Americans were even more generous than in Western Europe, for they allowed their allies full participation in the benefits of freer trade, while at first letting them protect their own markets as much as they liked; the Japanese were also allowed to spend next to nothing on defence.

Elsewhere in the world – in what we can now call the South – the changes which resulted from the long depression-crisis were less radical than in the North, though superficially some were most impressive. The South Asian countries, from the Mediterranean to the Pacific, quickly became independent, and their new regimes continued the policies of industrialisation which had been virtually forced on their predecessors by depression and war; the structures of power (with brown faces substituted for white) and the distribution of wealth, were for the most part little changed. In Latin America, already politically independent, most countries emerged from the crisis into the upswing with clearly-defined policies of import-substituting industrialisation. That these policies were pursued indicated that the export-oriented landowners (of, for example, Brazil, Uruguay and Argentina) had lost at least some of their power, in various forms of semi-revolution; but they had lost none of their land, unlike their counterparts in East Asia, and this made a lot of difference in the decades which followed. At all events, weakly based as the South's industrialisation was, politically, socially and economically, it could now proceed in an unusually helpful international climate – of peace, and favourable terms of trade (see chapter 7).

With this impetus, the decade of the 1950s produced the fastest growth so far recorded in the world economy, and a boom almost everywhere (see Figure 11.1 and Table 11.1). Practically the only exception was the United States itself, where from 1956 onwards growth slackened and unemployment rose: a Kuznets downswing in the middle of the Kondratiev upswing. This can be ascribed partly to (US-sponsored) success elsewhere, eroding her strength in international competition. At the same time, US industry was by now operating close to the existing 'technological frontier', which was no longer advancing fast, since the possibilities of Fordism were near to exhaustion. But there was also a hint of more general problems which would trouble the world in future. The movement towards equality had not been thrown back, but it had (as we saw) been checked, and this limited the scope for the further diffusion of Fordist consumption and production – within its own Deep South, for example. The mini-depression produced a mini-depression crisis in the country. The most obvious result of this crisis was that the domestic conservatism and international caution of Eisenhower lost support, in favour of the domestic reformism but international self-assertion of Kennedy. At first it was Kennedy's aggressive foreign policy which was the more apparent (the attack on Cuba, increased military spending, the commitment to Vietnam), but by 1963 the balance was restored, under pressure from what I take to be the second result of the mini-depression crisis – the upsurge of political activity among the blacks, who had seen twenty years of steady economic progress interrupted in the late 1950s. The new mood among the blacks gave strength not only to the Civil Rights campaign, but to liberal causes generally, and by 1964, under Kennedy's successor Johnson, there was again a majority in public opinion and in Congress for a measure of egalitarian reform. The 1964–8 period extended the progress made in the early 1940s; there was substantial redistribution of income through taxation and public expenditure,[14] and effective laws were passed against racial discrimination. One effect was to reduce inequality of income again, after tax at least, while levelling up social indicators of inequality like the high school drop-out rate;[15] another was to contribute to the prolonged upswing of 1961–7.

It was not only in the United States that fiscal redistribution reduced inequality: most of the Western European countries reacted to their remarkable rises in incomes, and to their first serious post-war recessions (briefer and later than in the USA, in about the mid-1960s) by increasing taxation and public expenditure.[16] This second instalment of the building of Welfare States came, in Europe, mostly in the late 1960s and early 1970s, and helped prolong the boom. So did immigration: during the 1950s expansion in Western Europe had threatened to exhaust domestic supplies of labour, and immigrants from the old colonial empires and the Mediterranean

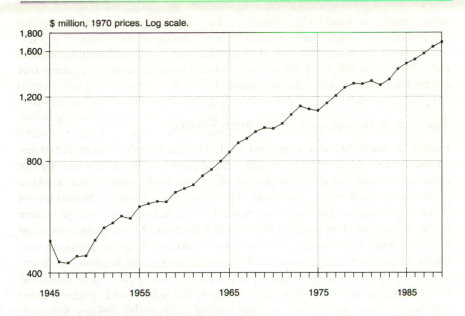

$ million, 1970 prices. Log scale.

Figure 11.1 US GNP, 1945–89
Source: Mitchell (1983); OECD *Economic Outlook*, June 1990

Table 11.1 Rates of growth of gross domestic product[1] in France, Germany, UK, USA and Japan, 1937–89, (% per annum)

Period	France	Germany	UK	USA	Japan[6]
1937–50[2]	1.4	1.0	1.7	4.4	−2.2
1950–60[3]	4.5	7.4	2.7	2.8	8.8
1960–69[4]	5.4	4.4	2.9	4.3	11.1
1969–73[5]	5.5	4.3	3.1	3.3	8.8
1973–79	3.0	2.4	1.6	2.7	4.1
1980–89	2.1	1.9	2.2	2.7	4.2
(1984–9	2.8	2.7	3.8	3.4	4.5)

Source: Solomou, 1987; Maddison, 1982; OECD Economic Outlook, June 1990
Notes: 1. GNP in US, Japan and Germany, 1980–9.
   2. Germany 1938–52; UK and USA 1937–51.
   3. Germany 1952–60; UK 1951–61; USA 1951–9.
   4. UK 1961–8; USA 1959–66.
   5. UK 1968–73; USA 1966–73.
   6. Japanese periods are not all peak-to-peak.

countries were welcomed (though, except in Britain, without an invitation to settle).[17]

THE UNDERMINING OF THE BOOM

There is of course a lively debate over what brought the long post-war upswing to an end. Mandel, as we saw in Chapter 6, treats the central cause as an upsurge in workers' militancy in the class struggle, due largely to the disappearance of mass unemployment as a weapon in the hands of capital: the effect was to reduce the rate of profit, damage capitalists' confidence, and reduce their willingness to invest. I have already argued against this explanation; here I will offer my own.

The crisis of the upswing in Northern politics

It may be useful for our argument to divide the populations of Northern countries into three groups of not very different size: a top 'third', the middle class and the rich; the middle third, the more prosperous working class; the bottom third, the poor. The triumphs of social democracy in Western Europe, and of liberalism in the United States, were brought about by an alliance of the middle third with the bottom. As we have seen, they gained a great deal through this alliance – initially. Broadly speaking, the Welfare State in its early forms, in Britain and the United States for example in the late 1940s, took from the top third to give to the rest; so in effect did the upsurge of mass unionism of that time. What followed, under mainly right-wing governments, was not the rolling back of the Welfare State – it was too popular for that, and its institutions too well-entrenched – but a gradual diversion from its original purposes, as its institutions grew and matured. Education spending, for example, was initially almost all on schools, and thus benefited the lower two-thirds roughly in proportion to their numbers – but as time went on an increasing share of the budget went to higher education, where working-class students were decidedly in a minority, at least among those who completed their courses. Where health care was funded by the State, as in the British National Health Service, there was a similar development: the middle class, confident and well-informed, learned to get more out of the service than the poor did.[18] Other state spending twisted in the same direction – as when urban motorways built with capital-intensive equipment ruined inner city neighbourhoods so that suburban commuters could drive easily to their downtown offices; and military spending, which in the 1940s had paid a mass army using for the most part rather simple mass-produced equipment, increasingly fed a military-industrial complex with fewer and fewer privates and production workers, and more and more generals, high-paid workers, and profits.[19]

And who paid for this ever-more expensive state machine? The top third, less and less; the bottom two-thirds, more and more. No one actually said in so many words that henceforth the wealthy would pay less tax on their incomes, or the corporations on their profits – the rates of tax were in general kept high; but there was a gradual multiplication of allowances, and a gradual learning how to use them for tax avoidance. Nor did anyone campaign on the platform that the working class paid too little tax, and should pay more; but as their money incomes rose with growth and inflation, they were caught by the progressive tax system which had been designed to milk their masters. As a result the middle third began to see less and less advantage to themselves from the growth of the state's activities. This had the effect, in politics, of giving an opening to the New Right to campaign on a platform of cutting back the state, and forge an alliance, in effect, of the top two-thirds. It had the effect, in industry, of leading the middle third (who were, for the most part, unionised) to push harder for wage increases which would compensate them for higher taxation. This latter development has to be seen in the context of other changes which were taking place in industry.

The crisis of the upswing in Northern economics

We saw earlier how the depression-crisis ended with a 'reintegration' of Northern industry, through an acceptance by management of the unions as representatives of the workers. By the late 1960s there had been in most Northern countries a far-reaching move back towards 'disintegration'. As always, the ebb tide was not a mere reversal of the flood. Disintegration this time was not so much between employers and employed, as *within* each side. On the employer side, with the growth of increasingly large and bureaucratic firms, and the new patterns of shareholding, management had become more independent of shareholders in day-to-day control. On the other side, two factors had combined to separate the union hierarchies from the rank and file: after some twenty years of renewal and growth the trade union movements had stabilised; and the increasing size and complexity of the workplace drew members' attention away from wider union issues. Union disintegration in this form, together with dissatisfaction at the growing 'tax wedge', was largely responsible for the shopfloor militancy of the late 1960s and early 1970s in Western Europe (and the paler US version which faded earlier). It confronted managements which competed with one another on price less than before, and were thus more able to make concessions to their workers at the expense of their customers. This was one of the two main causes of the increase in inflation in the early 1970s (for the other, see below).[20]

There was also an international element to the economic crisis: the problem of exchange rates, which arose from the liberalisation of trade and payments in the upswing, and the consequent mass of 'hot money' which flowed in and out of countries according to expectations of changes in the exchange rate. (We can label this 'international economic disintegration' in one form.)

We can take the argument beyond this point only if we take account of elements of the Northern crisis which were of Southern origin; so let us pause to examine those.

The 'oil shocks' and the crisis of the upswing in the South

The more advanced Southern countries had emerged from the last depression crisis set on industrialising and thus freeing themselves from the dependence on primary products which had brought them to bankruptcy in the 1930s; even the less advanced equated industrialisation with development and wanted some for themselves.

At the beginning of Southern industrialisation, in the 1930s and 1940s, the import-substituting industries were those of the steam, and steel-and-science styles – textiles, then steel. It was when the emphasis began to shift to Fordist products, and Fordist processes, that certain problems which are bound to arise anyway in a situation of technological dependence, rapidly became acute. The characteristics which made the Fordist style a difficult one to diffuse from the United States into the rest of the core, made it a thoroughly *inappropriate* style for most countries below the core in the technological hierarchy. The factor proportions it used were just the opposite of the 'endowment' available: it required much energy and raw materials, many qualified engineers and (in the 'upstream' industries) skilled workers; little unskilled labour. The large scale of production it demanded was difficult for even a large semi-peripheral country to reach, given the restrictions of its home market, and made it inevitable that the few firms which came near 'optimum scale' would have monopoly power. Thus what might be called 'independent Fordist development' was bound to be extremely difficult. The concentration of economic power in the hands of those with the necessary capital and/or skills made both for inflation and for increasing inequality – and the latter obstructed precisely that broadening of the market which continued growth required.[21]

In the less advanced Southern countries, particularly in Africa, industrial development on anything like these lines was really quite hopeless, and where attempted required costs in imported capital and components which only added to the strain imposed on the economy by the urban elite's insatiable demand for imported luxuries and arms. The crisis this had caused by the late 1960s in many of these countries was essentially the same as that which they are suffering now, only less severe; there was something of a pause in their difficulties during the 1970s, thanks to heavy borrowing, and to the brief upturn in primary product prices.[22]

In the more advanced Southern countries, however, it seemed possible to make a success of industrialisation by changing the strategy. First, it seemed that the shift away from primary products had gone too far. Why not take advantage of the rather favourable terms of trade now obtainable for them? The revenue could be used to give fresh impetus to industrialisation; and so there was an increase in investment in the primary sector. Second, instead of 'independent Fordism' it seemed attractive to seek a role in 'global Fordism' which suited the semi-peripheral country's *factor endowment*: in other words, to specialise in those industrial activities which made intensive use of semi-skilled labour, getting whatever economies of scale were necessary by selling on the world market, and using the foreign currency earned to buy high technology products, or the expertise required to produce them, from the core.[23]

This proved to be a jump from the frying pan into the fire. In the first place, success in selling cheap labour products demanded that the labour be as cheap as possible, so the wages of industrial workers had to be reduced. As we saw in Chapter 7, this was feasible without immiserising the poor only in the few countries which had had a thorough land reform, as in Korea and Taiwan (and in Hong Kong, which drew on Chinese labour). Elsewhere, it was not only disagreeable, socially: it also reduced the scope for mass production for the home market even further. Moreover, the dictatorial apparatus which had to be set up in order to persuade the workers to accept lower wages proved in most cases an extraordinarily corrupt and inefficient system of government (*vide* Argentina, Brazil, etc.). Second, while textiles, steel, etc., could generally be produced and sold on the world market independently of core firms, this was not true of Fordist products. Semi-peripheral countries could only break into the world market here by accepting partial or complete multinational control and ownership. This proved to be an expensive bargain, in terms of the outflow of profits, and also the cost of equipment and components which the multinationals chose, unnecessarily, to foist on their satellite enterprises. Finally, there was once again a steadily increased dependence on the world market, which was likely to have the same results, before long, as the build-up of primary product exports: increasing supply meets declining or static demand, in a competitive market, and the price falls.

For a time, however, it seemed like a solution to the crisis, and it earned for the countries who chose it (for example Mexico and Brazil) the optimistic label of Newly Industrialising Countries, alongside the 'Four Little Tigers', South Korea, Taiwan, Hong Kong and Singapore, for which optimism was more soundly based.

The other group of Southern countries for which optimism seemed justified in the 1970s were of course the oil exporters. I have explained the 'oil shocks' in considerable detail elsewhere;[24] there is no room for detail here, only for a summary which stresses the way in which they can be seen as a natural part of the crisis of the (late) upswing. As we saw in Chapter 7, there is a tendency in the upswing for the pattern of world production of any commodity to move towards specialisation according to comparative advantage. In the case of oil, this meant the concentration of production in a small group of richly-endowed Southern countries; in the latter stages of this process, during the 1970s, there was a large reduction in high-cost US output. Those in the West who encouraged this shift were rightly confident that there was ample production capacity to meet world demand, but they ignored the fact that the concentration of output gave some producers so much revenue that they could easily afford to cut back production – which after all merely *postponed* the extraction of the oil – and by doing it together they raised the price so much that their revenues increased further. (The activities of OPEC are of small importance in this context in comparison with the incentives for restraint affecting the major Southern producers as individuals.).

Resumé: the initial causes of the downswing

The crisis we have been examining was a complex one, but its immediate consequences for the world economy were quite simple: from about 1972, rapidly rising inflation, and from 1974, rapidly rising unemployment. These twin miseries, not hitherto found together, arose mainly from the oil shock and the industrial relations crisis. Both the shock and the crisis were obviously inflationary, the one working first through prices, the other first through wages, and combining in the classic wage-price spiral. Both were also deflationary, in the sense of reducing demand: the shock directly, because (as I argued in Chapter 7) it redistributed income to countries which, at least at first, were rather disinclined to spend it; the crisis indirectly, because governments respond to inflation – however caused – by deflating demand.

Had there been nothing more than this at work, the downswing would not have lasted very long. We shall see later how one country after another got its industrial relations crisis under control, most of them before the end of the 1970s; we saw in Chapter 7 how the oil shock too, though repeated in 1979–80, soon began to lose its deflationary effect, even before it was reversed in 1986. Yet the downswing continued: indeed, taking South, East and North together, it intensified.

CAUSES OF THE DEPRESSION CRISIS OF THE 1980s

You must be cruel to be kind – English proverb.

It is time to look again at changes in technology. We saw in Chapter 2 how the microelectronics paradigm was slow, and the biotechnology paradigm slower, to break through the crust of Fordism. Nonetheless, a new technological style was definitely crystallizing during the 1970s, and was beginning to have important economic effects. The demand for the products of the new electronics sector was increasing extremely rapidly, and output there was limited mostly by the shortages of skilled manpower which constrained the growth of production and the development of new products. On the other hand, some key industries saw the pattern of Northern demand switching away from them: Fordist industries like 'white goods' and (cheaper) vehicles, and pre-Fordist ones like steel, textiles and construction. Such a switch, if it had merely arisen from the normal course of technical development and economic growth, would have been fairly slow, and its effects – surplus capacity and unemployment in 'old' sectors, shortages of capacity and skills in 'new' ones, would have been relatively mild. In the event the switch in Northern demand, by the early 1980s, was rather sharp, because of increasing inequality, higher military spending, and the baby slump: the 'old' sectors depended disproportionately on the poor and large families for their market; military spending went increasingly to the 'new' sectors. That was not all: a number of the 'old' sectors in the North began rather suddenly to face competition from the South, as Southern industries built up with the original intention of supplying domestic demand swung towards earning foreign exchange from the North. Such goods as the South could still afford to buy from the North – as its terms of trade worsened and its debt burden mounted – had an increasing 'high-tech.' component: weapons, for example. Even then, the sudden change in industrial structure required in the North could have been managed reasonably well if the majority of the 'baby-boomers' now coming onto the labour market had gone into 'high-tech.' jobs in the new sectors. For that, however, their education was inadequate, particularly in the UK and USA.[25] So the 'mismatch' of available skills and capacity, to required skills and capacity, became extreme.

The drift of the argument so far is that the arrival of the new style *in itself* did relatively little to increase inequality and depress demand: the damage was mostly done by the changes going on in the environment at the time. It is however commonly believed that, in industries run on the new lines (described in Chapter 2), the pattern of employment, and the structure of firms, makes for greater inequality, and more employer power, than in the Fordist style. Again, I propose to argue rather differently.

It is clear, to start with, that large plants, as well as large firms, were characteristic of Fordism; and in those large plants, and large offices, there was a high proportion of three *middle* strata of employees: non-manual workers of a clerical nature, skilled manual workers, and semi-skilled workers responsible for expensive equipment. Workers of all three categories were in contact with or close to large numbers of their peers, which provided them with good conditions for union organisation – except perhaps the non-manual workers, whose closer relationship to management tended to reduce both incentive and opportunity for alignment with other wage-earners. With the help of unionisation, the semi-skilled workers had been able to move up to a more-or-less privileged position, like the rest. Some of this has certainly changed; it makes sense now for both factories and offices to be far smaller, in terms of numbers of employees, than they used to be, even if the size of the *firm* does not change.[26] But what category are these fewer employees in, and in what relation to each other? It is commonly argued that the work-force is becoming polarised between two groups – towards the top, management and its henchmen, computer programmers and other highly-skilled people – and the others, towards the bottom, who by and through the computer are so closely controlled that they lose discretion and skill: the operative in charge of a lathe now merely watches it operating under computer control. Trade unions have no place in this arrangement: the higher group naturally share power and feel no need for union organisation, while those at the bottom are too weak and fragmented to be able to insist on it.[27]

This view is certainly not nonsense: it is based on observation of some sectors of (particularly US) industry. But such a pattern is not likely to become the dominant organisational facet of the new technological style, for it is relevant to only one part of the industrial landscape and is not ideal even for that. We must remember that the distribution of employment among sectors is always changing. Once a sector can be mechanised in the way described, it will tend to become rapidly less important; those which are producing the equipment with which to mechanise, in ever-newer forms – CNC machine tools, microprocessors, etc. – will tend to become more important, being almost always much less susceptible to mechanisation. Taking the (world) economy as a whole, the tendency is not so much to a polarisation into skilled and unskilled, as to a general shift into more and more highly skilled employment. This move is accelerated if management, instead of *deskilling* production workers, *reskills* them, with (for example) the techniques of computer programming and repair and maintenance – which raises the productivity of both labour and capital at the cost of leaving shopfloor workers a share of power. Such a sharing is inherent anyway, in the type of structure which makes the most of the new technological style: the *participative* one. The use of worker participation in decision-making, at lower levels at least, is the radical organisational innovation which corresponds to the technical ones described already.[28]

The polarised arrangement described above, which exploits the new style to increase management power, can at best only be efficient statically, not dynamically: it is bound to be a disadvantage in the continuous process of technical change which is now the norm; and it could never be even statically efficient in the most high-technology, capital goods industries which the Japanese are now coming to dominate. Their success in these areas has been based on the intelligent – and educated – participation of virtually the whole labour force, both in day-to-day co-ordination and in technical development.[29] Helped by the peculiarities of Japanese Confucian culture, this essentially egalitarian feature has been successfully introduced into what remains in many ways an extremely hierarchical, deferential system; Western firms, on the other hand, can only make participation work by going more or less 'the whole hog' and drastically reducing hierarchy and deference, as in some high-tech. US firms like Hewlett-Packard, or Swedish industry in general. The classic Fordist-Taylorist US firm is, of course, organised on very different lines, and just the point when it needed to evolve in the direction of participation, social trends in the United States were nudging it the opposite way: as we saw earlier, a huge influx of under-privileged and under-educated Hispanic immigrants were becoming available to fill the lower-paid jobs and helping to depress their pay and status further.[30]

We have here an instance of a general proposition about the long wave in the twentieth century: that at just the point where a renewed movement towards equality is needed in the North, to stimulate expansion in general and the diffusion of the new style in particular, the tide starts to flow the other way. This ebb tide is clearly connected to the outcome of the crisis of the upswing; to that we now return.

The outcome of the crisis of the upswing in the North

The Northern crisis of the upswing, as described so far, was a political crisis, of the liberal/social democratic coalition, and an economic crisis, with several facets: minor crises in exchange rates, industrial relations and in the relations between management and shareholders, and a major crisis of inflation.

The responses to the crisis varied in their speed and effectiveness, according to the aspect they were addressing. The exchange rate problem was dealt with, from 1973 onwards, by a switch from fixed to flexible rates, intended to absorb, and to a certain extent deter, speculative movements. The outcome was disappointing: speculators proved less intelligent than central bankers had hoped and caused huge swings in exchange rates. Moreover, the new regime, in a situation of nearly-free trade, drastically altered the balance of advantage for most governments in their management of the economy. Under fixed exchange rates, it paid to use expansionary monetary and fiscal policy to maintain high employment and economic growth – the voters preferred things that way. Under flexible exchange rates, however, tight monetary and fiscal policies, although they reduced employment, which the voter did not like, pushed up the exchange rate, which led to lower inflation and higher real wages, at least for a few years – and the voter thoroughly approved of that.[31] (The United States was something of an exception: its size, relatively small dependence on trade, and possession of the major reserve currency allowed it to follow expansionary policies with relative impunity.)

The crisis in industrial relations provoked a variety of responses according to the peculiarities of the country's system. The general aim of management was to restore at least the degree of control they had had before: in the United States, always relatively anti-union, that meant in many cases getting rid of unions, with the help of the new style; in most European countries, on the other hand, firms sought rather to tighten up central control of their payments systems, and to undercut unofficial shopfloor organisation by improving formal channels for participation. The response of union leaders was to try to improve their links with the shop floor, and to make sure that they were at least as militant on the workers' behalf as the shopfloor leaders were – at least so long as shopfloor militancy stood a chance of success; as and when management tightened their own control, there was less need to worry about successful unofficial action.[32]

The 'disintegration' between shareholders and management had only become a serious problem in Britain and the United States, and it was in those countries that one can find evidence of a clear-cut response. The institutional investors who now dominated the market for shares became much less tolerant of poor managerial performance, as reflected in profits – they were forced to be, because their own performance was more and more under scrutiny; but they reacted not as the traditional large shareholder might have done, by intervening directly to force changes on management, but in an arm's length manner, by selling their shares – either piecemeal on the stock market, or to a take-over bidder. Any firm treated thus would suffer, immediately and certainly, through difficulty in raising finance, and probably, before long, by being swallowed by a corporate predator. Management had to seek to avoid this fate by improving its performance – on the face of it a highly desirable response; but unfortunately, as I have argued elsewhere,[33] the pressure was for good performance *in the short run*. All kinds of investments and outlays which could not be expected to pay off *soon* became less attractive than before; this particularly affected training and new product development (except that funded by the military), and made the skills and capacity mismatch even worse.

We come now to the response to the crisis as it showed itself at government level. The balance of political forces was slow to change and so the economic crisis of which inflation was the primary feature was tackled at first by the old politicians under the old political dispensation. They chose to depress demand somewhat – or rather, to allow the oil price rise to act like an extra tax to depress demand, without taking action to offset it – and to rely, where inflation threatened to get out of control, on incomes policies of one sort or another. They were also happy to see the commercial banks taking in the oil exporters' surplus funds and 'recycling' them to the non-oil exporting South, which was thus able to keep up, or even increase, its imports from the North. As time went on, however, the pressures on the politicians changed, and they either changed accordingly, or were replaced. The electoral pressures changed, as I have argued, because of the break-up of the old alliance of the 'bottom two-thirds': the prosperous working class could be won by a new Right promising tax cuts, while a part – in some countries, like France, Switzerland and the USA, a substantial part – of the bottom third were immigrants without votes (or, as in the USA, so alienated from the political system that they did not use their votes). The pressures on politicians from business changed. Earlier, when they had sold mostly in the home market, their main interest had been the maintenance of home demand. Now, the stronger (and thus more influential) firms were at least as much interested in demand abroad. Where (as in Germany and Japan) their emphasis was still on exporting from their plants at home, they demanded that their currency be not allowed to get too 'strong' (i.e. with an unfavourable exchange rate); where (as in Switzerland, Britain and the United States) the emphasis was on multinational operation, with production largely abroad, that did not matter. Both exporters and multinationals demanded first and foremost low taxes and a minimum of government interference – again, wind in the sails of the New Right.

Whatever the specific pressures on them, politicians and bureaucrats naturally like to see themselves as acting according to some coherent body of economic doctrine of which they can offer some simplified version to the electorate and the other groups they have to satisfy. When today's doctrines – in this case Keynesian – seem discredited, they have to look for new ones. Genuinely new ones are hard to find, and when found seem dangerous – the alternative is to take up old doctrines, tarted up. That option was particularly attractive to the new generation of opinion-formers and policy-makers on the Right, for (as I argued in Chapter 3) they had no personal experience of the results of pre-Keynesian policies, and were easily persuaded that current difficulties were due to Keynesian meddling with the market mechanism. Thus it was that monetarism returned to the position of influence it had enjoyed before the 1930s Slump, and (in one or other of its various versions) resumed its dominance of the treasuries and central banks of the world, preaching less interference in markets – by unions, and by the state, whether through taxation, public expenditure and ownership, or restrictive legislation. At the same time, it called for the control of inflation by tight monetary and fiscal policies, for it denied that these could be responsible for unemployment – which it blamed on the distortion of labour markets by collective bargaining, minimum wages, and unemployment benefits.[34]

There were many Keynesians in office who resisted, but their policies, at least in Europe, could not achieve the old results. Once, reflationary fiscal and monetary policies had produced big increases in employment and income and only a small rise in inflation; now, any increase in home demand produced a smaller increase in home output than before. A greater proportion was now diverted (with free trade) into increased imports. That in turn hurt the balance of payments. The fall in the exchange rate which followed, ensured that there would be a large increase in inflation.[35] (*Vide* France after 1981.) It did not go unnoticed that governments following deflationary policies were re-elected (like the British Conservatives in 1983 and the centre/right coalition in Germany in 1986) while those who had tried to reflate were defeated, like the French Socialists in 1986. (The United States was something of an exception, because, as I said above, its situation was exceptional. We shall look at US policies below.)

Population feedback and the rate of saving

It is time to consider how far changes in birth-rates and migration may have contributed to the downswing in the North. Most European countries sharply reduced immigration in the early 1970s (in the British case a little earlier),[36] hoping to reduce the oversupply of labour in general and less-skilled labour in particular; but most immigrants who had already arrived were able to stay, and with their high birth-rate went on adding to the 'underclass' to which most of them, through discrimination or low skills, belonged. While at least the supply of *new* immigrant labour was declining, in Europe, the supply of new female labour, also mostly less-skilled, increased rapidly during the 1970s: new attitudes, and social disintegration, put women under more pressure to work, and the 'baby slump', not by coincidence, gave them more opportunity. The baby slump, together with the previous baby boom, had implications too for the rate of saving, as we saw in the Appendix to Chapter 5. From about the age of 30 to some point in their 60s, people tend to have a high rate of net saving, particularly nowadays, through 'funded' pensions schemes; just how high depends partly on the demands their children are making on them. By the end of the 1970s there was a conjunction of demographic factors tending to raise the savings rate: the proportion of 30- to 65-year-olds in the population of most Northern countries was unusually high, and those of them with dependent children had a rather large proportion of them in the age range of least financial strain, 5 to 15.

THE NORTHERN 'KUZNETS UPSWING' OF THE LATE 1980s

By 1990 the outlook for the North seemed to many rather brighter than at any time since the downswing began. The national incomes of the OECD countries had been growing for several years at a quite respectable rate (Table 11.1 and Figure 11.1); profits were high, real wages increasing and inflation low. Unemployment, while still very high in most countries, was falling, on the whole, and with the 'baby slump' beginning to reach the labour market it would soon be only the quality, not the quantity, of the young labour force which would be worrying.

What had gone right? And was it still fair to talk about a depression or a crisis, let alone a depression-crisis? If there is credit to be given for the 'recovery' in the North, it must go mainly to the United States. As we saw above, the pressures on policy-makers there were unusual. While by the end of the 1970s they were strongly influenced by the New Right, they were reminded in the recession of 1981 that deflation in the US was as unpopular as ever; and they were committed to a large increase in one of the major components of US expenditure, defence. Since at the same time the New Right believed in low taxes on the rich, and there were limits to the scope for squeezing government spending, it was rather difficult to achieve their proclaimed goal, a balanced budget; and failure to do so was not very embarrassing, since Congress and President could each blame the other. The result was a sort of 'military Keynesianism', deficit-led reflation. The Federal Reserve Bank of New York, the US central bank, reacted to the fiscal 'spree' by raising US interest rates; this led to overvaluation of the dollar, which combined with high demand to create a huge trade deficit, benefiting other Northern countries, and allowing the South to avoid the utter bankruptcy which would otherwise have resulted from the high interest on their debts (see Table 11.3).

Pleasant as it was for the rest of the North to have the USA to take on the role of 'locomotive', the twin deficits, on the budget and the balance of payments, were extremely worrying to American policy-makers. In 1984 they passed the Gramm-Rudman Act, which set targets for reducing the fiscal deficit (to zero by 1993) and provided a nearly-watertight mechanism for keeping to them. More urgently, they tackled the overvaluation of the dollar. James Baker, Treasury Secretary from 1985 to 1989, found it possible to get the key central banks to act together to win back from 'the markets' a measure of control over exchange rates and to bring down the dollar, forcing up the yen.

The Baker devaluation had an odd effect. It might have been – and was – expected to have a big effect on the US deficit, and little effect on world demand. But this would imply a corresponding fall, for the Americans' main trading partner, Japan, in the huge trade surplus which had maintained its level of demand. The Japanese government, faced with the danger of a severe recession, showed itself not to be *New* Right at all, but Old: at the head of a still-integrated economy it was under pressure to maintain demand for home industry, never mind how, and it resorted to standard Keynesian methods; meanwhile, Japanese exporters were responding remarkably well to the rise in the yen, and lost much less than expected. At about the same time the British government also made a change of policy: while proclaiming the infallibility of its past policies, it had discreetly dropped its tight control of the money supply. High interest rates remained, but they proved little disincentive to borrowing by consumers in a credit market freed from all restraint and buoyed up by the 'wealth effect' of a boom in house prices. (There was a similar 'explosion' in personal debt, for similar reasons, in the USA. For the results in both countries see Tables 11.2 and 11.3.) The changes in Britain and Japan, and the 'locomotive' effect of the continuing US deficit, balanced the deflationary policies grimly adhered to by Germany and its neighbours.[37] Even the New York Stock Market crash of October

1987 helped, for governments and central banks, fearing a repetition of 1929, relaxed their monetary and fiscal 'stances'; in the event the crash had little effect on demand, which was more than compensated by the 'authorities'' responses. Demography helped too: in most countries the 1960s baby boom was now reflected in an unusually large proportion of 15- to 30-year-olds, who did much to cut their parents' rate of saving, and incurred a great deal of debt on their own account for education and housing.[38]

Crisis? What crisis? The Northerners, their confidence returning, were inclined to forget that they owed their increasing prosperity largely to the misery of the South and East, whose terms of trade, once the oil price came into line with the rest, were at least as bad as they had ever been, and who were forced by their enormous debt burdens to spend even less on imports

Table 11.2 Net household saving as a percentage of disposable household income, 6 major Western countries, 1973–89

Period	USA	Japan	Germany	France	Italy	UK
1973–80	8.1	20.1	13.3	19.1	25.5	11.2
1981–84	6.6	16.8	12.1	16.4	19.9	11.1
1985–89	4.4	15.4	12.3	12.2	14.5	5.8

Source: OECD Economic Outlook, June 1990
Note: Gross household saving in France, Italy and UK.

Table 11.3 Current balances as a percentage of GNP/GDP, 6 major Western countries, 1972–89

Period	USA	Japan	Germany	France	Italy	UK
1972–80	0.0	0.4	0.7	0.1	−0.4	−0.6
1981–84	−0.9	1.4	0.7	−1.0	−1.0	1.5
1985–88	−3.2	3.6	3.8	−0.2	−0.4	−0.8
1989	−2.0	2.0	4.4	−0.4	−1.3	−4.1

Source: OECD Economic Outlook, June 1990
Notes: US, Japan, Germany, percentage of GNP; France, Italy, UK, percentage of GDP.

from the North than their exports earned from it.[39] It was argued in Chapter 7 that this would tend on balance to decrease aggregate demand in the North. So it did, in the late 1970s and early 1980s.[40] However, in the middle and late 1980s the deflationary effect was small, particularly in the UK and USA. Since these countries had unregulated credit markets and housing markets dominated by owner-occupiers, rises in real incomes (at the expense of the South and East) led to higher house prices and contributed to the borrowing spree mentioned above. Low import prices also helped marvellously to reduce Northern inflation,[41] and this in time encouraged even right-wing governments to take a more relaxed view of reflation. And when does a borrowing spree reach its peak? At the top of a Kuznets upswing.

CONCLUSION

If there was still a crisis of the world economy, it was now mostly the South and East which felt it, and its course would be determined largely by their responses to it. We must turn our attention, then, to the South and East. We begin with the Soviet Union, because in its case there is something to add to the explanation in Chapter 7 of the *causes* of the crisis. There as elsewhere revolutionary reformers had degenerated, in Jaček Kuron's words, from Jacobins pursuing their programmes to mandarins protecting their privileges; but in the Soviet Union as nowhere else this process was inhibited by an external factor: competition with the West in general and the United States in particular. There remained, throughout and in spite of the degeneration, a dynamic core within the Soviet bureaucracy which was determined not to be defeated in this competition. During the 1970s, as the microelectronics paradigm began to crystallise in the West, it became clear that a Soviet Union run on existing lines would before long be left hopelessly behind, unable to cope with the new style. The 'dynamic core' opted for whatever reforms were necessary to avoid defeat; led by the head of the KGB, Yuri Andropov, it got its chance on Brezhnev's death in 1983. The reformers were divided as to how far to go, and obstructed by the bureaucracy around and below them, but they had a trump card in argument which silenced all opposition: 'Well then, how do *you* propose we get out of this mess?' Even silenced, their opponents within the bureaucracy could still be beaten only by going outside it, appealing to the 'intelligentsia' and the working class. The reformers therefore embarked, under Gorbachev, on far-reaching political and cultural changes which put at risk, ultimately, not only the privileges of the bureaucratic elite, but even the power of the Communist Party.

The upheaval taking place in the Soviet Union, and its erstwhile 'empire' in Eastern Europe, is worthy of a depression crisis. We can be confident that it will result, appropriately, in far-reaching reintegration, as ossified dictatorial bureaucracies are replaced by institutions which are responsible and responsive to *someone*, whether voters, workers or consumers. (The increase in inequality of income due to market relationships may or may not be outweighed by the loss of economic privileges by the *nomenklatura*; that matters little compared to the levelling of *power*.) In addition, the opening to Western trade and technology, though not without long-term dangers, will stimulate growth. But it will be at least five years, perhaps ten, before any real upturn becomes apparent.

The crisis in most of the South is, in economic terms, as serious as in Eastern Europe – I have described and analysed it in Chapter 7. Yet it would be premature to predict any revolutionary upheaval in the South in general or any large Southern country in particular. Those in power are supported by ties within their countries, and between them and the North, which have not broken: they will not be easily overthrown. Nor is it, for the time being, easy to envisage those in power choosing any radical change of economic strategy such as took place in the 1930s without any real upheaval in countries like Brazil. The terms of trade with the North are now, no doubt, dreadfully unfavourable, but a switch to import-substituting industrialisation as in the 1930s is impracticable for any individual country; what is practicable, the South-South option – in other words collective import-substitution, buying from one another rather than the North[42] – would require political cohesion among Southern countries of which there is as yet no sign at all. Likewise, although there is little hope of the South ever repaying more than a fraction of its huge debts, there need be little fear of sudden, wholesale default – which could lead to the disruption of world trade and finance – because unless the central and commercial banks of the West behave with extreme crudity, no one Southern country could expect to gain from default on its own; and collective default, again, would require political cohesion.[43]

If there is little change taking place, or imminent, in Southern power structures or economic strategies, there can be little prospect of improvement in the South's terms of trade. Even if, with rock-bottom prices, its supply of primary products and low-technology manufactures turns down, Northern demand for these Southern exports may fall at least in proportion. The microelectronics paradigm has a tendency to economise on energy and materials, even at low prices, and the demand for some minerals is likely to suffer also from cuts in armament production. Even the demand for labour-intensive manufactures may increase more slowly than in the recent past, for the North is mastering the problems of mechanising these processes to the point where it pays to keep them at home as part of a Just In Time network (a tightly-coordinated system of supply which makes stockholding unnecessary but requires suppliers to be within about 100 kms).[44] Moreover the 'opening up' of Eastern Europe offers a new source of low-wage competition with close and privileged links with Western Europe.

The stage was then set, by 1990, for the final terrible act of the depression crisis. This time, as in 1929, the impulse came from the core of the world economy. (Not that the South was prosperous, of course, but its weakness was not new, nor was the deflationary effect of its lack of purchasing power. Likewise, the collapse of the Eastern European economies had no obvious depressing effect on the rest of the world.) A large part of the deflationary dynamic in the North can be summed up as a Kuznets downswing: that is, the reaction to a period of some 8–10 years of strong growth which has overreached itself through over-borrowing, over-building and over-consumption based on a speculative bidding-up of land and other asset values.[45] Such was most to be expected in the three major economies which had been most reckless in financial deregulation during the 1980s: the US, the UK, and Japan. The first two, burdened by external deficits as well as internal debts, turned first, in 1989/90; the Japanese powerhouse roared on another year, to ludicrous heights of assets overvaluation. Then it turned too, beginning a financial implosion reminiscent of Wall Street after 1929. Meanwhile Germany had avoided the excesses of the Kuznets upswing, with France and other neighbours, by deregulation. Now its reunification delayed the downswing, by suddenly pumping the savings of the East into demand in the West. The effect of this however was to push up interest rates. This had a depressing effect throughout Europe, and as the East German spree faded out in 1992 it ensured that the recession would be severe.

At last the doomsday scenario had arrived – a Slump to be compared with that of the 1930s. The key elements were the same in the early 1990s as in the early 1930s: in the North a new technological style with great potential, stood largely balked by an obsolete socio-institutional framework; the one major Northern country whose fundamental institutions were suited to the new style, which had thus become a dynamic economic power on which the rest of the world had relied for credits, had fallen into utter disarray financially, and consequent deep recession.[46] The rest of the world was desperately vulnerable to Northern slump: East and Central Europe (starting this time at the Oder rather than the Rhine) was politically and economically shattered; most of the South was racked by debt and rock-bottom export prices.

In some respects the prospects were less depressing in the early 1990s than sixty years earlier. The world was not on its way into the second phase of a global war, although there were serious military dangers in some Eastern and Southern countries, including, alarmingly, the ex-Soviet Union. On the contrary, the Pax Americana inaugurated in 1945 was not yet over, and its institutions worked after a fashion: that, and the influence of multinational companies, made a 1930s-style outbreak of protectionism unlikely, in spite of the difficulties over the GATT talks. Something had certainly been learned from the experience of the last Slump: the teaching of Keynes, that at such times large budget deficits were inevitable and indeed helpful, had been remembered, after a brief lurch into pre-Keynesian rhetoric in the 1980s.

Just as most generals would be fully competent to refight the last war, most politicians and central bankers are probably capable of coping with the last Slump. The problem is that this one is different. With public sector debts and deficits already alarmingly high, simple Keynesian reflation presents new dangers. To reflate without increasing public sector deficits is harder; it is necessary to remember another insight of Keynes, which most are determined to forget – that the poor spend more out of extra income than the rich: so one should take from the rich and give to the poor. There is one more novelty in this slump, a more dramatic one which shall be discussed only in the final chapter.

Chapter 12

The way to the next upswing

The end of all our journeying
Will be to arrive where we started
And know the place for the first time.
(T. S. Eliot, *Little Gidding*)

RETROSPECT: A RÉSUMÉ OF THE HISTORICAL ACCOUNT

I have deployed five main explanatory factors in explaining the ups and downs of the world economy over the last two centuries:

1 The succession of new technological styles, and the cycle of 'mismatch', crisis and 'rematch' (linked to fluctuations in economic and political integration) to which they tend to lead;
2 Population feedback: the effect of economic growth and technological change on the growth and movement of population, and the effects of these on economic growth;
3 Monetary feedback: the effect of economic growth and technological change on real interest rates, and of real interest rates on growth;
4 Inequality feedback: the relationship between economic growth and technological change, on the one hand, and internal and international inequality, on the other;
5 The 'long cycle' in international relations, with the rise and decline of 'world powers' and the 'global wars' which end with the appearance of a new world power.

I have also pointed, on occasion, to the effects of peculiarities of particular technological styles.

Since the economic, social and political structures of individual countries, and the world in general, have been changing rather rapidly during the last 200 years, I did not attempt to put forward *one* model of the dynamics of the world economy, but rather to show how its dynamics had *evolved*, and to show how this could account for changes in the way growth rates, prices, etc. have fluctuated. The main changes in dynamics involved:

(a) The evolution of the feedback processes. There was a great increase in the importance of inequality feedback ('pro-cyclical'), a changing direction of population feedback (first weakly, then strongly 'counter-cyclical' and later 'pro-cyclical') and an increasing lag in monetary feedback, which was at first only briefly pro-cyclical, early in each upswing and downswing, and later had this effect for longer periods;

(b) Irregular changes in the effects of new styles – for example, the water style showed unique geographical selectivity.

(c) The effect of the 'long cycle' and its irregularities. Its length meant that the second half of the nineteenth century – and we may expect, the second half of the twentieth! – had no global war. Its irregularities meant that the global war at the beginning of our period was particularly long and ended with a particularly conservative settlement; and that the last global war had two widely-spaced 'acts'.

Throughout, wars, revolutions and other crises were given their due as explanatory factors, but were brought 'inside' the explanation by linking them with the 'long cycle' on the one hand, and mismatch and disintegration on the other.

Let me recall, then, how I accounted for the most striking changes in economic rhythms.

We can begin at the beginning with the first style, and its failure (so far as we can tell from the statistics) to induce a long wave in economic growth. It certainly seems to have induced a (mixed) crisis, in the shape of the French Revolution and the subsequent wars and upheavals, but the whole affair was exceptionally long drawn out, so that diffusion went ahead unhindered in Britain, and in the USA, while it was largely blocked on the continent of Europe. The length of the crisis was explained by its involving a 'global war', and worse, one where the 'retiring' world power, Britain, was to emerge as the new world power, and thus had to confront its 'continental challenger' France without the help of a vigorous ally such as it had in the next global war. The re-emergence of Britain from 'retirement' also meant that the ultimate resolution of the crisis, in the peace settlement of 1815, was conservative, even reactionary. The peace settlement was indeed peculiarly unfortunate, in view of the geographical 'choosiness' of the water style – it deprived France, the Continental country which should have led in the diffusion of the style, of just those territories best adapted for it, and handed over much of them to another state, Prussia, which was not yet ready to make good use of them.

The second, 'steam transport' style also provoked a 'mixed' crisis on the continent of Europe, in the late 1840s, having already diffused there to some extent. This crisis, involving no global war, was resolved quite quickly, and that opened the way for an international boom – assisted by low interest rates (monetary feedback) and an upsurge of migration which had causes in common with the crisis. At this point two counter-cyclical processes begin to play a role:

1 Population feedback, which has a strongly counter-cyclical character from the 1840s to the end of the century: the boom in Europe led to a sharp cutback in emigration, and this helped to undermine the boom overseas, particularly in the USA.
2 Monetary feedback, which swung round because of the rapid inflation of the early 1850s. This was largely due to the expansion, but certainly exacerbated by the Crimean War, itself a consequence of the mixed crisis of the late 1840s. The crisis had worked to the advantage of the leading reactionary power, Russia; and three of the the main progressive powers, Britain, France and Sardinia-Piedmont, combined to 'put Russia in its place'.

We have also, from this point, to take account of the powerful Kuznets cycle in the United States, some nineteen years in length and apparently regulated by climatic fluctuations. This led to the American crash of 1857 which had repercussions in Europe.

In the 1860s another counter-cyclical factor makes its appearance: the crisis of the upswing. There was no *world* crisis of the upswing because there was no world 'Kondratiev' upswing; but two major countries did have an upswing of appropriate length and strength. The first was the United States, in which the steam transport style diffused rapidly throughout the 1840s and 1850s. This led to the tipping of the delicate balance between free and slave states decisively in favour of the free, and thus to the outbreak of the Civil War in 1861. Thus scarcely had the world boom resumed, when it was brought to a halt again. Prussia too experienced a great boom after 1849, which by the early 1860s threatened likewise to tip the balance against the reactionary element, in this case the Junkers; they saved themselves by three successful wars, culminating in that against France in 1870–1, which being short did much less economic damage but had important long term consequences.

Thus a period of some ten years which would otherwise have formed the middle of a 'long upswing' was condemned to rather slow growth by *fast negative* population and monetary feedback, and by some 'crises of the upswing' rather before their time. The boom resumed in the mid-1860s but was brought to a halt again after 1873 by a Kuznets downswing exacerbated by more negative population feedback, high interest rates – monetary feedback again – and the (mostly international) imbalances produced by the arrival of the new style, no.3. Chance factors – climate and crop pests – were also deflationary in Europe in the late 1870s and the 1880s.

Just as we had to explain the lack of a long upswing after 1850, so we had to account for the fact that the 'great depression' of 1873–96 has now been shown to be no such thing. At this point population feedback is crucial: the peace and prosperity of the 1850s led, some twenty years later, to the arrival of an unusually large 'cohort' of young adults on both sides of the Atlantic. This gave a particular stimulus to economic growth because many of the European contingent, 'pushed' by the downswing in Europe, went, in an upsurge of migration, to the Americas, where they could be most productive. (This largely accounts for the fast growth of the 1880s in the USA.) Monetary feedback was also, once again, playing a counter-cyclical role from the 1880s onwards. We have further to take account of (and explain) the absence of any really disruptive crisis in the 1873–96 period. The impact of the steel and electricity style might have been expected, in various ways, to lead to economic and political mismatches, to the point of causing another mixed crisis. That no such crisis erupted is due largely to the effect of the preceding crises of the upswing and their outcomes: the 'progressive' side won in the United States; the losers in the European wars (notably Austria-Hungary and France) were driven by defeat into reform, and the winners (Prussia and Piedmont) were led to reform by the reunification of their countries. (We might also mention the (slow) reforms in Russia due to defeat in the Crimean War, which were also bearing fruit by the 1880s.) Another important change was due to the diffusion of the steam transport style: bad harvests could no longer lead to the famines which had touched off the mixed crises in 1789 and 1848. As a result the industrial and industrialising countries got through the period without acute crisis, making minor adaptations which eased the diffusion of the new style – but not making the major reforms which were required, in most cases, really to come to terms with it.

At all events the reforms were enough for economic purposes (except in Britain), and with monetary feedback producing low real interest rates they made possible the steady diffusion of the steel and electricity style. As a result there was a modest but distinct acceleration of world growth after about 1896 – the first real long upswing, as it turns out. But what of the fast negative population feedback which might have been expected to help bring that upswing to an early end? That did not materialise because population feedback was beginning to change its character: the main source of emigration was now Southern and Eastern, not North-Western, Europe, and this meant that:

(a) 'Pull' factors were particularly strong, because the difference in wage levels between America and (Southern and Eastern) Europe was so large as to be attractive even when the migrants could find work at home.

(b) 'Push' factors were still at work, in fact, late in the upswing, because it was only at that point that diffusion of the new style began to affect the peripheral regions of Southern and Eastern Europe.

Monetary feedback too was much slower than before to turn counter-cyclical – there was no war of the importance of the Crimean War to accelerate the (gentle) inflation of the period, and there were African miners whose wages could be depressed to keep gold production increasing.

What did, of course, ultimately bring the upswing to an end, was that greatest of all 'crises of the upswing', the First World War. That crisis was explained partly by well-documented political disintegration in Russia, Austria-Hungary and Germany – particularly Germany – and partly by Germany's appearance as continental challenger to Britain in the long cycle. It was shown that it did not lead to reintegration, but rather the contrary, partly because the new or emerging world power was not yet ready to act the part. Its outcome, moreover, combined with the arrival of the Fordist style in the United States to increase international imbalances and inequalities; which brings us to inequality feedback. This was now becoming decidedly pro-cyclical, as was population feedback (the change there was completed by the US legislation of the early 1920s which effectively abolished 'push' factors in the most important stream of migration). With monetary feedback at first pro-cyclical, it becomes easy to understand the severity of the depression after 1929; and that in turn, with political disintegration far advanced, was bound to create a savage depression crisis.

The acuteness of the depression crisis made for a correspondingly complete catharsis: there were far-reaching reforms, which at an international level were largely due to the fact that at the end of a global war a truly new world power was finally prepared to take a corresponding role. By now all the feedback processes were pushing in the same direction: low real interest rates, low inequality, far-reaching reintegration, all launched the post-war upswing, and high birth-rates and migration helped to prolong it. The extent of the political and social reintegration with which the upswing began helped to delay the crisis of the upswing (so did the late arrival of the style no. 5, explained in Chapter 2) and to make it relatively mild; of course there was at this point no question of a global war. As a result, instead of interrupting the upswing, the crisis inaugurated the downswing, to which all the feedback processes contributed – particularly inequality within the South and between it and the North.

THE OUTLOOK

> No man is an island, entire of itself... Any man's death diminishes me, because I am involved in mankind. And therefore never send to know for whom the bell tolls. It tolls for thee.
>
> (John Donne, *Devotions upon Emergent Occasions*, Meditation XVII)

The ecological crisis and the North–South relationship

I promised at the end of the last chapter to discuss a novel feature of this Slump which had not entered the analysis before. In a general sense it is as certain now as it was in the 1930s that the depression crisis must get worse before it is resolved, for (now as then) we have, nationally and internationally, very high inequality and very low integration. 'When the rich get too rich, and the poor, too poor, something happens'. But what? The wheel turns, but it also moves on, so that when we return to its lowest point, it is not the same nadir as last time. War this time is not to be expected (nor is it worth discussing the consequences if we were to slip into one). However, high inequality and low integration have led to the accentuation of a very different crisis, against which we shall have to struggle for the rest of the century and beyond: the crisis of the world's ecology, of man's relationship with nature.

It may seem unreasonable to bring into the framework of our model a crisis which has been brewing for many decades now: for example, the level of carbon dioxide in the atmosphere, which is (at present) the main cause of the 'greenhouse effect', has been rising at an accelerating rate since the beginning of the Industrial Revolution, and has causes (the burning of fossil fuels, and the clearing of forests) which cannot simply be ascribed to low integration and high inequality! Nor can the other alarming trends – the spread of deserts, soil erosion,[1] falling water tables, and the mounting pressure of population on the good land that remains – be explained purely in such terms. Nonetheless, inequality and disintegration have done much to accelerate these trends. Take Brazil, for example, a large country currently estimated to be destroying its huge Amazonian rainforest at the rate of 4 per cent per annum, and thereby contributing (among other horrors) largely to the greenhouse effect. Brazil has long had a highly unequal structure of power and distribution of income, which accounts partly for its very rapid rate of population growth and entirely for its failure to carry out a land reform.[2] While millions of hectares lie uncultivated, or undercultivated, on the great estates, the landless are forced to take the only land unguarded: the rainforest. Alongside them – often robbing them at gunpoint of the land they have cleared – are ranchers, eager to profit from the country's, and the world's, taste for lean beef. The government in Brasilia has presided limply over this Faustian orgy, political disintegration personified. The countries of the West – Brazil's main creditors, customers and suppliers, and as such with enormous potential influence over its policies – have stood by, concerned first and foremost to avoid default by Brazil on its huge debts and a leftward shift in its political complexion.[3] The case of China is less typical and much less well known but even more important, given the country's size. A Stalinist dictatorship has through four decades of political twists and turns pursued a policy of rapid industrialisation. The decision-takers at the top were free of any control from below; in turn they created a system in which industrial managers treated energy as virtually free and pollution as harmless, and in which peasants had no interest in the future of the land they tilled but did not own. The result was a movement towards ecological disaster comparable with that of Brazil.[4] The influence of the West on China is less than on Brazil or most other Southern countries, but since the 'opening up' in the late 1970s it has been considerable; it is not being used to try to change internal policies because of China's position in international power politics.[5]

What is involved here is not only internal but international inequality and disintegration: the South's desperate position in its debt and terms of trade *vis-à-vis* the North drives it to forget its long-term interests, and the world has not yet evolved a set of international institutions and relationships which reflect and address the ecological interactions between countries.

Let us look in more detail at the immediate, and ultimate, causes of the ecological crisis. Everywhere in the South population growth has something to do with it; and everywhere in the South (as we saw in Chapter 5) fast population growth is due to a movement towards Northern levels of public health and nutrition, without the North's mass education, comparatively low inequality, and relatively high status of (young) women. (Where the latter has been achieved, as in Taiwan, population growth has virtually stopped.) What was needed were reforms more or less in the manner of Taiwan; but in the absence of such reforms, the immediate goal of feeding the extra billions was achieved in part by clearing forests for cultivation, in part by the 'Green Revolution's' intensification of agriculture. The Green Revolution consisted of the introduction of new types of grain (etc.) which gave high yields when liberally supplied with fertiliser and water (and pesticides).[6] Not only did it contribute to inequality by favouring the large farmers who had good access to these inputs; there was also a price to be paid for their use. Where the water required was supplied from wells (as in most of India and Central China) the water table has been dropping alarmingly; where there was an adequate supply of river water (as in Iraq) there is often increasing salination. Thus while the new land, won from the forests, is usually naturally unsuitable for prolonged agriculture or pasture, the old land is threatened with becoming unsuitable too; and it is also increasingly at risk from drought and flood due to the destruction of the forests. That is not all. It is now becoming known that, besides carbon dioxide, there are other 'greenhouse gases' whose build-up is currently contibuting as much to the warming process: oxides of nitrogen (NOx), methane, chlorofluorocarbons (CFCs), and ozone near ground level. (CFCs cause the depletion of ozone in the stratosphere, and NOx contribute for good measure to smog and acid rain.) The major source of NOx, besides car exhausts, is nitrates in the soil, mainly from artificial fertilisers; methane comes from the digestions of cattle and sheep, and from paddy fields, as well as from oil and gas well leaks.[7] Thus the intensification of farming, and its extension, particularly through stock-rearing and rice-growing, are contributing to the greenhouse effect not only through carbon dioxide from forest clearance, but also through methane and NOx. Meanwhile the desperate attempt to industrialise the South, in order to provide foreign exchange, and jobs for the surplus rural population, produces all the 'greenhouse gases' in large quantities. It might be reassuring to know that these gases (except for carbon dioxide) are naturally broken down, in the atmosphere, by the action of hydroxyl ions; however, these hydroxyl ions are themselves being destroyed, increasingly, by the rising levels of carbon monoxide, produced by vehicle engines and incomplete combustion of all kinds. Here again, the South is making an increasing contribution to the problem.[8]

No man is an island, and no country either. The misery of the South, as I have tried to show earlier in this book, owes much to the nature of its links with the North, and it is currently contributing something, through the terms of trade, to the North's affluence. Yet we now see that the North is soon likely to pay dearly – the 1988 drought in the US Midwest was a first hint – for the state of the South.[9] (It is already paying in another way, through drugs: in Latin America the export of cocaine, and in South Asia that of heroin, offer earnings that legal exports cannot, fostered by corrupt dictatorships which enjoy Northern support because they are reliably anti-communist, like that of Noriega until recently, and Zia ul Haq until his death. Likewise, the domestic equivalent of the South, the Northern underclass, takes its revenge through drugs and crime.) As the ecological crisis worsens, and clearly threatens – or already damages – Northern interests, we can look forward to a transformation of Northern attitudes to the South – and of course to a change in the North's attitudes to its own ecological actions. These two changes, as we shall see, can be expected to interact.

What is to be done, then, to protect us from the Four Horsemen of the Apocalypse now riding across the South and threatening the North? We can state some of the changes needed in physical terms, and then consider what social and technological reforms are required to bring the physical changes about. The greenhouse warming, and ozone depletion, must be drastically slowed down. This requires (among other things):

(a) a reduction in fossil fuel consumption and in loss of forest cover;
(b) a check to the extension of cultivation, particularly for stock-rearing and rice-growing;
(c) a turn away from nitrogen-based fertilisers;
(d) a clean-up of combustion processes in general, including vehicle emissions; and
(e) a drastic reduction in the use of CFCs (mainly because of their threat to the ozone layer, but also because they contribute to global warming).

(a), (b) and (c) seem the most difficult to bring about, and none the easier when we look at them together: if we set our faces against the destruction of the forests and the extension of cultivation, how can we also (to curb NOx) reduce the use of nitrate fertilisers, currently a vital ingredient of the intensification of cultivation? Moreover, the best-known alternative to fossil fuels is nuclear power. This is already unpopular in the North on grounds of cost and danger, and deservedly so: it would be hard, then, to accept nuclear energy as an alternative to fossil fuels in the North. But an alternative to fossil fuels is also sorely needed in the South, where most of the new growth in energy consumption is taking place. Are we then to see the South paying enormous sums of foreign exchange to the North in order to cover itself with a network of nuclear power stations which will provide large quantities of plutonium, either to be extracted for use in nuclear weapons, or to remain, waiting only for a conventional war to be vented into the atmosphere by a few well-aimed bombs?[10] Such a prospect almost makes one soften towards drought, hurricanes and melting ice-caps.

Yet, surprisingly, there is nothing impossible about these measures of protection, once the political will is there. The North, like its Southern imitators, is extraordinarily wasteful of energy, and could cut its use of it by half or more without any really painful effects on cherished lifestyles, by using existing technology – much of it the outcome of the microelectronics revolution which has greatly reduced the cost of measurement and control apparatus.[11] (One of the economies will involve a change of emphasis in the transport systems, to be discussed later in this chapter.) What is more, it is just beginning to develop, as sources of electricity, the virtually limitless power of the wind, waves, and sun. Enough has been done in this direction to show that, with an investment on the same scale as that in nuclear energy, wind, wave and solar power can be made tolerably cheap, if not (perhaps) as cheap as 'fossil' electricity at current prices; and wind and solar power are both particularly suitable for the small-scale generation needed in the South.[12]

There are good prospects, too, as we shall see below, for a 'technological' solution to the problem of soil fertility without nitrate fertilisers; and such solutions to the problem of NOx through combustion have already been found.[13] The most intractable problem is that of protecting the forests. Here technology is secondary: it is social and political reform which must come first. As the comparison of Taiwan and Brazil shows, the first essential is thoroughgoing land reform, backed by programmes for mass education and rural development. After that, birth control becomes feasible. The forests can be protected once people are no longer being driven from existing rural settlements by overpopulation and landlessness.

These suggestions must seem absurdly naïve. Almost all Southern governments neglect the rural population in general, and the rural poor in particular: will they now change their policies and priorities utterly? Not willingly, to be sure. But as long as they continue as at present, we march on towards ecological disaster: Northern self-restraint alone will not be enough. Once Northern governments, informed themselves and facing an informed public opinion, have taken the difficult decision to turn their own economies towards 'sustainability' they will have gained the right to urge their Southern counterparts to act in the interests of the planet. As I pointed out above, countries which are at once the South's main creditors, customers and suppliers, can exert almost irresistible pressure; on the other hand, the recipients of that pressure represent interests in Southern society which have everything to lose from the necessary reforms. Still, all that obstinate Southern governments will have to offer their peoples will be more of the misery they have endured in the last decade, plus the effects of 'eco-disaster' – drought, flood and hurricane – and of whatever sanctions the North imposes. It is, I predict, at this point that the political log-jam in the South will be broken, and that in their despair Southern societies will begin to drag themselves towards what Robert Riddell (1981) calls 'ecodevelopment', emphasising small-scale industry using labour-intensive technology and closely linked with local agriculture. If they have as yet done little in this direction, it is because ecodevelopment is not attractive to powerful social groups, as the Bolshevik 'solution' once was to the intelligentsia and the industrial working class in Russia and elsewhere. (That 'solution', of central-ised state power in the economy and elsewhere, is part of the disease, as in China, not part of the cure.) Its triumph will take time – time for the groups which will gain most by it (peasants and small entrepreneurs) to organise, time for some in other groups to realise that there is no other way out of the crisis, time for the necessary technology to be further developed and begin to diffuse.

It is possible that a breakthrough may be made before long in Latin America, where the Catholic Church's *base communities* and the liberation theology which inspire them, offer the right organisational and cultural milieu for appropriate technology – their inspiration coming from a provincial carpenter whose recorded opinions suggest that he would have approved. (There is no reason why traditionalists should object to the church taking a hand in the diffusion of new technology, since that was one of the main roles of the monastic orders in the West between the fifth and thirteenth centuries!). The Latin American countries have, moreover, a large enough community of scientists and technologists to make rapid progress in appropriate technology once they are persuaded to devote themselves to it – not that persuasion will be easy.[14] Likewise China may soon be ripe for change: oriental Stalinism may not last long after the fall of its mentors, and its own disgrace; its successors will have a tradition of appropriate technology to draw on.

Paradoxically, although they will be turning away from so-called 'modern' industry using Northern technology, the Southern 'ecodevelopers' will depend crucially on technological help from the North. Only the North can develop, soon enough, machinery like that required for solar power; groups like Intermediate Technology in Britain will be invaluable in developing labour-intensive techniques; but the most important technological help will be in the most basic agricultural area, seeds. The new biotechnology paradigm – drawing heavily on genetic engineering – can, and must, for example, soon produce new strains of key food species which are pest-resistant, not too thirsty, and with the legumes' capacity to play host to nitrogen-fixing bacteria. Salt-resistant strains are also urgently required. Much of the necessary research is under way already. When such new strains are available they will much increase food production per hectare, reduce NOx emissions – and cut the market for pesticides and fertilisers.[15]

The outlook for the North

The North will be shaken both by the ecological crisis and by the South's reaction to it. Although the net consequences of the greenhouse effect are hard to predict, there will probably be a loss of Northern food production through drought in the North American grain belt and the Ukraine; there will also be increasing damage to crops and buildings from hurricanes, typhoons, etc.[16] Huge expenses will have to be incurred to protect the low-lying parts of the North from the rising sea, and water from salination. These are losses from the greenhouse effect as it happens; but in addition, if the world is to be saved from utter disaster, the North will have to spend further enormous sums in order at least to slow the warming (and ozone depletion) down: on research and development, and on investment in new energy, transport, and agricultural systems, on housing and reforestation. There are expensive implications for virtually every aspect of production and consumption, in the short run, although in the long run we will be very much better off for the change. (The damage done and the expense of checking it would be much less if drastic action were taken at once; but of course, as in the 1930s, those in power are trying to haggle with history, and we shall all end up paying more for less.)

The North will also lose greatly from its new relationship with the South (and East). Not only sticks, but carrots will be required to bring about the necessary changes in Southern and Eastern policies: the writing off of debts, certainly, if the South does not default first; the supply, gratis or very cheap, of equipment for pollution control, and renewable energy systems; large-scale aid for the development of small-scale technology and 'eco-friendly' agriculture. The terms of trade will also deteriorate – not for minerals or low-technology manufactures, for the reasons already given, but for tropical agricultural products, because the South will need virtually all its land for forest or to feed itself; tropical timber, in the same way, will become scarce and dear.

The economic and political effects of these changes are likely to be far-reaching. Doctrinaire conservative governments will look extremely odd, clothed in green, and be thoroughly confused by the extent to which they have to intervene in the activities of their corporate supporters. They will also find it impossible to deliver rising living standards to their electorates without the large 'peace dividend' which would come from wholesale disarmament: that too would cause much doctrinal confusion and corporate distress. That is bad news for the doctrinaire Right; what is good news for most of us is that there are already the first signs of a move towards a new social consensus in favour of egalitarian reform. For two things are becoming clear in virtually every Northern country. First, the baby Slump is already reducing the flow of young people on to the labour market, and the number of old people off the labour market is rapidly increasing – with a flood of 'baby-boomer' retirements to start around 2010: so in the long run it is labour shortage, not surplus, we have to fear. Now a crude shortage could be filled by immigration; but – the second point – for the requirements of new technology, and for success in international competition, it is highly skilled and versatile labour that is needed, and is already in short supply. No country can afford to let a large proportion of its children grow up unfit for skilled jobs because of poverty or social disintegration; nor can it afford to leave millions of adults to rot, unskilled, ill-prepared to adapt to changing demands, and demoralised. Businessmen in many industries are now having to look increasingly hard for skilled manpower, and they are already beginning to put pressure on governments to improve not just the training but the general educational level of their recruits: it will not be long before they begin to realise that this cannot be done without social reform. Let me now set out a 'package' of reforms such as might form the basis of a new social consensus such as last developed in the 1940s, and would make possible the launching of a new upswing in the North, as the world economy begins to struggle out of its ecological crisis.

REFORMS FOR THE NORTH IN THE 1990s

The reforms must have the following objectives:

(a) To restore full employment;
(b) To reduce inequality of income and wealth;
(c) To help restore ecological balance;
(d) To increase economic and social integration;
(e) To release the potential of the microelectronics and biotechnology 'style'.

These objectives turn out to be interconnected to a large extent – two or more of them promoted by one policy measure, or one of them, when achieved, promoting the achievement of another; but it will still be helpful to present the package according to the *primary* aims of the measure described.

Restoring full employment

My first remedy is simple and (to my mind) obvious: give the unemployed work, or training, or (better still) work *and* training. It is wasteful and demoralising for millions of people who could do work of some kind to be paid to do nothing. The idea that the recipients of welfare benefits should be expected to work in return is hard to criticise in principle, but it is easy to criticise many of the schemes which have been implemented. In some, the work required has been degrading and/or the training negligible, in others, 'workfarers' have been used to provide cheap labour competing with those in normal employment. But both dangers can be avoided – and have been, in Sweden and Massachusetts, for example.[17] There is of course no shortage of jobs which urgently need doing.[18] Given the shortage of skills, however, it is probably best to put at least as much emphasis on training as on 'substitute' employment: the experience in Sweden and Massachusetts is that if enough is spent on retraining, the jobs required will usually be available.

The training or retraining of the unemployed is merely an element of the massive effort required in education, which will in future have to be concentrated increasingly on adults, and linked to retraining and the 'upgrading' of skills: the emphasis will have to be on education for adaptability, since any specific skill may soon become obsolete. In economic terms, this amounts to the accumulation of human capital, which because it is *complementary* to most private investment, will encourage it. There are other more tangible complementary investments which governments should undertake. Ian Mackintosh has proposed the construction of a Eurogrid, a Europe-wide, broad-band communications network, based on optical fibres, which will stimulate a huge increase in demand for information services and for the equipment necessary to satisfy that demand.[19]

Another way of stimulating private investment is to make it more costly for individuals and firms *not* to invest in certain ways. Tighter laws on pollution (or taxes – see below) would increase investment in pollution control equipment. Tight regulations on energy saving, particularly in private houses, would have a big effect.[20] The simplest and most general measure, however, is 'cheap money' – low interest rates such as prevailed in the 1940s, at the beginning of the last upswing. As well as stimulating capital spending in general, this should reduce the 'short termism' which is inhibiting corporate spending on training and new product development, particularly in the United States and Britain. To the extent that the State needs to borrow for reflation, 'cheap money' will ease the burden upon it. There is a snag, however: low interest rates will tend to increase two other categories of spending which are not so obviously desirable: personal consumption, and speculative hoarding of assets, particularly land. I shall deal with these problems, and propose solutions, below.

Reducing inequality

We have to be rather wary of relying heavily for redistribution of income and wealth on progressive income taxation. High rates of income taxation probably do not much discourage work in general,[21] but they certainly do distort people's pattern of work and pay towards that which is hidden from, or treated kindly by, the taxman, and that is damaging.[22] Better not to raise income tax progression very much from the new low levels; but to raise thresholds below which tax is not paid, so as to help the poor and reduce the 'poverty trap' effect; and to raise the effective rates paid by the rich by reducing tax allowances like interest relief on house buying. In addition, there is scope, by computerisation and expansion of the tax inspectorate, and far more severe punishment of tax evasion, sharply to increase revenue raised from the affluent. (Those who owe their affluence partly to a subsidised higher education, can be required to pay back that subsidy over the years, through a 'graduate tax' – payable in whatever country they may have chosen to live.) Better than steeply progressive income taxes are taxes on wealth, whether on inheritance (the traditional British preference) or annually by a 'wealth tax' (used in a number of European countries). These too, if intended to raise much revenue, can have a distorting effect. One kind of wealth tax, however, has no distorting effect, because it is practically impossible to avoid whatever you do: the tax on the value of land. Such a tax is already in use in (among other places) Pennsylvania and New South Wales. Land taxation indeed offers much more than a harmless way of raising money. It would be highly redistributive in most countries. It would much reduce the incentive for a corrupt relationship between property developers and those administering planning control (and zoning systems), since it would cut, even perhaps eliminate, the gain to the owner from permission for change of use. And since it would make speculative hoarding of land prohibitively expensive, it would make for much more efficient use of scarce urban land: less dereliction of unused properties, more construction jobs available in the inner cities, less suburban sprawl.[23] A side-effect would be a reduction in house prices and thus in consumer borrowing out of capital gains anticipated by the owners. The mild deflationary effect of this would be amply compensated by the reduction in the debt burden to which it would lead, and it would free governments to reduce interest rates as proposed above.

The land tax sets the example: look for taxes which, besides raising revenue, improve both the distribution of income and the allocation of resources in the economy. Another such tax, or charge, is *electronic road pricing*.[24] The principle involved is that users of anything in short supply should pay, this providing them with an incentive to economise, and thus relieving the shortage. Road space, particularly in urban areas at peak hours, certainly is in short supply, and should be priced accordingly. (Road pricing can also of course reflect the polluting and 'greenhouse' effects of motor vehicles; see below.) Technically it is not difficult, now: equip each vehicle with its own electronic 'number plate' emitting its own 'call sign', and have that emission picked up by sensors at intervals along the roads, connected to a central computer, which would issue road bills every month or every quarter, just like telephone bills. Consider the advantages: the system could easily be used to reduce all kinds of 'autocrime', from speeding (the sensors would register it, every time) to theft (the route and position of stolen vehicles could be quickly discovered) to abductions and robberies (similarly).[25] Charges set at the right level would eliminate congestion and greatly improve the economics of public transport by increasing the demand for it while at the same time (in the case of buses) drastically reducing delays (which would further improve its attractiveness). The huge expense and social and environmental devastation of road building could be eliminated in urban areas and much reduced elsewhere; further large savings could be made in subsidies to public transport; policing costs would fall sharply. Thus although the capital cost of installing the road pricing system would be substantial (and thus a useful source of employment at precisely the right time), once installed, it would allow very large savings in public expenditure.

The leveling effects of road pricing may be less obvious, particularly in countries like the United States where every adult expects to own an automobile. But it is not the *ownership* of a vehicle which is made more expensive, only its use: indeed, with insurance premiums reflecting a sharp fall in accidents and theft, a low-mileage motorist might actually save money. The typical residential pattern in the USA and Britain (not everywhere on the continent of Europe) has the middle class in the outer suburbs commuting to work in downtown offices through inner suburbs and city neighbourhoods inhabited by the poor. The poor have suffered greatly over the last few decades from the deterioration and increasing expense of public transport, and from the disproportionate exposure of their neighbourhoods to the noise, pollution and danger caused by heavy urban traffic. This trend would be reversed, and once people had adapted to the new situation, it would be the more affluent only who chose the expensive luxury of driving long distances at peak hours. Other affluent commuters, who prefer, or may come to prefer, to commute by rail from the suburbs, could be obliged to pay much increased fares at peak hours, without any danger that they would defect to the roads; meanwhile buses, used by the poorer, could be kept cheap. We should not forget, at this point, the contribution to inequality made by the 'malfunctioning' – or 'male-functioning' – of the family. It is a paradox of the spread of private transport (with the consequent decay of public transport and danger of walking and cycling) that it has made children, from say 8 to 18, less mobile, and less independent, than before – their mothers too, in 'one car' families. Road pricing would raise the real living standards of that fragment of the 'nuclear family' which has suffered most from 'nuclear fission' in recent years.

One commonly overlooked source of inequality is the penal system. It is well known among criminologists that the poor – and above all blacks – are more likely to be sent to prison for a given offence than the more privileged.[26] Prison means not only present misery, and family breakdown, but also a shattering blow to future earning power. To raise up the poor, we need not only fewer and shorter prison sentences in general, but less discrimination in sentencing against the poor. To achieve this will certainly require the 're-education' of those (privileged) who run the penal system – partly by the very public monitoring of their decisions, for such discrimination. In addition, it will require the reform of the conventional alternative to prison, the monetary penalty, fines. Minimum and maximum fines are set for each offence, regardless of the affluence of the offender, and this means not only that poor offenders pay proportionately more, but also that (being seen as less likely to pay at all) they are more often sentenced to prison instead. The obvious reform is to set minima and maxima in terms of so many hours' or days' earnings for the offender.[27]

As the state raises taxes in a more egalitarian way, it must make the same shift in the bias of its spending. That will follow from the expansion, and change in direction, of spending on education and training, as already proposed: the beauty of such a policy is that the reduction in inequality is likely to be permanent, since the poor are enabled to earn more for themselves in future. Education is a benefit in kind which can easily be given directly by the State to the child; but for most of their welfare, and future effectiveness socially and economically, children depend on their parents. Another, fairly effective way of reaching children is to give money to their mothers (or to whoever is the 'primary carer'). There is much debate currently over whether to 'target' benefits to the poor, or to make them universal – the more certain, but the more expensive, arrangement. I believe that the universal system should be used, and generously, not only because otherwise many poor families will be missed, but because of the malfunctioning of many more affluent ones: the money simply fails to pass from the father to the mother.[28]

Another necessary aspect of a levelling strategy is to reduce spending in areas where it gives the poor little benefit. I have already shown how road pricing would make large economies possible in road building, and allow public transport to become profitable rather than a drain on the public purse. Grants and tax allowances to corporations (particularly multi-nationals) to attract them to competing countries and regions offer further scope for economy. A process of what might be called disarmament is required in this area, relying on tightly drawn rules, policed by a central authority (the EEC in Europe, the Federal Government in the USA) – and on the success of reflation, which will reduce the pressure to attract firms at almost any cost. The greatest savings, however, should come from (literal) disarmament. As I have already pointed out, the beneficiaries of military spending are now mainly the employees and shareholders of high-technology firms in electronics and aerospace, while the cost is borne in the short term by the taxpayer and in the long term by the civilian economy, starved of highly-skilled manpower. What first made disarmament attractive to Western public opinion, of course, was the arrival of a Soviet government which obviously needed and wanted to reduce the military burden on its economy. However, the case for economies in defence does not require a Gorbachev or Yeltsin in the Kremlin, only the realisation that the purpose of Soviet military strategy, like that of the West, has long been defensive and would remain so even under less friendly leaders.[29] The mutual recognition of this fact, and the availability of exclusively defensive strategies and tactics, opens the way to huge reductions in military spending.[30]

Ecological measures

It is fortunate that our increasing awareness of the dangers of pollution is matched by an increasing capacity to measure pollution as it takes place. This makes it possible, for a wide range of substances, either to impose legal limits on discharges into the air or waterways, or to tax them. Taxes seem distinctly preferable where industrial pollution is concerned: they keep up the pressure for reductions even when the polluter would be below any limit, and they could be net raisers of revenue, while legal limits merely cost money for policing. They should of course include a 'carbon tax' on fossil fuels to reflect contributions to the 'greenhouse effect'. Small-scale polluters – households, motorists – would have to be governed by regulations – as now, but more tightly. Both categories would have to spend more on control measures, and thus increase effective demand. Electronic road pricing, too, would tend to reduce pollution and the greenhouse effect by causing a shift from private transport to walking, cycling and public transport – also by virtually eliminating traffic jams and speeding.

Economic reintegration

Three points of *micro*economic disintegration have been identified. The first was between the State and the rest, both individuals and firms; this can be dealt with by the changes in taxation policy proposed above, to remove (or drastically reduce) distortions in incentives. The second was between shareholders and managers of businesses; the third, between managers and workers. There is one simple and effective way of dealing with both these problems at once: to give workers an important stake in ownership and control. There are various ways for firms to do this, and various ways for government to induce them to – ranging from straightforward compulsion to tax relief. A formal share in ownership is not necessary: the elements which are necessary, or highly desirable, are first, 'local participation' (in decisions immediately affecting the individual worker); second, 'distant participation' (through elected representatives, in the control of the firm); third, a share in profits, in some form. Japanese industry already has the first and the third, West German industry the first to some extent, and the second (through the works council and the supervisory board). No country yet, to my knowledge, has all three; these countries have benefited greatly from their partial solutions. Another, complementary, way to reintegration in industry is reduction in the size of firms. I shall argue below that there is considerable scope to achieve this in the new 'style', and outline the policies required.

I also found two macroeconomic expressions of disintegration. The first is essentially intra-national – inflation – which is due largely to the market power of large firms, and will therefore be much alleviated by the changes in the microeconomy.[31] The second is international – the wild movements of exchange rates, and the difficulty of following an economic policy disapproved of by the 'markets'. As I once expressed it, 'either the market must shrink, or the state must grow':[32] that is, either the freedom of trade and movement of capital must be reduced, or economic policy must be controlled more by supra-national institutions. The latter can be achieved within Europe by giving more power to the European Community *vis-à-vis* its components, but otherwise seems impracticable. As to the former, it seems feasible for states, including the Community, to take more control of capital movements and exchange rates; but to reverse the movement towards free trade seems politically unthinkable. However, the taxes proposed on pollution and congestion will sharply increase the price of transport, and that will tend to cause 'market shrinkage'.

Easing the way for the new 'style'

Any perspective of reform in the North must have the microelectronics paradigm in the middle of it. We have to reorganise our arrangements to make the best of microelectronics, and the drift of the argument so far is that policies which are socially just and ecologically sound will not *inhibit* but *promote* the full development and diffusion of the microelectronics paradigm. That drift will be the stronger when we have looked at the future role of the small firm. Small firms have a levelling tendency because they are unlikely to be able to earn monopoly profits, and because they provide little scope or excuse for a large differential in pay between bottom and top. There are, happily, certain trends at work to help them.

There are, first, two changes in attitude:

1 The decline of deference. There is an increasingly egalitarian climate in social and personal relationships. People increasingly resent and rebel against hierarchies of authority, except to the extent that their 'superiors' have clearly earned their positions on ability for the task in hand, *and* carry their rank very lightly:

2 The insistence on 'self-realisation'. There is less and less interest in making

money and in earning the respect of others, and more and more in 'living as I like', in fulfilling oneself by using one's own abilities and following one's own interests (the Netherlands and Britain lead here, while Japan lags behind).[33]

These trends favour small firms because they are best suited to an atmosphere of participation, a spirit of community, and a satisfyingly varied set of tasks in which individuals can see how their contribution fits into the work of the whole organisation. They are matched by two favourable changes in circumstances:

3 The improvement in communications and computing;
4 The cheapening and increasing flexibility of capital goods.

The changes in attitude, plus the improvement in communications and computing, can be given credit for the rise of 'networking': the development of networks of individuals, within and outside organisational hierarchies, linked together by telecommunications and a certain camaraderie, and having in common some access to electronic systems for information storage and retrieval, and an aversion to 'using the proper channels'. Whatever you want in the way of information – that most vital modern commodity – can be quickly got from a pal in the 'network'. Networking is already strong in the United States[34] and is catching on fast in Western Europe; it will be much encouraged by the optical fibre network proposed above.

A further favourable change still to come will arise from 'ecotaxation'. The sharp rise in transport costs envisaged will encourage firms to cater to relatively small local or regional markets. 'Ecotaxes' in general will discourage the mass production of consumer goods like cars, with a marked shift of expenditure patterns towards services (including repair and maintenance) in which small firms are strong.

In most sectors firms are generally larger than efficient production requires,[35] and the five trends just outlined – four under way, the fifth in prospect – will reduce the 'minimum optimum' scale of production further. The main advantages of large firms, particularly multinationals, are in finance, bargaining power, market dominance and research and development. The first three reflect no benefit to the community at large, and government policy should seek to take them away, or offset them: for example, governments should, as I have said, agree to reduce their competitive armouries of 'incentives' to firms which benefit large firms more than the rest; the moves to worker participation should eliminate their scope for profiting at their workers' expense; and there should be much tighter rules on monopolies and mergers, leading to forced breakup of some large firms. The advantage to research and development, on the other hand is a genuine one, and they deserve to derive advantage from it; but their advantage should be reduced by government support for independent research institutions, and expanded activity by its own R&D organisations.

These changes in circumstances and policies can lead to a challenge to the large multinational, as the dominant type of economic unit, from a new species of organisation: small participative firms, led by technologist-entrepreneurs, with highly flexible workers. Those workers producing goods would still be working in a factory, with the new highly productive and flexible equipment, which many or most would know how to operate *and* maintain *and* repair *and* programme; those producing services of one sort or another (which might be everyone in a 'software' firm) would do much of their work from home. To be able to compete effectively with large firms in areas where production is not very small-scale, a small firm must be very specialised. That means it must buy in, rather than provide itself, almost all the services and components it needs; the natural suppliers of such things are other small firms, which it will be able to reach more easily through optical fibres communications and networking.

Specialisation also means that firms are likely quite frequently to suffer what Kay (1984) calls *catastrophes* – a sudden loss of market for one product which cannot be cushioned by the existence of other lines. A change in the role and regulations of the state is required to ensure that catastrophe is not often lethal. To survive a catastrophe, a specialised firm must be able to make a rapid change of direction – changing its product and probably reducing its work-force, at least for a time; unless the existing work-force is very adaptable indeed there will also have to be considerable turnover of employees. It follows from this that small firms are likely to be handicapped more than large by restrictive rules on redundancy (we may note on the other hand that there is no reason why they should not be subjected to strict rules on minimum wages, and against discrimination by race or gender). Rather than impose on firms responsibility for continuity of employment, the State should take that responsibility itself, with the measures already discussed, for training and 'interim' employment. Paradoxically, greater instability of employment with any one firm might coexist with greater stability of the family and the local community. Now, large firms and state organisations of similar size insist, as a condition of employment or at least of promotion, on willingness to move hundreds, sometimes even thousands of miles, every few years with devastating social and psychological effects. In future, it would be much easier to make a commitment to stay put – one's employer would have only one base and would be unlikely to move, and if by mischance a 'catastrophe' forced it to shrink or mutate to the point where one lost one's job, one would retrain, take interim employment or take a turn with child care, etc., until a suitable job became available in the locality.

It may seem inconsistent to look forward to a much increased role for the small firm, and at the same time to the discharge of some new and very heavy responsibilities by 'the State'. Is not the State the largest organisation of all, and has it not shown itself the natural friend of the larger organisations in the private sector? Perhaps; but that speaks for a shift of responsibilities as far as possible to the lower levels of government. Changes in technology, and 'eco-taxation', particularly of transport, will encourage small size in government as in industry – and so will the greater stability of communities foreseen here, as it encourages participation in local affairs. What stands in the way is not practicality but tradition – to be precise, *two* traditions: the European tradition of centralised government, which the Left has inherited and tried to make redistributive, and the American tradition of non-interventionist government, with very little central redistribution of funds. Political power in the United States is admirably decentralised, but so are its sources of revenue: those communities where there is a particular need to intervene to help the poor, and where there might be the political will, lack the money to do it. Graft European redistribution (on automatic principles that deny the central government any blackmailing power) on to American local democracy, and you have roughly what you need.[36]

CONCLUSION

This chapter has proceeded from retrospect to prospect, and then from prediction to prescription. A move from what *will* be to what *should*, is bound to be an awkward one – in this case the sceptic might say it took the form of a leap from alarmism to wishful thinking. Is it not naïve to imagine that any government – let alone governments in general and together – will enact such a set of radical reforms, many of which run counter to the trends and policies of twenty, fifty, even a hundred years? Yes – *if* the predictions are alarmist. It will take a worse situation than we have at present to produce the rosy outcome here foreseen. Although, as I have argued, there are trends working in favour of agreed reform – trends in Northern demography and some aspects of technology – there are also formidable obstacles. These will only be budged if and when the crisis – now essentially an *eco*-crisis – gets a good deal worse. But until they are budged it will get rapidly worse: that is the basis for grim optimism.

The proposals put forward will fit rather better into the agenda of the Left and Centre than that of the Right, though the latter will approve the insistence on the need for incentives and respect for market forces. But they should not be regarded as either Left or Right, rather as the basis for a new consensus – a consensus which will not be reached without a good deal of conflict on the way. The reforms which ended the last depression crisis were made possible by a degree of unity, in support of levelling measures, among the 'bottom two-thirds', and an understanding between the leaders of this coalition, on the one hand, and bureaucrats and big business, on the other. The reforms which will sooner or later end this depression crisis, will, I believe, have a similar political basis: there will be broad coalitions, in North and South, in support of programmes which promote equality, ecology and market forces at the same time; again this programme will require an understanding between the Left and Centre and business – large firms reluctantly, the new entrepreneurs enthusiastically. The way to the new political consensus – to political 'reintegration' – will vary among countries. In most of the South it will require first the obvious bankruptcy of the old order, the ripening of the technical conditions for ecodevelopment, and pressure from the North: then there will have to be a revolution of some sort before a new order, dominated by peasants and small business, takes over. For the North the path will be easier. In most of Europe, the reforms could be implemented by Left and Centre parties which succeed in bringing their programme up to date. (The same opportunity may exist in Japan, although Japan's economy has less need for reform.) A greater change is required in the United States, since the whole political spectrum there lies further to the Right; on the other hand, three shocks are likely during the next decade which may well produce such a change. The first is what might be called the hangover after the spree of the 1980s, in which the economy has to adjust to its new status as a major international debtor, largely controlled by foreign firms, lagging in many areas of technology, and forced to curb its consumption in order to satisfy its creditors. The second is ecological and less certain: the United States seems the most vulnerable of the major countries of the North to the greenhouse effect: in particular to the likely shift in rainfall patterns, and the increase in frequency, ferocity, and range of hurricanes. The third is by origin demographic: massive immigration, mostly illegal, from Latin America has produced a large and rapidly growing Hispanic minority whose potential voting strength is being further increased by the 'legalisation of the illegals'. The Hispanics are particularly vulnerable to any economic downturn, and if such a downturn coincided with revolution in their countries of origin, they might be radicalised rather suddenly; their new mood might be infectious. A conservative consensus which involves the voluntary abstention from voting of most of the poor, is necessarily rather fragile.

To sum up: we must reverse the conventional wisdom of the 1980s, that 'you must be cruel to be kind'. It never paid, in the long term, to make the poor and weak, poorer and weaker: that could only reduce the good they can contribute, and increase the harm. Great harm they can certainly do, and now more than ever. The rich of the USA have new cause to remember that, as they shrink from the hot tongues of crime and drugs licking out from the inner cities. No man is an island – no affluent suburb either. Policies which tolerate and even encourage great inequality of income and power are particularly wasteful in the face of a new technological style which demands an unprecedented level of education and participation right across the working population – as demonstrated by the success of the country with the highest level of mass education and participation, Japan. To borrow Talleyrand's phrase, it is worse than a crime, it is a mistake for the powerful to allow many millions of their young compatriots to be brought up in conditions of deprivation and hopelessness. It will pay to ensure that all are paid decent wages and have an effective say in the running of their workplaces. But inequality and disintegration are a threat not only within countries, but across the planet: we shall only be able to cope with the ecological crisis which is now almost upon us if we tackle them at that level. We find ourselves in the worst depression-crisis yet, which will force us to the most radical transformation of our institutions: if that goes far enough, it may yield not just an upswing to surpass the last, but an end to the long wave altogether.

Notes

INTRODUCTION

1 Bairoch and Levy-Leboyer, 1981.
2 Banks, 1989.
3 In a pioneering unpublished study of Malawi during the early 1980s, James Howe found precisely that (personal communication).
4 See also Pearce *et al.*, 1989, particularly Chapter 4.
5 In E. H. Phelps Brown, 1972, 'The Underdevelopment of Economics', *Economic Journal*, March, pp. 1–10; address given 8 July 1971.

1 THE LONG WAVE DEBATE

1 See Juglar, 1862.
2 Kuznets, 1930.
3 Indeed after the mid-1950s there was a switch to a new, opposite relationship between the luni-solar tide and rainfall, so that droughts were concentrated in periods when they would previously have been least expected.
4 This would not have happened had those 'luni-solar tides' affected European agriculture as they did American, but it appears they did not.
5 There is, it is true, a climatic 'wave' of some fifty-four years in length; but no one has come anywhere near showing how it could have 'powered' a long wave in economic growth rates.
6 See Mandel, 1980, 1983.
7 Kondratiev, 1925, p. 536 of 1979 reprint.
8 C. Freeman, J. Clark and L. Soete, *Unemployment and Technical Innovation* (London: Francis Pinter, 1982), pp. 64–8.
9 Giovanni Dosi, also at SPRU, developed a similar, and well worked out, concept of new technological *paradigms* (patterns) which shaped the 'normal trajectory' of technical change in whole industrial sectors (Dosi, in Freeman (ed.) 1984).
10 Mandel, 1983, p. 199.
11 See, for example, Aglietta, 1979; Boyer and Mistral, 1978; Lipietz, 1984.
12 Perez, 1983, p. 361.
13 Ibid.
14 Ibid. See also Perez, 1985, for an excellent summary of the theory, a description of the new 'technological style', and a consideration of the implications for developing countries.
15 Kondratiev, 1935 [1979], p. 536.
16 See Modelski, 1987.

17 Immanuel Wallerstein has a similar concept of *hegemony*; see e.g. Wallerstein, 1983.
18 In fact the model does not call for a challenger at so early a stage in the long cycle, and events in the 1980s have suggested that the USSR may not keep even the semblance of such a status for long.
19 For completeness, there is of course the possibility of varying the direction by changing the effect *of growth on factor X*.

2 TECHNOLOGICAL STYLES

1 Quotations from pp. 31–5 of Perez, Chapter 2 in Freeman (ed.), 1986.
2 C. Perez, 'Towards a Comprehensive Theory of Long Waves', paper presented at the IIASA meeting on 'Long Waves, Depression and Innovation', Siena-Florence, 26–9 October 1983.
3 Adam Smith, *Wealth of Nations*, vol. 1, p. 33 of the Campbell and Skinner edition (Oxford: Clarendon Press, 1976). For a comparison of costs of water carriage (by river) with those of carriage by road, see Willan, 1964, pp. 119ff.
4 Reynolds, 1983; Stowers, 1958.
5 As Maddison, 1982, points out, the Dutch had led in the development of windmills and even used them for powering industrial machinery. But this was very much a second-best solution, given the unreliability of wind power. So were tidemills (Reynolds, 1983, p. 123).
6 Rolt, 1969, pp. 2–3.
7 Willan, 1964, pp. 88–95.
8 Ibid., 1964, p. 4.
9 Landes, 1969, pp. 46–7.
10 Reynolds, 1983, pp. 267ff.
11 Walter Vincenti's term, quoted by Reynolds, 1983, p. 232.
12 Rees, 1819, quoted by Reynolds, 1983, p. 282.
13 Reynolds, 1983, p. 309.
14 Reynolds, 1983.
15 H. R. Schubert, 1958, 'Extraction and Production of Iron and Steel', p. 100ff. in Singer, *et al.*, vol. IV. Note that coke was only clearly superior to charcoal once higher-powered bellows had been introduced into blast-furnaces – water-powered in the 1760s, steam-powered in the 1770s (*ibid.*).
16 Schubert, *op. cit.*, pp. 105ff. The key patents were secured in 1783 and 1784.
17 See H. W. Dickinson, 1958, 'The Steam Engine to 1830', Chapter 6. in Singer *et al.*, vol. IV.
18 Musson and Robinson, 1969, Chapter 12.
19 The price of coal in Manchester is said to have halved after the completion of the Bridgewater Canal in 1761. There was a similar fall in price at Birmingham in 1772 for the same reason (Hadfield, 1974, p. 95).
20 Andrew Ure, quoted in Arnold Pacey, 1983, *The Culture of Technology* (Oxford: Blackwell) p. 19. See also Sidney Pollard, 1965, *The Genesis of Modern Management* (London: Edward Arnold).
21 R. G. Wilkinson, 1973, p. 159–60.
22 Ibid.
23 Hadfield, 1974, pp. 171–4.
24 Ayres, 1987, p. 3.
25 On the improvements in sailing ship technology, see C. S. Graham, 1956, 'The Ascendancy of the Sailing Ship', *Economic History Review* (Series 2), 9: 74–88: on the improvements to the steamship, S. C. Gilfillan, 1935, *Inventing the Ship* (Chicago: Follett). The fares are quoted from Thomas, 1973, p. 96.

26 R. W. Fogel, 1964, *Railroads and American Economic Growth*, Baltimore, has questioned the value of the railway to the United States (and by implication to other countries). For a damning criticism of his arguments and methodology, see G. N. von Tunzelmann, 1978, *Steam Power and British Industrialisation to 1860* (Oxford: Clarendon Press) Chapter 3.

27 Reynolds, 1983, pp. 338ff. This followed Poncelet's dramatic improvement of the undershot wheel in 1824.

28 Quoted in Reynolds, 1983, p. 328.

29 Temin, 1964, quoted in Reynolds, 1983, p. 329.

30 Reynolds, 1983, p. 328.

31 Ibid., p. 329.

32 Ibid.

33 For example, 'In Germany it was the southern centres, Bavaria, Wurttemberg and Baden – with their new joint-stock companies and, interestingly enough, their persistent use of water power in conjunction with steam, that took the lead in cotton' (Landes, 1969, p. 213). See also Reynolds, 1983, p. 329.

34 Peter Hall and Paschal Preston, 1988, *The Carrier Wave* (London: Unwin Hyman) pp. 38–42.

35 The priority of the British inventor Bessemer has been disputed in the USA; but if the American Kelly did invent the converter at the same time, as claimed by Ayres, 1987, and others, he certainly did not develop it so successfully.

36 R. F. Tylecote, personal communication.

37 In 1819 steel prices were above £100 per ton; by 1850 Swedish steel prices were down to £50–£60 per ton, and *puddled* steel was (in Germany) about £22 per ton – but the latter, invented in Germany, was unsatisfactory for most uses, and hard to make from British pig-iron (Landes, 1969, pp. 251–2).

38 The best brief account of this transformation of steelmaking is in Landes, 1969, pp. 249–62. I have also drawn on Carr and Taplin, 1962.

39 Carr and Taplin, 1962, p. 50.

40 Landes, 1969, p. 255.

41 Carr and Taplin, 1962, p. 29.

42 Ibid., p. 96.

43 By Robb, in Singer *et al.*, vol. V.

44 Temin, 1964, p. 284.

45 Landes, 1969, p. 277.

46 Reynolds, 1983.

47 Landes, 1969, p. 291.

48 Mitchell, 1978 and 1983.

49 Perez, in Freeman, 1986, p. 47.

50 Cheap steel also played a major part, however, as Christopher Freeman has pointed out, in 'The Third Kondratieff Wave: Age of Steel, Electrification and Imperialism', paper presented to colloquium on 'The Long Waves of the Economic Conjuncture', Brussels, January 1989.

51 Jarvis, 1958.

52 Ibid.

53 The old exception was weapons; the typewriter and the bicycle followed in the second half of the nineteenth century.

54 As in sewing machines (by 1870) and bicycles (1890s), following the lead of small arms (from the 1820s in the USA) (Landes, 1969, p. 308).

55 K. R. Gilbert, 1958, 'Machine Tools', Chapter 14 in Singer *et al.*, vol. IV.

56 In fact the first improved tool steel was produced by Robert Mushet in 1868, in England. This was a manganese steel and self-hardening, cutting out the need for constant sharpening and hardening required with the old carbon steel tools. (The

contribution of the open-hearth steel-makers was to make Mushet steel much cheaper.)

This tool steel made it possible both to increase the speed of operation of machine tools, and to machine the newly introduced manganese steel produced by the Bessemer and Siemens-Martin processes. The major experiments in this field were however carried out in the United States by Frederick W. Taylor, working with Maunsel White of the Bethlehem Steelworks. Taylor experimented both with different methods of using existing tool steels, and with the development of new materials, and over a period of twenty years greatly altered engineering practice in both these directions. Taylor and White replaced the manganese in Mushet steel with chromium, increased the tungsten content, and finally added silicon.

This new alloy allowed the cutting speed of the tools to be increased from under 30 feet per minute to approximately 80–90 feet per minute. Taylor and White concluded their experiments by adding vanadium to the alloy, further increasing the strength of the tools. The result of these improvements was greatly to increase the speed of feed of the cutting tool, unfortunately far beyond the strength of the existing machine tools, which fell to pieces when run at the new speeds. After the introduction of the new high-speed tool steels, as they were called, from 1900 onwards, all machine tools were therefore gradually redesigned to cope with the higher speeds, and thus the greater strength and stability which was required.

(Roderick Floud, 1976, *The British Machine Tool Industry, 1850–1914*, Cambridge: Cambridge University Press, pp. 24–5.)

57 Perez, in Freeman, (ed.) 1986, pp. 38–41.
58 In fact Burton's cracking process, developed in 1913, did a great deal to ensure cheap fuel, since it doubled the gasoline yield per barrel of crude oil (Ayres, 1987, p. 15).
59 Landes, 1969, p. 442.
60 Perez, 1986, *op. cit.* p. 42.
61 Ibid.
62 Reich, 1985.
63 Rothwell, in Freeman (ed.) 1986, and Kaplinsky, 1984.
64 Tables 2.4 and 2.5, 'Cost and capacities of alternative transmission technologies', from Kaplinsky, 1984, pp. 90–1.
65 Kaplinsky (1984).
66 Arnold and Senker, in Sharp (ed.) 1983; Kaplinsky, 1984.
67 Lund *et al.*, 1983, quoted in Kaplinsky, 1984, p. 30, para 2.
68 Kaplinsky, 1984, Chapter 4.
69 Lambert, 1983, quoted in Kaplinsky, 1984, p. 103.
70 Perez, in Freeman, 1986, p. 33.
71 Ibid.
72 Sharp, 1983, p. 163.
73 Sharp, 1983.
74 Chandler, 1977.
75 As Williamson, 1970, has argued.
76 Landes, 1969.
77 Williamson, 1975.
78 Ubbelohde, 1958; Musson and Robinson, 1969.
79 See, for example, Geoffrey Tweedale, 1987, *Sheffield Steel and America: A Century of Commercial and Technological Independence* (Cambridge: Cambridge University Press) on the transmission of steel-making techniques.
80 Landes, 1969, pp. 149–50.

81 Ahlstrom, 1982.
82 Quoted in Ahlstrom, 1982, p. 29.
83 Landes, 1969, p. 151.
84 Carr and Taplin, 1962, p. 31.
85 Landes, 1969, p. 274.
86 'Appear' – at least when Beer wrote, BASF and Hoechst had said little about what they had been doing with those chemists. At all events, their more backward rival Bayer had such labs from 1886 (J. J. Beer, 1958, 'Coal Tar Dye Manufacture and the Origins of the Modern Industrial Research Laboratory', *Isis*, vol. 49, pp. 123–31).
87 See Landes, 1969, p. 275.
88 Reich, 1985.
89 Ibid., p. 19.
90 Ibid., p. 29.
91 Ibid., p. 41.
92 Ibid., pp. 43–5.
93 Landes, *op.cit.*, Chapter 5.
94 On the successes of the Scandinavian countries, Italy, and even Hungary, in the 1870–1914 period, see I. Berend and G. Ranki, 1982.
95 Berend and Ranki, *op.cit.*
96 See Mitchell, 1978, Table 20; and Chapter 8, below.
97 Reich, 1985.
98 Christopher Freeman, 1974, *The Economics of Industrial Innovation* (London: Penguin).
99 Arthur Meidan, 1986, *Handbook of Business Policy* (Bradford: MCB).
100 Christopher Freeman, *op.cit.*
101 See my 'Unionisation in the Long Wave' (Tylecote, 1990) and later chapters.
102 R. Baker, 1976, *New and Improved ... Inventors and Inventions that have changed the Modern World* (London: British Museums Publications).
103 On that reasoning one might have expected it to have waited until after 1815; but there was rather more order in most of Western Europe in 1800–10 than in the previous decade.
104 The impact of global wars – specifically the First and Second World Wars – may well explain Solomou's failure to find a long wave fluctuation in innovations either.

3   INTEGRATION, DISINTEGRATION AND CRISIS

1 In fact, given that prices now are rising, which tends to erode the value of outstanding public debt, while then they were falling, and thus increasing that value, the fiscal stances, in terms of the rate of change of real public sector debt, are much the same.
2 Centre for Incentive Taxation, *Economic Intelligence* no. 7, September 1988.
3 Ernesto Screpanti, 1986, 'Some Demographic and Social Processes and the Problem of Kondratieff Cycle Periodicity', paper presented to the Siena long wave Workshop, December (and included in Goodwin *et al.*, eds, 1989) has usefully surveyed the literature on this issue, some of which argues that a generation is formed or influenced by its environment from birth to young adulthood, while others stress the later period which I propose.
4 Tylecote, 1987.
5 This was noted with something like derision by Japanese observers like Akii Morita of Sony, who pointed out that their own firms used profit-based bonuses

to motivate *workers*, never managers – it might distract them from their relentless pursuit of the long-term success of the firm (*War of the Worlds*, BBC Radio 4, 6 October 1985).

6 Istemi Demirag and Andrew Tylecote, 1990, 'The Influence of Accounting Numbers, Organisational Structure and Culture on Short Term Pressures and Innovation', *University of Sheffield Management School Discussion Paper* no. 90.3.

7 In fact the most likely solution to this problem within Europe is the harmonisation of tax and subsidy rates managed from Brussels. See the final chapter.

8 Another disintegrating development is the degeneration of attitudes. After a new 'social contract' is made between government and governed at the end of a depression crisis, high taxes may be paid almost gladly while the mood of reconciliation lasts. As time passes, the social contract is forgotten and selfishness and resentment become dominant: evasion turns from vice into sport. Such differences in attitudes exist between countries as well as over time and explain how for example Sweden manages with only modest evasion of tax rates which would drive Americans to prodigies of infuriated ingenuity. (I am indebted to John Westergaard for this point.)

9 Barbara Ehrenreich, 1984, *The Hearts of Men* (New York: Doubleday and London: Pluto Press).

10 Maggy Mead-King, 'Unpaid Dues', *Guardian*, 1 March 1988, p. 20.

11 Mead-King, *op.cit.*

12 Arvonne Fraser of the University of Minnesota's Hubert H. Humphrey Institute, quoted in Mead-King, *op.cit.*

13 Mead-King, *op.cit.*

14 Clare Dyer, 'Children "suffer long-term hurt from divorce"', *Guardian*, 14 September 1989. The evidence for Britain is discussed by Mavis Maclean and M. E. J. Wadsworth (1988) 'The Interests of Children after Parental Divorce: a long-term perspective', *International Journal of Law and the Family*, 2: 155–66.

15 Its effects on the next generation of adults are evident: to the ones documented above I would add crime, and drug-taking; perhaps also the rapid spread of AIDS. AIDS appears now to be spreading fastest in those countries, like the USA and Brazil – and those social groups – where the other signs of social deprivation are most evident.

16 One sign of hope, at least, was that women appeared to be more and more conscious of their underprivileged position, being for the first time, almost everywhere, more inclined than men to vote for the left.

4   MONETARY FEEDBACK

1 There was some persistence of trade barriers after the World Wars of this century.

2 Rostow, 1978, p. 124

3 Solomou, 1987, p. 76.

4 Mathias, 1969, p. 221 and Rostow, 1978, p. 123 ff.

5 Mathias, op.cit., p. 455.

6 Solomou, 1987, p. 76, ascribes the rapid price fall of 1848–51 to the 'war-revolution era'. This seems to me quite implausible: apart from the downward trend, the fluctuation in prices in France between 1845 and 1851 is very well explained by bad followed by good harvests – see Rostow, 1978, p. 128; the bad harvests touched off the revolutions.

7 Rostow, 1978, p. 149.

8 Solomou, 1987, p. 75.

9 Mathias, 1969 p. 455.

10 Steel rails not only lasted longer, they allowed higher speeds. Steel ships were admittedly not general at this period – but as we saw in Chapter 2, wrought-iron plates had fallen a long way in price too, by the mid-1870s.

11 Rostow, 1978, pp. 148–9: the US wheat price fell from a peak of 2.945 dollars per bushel in 1866 through 1.787 in 1873 to 1.253 in 1880 (p. 150).

12 Solomou, 1987, p. 83.

13 Lewis, 1978.

14 See Solomou, 1987, Table 6.9.

15 See my 'Unionisation in the Long Wave' (Tylecote, 1990) and W. A. Lewis (1980), 'Rising Prices: 1899–1913 and 1950–1979', *Scandinavian Journal of Economics*, 82, 4, pp. 425–36.

16 See Tylecote, 1981, Chapters 2 and 3.

17 Minsky, 1982a.

18 See Kondratiev, as reprinted in *Review*, Spring 1979, pp. 541–3, and Vilar, 1976. Solomou, 1987, p. 83, cites Kitchin, 1930, as estimating that the world monetary gold stock increased by 3.47 per cent p.a. from 1890–1913 after deductions for industrial use and flows to India, China and Egypt; he finds that the evidence, at least for Britain and America, suggests a faster growth of overall money stock for 1890–1913 than for 1873–90.

19 See Immanuel Wallerstein and William G. Martin, 'Peripheralisation of Southern Africa, II', *Review*, vol. III, Fall 1979, pp. 193–207.

20 Solomou, 1987, p. 82.

21 Ibid.

22 I. Fisher, 1933, 'The Debt-deflation Theory of Great Depressions', *Econometrica* 1, pp. 337–57.

23 See Pamuk, 1982, on the effect on the Ottoman Empire.

24 Solomou, 1987, p. 83.

25 Minsky, 1964, p. 325.

26 See also Friedman and Schwartz, 1963, Chart 62.

27 Solomou's Table 8.2, p. 156, taken from Minsky, 1984, 'Banking and Industry Between the Two Wars: the United States', *Journal of European Economic History* 13 (2) pp. 235–72.

28 Solomou, 1987, pp. 155–6.

29 Ibid.

30 Solomou, 1987, p. 156, quoting Goldsmith, R. W., 1984, 'The Stability of the Ratio of Non-financial Debt to Income', *Banca Nazionale del Lavoro Quarterly Review* 150, pp. 285–305.

31 In Hyman Minsky, 1982, *Inflation, Recession and Economic Policy*, Brighton: Wheatsheaf.

32 Herman van der Wee, 1987, *Prosperity and Upheaval in the World Economy 1945–1980* (London: Pelican) Chapters XI and XII.

33 Friedman and Schwartz, 1963.

5 POPULATION FEEDBACK

1 Simon, 1976.

2 Russell, 1982, chapter 2. It is true that these three fluctuations all began before the economic turning point; but it is unlikely that the baby boom or Slump in question would have lasted long enough to have much impact, were it not for the change in the economic situation.

3 It could also explain other changes in pattern. Thus J. A. Banks, in *Prosperity and Parenthood*, 1954, ascribed the onset of the 'small family' pattern among British

upper- and middle-class couples from the 1870s to a clash between steadily increasing material expectations on their part and the new economic uncertainty they saw in the downswing of the 1870s. Again, once the 'small family' pattern had spread widely across classes – by about the mid-twentieth century in Britain – one might expect the most secure and confident more often than others to choose to have an extra child. Just such a trend became visible, at least in Britain, from the 1960s, when professional couples showed rather higher fertility than skilled and partly-skilled working-class couples (John Westergaard, personal communication).

4 Easterlin, 1961.
5 Keyfitz, 1972.
6 Keyfitz, op.cit..
7 Russell, 1982, p. 12.
8 Holsinger and Kasarda, 1976; de Tray, 1976.
9 Dixon, 1976.
10 See, for an explanation on these lines, Butz and Ward, 1979.
11 Thomas, 1973.
12 See Findlay and White, 1986; Thomas, 1973.
13 The greatest improvement was not, surprisingly, in steamships, so much as sailing vessels, until well into the 1850s – and later, on the longer routes (see Chapter 2).
14 For one of the better attempts see Moses Abramovitz, 1961, 'The Nature and Significance of Kuznets Cycles', *Economic Development and Cultural Change*, 9: 225–48.
15 See, for example, Dudley Baines, 1985, *Migration in a Mature Economy* (Cambridge: the University Press).
16 Crewdson, 1983.
17 Crewdson, 1983; Vining, 1982.
18 On the causes of the migration, see Etienne van der Walle, 'France', and Robert Lee, 'Germany', both in W. R. Lee (ed.), 1979, *European Demography and Economic Growth* (London: Croom Helm). Van der Walle (p. 136) quotes Robert Laurent:

> Increasing demographic pressure and the ensuing bitter competition for jobs and for the ownership of land, on the one hand, and the decay of rural industries on the other hand, were worsening the living conditions of the lowly people.

For the fall in the French birth rate in the late 1840s, see J. C. Toutain, 'La population de la France de 1700 à 1958', *Cahiers de l'Institut de Science Economique Appliquée*, Supplement no. 133, Series AF,3 (January 1963), p. 130.
19 The feedback effect may have been somewhat complicated by an 'echo' of the 1850s 'baby boom' tending to produce another such boom in the late 1870s and 1880s, thus cancelling out the effect of the recession.
20 The post-Keynesian onslaught on neo-classical doctrines regarding the effect of reductions in real wages began with Joan Robinson, 1953, 'The Production Function and the Theory of Capital', *Review of Economic Studies*, no. 2. A fairly recent summary, from the post-Keynesian point of view, is by Richard Chase, 'Production Theory', pp. 71–86 in A. S. Eichner (ed.), 1979, *A Guide to Post-Keynesian Economics* (New York: M. E. Sharpe).
21 See King (ed.), 1986.

Appendix

1 Akin to the funded pensions system as a method of forcing people to save for retirement, and abstain from consumption in the meanwhile, is the practice, with similar tax advantages, of buying a house with borrowed money. The loan has to be repaid before retirement, so the pattern of accumulation of wealth is similar to pension rights; the difference is that there is no automatic running down of the assets acquired, although of course if the retired person no longer needs, or can afford, the house, it can be sold. Since there is an almost universal trend away from rented accommodation towards owner-occupation, here too is an element of forced, and partly disguised, saving which is on the rise. (On the USA, for example, see Russell, 1982, pp. 110–19.)
2 Huhne, Christopher (1988) 'The credit boom will deflate – and puncture Mr Lawson's boom', *Guardian*, 16 November, p. 15. Norbert Walter, 1988, 'Demographic factors and economic momentum', *Deutsche Bank Bulletin*, October.

6 INEQUALITY FEEDBACK (1): IN THE NORTH

1 It is not too hard to make allowance for the fact that bigger countries will, other things being equal, have greater inequality because of spatial differences, and that if countries A and B unite, the new country AB will probably show greater inequality than either of its components.
2 The most popular measure of inequality of income among persons or households within one country is the Gini coefficient, which has a lower limit of 0 for total uniformity and an upper limit of 1. Gini coefficients are calculated as follows: Arrange the (standardised) incomes of all households in the country, in order of size. Then, starting from the lowest income, add the incomes of successive households, finishing with the highest, and as you go, calculate and

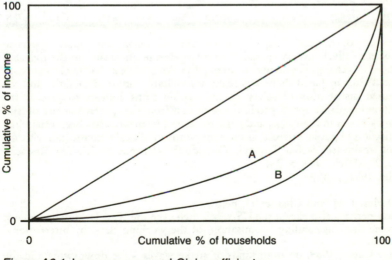

Figure A6.1 Lorenz curves and Gini coefficients

plot the percentage of total income you have reached. You will describe a line which rises more and more steeply as the incomes you are adding get larger (see Figure A6.1).

These are Lorenz curves. If the distribution of income is relatively equal, they will look something like curve *A*; if it is much more unequal they will be nearer curve *B*. The Gini coefficient is the area between the Lorenz curve and the 45° line, as a proportion of the whole area below the 45° line. For standardised household inequality, a Gini coefficient of 0.3 counts as low, a coefficient of 0.5, as high (which, for those with no taste for the principles of statistics, is all that is necessary). The Gini coefficients I quote will be for this type of inequality, unless otherwise stated. One figure, of course, cannot touch the subtleties of inequality. For example, a redistribution from the very rich to the middle class will show up as a lower Gini coefficient even if (say) the bottom 50 per cent of households gain nothing. But the Gini coefficient is crisp, and available (for many Northern countries at least since the beginning of this century, and for the South more recently). If used with care it will do: if there are big differences in it between countries, or big changes in the same country over time, then we can be fairly sure that any other measure of household income inequality would give much the same picture.

3 It may be, of course, that the failure to pool incomes after the break-up of a family is only the tip of the iceberg: the male selfishness it reveals is presumably at work within families which have not (yet?) broken up.

4 See Bornschier, 1983.

5 See Lenski, 1966.

6 Tylecote, 1990.

7 Ibid.

8 Ibid.

9 Bisson, 1954.

10 See review of Frank Levy, 1988, *Dollars and Dreams: The Changing American Income Distribution*, (New York: Basic Books) by Robert Kuttner in *Guardian Weekly*, 28 February 1988, p. 20.

11 See also Maggy Mead-King, 'Unpaid Dues', *Guardian*, 1 March 1988, p. 20.

12 The burden of increased inequality in continental Europe and Japan appears to have been relatively evenly spread. A more modest political shift to the right has produced less change in policy than among the 'Anglo-Saxons'. (On Germany see Welzk, 1986.) In Japan there was really no welfare state to dismantle, and the egalitarian distribution of salary income within firms appears to persist; the growth in inequality appears to have arisen first from the spectacular rise of land and stock prices in the 1980s, and perhaps second from what has been called 'the privatisation of public interest' as the conservative political elite merged with the elite of wealth (see Stefan Wagstyl, 'Outside the charmed circle', *The Financial Times*, 20 March 1989, p. 23).

13 Mandel, 1983, p. 199.

14 Ibid.

15 See Davies, 1984, and Chapter 11, below.

16 We may perhaps also except the USA; but then even the New Deal there had not overcome the longstanding 'atomisation' of the working class, by international standards.

17 See also Gattei, 1989, on both kinds of strike waves – the downswing and the upswing type.

18 Tylecote, 1981.

19 Tylecote, 1981, Chapter 3; Crouch and Pizzorno (eds), 1978.

20 The change between the late 1870s and the early 1900s presumably also reflects the switch around 1880 from a free trade regime with intense international competition, to a high degree of protectionism.

21 They may alternatively adjust to excess capacity by mergers and/or cartels which limit competition. Moreover, during a downswing, a great deal of physical capital will become valueless, either because of the fall in demand or because of the new technology, diffusing at this time, which makes it obsolete. Once a firm's accountants recognise this fact, they *write down* the value of the firm's assets – which means that a given profit, in future, represents a higher rate of return. The writing down reduces the mass and share of recorded profit, while it is taking place, and thus shows a spurious recovery in the share, when it is finished.

22 Hill, 1979; Martin and O'Connor, 1981.

23 The small loss of some Southern markets would have been balanced by the supply of certain components to the Southern industry.

24 This is consistent with the observed fall in *average* rates of profit taxation. What happened is that while marginal rates (until recent 'reforms') rose, tax allowances multiplied.

25 Also, for an *individual* economy, exports. For the world economy of course, changes in foreign trade cancel out. Nevertheless, as we saw when discussing the North-South relationship, it may be that increased exports from the North, financed by outflows of capital, contribute to the upswing; and the reverse, to the downswing.

26 Hannah, 1986, pp. 124–5.

27 Pitelis, 1986.

28 Habakkuk, 1962; Elsenhans, 1983.

29 Habakkuk, 1962, pp. 24–5.   In fact, it is commonly found that labour saving inventions are preferable – offering lower total costs – even in countries where the labour on which they would economise is relatively cheap; nonetheless, such countries (like England compared to America in Habakkuk's study) do not adopt them, or do so only with a delay. What may be forgotten in considering such cases is the cost of change. Where the new methods have not yet been developed there is the research and development to be done. Even where they have been pioneered already somewhere else there is the cost of acquiring the information, and of mastering the new methods in the firm in special circumstances. All these things require work, and most of those involved are managers and highly skilled workers. The more expensive is their work – relative to that of those to be displaced – the less attractive is the move.

30 Unlike the South today, there is no reason to suppose that industry in general paid better than agriculture, since there was in the nineteenth century North not the divide between an impoverished countryside and a privileged city society using high technology got from the North, and benefiting from State subsidies, that we see in the South today (see next chapter).

7 INEQUALITY FEEDBACK (2): INTERNATIONAL AND IN THE SOUTH

1 Howard, p. 34, in Hedley Bull and Adam Watson (eds), 1984, *The Expansion of International Society* (Oxford: Clarendon Press).

2 See O'Brien, in Bull and Watson, *op. cit.*, p. 46.

3 On China's long superiority over the West, see Joseph Needham's *Science and*

Civilisation in China, particularly volumes IV and V (Cambridge: Cambridge University Press, 1986).

4 The possibility of so imposing themselves dawned on them in India in 1746, after Dupleix's crushing victory at Madras, but in China, not until well into the nineteenth century (Howard, *op.cit.*).

5 The British had a long-standing problem of finding exports (other than silver) with which to pay for their imports from China; a problem which, notoriously, they resolved with opium in the 1820s (Gong, Chapter 11 in Bull and Watson, *op.cit.*).

6 O'Brien, in Bull and Watson, *op. cit.*, p. 59.

7 On the increasing economic disparities among nations in general, and between North and South in particular, see Bairoch, Chapter 1, in P. Bairoch and M. Levy-Leboyer, 1981.

8 Howard, *op. cit.*

9 See Watson, Chapter 1, in Bull and Watson, *op. cit.*

10 See Walter Rodney, 1972, *How Europe Underdeveloped Africa* (London: Bogle-l'Ouverture).

11 For a recent attempt to divide the world economy into three categories, concentrating on the intermediate one, see Giovanni Arrighi and Jessica Drangel, 1986, 'The Stratification of the World Economy: An Exploration of the Semiperipheral Zone', *Review*, X, Summer, pp. 9–74.

12 See for example Giovanni Arrighi (ed.), 1985, *Semiperipheral Development: the Politics of Southern Europe in the Twentieth Century* (Beverly Hills: SAGE).

13 See Andrew Tylecote, 1985.

14 Ibid.

15 The assignment to categories is mainly based on the gross national product (GNP) per capital and industrialisation data in Bairoch, 1976, 'Europe's Gross National Product, 1800–1975', *Journal of European Economic History* 5(2); *idem*, in Bairoch and Levy-Leboyer, 1981; and Maddison, 1982, Table 1.4; I have however altered the ranking slightly to take account of Sweden's strength in the (relatively high technology) iron and steel industry. See (on this and other points of detail) Berend, I. and Ranki, G., 1982.

16 See again Bairoch, *op. cit.*, Maddison, *op. cit.*, and Berend and Ranki, *op. cit.*

17 For the relevant income data, see again, Maddison, Bairoch, and Berend and Ranki.

18 See Tylecote and Lonsdale-Brown (1982).

19 See historical section, below.

20 Until around 1930 population growth in the less-developed countries had been slower than in the developed ones; from then on it was faster, and the differential in growth rates has increased steadily: in the 1960–70 period it was 2.4 per cent p.a. against 1.0 per cent (Bairoch, 1975, p. 6). Bairoch found a continuing widening of the gap in per capital GNP between developed and non-communist less-developed countries between 1953 and 1970 and expected it to widen even more quickly in the following decade. This it clearly did.

21 See below.

22 See Bequele and van der Hoeven, 1981, for example, on recent developments in Sub-Saharan Africa.

23 See Muller, 1977.

24 This subtraction is only relevant if the assets really are of value to the South – not just to ex-Southerners who have moved North.

25 So long as prices for low-technology products are relatively low, there is likely to be a shift to high-technology production even without HTB in the strict sense.

26 A remark attributed to the Polish Solidarity leader, Jaček Kuron (see also Voslensky, 1981).

27 See previous chapter.

28 The stream of people leaving the countryside for the towns, in almost every 'developing' country, are not necessarily going into the high-technology sectors. They are much more likely to be heading for what is called the urban 'informal' economy, where they subsist mostly by self-employment and casual employment at levels of technology, and income, very similar to those in the rural areas.

29 The rich in the rural areas may get more land, use new agricultural methods more effectively on the land they have, drive down the wages of the labour they use. In the higher-technology sectors, the gap between the owners of firms, together with their higher-paid employees, and the lower-paid workers, may widen.

30 See Tylecote and Lonsdale-Brown, 1982.

31 See O'Brien and Keyder, 1978, for quotations from Young, on the faults of the French peasant, and for their own defence of him; and Stolper et al., 1967, on the German Social Democrats' preference for large-scale agriculture.

32 Elsenhans, 1983.

33 Tylecote, 1985.

34 Fei, Ranis and Kuo, 1979.

35 Michael Sanderson, in *Education, Economic Change and Society in England, 1780–1870* (Macmillan, 1983) argues that the education of the poor was something of a luxury in late eighteenth century England, because the technology of the time did not require most manual workers to be literate or numerate. Even he, however, concedes that this was no longer so by the end of his period.

36 See, for example, Galvao and Tylecote, 1990, on Brazil.

37 There are relatively equal countries like Sri Lanka which seem to lack the necessary technological capacity, perhaps due to British rule and its anti-manufacturing educational legacy, quite different to that of the Japanese in Korea and Taiwan. One can also explain the Sri Lankan failure in terms of disintegration, politically and economically, between the (mainly peasant) Buddhist Sinhalese majority, who came after independence to control the State, and the Christian and Tamil elites who had most of the capital, technical expertise, and entrepreneurial capacity.

38 Macpherson, 1987.

39 Fukutake, 1982.

40 Dore, 1959; Bisson, 1954; Sasaki, 1981.

41 Dore, 1965; Kawano, 1965.

42 Tsuda, 1972.

43 See Sasaki, 1981.

44 Ray, 1987.

45 The present author recognised this at the time (Tylecote, 1986a) and was almost alone in his pessimism about growth prospects for 1986–8.

46 See Tylecote, 1977; Roncaglia, 1985.

47 Berend and Ranki, 1982, p. 118.

8   A HISTORICAL ACCOUNT, 1780–1850

1 van Neck, quoted in Cameron, 1985.
2 Marczewski, quoted in Cameron, 1985.
3 Wilkinson, 1973, 118ff.
4 Ibid., pp. 149–158.
5 Landes, 1969; Elsenhans, 1983.
6 Cf. Price's verdict on France: 'Overpopulation, and lack of alternative employment, created a docile labour force whose low wages maintained the labour costs of production at a low level and so created a disincentive to modernisation' (Price, 1981, p. 105).
7 Here low inequality took the form of many 'middle incomes' despite a wide range from top to bottom. If the data cited by Phelps Brown (1988, Chapter 11) is accurate, not only was Britain relatively equal by international standards, but it was a good deal more equal in 1759, just before its growth accelerated, than in the previous century, or the next.
8 Berg, 1985, pp. 53 and 119.
9 Landes, 1969.
10 Price, 1981, p. 145.
11 Ibid.
12 Quoted in Landes, 1969.
13 The truth and force of this anecdote is supported by the recent scholarship of Peter Jones (1988) in *The Peasantry in the French Revolution*, (Cambridge University Press). He found that the main obstacle to economic advance in the French countryside was the large estate, often run on rentier lines (pp. 125–7).
14 Labrousse *et al.*, 1970, *Histoire economique de la France*, II, p. 193.
15 Ibid.
16 Labrousse *et al.*, 1970, *Histoire Economique de la France*, II, pp. 657–89.
17 Labrousse *et al.*, 1970, *Histoire economique de la France*, II, p. 249.
18 In the north of France at least. In 1789 the price of grain in Champagne/Lorraine was 60 per cent above the long-term average. It is a telling comment on the expense of transport in France that the grain market in the South was effectively quite separate (*Histoire economique de la France*, II, p. 44.)
19 Ibid.
20 Lafayette and Brissot, for example, according to T.C.W. Blanning (1986) *Origins of the French Revolutionary Wars* (London: Longmans).
21 See for example Trebilcock, 1981, p. 30, and Blanning, 1983, on the Rhineland; see Frank Huggett, 1969, *Modern Belgium* (London: Pall Mall Press) Chapter 1, and E. H. Kossmann, 1978, Chapters 1 and 2, on Belgium.
22 The Revolutionary period disrupted industrial activity due to a lack of internal stability and the losses of overseas markets and, more significantly in the long term, through the consolidation of the economic situation of the small peasant. This inhibited overall structural change.

(Price, 1981: 94)

23 Caron, 1979, p. 38.
24 A start to putting this right was made in the 1820s and 1830s: after the 1821 and 1836 laws, secondary road building increased enormously; the Becquey programme of 1822 began an era of canal building, and 2,000 km, of navigable canals were opened up between 1830 and 1848 (Caron, 1979).
25 Alan Milward and S. B. Saul, 1979, *The Economic Development of Continental Europe, 1780–1870* (London: Allen & Unwin).
26 Soboul, 1989, pp. 402–3.

27 See Soboul, 1989, pp. 498 ff.
28 Tactically, the British showed that a line with an improved rate of firing and a forward screen of riflemen could cripple almost any attack in column. Logistically, they showed that once the French were on the defensive their economical methods of supply merely gave them the extra problem of guerrilla attacks on their rear.
29 Cf. Price, 1981, on the French linen and woollen industries: 'The Wars of the Revolution and Empire closed many of their overseas markets, with disastrous effects ...' (p. 129).
30 Caron, *op.cit.*, p. 35.
31 Leon *et al.*, 1976, *Hist. econ. de la Fr.*, III, p. 154.
32 See, for example Blanning, 1983.
33 Trebilcock, *op.cit.*, p. 34.
34 He not only won all his battles but was extremely parsimonious with his soldiers' lives. It is unfortunately only after a long succession of defeats that British governments take their armies out of the hands of aristocratic English incompetents and hand them over to such intelligent parvenus.
35 Lebrun *et al.*, cited in Cameron, 1985, p. 10.
36 Lebrun, *op. cit.*; Cameron, 1961.
37 Leon *et al.*, 1976, *Hist. econ. de la Fr.*, III, pp. 155–6.
38 R. J. Carbaugh, 1985, *International Economics* (Belmont, California: Wadsworth) Chapter 7.
39 M. Lutfalla, 1983, 'La desinflation en Occident: sommes-nous en 1815?' *Revue d'economie politique*, no. 2, pp. 211–32.
40 The British ban on emigration of skilled workers had been dropped in 1825, though some machinery exports were prohibited until 1842 (Henderson, 1972, p. 7).
41 Mathias, 1969, p. 281 ff.
42 See, for example, Alex Wilson, 'Chartism', in J. T. Ward, 1970, *Popular Movements c. 1830–1850* (London: Macmillan).
43 Mathias, 1969, p. 297 ff., and Chaloner, 'The Agitation against the Corn Laws', in Ward, 1970.
44 C. H. Hume, 'The Public Health Movement', in Ward, 1970, *op.cit.*
45 Berg, 1985, pp. 193–4 and G.N. von Tunzelmann, 1978, *Steam Power and British Industrialisation to 1860* (Oxford: Oxford University Press), find that the diffusion of the high pressure steam-engine was encouraged by the Ten Hours Act.
46 Leon *et al.*, 1976, *Hist. Econ. de la Fr.*, III, pp. 155–6.
47 Pinkney, 1986.
48 Caron, *op.cit.*, p. 95.
49 Quoted in Pinkney, *op.cit.*, p. 24.
50 Ibid., 1986, p. 56.
51 Henry Hobhouse, 1985, *Seeds of Change: Five Plants that Transformed Mankind* (London: Sidgwick & Jackson).
52 There was no potato crop in 1846, and only a poor one in 1847 (G. Stedman Jones, 1977, p. 79 in 'Society and Politics at the Beginning of the World Economy', *Cambridge Journal of Economics*, 1, pp. 77–92).
53 There were poor grain harvests in 1846, and in some areas in 1847. The price of rye bread in Germany increased 115 per cent between 1844 and 1847; in north France grain prices rose between 100 and 150 per cent in 1847–8 (Stedman Jones, 1977).
54 Trebilcock, *op.cit.*, p. 152.
55 Caron, *op.cit.*, p. 57.

56　Trebilcock, *op.cit.*, p. 152.
57　Ibid., p. 155.
58　Caron, *op.cit.*, p. 95.
59　Kitchen, 1978, pp. 84–5.
60　As Kitchen, 1978, pp. 84–6, points out, some reforms continued. In Prussia the 'direction principle' in the coal-mines was abolished in 1851, an example of a general tendency for the state to withdraw from direct control of the economy. Restrictions on the formation of joint-stock companies and co-operatives were relaxed. The general liberal tendency of policy was encouraged by the fact that the three-class franchise brought in in 1849 to ensure aristocratic dominance quickly turned out to do no such thing.

9　A HISTORICAL ACCOUNT, 1848–1896

1　1850 is a 'cheating' date, in the sense that it is not the peak of a Juglar short cycle, but it cannot be helped – the data do not go back any earlier. Even if we took 1845 instead, as perhaps we should, the growth rate would be high.
2　van Duijn, 1983, p. 156.
3　Rostow, 1978, p. 146.
4　Murphy, 1973, Table 11.20.
5　Note that the Civil War did *not* affect gold output or world interest rates because its inflationary effects were, by and large, restricted to the USA, whose currency duly fell against sterling and gold; the inflationary effects of the Crimean War were significant precisely because they affected the main reserve currencies, which were tied to gold.
6　It has been argued that the Erie Canal of 1826, followed by the development of steamboat navigation on the Mississippi and its tributaries, was as important as the railway in launching the industrial development of the West. But if we assimilate the immigration and the steamboats to the railways as aspects or consequences of the steam transport style, the three together can be taken as decisive.
7　James M. McPherson, 1987, *Battle Cry of Freedom: The Civil War Era* (Oxford: Oxford University Press).
8　The phrase 'pre-emptive counter-revolution' is Arno Mayer's, coined to explain the next great conflict.
9　Christopher Freeman, 1989, 'The Third Kondratieff Wave: Age of Steel, Electrification and Imperialism', paper presented at international colloquium on long waves at Vrije Universiteit, Brussels, 12–14 January, 1989.
10　Between 1811, when emancipation first became possible, and 1848 only 240,000 Prussian peasants had bought their freedom; between 1848 and 1865 640,000 did so (Wehler, 1985, p. 13).
11　Wehler, 1985, p. 23.
12　Ibid., p. 24.
13　Ibid., p. 25.
14　Ibid., p. 27.
15　David F. Good, 1984, *The Economic Rise of the Hapsburg Empire*, (Berkely: University of California Press).
16　Taylor, 1961, pp. 116–7.
17　Taylor, 1961, pp. 136–7.
18　S. N. Solomou, 1986, 'The impact of climatic variations on British economic growth, 1856–1913', *Climatic Change* 8: 53–67.
19　Solomou, 1987, Chapter 6.
20.　Ibid.
21　Wehler, 1985, p. 36.

22 Solomou, 1987, p. 112.
23 Solomou, 1987; Wehler, 1985.
24 Thomas, 1973, Table 98.
25 Ibid., Table 96.
26 Solomou, 1987, p. 126.
27 Saul, 1969.
28 Wehler, pp. 34–51.
29 As we saw in Chapter 7, Denmark also responded very successfully by agricultural innovation and commercialisation; so did the Netherlands.
30 Wehler, 1985, p. 107.
31 Hans Rosenberg, 1967, 1976 *Grosse Depression und Bismarckzeit*, Berlin.
32 The Reich only contributed to the old age and disability insurance (Stolper *et al.*, 1967, pp. 45–60).
33 By Lance E. Davis and Robert A. Huttenback, 1986, *Mammon and the Pursuit of Empire: The Economics of Imperialism, 1869–1912* (Cambridge: Cambridge University Press).

10 A HISTORICAL ACCOUNT, 1896–1945

1 See Solomou's chapter in Goodwin, di Matteo and Vercelli, 1989.
2 Mitchell, 1983.
3 Mitchell, 1978, 1983, shows the USA as having in 1900 238,000 university students against Germany's 48,000 (with a total population less than double). The disparity in the secondary schools would have been greater.
4 Trebilcock, 1981.
5 Wehler, 1985, p. 34.
6 Trebilcock, *op. cit.*, p. 72.
7 Ibid.
8 Wehler, 1985, p. 44.
9 Kuznets, 1963; and see my Figure 6.1.
10 Wehler, *op. cit.*, pp. 241 and 139.
11 Wehler, *op. cit.*, p. 142.
12 Wehler, *op. cit.*, pp. 164–5.
13 Eley, however, in his Chapter 5 in Evans (ed.), 1978, speaks of 'the deterioration of German capitalism's position in the world market, especially after 1911' (p. 128).
14 See Eley, Chapter 5 in Evans (ed.), 1978.
15 See Owen, Chapter 3 in Evans (ed.), 1978.
16 Wehler, *op. cit.*, p. 196.
17 Eley, Chapter 5 in Evans (ed.), 1978, pp. 128–9.

> In 1900 the Pan-Germans were dismissed as 'beer-bench politicians', the radical peasants of Central Germany were scorned as 'gutter anti-semites', and the extremist agrarian agitators attacked as 'irresponsible meddlers'. By 1913 the Agrarian League had reshaped the Conservative Party in its own image, the anti-Semites had been successfully assimilated to it, a new national Mittelstand had given its annual congress for the announcement of a new right-wing front, and the Pan-Germans had become important intermediaries between industrialists and agrarians. Something had clearly happened in the meantime.
>
> (Eley, p. 131)

18 Bartlett, 1984, p. 79.

19 Wehler, *op. cit.*, p. 199.
20 Taylor, 1961, p. 186.
21 Fritz Fischer, 1967, *Germany's War Aims in the First World War* (London). See also W. Schieder (ed.) *Erster Weltkrieg* (Koln, 1969).
22 Wehler, *op. cit.*, pp. 210ff.
23 See, for example, the arguments in A. J. P. Taylor, 1948, *The Hapsburg Monarchy 1809–1918* (London: Hamish Hamilton).
24 Arno Mayer, 1981, *The Persistence of the Old Regime* (London: Croom Helm). Mayer argues that the landowning aristocrats had clung to power throughout Europe; but his case is clearly weaker for Britain and France.
25 Wehler, *op. cit.*, p. 220ff.
26 See Chapter 6; and Wehler, *op. cit.*, pp. 202–3.
27 Margot Asquith, quoted in A. J. P. Taylor, 1965, *English History, 1914–1945* (Oxford: Clarendon Press).
28 See Chapter 6.
29 M. C. Kaser and E. A. Radice, 1985, *Economic Structure and Performance between the Two Wars*, vol. I of *The Economic History of Eastern Europe, 1919–75* (Oxford: Clarendon Press).
30 See, for example, Galvao and Tylecote, 1990, on Brazil.
31 See Aldcroft, 1977, Chapter 9.
32 See Chandler, 1977.
33 Much of the increase in industrial concentration in the 1920s was due to vertical integration, which as Oliver Williamson has argued, in *Markets and Hierarchies* (New York: Free Press, 1975) increases with an increase in environmental and technological uncertainty.
34 By the same token, Fordist style production in France helped to undermine the French unions and to allow the increase in inequality described earlier.
35 Unemployment and underemployment was serious, since the labour force recovered more quickly from the slaughter than employment did from the devastation.
36 They should also have had some adverse effects on the US economy, following the argument which gave high rates of immigration credit for stimulating growth there; but these are unlikely to have been large, for two reasons. First, the new restrictions did not apply within the Americas, and considerable immigration now took place from Mexico (some also from Canada); there was even more internal migration, of impoverished rural whites from Appalachia and rural blacks from the South, to the industrial areas, which had effects not dissimilar to international migration. Second, as I have already argued, in a mature industrial economy fast growth of the labour force from whatever source will do much less to quicken the growth of the economy than it had done in the United States of the nineteenth century.
37 Friedman and Schwartz, 1963.
38 Aldcroft, 1977, pp. 250–1.
39 Aldcroft, *op. cit.*, p. 251.
40 Cited in Aldcroft, *op. cit.*, p. 221ff.
41 The main reason for this is that Northern productivity increases faster than Southern (see Spraos, 1983).
42 Aldcroft, 1977, pp. 251 ff.
43 See Aldcroft, *op. cit.*, Chapters 9 and 11.
44 At this point in the diffusion of the new style we can take it that industrial productivity was rising faster than theirs.
45 R. J. Overy, 1982, *The Nazi Economic Recovery, 1932–8* (London: Macmillan).
46 Aldcroft, *op. cit.*.

47 See for example Aglietta, 1979.
48 The boom had been particularly in construction, delayed by the war.
49 See Pitelis, 1986, Table 1.
50 Friedman and Schwartz, 1963.
51 Overy, *op. cit.*, p. 56, has argued that the slow rate of growth of German industrial productivity under the Nazis was largely due to the suppression of both national and international competition.
52 See, for example, David E. Kaiser, 1980, *Economic Diplomacy and the Origins of the Second World War* (Princeton NJ) on the industrialisation of Eastern Europe during the 1930s, with Western capital.
53 See, for example, H. A. Turner, 1969, 'Big Business and the Rise of Hitler', *American Historical Review*, and B. Weisbrod, 1979, 'Economic Power and Social Stability Reconsidered: Heavy Industry in Weimar Germany', *Social History*.
54 Stolper *et al.*, 1967.
55 Stolper *et al.*, pp. 110 ff.
56 Ibid.
57 Overy, *op. cit.*, p. 60, finds a 20 per cent increase in consumption of rye bread by working-class families between 1927 and 1937, while their consumption of wheat bread, eggs and meat fell.
58 Overy, *op. cit.*.
59 Bartlett, 1984, p. 199; J.-P. Azema, 1984, *From Munich to the Liberation, 1938–44* (Cambridge: Cambridge University Press) p. 6.
60 At the time of Munich, the Soviet Union indicated a willingness to join an alliance agaist Germany; the overture was ignored (Bartlett, *op. cit.*, p. 200).
61 They did not think the Siegfried Line could hold out more than three weeks (Bartlett, *op. cit.*, p. 199).
62 Bartlett, *op. cit.*, pp. 200–1.
63 Bartlett, *op. cit.*, p. 201.
64 I am acutely aware that this account of the reasons for the abandonment of Czechoslovakia is highly controversial. Recent work has stressed the attachment of the British government to 'Empire solidarity' and its difficulty in persuading all its Dominions to support a determined stand against Hitler (see for example Ritchie Ovendale's Chapter 8 in Boyce and Robertson (eds) 1989). It is also well known that British strategists gravely underestimated the military value of Czechoslovakia and (to a lesser extent) the Soviet Union in 1938 (Milan Hauner, 'Czechoslovakia as a Military Factor in British Considerations of 1938', *Journal of Strategic Studies*, vol. 1 (1978), pp. 194–222, and Kaiser, 1980). But people believe what they desperately want to believe, even when it is obviously untrue. It is known, for example, that French strategists wilfully disregarded intelligence information about Russia and Czechoslovakia's military strength (Robert J. Young, French Military Intelligence and Nazi Germany', in *Knowing One's Enemies*, E. R. May (ed.) pp. 297–308). Nor did the British and French wish to know how willing the Soviet Union was to help. Boyce in the introduction to Boyce and Robertson (eds), 1989, summarises the implications of recent work by Jonathan Haslam (*The Soviet Union and the Struggle for Collective Security in Europe, 1933–39*, London, 1984):

> As interesting as the precariousness of the collective security policy is the intensity and apparent sincerity with which it was pursued, and the frustration caused by the refusal of the western powers to grasp the outstretched Soviet hand. If A.J.P. Taylor is right that the Second World War was the unnecessary war, he is also right in pointing to the failure to create an Anglo-French-Soviet

alliance as one of the missed opportunities for averting it. Haslam indicates that anti-Communism, discounted in most studies of British (but not French) appeasement, indeed was a major obstacle to agreement. (p. 17)

See also Williamson Murray, 1984, *The Change in the European Balance of Power, 1938–39: The Path to Ruin* (Princeton, NJ: Princeton University Press).
65 In American terms, I know, the Administration and Congress were by this time controlled by liberals. I am using 'conservative' in a very general sense.
66 See Chapter 6, and Williamson and Lindert, 1980.

11   A HISTORICAL ACCOUNT, FROM 1945 TO THE PRESENT

1 Solomou, 1987.
2 One study finds a rise in labour's share of income in the non-primary sector from 48.7 per cent in 1934–40, to 70 per cent at the beginning of the post-war period (Minami and Ono, 1981, pp.309–24).
3 See Sasaki, 1981.
4 K. M. Bolte, 1959, *Sozialer Aufstieg und Abstieg* (Stuttgart).
5 See, for example, Volker Berghahn, 1988, *Modern Germany* (Cambridge: Cambridge University Press).
6 Hilary Footitt and John Simmonds, 1985, *France 1943–1945* (Leicester: Leicester University Press).
7 See Paul Furlong, 'State, Finance and Industry in Italy', Chapter 5 in Andrew Cox and N. O'Sullivan (eds), 1986, *State, Finance and Industry* (Brighton: Wheatsheaf).
8 Douglas Ashford, 1986, *The Emergence of the Welfare States* (Oxford: Blackwell); Malcolm Sawyer, 1982, 'Income distribution and the Welfare State', Chapter 7 of Andrea Boltho, *The European Economy* (Oxford: Oxford University Press). There was indeed land reform of a sort – the 1947 Town and Country Planning Act's appropriation of 'development values' and rights in the land – but this was promptly reversed when the landowners' party returned to power in 1951.
9 The United Nations, *Economic Survey of Europe, 1969*, Table 5.11, gives earnings of male wage-earners in agriculture as percentage of manufacturing, 1938, 1948: Denmark 44, 65; West Germany 64, 66; Italy 43, 58; Netherlands 61, 83; Norway 42, 76; Sweden 50, 70; Switzerland 42, 47; UK 48, 72.
10 The United States, not the most favourable example for my argument, saw the share of national income taken by corporate profits rise from 5.3 per cent in the depressed 1930s to 14.3 per cent in the prosperous year of 1950; but the share of rent fell from 4.3 per cent to 3.0 per cent, and that of net interest from 6.9 to 1.0 per cent, with the result that 'Total Capital Income' was only up from 16.5 per cent to 18.3 per cent (Lars Osberg, *Economic Inequality in the United States*, Armonk, NY: M. E. Sharpe, 1984).
11 Henry Pelling, 1960, *American Labor* (Chicago and London: University of Chicago Press).
12 See Mandel, 1980, and Tylecote, 1990, 'Unionisation in the Long Wave'.
13 On the geopolitical aspects of these and later developments see Bartlett, 1984; on their economic aspects see Van der Wee, 1986.
14 See Martha S. Hill, 1985, 'The Changing Nature of Poverty', *Annals of the American Academy of Political and Social Science*, 479, May, pp. 31–47.
15 Williamson and Lindert, 1980.
16 See Sawyer, op. cit.
17 W. R. Bohning, 1972, *The migration of workers in the United Kingdom and the*

European Community (Oxford: Oxford University Press for the Institute of Race Relations).

18 See R.Goodin *et al.*, 1987, *Not only the Poor: the Middle Classes and the Welfare State* (London: Allen & Unwin).

19 Mary Kaldor, 1983, *The Baroque Arsenal* (London: Abacus).

20 See Tylecote, 1981. To the extent that the buck could be passed to the consumer, shopfloor militancy should not be blamed for the (rather small) fall in (recorded) profits. As we saw in Chapter 6, there are other good explanations for this.

21 Alain Lipietz, 1982, 'De la nouvelle division internationale du travail à la crise du fordisme péripherique', CEPREMAP Working Paper no. 8225.

22 This was due to the neglect of primary production while the emphasis was on industrialisation.

23 Lipietz, *op. cit.*

24 Tylecote, 1977; and 1986 'The Oil Price in the Long Wave', mimeo.

25 On the situation in the USA, see the National Science Board Commission on Precollege Education in Mathematics, Science and Technology, *Educating Americans for the 21st Century: A Report to the American People and the National Science Board* (Washington DC, 1983). For causes, see social disintegration and the growing 'underclass'. The US shortage in areas like engineering is now acute, and its efforts to cope with it by recruiting from abroad are accentuating the Southern crisis – see Chapter 7.

26 Best, 1990.

27 Barry Wilkinson, 1983.

28 Wilkinson, 1983; H. H. Rozenbrock, 1974, *Computer-aided Control System Design* (London: Academic Press).

29 See Christopher Freeman, 1987.

30 See Chapter 5.

31 See Tylecote, 1981, Chapter 2, and Michael Stewart, 1983, *Controlling the Economic Future: policy dilemmas in a shrinking world* (Brighton: Wheatsheaf).

32 See Chapter 6.

33 Tylecote, 1987.

34 On the fall and rise of monetarism (broadly defined) see Phyllis Deane, 1989, *The State and the Economic System* (Oxford: Oxford University Press) Chapters 8 and 9.

35 See Stewart, *op. cit.*, 1983 and Tylecote, *op. cit.*, Chapter 2.

36 Tylecote, 1990, 'Unionisation in the Long Wave', *op. cit.*

37 Sweden by contrast merely returned to its old successful combination of Keynesianism plus a low exchange rate and a 'social contract'.

38 See Chapter 5, Appendix.

39 See Chapter 7. By way of example, the GNP per capita of Latin America as a whole was 6.5 per cent less in 1988 than in 1980. About 4 per cent of GNP was transferred abroad in 1988 ($29bn.) in debt repayments and interest (mostly the latter). Debt levels stood at $401 bn – $9 bn down from 1987 (*The Financial Times*, 21 December 1988, p. 8, quoting from ECLA preliminary report for 1988).

40 This also helps to account for the disappointing growth rate just after the oil price collapse of early 1986 (see Tylecote, 1986a).

41 Beckerman and Jenkinson, 1986, argue that by comparison the effect of unemployment was insignificant.

42 See Jerker Carlsson (ed.), 1982, *South-South Relations in a Changing World* (Uppsala: Scandinavian Institute of African Studies) particularly Carlsson's introduction, and C. V. Vaitsos, 1978, 'Crisis in Regional Economic Cooperation (Integration) in Developing Countries: a Survey', *World Development*, vol. 6, no. 6, June.

43 See for example J. Bulow and K. Rogoff, 1989, 'A Constant Recontracting Model of Sovereign Debt', *Journal of Political Economy*, vol. 96, February.
44 Alan Altshuler *et al.*, 1984, *The Future of the Automobile* (Cambridge Mass: MIT Press).
45 See Centre for Incentive Taxation, *Economic Intelligence*, Issue 20, 1990, p. 1 and p. 4. This journal deserves great credit for correctly analysing the Kuznets upswing and correctly forecasting the current downswing.
46 The resemblance of 1980s Japan to 1920s USA extends beyond the financial system, to a political and economic system which has in the last decade begun progressively to increase inequality of income and wealth. See for example Stefan Wagstyl, 'Outside the charmed circle', *The Financial Times*, 20 March 1989, p. 23.

12 THE WAY TO THE NEXT UPSWING

1 This is currently running at such a rate as to deplete one-third of the world's arable land in the next twenty years; see Bernard Leblond and Laurent Guerin, 1988, *Soil Conservation: project design and implementation using labour-intensive techniques* (Geneva: International Labour Office).
2 See Galvao and Tylecote, 1990.
3 See Susanna Hecht and Alexander Cockburn, 1989, *The Fate of the Forest: Developers, Destroyers and Defenders of the Amazon* (London: Verso).
4 See Katharine Forestier, 1989, 'The Degreening of China', *New Scientist*, 1 July, pp. 52–5. On the contrasting record of Taiwan's management of its forests, see Anton Galli, 1987, *Taiwan ROC: A Chinese challenge to the world* (London etc.: Weltforum, particularly p. 28.
5 The gentle reaction of the Bush Administration to the bloodbath of Tiananmen Square and its aftermath exemplified this approach.
6 See Robert Riddell, 1981, p. 70.
7 Termites are also a major source of methane; and since they feed on dead wood, they provide another link with forest clearance.
8 See Joe Farman, 1987, 'What Hope for the Ozone Layer Now', *New Scientist*, 12 November, pp. 50–4; Michael McElroy, 1988, 'The Challenge of Global Change', *New Scientist*, 28 July, pp. 34–6; Lionel Milgrom, 1988, 'Alternative CFCs pose problems near the ground', *New Scientist*, 31 March, p. 33; Veerabadrhan Ramanathan, 1988, *Science*, vol. 240, p. 293. The Chinese contribution to the greenhouse effect is large and growing: it is the third largest producer and consumer of fossil fuels in the world and 70 per cent is coal, which has the highest carbon content (see Vaclav Smil, 1988, *Energy in China's Modernization* (New York: East Gate)).
9 For the connection between global warming and the Midwest drought of 1988, see *New Scientist*, 8 September 1988, p. 30, 'The Man who Predicted the American Drought.'
10 There are also, of course, the more familiar dangers of accidents and other sources of radiation leakages.
11 See Jose Goldemberg *et al.*, 1988, *Energy for a Sustainable World* (New York: Wiley). Smil, *op. cit.*, shows how China alone wastes huge quantities of energy through low conversion efficiencies, resulting largely from underpricing.
12 On wind energy see e.g. D. S. Milborrow (ed.), 1988, *Wind Energy Conversion* (London: Mechanical Engineering/British Wind Energy Association). On solar energy see Bernard McNelis *et al.*, 1988, *Solar-powered Electricity* (London: Intermediate Technology Publications/UNESCO); and Clive Cookson, 1988, 'A Commercial Breakthrough for the Sun', *The Financial Times*, 15 December, p.

18. Once such technologies are providing cheap electricity to the rural population, the way is open for the wide diffusion of highly efficient (but cheap)
cooking   stoves   already   developed,   using   local   supplies   of   wood
economically: these are currently shunned, in favour of the wasteful open
fire, because of the light which the latter provides, for cooking at night. There
are also stoves using methane from 'digesters' of sewage and other wastes,
already common in China.

13 See D. Mackenzie and D. Searle, 1988, 'Pollution Treaties Upstaged by German
Technique', *New Scientist*, 12 November, p. 23.

14 The support of much of the Catholic Church – part of the hierarchy and most of
the grassroots – for Luis da Silva, the most left-wing of the main candidates in the
Brazilian presidential election of 1989, was a notable sign of commitment to
reform: da Silva's party had included Chico Mendes, the Amazonian activist
murdered in 1988, and was committed to land reform.

15 See Iftikhar Ahmed, 1988, 'The Bio-revolution in Agriculture: key to poverty
alleviation in the Third World?', *International Labour Review*, vol. 127, no. 1,
pp. 53–72; Anne Charnock, 1988, 'Plants with a Taste for Salt', *New Scientist*,
3 December, pp. 41–5; Steve Connor, 1988, 'The Battle for Britain's Biotechnology', *New Scientist*, 11 August, pp. 48–50; *New Scientist*, 28 January 1989,
p. 34.

16 Christopher Joyce, 1988, 'America counts the cost of global warming', *New
Scientist*, 29 October, p. 26; ibid., 1988, 'Underwater methane could fuel global
warming', *New Scientist*, 17 December, p. 9.

17 On the Swedish system see 'Sweden's Economy: the nonconformist state',
Economist, 7 March 1987, pp. 19–24. The employment of others can be
safeguarded if the work is done for some public sector employer – normally the
local authority – in areas which do not much compete with the private sector; all
employers have to do then is to commit themselves to maintaining or increasing
their 'normal' payroll.

18 In the care of the old and sick, and of children (in day nurseries, and as assistants
to teachers in schools); or improving the environment, cleaning the streets,
working in parks, repairing country footpaths...

19 Ian Mackintosh, 1986, *Sunrise Europe: the dynamics of information technology*
(Oxford: Blackwell). He estimates that cumulative installation costs over the
period 1990–2005 will be about $400bn, and that the investment will create an
additional demand for information technology products of one sort or another
amounting to a further $325bn. Clearly if it is worth doing for Europe it would
be worth doing also in the USA; it is *already* being done in Japan!

20 One method is to inspect every building every ten years (say) and/or when it is
put up for sale, and give it an 'energy rating' on a scale of 1 to 10 (such a system is
already in use in Denmark). Compulsion could be used to move buildings up the
scale by setting stiffer and stiffer minimum scores; but even without that, the
market, now better informed, would apply its own pressure for improvement. In
larger buildings it might even be made compulsory to install some form of CHP,
combined heat and power generation, which (at least in colder climates) offers a
safe, clean and cheap alternative to nuclear power (Nicholas Schoon, 1989, 'Every
Home a Power Station?', *Independent*, 10 July, p. 15). One reason for private
reluctance to carry out such investments, hitherto, is difficulty and uncertainty in
borrowing money for the long periods before they pay off: not only are real rates
of interest currently high, but nominal rates (before inflation is subtracted) are
higher, and with repayments on top, represent a heavy burden in the early years
of a loan. Government encouragement, through changes in tax rules among other
things, is required for 'index-linked' lending, in which only the real rate of

interest is paid, the money value of the principal being adjusted according to the rate of inflation: this reduces the strain on the borrower, and the risk to both borrower and lender.

21 See Jonathan Leape, 1988, 'Tax Cuts Do Not Work', *Employment Institute Economic Report* vol. 3, no. 9, July, pp. 1–4.

22 And if one country goes it alone with high tax rates it may lose people to other countries that it would rather keep.

23 On experience of land value taxation, and the case for it, see Fred Harrison, 1983, *The Power in the Land* (London: Shepheard-Walwyn), and Steven B. Cord, 1987, *The Evidence for Land Value Taxation* (Columbia MD: Center for the Study of Economics).

24 This was discussed in the UK in a government report in 1964, and advocated by Gabriel Roth, 1967, *Paying for Roads* (London: Penguin); more recently by A. A. Walters, *The Economics of Road User Charges*, World Bank Staff Occasional Papers no. 5.

25 If it is felt that the implications of this system for civil liberties are unacceptable, there is an alternative method using 'smart cards'; this cannot, on the other hand, help against 'autocrime'. In fact the Big Brother effect is exaggerated: Big Brother would know where your car was, not you; and the whole point of the exercise would be to induce people not to travel often in their own cars.

26 Moreover the offences they tend to commit are more severely punished than 'white-collar' crime. For a review of this (complex) area, as regards the poor in general, see for example Steven Box, 1987, *Recession, Crime and Puinishment* (London: Macmillan); as regards ethnic minorities, see Barbara Hudson, 1989, 'Discrimination and Disparity: the influence of race on sentencing', *New Community*, vol. 16, no. 1, October, pp. 23–34.

27 Such a system is already in use in Sweden, and is under review in Britain. See Pat Carlen and Dee Cook (eds), 1989, *Paying For Crime* (Milton Keynes: Open University Press).

28 Measures are also required to combat another threat to the family's proper functioning: debt. We saw in the last chapter how, at least in the USA and UK, demand had been kept up through the 1980s by a huge increase in the ratio of personal debt to income. Lower interest rates, though they would ease the immediate strain of debt, would further increase the temptation to incur it. One way to restrain this temptation would be to impose tight controls on the rates of interest which could be charged by lenders, relative to current market rates. At the same time there would be limits, particularly restrictive where children were involved, on the proportion of a family's income which could be demanded, in interest and repayments, by lenders taken together. Banks etc. could then only make a profit on their lending by being rather choosy about the recipients, and by restricting the amount they spent on seductive marketing of their loans. The end result would be a decided reduction in poverty, particularly that of children, due to parental extravagance.

29 See Michael McGwire, 1987, *Military Objectives in Soviet Foreign Policy* (Washington DC: Brookings).

30 See Egbert Boeker, 1987, *Defence in a Peaceful Europe*, ADIU report, vol. 9, no. 2, March–April, pp.1–4.

31 See Tylecote, 1981.

32 In Tylecote, *op. cit.*, Chapter 6.

33 See the surveys quoted in National Economic Development Council Long-Term Perspectives Group, 1987, *IT Futures – It Can Work* (London: National Economical and Development Authority).

34 John Naisbitt, 1984, *Megatrends* (London: Futura).

35 See Best, 1990, and Graham Bannock, 1981, *The Economics of Small Firms* (Oxford: Blackwell).
36 And we might get it: throughout Europe the Left has been paying more and more attention to local government in recent years (*vide* Mitterrand's decentralisation, and the strength of the British Labour Party, and the German SDP, everywhere but at the centre); in the USA what is required, once the Federal fiscal crisis is resolved, is for the Democratic majority in Congress to use its power to redistribute funds to the lower levels of government – also mostly Democrat-controlled.

Bibliography

Aglietta, M. (1979) *A Theory of Capitalist Regulation*, London: New Left Books.

Ahlstrom, G. (1982) *Engineers and Industrial Growth*, London: Croom Helm.

Aldcroft, D. H. (1977) *From Versailles to Wall Street, 1919–29*, London: Allen Lane.

Ayres, R. U. (1987) 'The Industry-Technology Life Cycle: An Integrating Meta-Model?', *International Institute for Applied Systems Analysis*, RR-87-3, March.

Ayres, R. U. and Miller, S. M. (1983) *Robotics: Applications and Social Implications*, Cambridge, Mass.: Ballinger Publishing Co..

Bairoch, P. (1975) *The Economic Development of the Third World since 1900*, London: Methuen.

Bairoch, P. and Levy-Leboyer, M. (1981) *Disparities in Economic Development since the Industrial Revolution*, London: Macmillan.

Banks, Ronald (1989) *Costing the Earth*, London: Shepheard-Walwyn.

Bartlett, C. J. (1984) *The Global Conflict, 1880–1970*, London: Longman.

Beckerman, Wilfred and Jenkinson, Tim (1986) 'What Stopped the Inflation? Unemployment or Commodity Prices?', *Economic Journal* 96 (381) (March) 39–54.

Berend, T. and Ranki, I. (1982) *The European Periphery and Industrialisation*, Cambridge: Cambridge University Press.

Berg, Maxine (1985) *The Age of Manufactures*, Oxford: Blackwell.

Bequele, Assefa and van der Hoeven, Rolf (1981) 'Poverty and Inequality in Sub-Saharan Africa', *International Labour Review* 119 (3) (May–June).

Best, Michael H. (1990) *The New Competition: Institutions of Industrial Restructuring*, Cambridge: Polity Press/Blackwell.

Bisson, T. A. (1954) *Zaibatsu Dissolution in Japan*, Berkeley and Los Angeles: University of California Press.

Blanning, T. C. W. (1983) *The French Revolution in Germany*, Oxford: Clarendon Press.

Bornschier, U. (1983) 'World Economy, Level of Development and Income Distribution: An Integration of Different Approaches to the Explanation of Income Inequality', *World Development* 11 (1) 11–20.

Boserup, Ester (1981) *Population and Technology*, Oxford: Blackwell.

Boyce, Robert and Robertson, Esmonde (eds) (1989) *Paths to War: New Essays on the Origins of the Second World War*, London: Macmillan.

Boyer, R. and Mistral, J. (1978) *Accumulation, Inflation et Crises*, Paris: Press Universitaire de France.

Butz, William P. and Ward, Michael P. (1979) 'Baby Boom and Baby Bust: a new view', *American Demographics* 1 (September) 11–17.

Cameron, Rondo (1961) *France and the Economic Development of Europe*, 1800–1914, Princeton: Princeton University Press.

Cameron, Rondo (1985) 'A New View of European Industrialisation', *Economic History Review*, second series, 38 (1) (February) 1–23.

Cardoso, E. A. (1979) 'Celso Furtado revisitado: a decada de 30', *Revista Brasileira de Economia* 33 (3) 373–97.

Caron, François (1979) *An Economic History of Modern France*, London: Methuen.

Carr, J. C. and Taplin, W. (1962) *History of the British Steel Industry*, Cambridge, Mass.: Harvard University Press.

Castellino, O. (1982) 'Italy' pp. 47–70, in Rosa, J. J. (ed.) (1982).

Chandler, Alfred D. (1977) *The Visible Hand: The Managerial Revolution in American Business*, Cambridge: Harvard University Press.

Coombs, R. W. (1983) 'Long Waves and Labour Process Change', in C. Freeman (ed.) *Long Waves in the World Economy*, London: Butterworth.

Cowling, Keith (1982) *Monopoly Capitalism*, London: Macmillan.

Crafts, N. F. R. (1983) 'British Economic Growth, 1700–1831: A Review of the Evidence', *Economic History Review* 36, 175–99.

Crewdson, J. (1983) *The Tarnished Door: The New Immigrants and the Transformation of America*, New York: Times Books.

Crouch, D. and Pizzorno, A. (eds) (1978) *The Resurgence of Class Conflict in Western Europe since 1968*, 2 vols, London: Macmillan.

Crouzet, F. (1967) 'England and France in the 18th Century', in R. M. Hartwell (ed.) *Causes of the Industrial Revolution in England*, London: Methuen.

Currie, Robert (1988) 'Lunar Tides and the Wealth of Nations', *New Scientist*, 5 November pp. 52–5.

Davies, Andrew (1984) *Where did the Forties go?*, London: Pluto Press.

Deane, Phyllis and Cole, W. A. (1962) *British Economic Growth, 1688–1959: trends and structure*, Cambridge: Cambridge University Press.

Deger, S. (1986) *Military Expenditure in Third World Countries: The Economic Effects*, London: Routledge & Kegan Paul.

de Tray, Dennis N. (1976) 'Population Growth and Educational Policies: An Economic Perspective', pp. 182–209, in Ridker (ed.) (1976).

Dickinson, H. W. (1958) 'The Steam Engine to 1830', Chapter 6 in Singer *et al.* (eds) vol. IV (1958a).

Dixon, R. B. (1976) *The Roles of Rural Women: Female Seclusion, Economic Production and Reproductive Choice*, pp. 290–316, in Ridker (ed.) (1976).

Dore, Ronald (1959) *Land Reform in Japan*, Oxford: Oxford University Press.

Dore, Ronald (1965) 'Land Reform and Japan's Economic Development', *The Developing Economies*, special issue, 3, 487–96.

Dosi, Giovanni (1986) 'Technology and Conditions of Macro Economic Development: Some Notes on Adjustment Mechanisms and Discontinuities in the Transformation of Capitalist Economies', in C. Freeman (ed.), *Design, Innovation and Long Cycles in Economic Development*, London: Francis Pinter.

D'Souza, V. G. (1985) *Economic Development, Social Structure and Population Growth*, New Delhi: Sage.

Duijn, J. J. van (1913) *The Long Wave in Economic Life*, London: Allen & Unwin.

Dunning, J. H. (1983) 'Changes in the Level and Structure of International Production: the last one hundred years', pp. 84–139 in Mark Casson (ed.) (1983) *The Growth of International Business*, London: Allen & Unwin.

Duran, Esperanza (ed.) (1985) *Latin America and the World Recession*, Cambridge: Cambridge University Press.

Easterlin, R. A. (1961) 'The Baby Boom in Perspective', *American Economic Review* 51, 869–911.

Easterlin, R. A. (1968) *Population, Labor Force and Long Swings in Economic Growth: The American Experience*, NBER: Columbia University Press.

Elsenhans, H. (1983) 'Rising Mass Incomes as a Condition of Capitalist Growth: Implications for the World Economy', *International Organisation* 37 (1) (Winter) 1–39.

Evans, Richard J. (ed) (1978) *Society and Politics in Wilhelmine Germany*, London: Croom Helm.

Fei, J. C. H., Ranis, G. and Kuo, S. W. Y. (1979) *Growth with Equity; the Taiwan Case*, Oxford: Oxford University Press.

Findlay, A. M. and White, P. E. (1986) *West European Population Change*, London: Croom Helm.

Freeman, C. (ed.) (1983) *Long Waves in the World Economy*, London: Butterworth.

Freeman, C. (ed.) (1986) *Design, Innovation and Long Cycles In Economic Development*, London: Frances Pinter.

Freeman, C. (1987) *Technology Policy and Economic Performance: Lessons from Japan*, London: Frances Pinter.

Freeman, C., Clark, J. and Soete, J. (1982) *Unemployment and Technical Innovation: A Study of Long Waves and Economic Development*, London: Frances Pinter.

Freeman, Richard R. and Medoff, James L. (1984) *What Do Unions Do?*, New York: Basic Books.

Friedman, Ed (ed.) (1982) *Ascent and Decline in the World-System*, London and Beverly Hills: Sage.

Friedman, Milton and Schwartz, Anna J. (1963) *A Monetary History of the USA, 1867–1960*, Washington DC: National Bureau of Economic Research.

Friedman, Milton and Schwartz, Anna J. (1982) *Monetary Trends in the United States and United Kingdom*, Chicago: University of Chicago Press.

Fukutake, Tadashi (1982) *The Japanese Social Structure: Its Evolution in the Modern Century*, Tokyo: University of Tokyo Press.

Galvao, Claudia and Tylecote, Andrew (1990) 'The Choice of Technology in Brazilian Industrialisation', pp. 84–104 in M. P. van Dijk and Henrik Secher Marcussen (eds) *Industrialization in the Third World: The Need for Alternative Strategies*, London: Frank Cass for European Association of Development Institutes.

Gattei, G. (1989) 'Every 25 Years? Strike Waves and Long Economic Cycles', paper presented to long wave Conference, Brussels, January.

Gelderen, J. van (1913) 'Springvloed: beschouwingen over industrieele ontwickeling in prijsbeweging' *De Nieuwe Tijd* 18, 253–77, 369–84, 445–64.

Gerschenkron, A. (1965) *Economic Backwardness in Historical Perspective*, New York; Praeger.

Gimenez, M. E., Greenberg, E., Markusen, A., Mayer, T. and Newton, J. (1977) 'Income Inequality and Capitalist Development: A Marxist Perspective', Chapter 10 in W. Loehr and J. P. Powelson, *Economic Development, Poverty and Income Distribution*, Boulder, Co.: Westview Press.

Goldstein, J. S. (1988) *Long Cycles: Prosperity and War in the Modern Age*, New Haven: Yale University Press.

Goodwin, Richard, di Matteo, M. and Vercelli, A. (eds) (1989) *Technological and Social Factors in Long Wave Fluctuations*, Berlin: Springer.

Gordon, D., Edwards, R. and Reich, M. (1982) *Segmented Work, Divided Workers: The Historical Transformation of Labour in the United States*, Cambridge, Cambridge University Press.

Greenough, William C. and King, Francis P. (1976) *Pension Plans and Public Policy*, New York: Columbia University Press.

Habakkuk, H. J. (1955) 'Family Structure and Economic Change in Nineteenth Century Europe', *Journal of Economic History* 15 (1).

Habakkuk, H. J. (1962) *American and British Technology in the 19th Century*, Cambridge: Cambridge University Press.

Hadfield, C. (1974) *British Canals*, Newton Abbot: David & Charles.

Hannah, Leslie (1986) *Inventing Retirement: the development of occupational pensions in Britain*, Cambridge: Cambridge University Press.

Hemming, Richard and Kay, John A. (1982) 'Great Britain', pp. 29–46 in Rosa, J. J. (ed.) (1982).

Henderson, W. O. (1972) *Britain and Industrial Europe, 1750–1870*, 3rd edn, Leicester: Leicester University Press.

Hill, Martha S. (1985) 'The Changing Nature of Poverty', *Annals of the American Academy of Political and Social Science* 479, May, 31–47.

Hill, T. (1979) *Profits and Rates of Return*, Paris: OECD.

Holsinger, Donald B. and Kasarda, John D. (1976) *Education and Human Fertility: Sociological Perspectives*, pp. 154–78, in Ridker (ed.) (1976).

Janssen, Martin C. and Muller, Heinz H. (1982) 'Switzerland', pp. 121–47 in Rosa, J. J. (ed.) (1982).

Jarvis, C. M. (1958) 'The Generation of Electricity', Chapter 9, and 'The Distribution and Utilisation of Electricity', Chapter 10 in Singer *et al.* (eds) vol. V (1958b).

Jevons, W. S. (1884) *Investigations in Currency and Finance*, London: Macmillan.

Jones, Peter M. (1988) *The Peasantry in the French Revolution*, Cambridge: Cambridge University Press.

Juglar, C. (1862) *Des Crises commerciales et leur retour periodique en France, Angleterre et aux Etats Unis*, Paris: Guillaumin.

Juttemeier, Karl-Heinz and Petersen, Hans-Georg (1982) 'West Germany', pp. 181–205 in Rosa, J. J. (ed.) (1982).

Kalecki, Michal (1954) *Theory of Economic Dynamics*, London: Allen & Unwin.

Kaplinsky, R. (1984) *Automation: The Technology and Society*, London: Longmans.

Kawano, Shigeto (1965) 'Economic Significance of the Land Reform in Japan', *Developing Economies* 3, pp. 139–57.

Kay, Neil M. (1984) *The Emergent Firm*, London: Macmillan.

Keyfitz, N. (1972) 'Population Waves' in T. N. E. Greville (ed.) (1972) *Population Dynamics*, New York: Academic Press.

Kindleberger, C. P. (1973) *The World in Depression. 1929–39*, London: Allen Lane/Penguin.

King, Russell (ed.) (1986) *Return Migration and Regional Economic Problems*, London: Croom Helm.

Kitchen, Martin (1978) *The Political Economy of Germany, 1815–1914*, London: Croom Helm.

Kitchin, J. (1923) 'Cycles and Trends in Economic Factors', *Review of Economic Statistics*, 5, 10–16.

Kitchin, J. (1930) *Report to Gold Delegation of the Financial Committee of the League of Nations*, Geneva.

Kondratiev, N. D. (1979) 'The Major Economic Cycles', translation, *Review*, 11 (4) 519–62. First published (1925) in Voprosy kon'iunktury, I, 28–79. An abridged English translation (1935) appears as 'The Long Waves in Economic Life', *R.E.S.*, XVII (6) 105–15.

Konrad, George and Szelenyi, Ivan (1979) *The Intellectuals on the Road to Class Power*, Brighton, UK: Harvester.

Kossmann, E. H. (1978) *The Low Countries, 1780–1940*, Oxford: Oxford University Press.

Kuhn, Thomas S. (1970) *The Structure of Scientific Revolutions*, 2nd ed, Chicago: Chicago University Press.

Kuznets, S. (1930) *Secular Movements in Production and Prices*, New York: Houghton Mifflin.

Kuznets, S. (1963) 'Quantitative Aspects of the Economic Growth of Nations, VIII: Distribution of Income by Size', *Economic Development and Cultural Change* 11 (2), part II.

Labrousse, E. *et. al.* (1970) *Histoire economique de la France, Tome II: Des derniers temps de l'âge seigneurial aux preludes de l'âge industriel, 1660–1789*, Paris: Presses Universitaires Françaises.

Lambert, R. (1983) 'Geared for a Rail Revival: General Electric in the U.S. goes for major investment', *The Financial Times*, 14 April.

Landes, D. S. (1969) *Prometheus Unbound: Technological Change and Industrial Development in Western Europe from 1750 to the Present*, Cambridge: Cambridge University Press.

Lane, D. (1971) *The End of Inequality? Stratification under State Socialism*, Harmondsworth: Penguin.

Lardy, N. R. (1978) *Economic Growth and Distribution in China*, Cambridge: Cambridge University Press.

Latham, A. J. H. (1981) *The Depression and the Developing World*, London: Croom Helm.

Lecaillon, J. *et al.* (1984) *Income Distribution and Economic Development*, Geneva: International Labour Organisation.

Lenski, Gerhard, E. (1966) *Power and Privilege: A Theory of Social Stratification*, New York: McGraw Hill.

Leon, P., Levy-Leboyer, M., Armengaud, A., Broder, A. *et al.* (1976) *Histoire economique de la France, Tome III: l'avenement de l'ere industrielle, 1789–1880*, Paris: Presses Universitaires Fançaises.

Lewis, W. A. (1978) *Growth and Fluctuations, 1870–1913*, London: Allen & Unwin.

Lipietz, Alain (1984) *L'audace ou l'enlisement*, Paris: La Decouverte.

Lund, R. T., Hall, L. and Horwich, E. (1977) *Integrated Computer Aided Manufacturing: Social and Economic Impacts*, Cambridge, Mass.: Centre for Policy Alternatives, Massachusetts Institute of Technology.

Macpherson, W. J. (1987) *The Economic Development of Japan c. 1868–1941, Studies in Economic and Social History*, London: Macmillan.

Maddison, A. (1982) *Phases of Capitalist Development*, Oxford and New York: Oxford University Press.

Mandel, E. (1980) *Long Waves of Capitalist Development: The Marxist Interpretation*, Cambridge: Cambridge University Press.

Mandel, E. (1983) 'Explaining Long Waves of Capitalist Development', Chapter 14, in C. Freeman (ed.) *Long Waves in the World Economy*, London: Butterworths.

Martin, W. E. and O'Connor, M. (1981) 'Profitability: A Background Paper', in W. E. Martin (ed.) *The Economics of the Profits Crisis*, London: HMSO.

Mason, E. S. (1980) *The Economic and Social Modernisation of the Republic of Korea* (Harvard East Asian Monographs, vol. 92), Cambridge, Mass.: Harvard University Press.

Mathias, Peter (1969) *The First Industrial Nation: An Economic History of Britain, 1700–1914*, London: Methuen.

Mensch, G. (1979) *Stalemate in Technology: Innovations Overcome the Depression*, Cambridge, Mass.: Ballinger.

Minami, Ryoshin and Ono, Akira (1981) 'Behavior of Income Shares in a Labor Surplus Economy', *Economic Development and Cultural Change*, April, 309–24.

Minsky, H. P. (1964) 'Longer Waves in Financial Relations: Financial Factors in the More Severe Depressions', *American Economic Review*, Papers and Proceedings, LIV (3) 324–35.

Minsky, H. P. (1982a) *Inflation, Recession and Economic Policy*, Brighton: Wheatsheaf.

Minsky, H. P. (1982b) 'The Financial Instability Hypothesis: Capitalist Processes and the Behaviour of the Economy', in C. P. Kindleberger and J. P. Laffargue (eds) *Financial Crises*, Cambridge: Cambridge University Press.

Mitchell, B. R. (1978) *European Historical Statistics*, London: Macmillan.

Mitchell, B. R. (1983) *American Historical Statistics*, London: Macmillan.

Modelski, George (1987) 'The Study of Long Cycles', in G. Modelski (ed.) *Exploring Long Cycles*, London: Frances Pinter, 1–16.

Muller, Mike (1977) *The Baby Killer: A War on Want investigation into the promotion and sale of powdered baby milks in the Third World*, London: War on Want.

Munnell, Alicia (1982) *The Economics of Private Pensions*, Washington DC: The Brookings Institution.

Murphy, Brian (1973) *A History of the British Economy, 1740–1970*, London: Longmans.

Musson, A. E. and Robinson, Eric (1969) *Science and Technology in the Industrial Revolution*, Manchester: Manchester University Press.

O'Brien, Patrick (1988) *The Economic Effects of the American Civil War*, London: Macmillan.

O'Brien, Patrick, and Keyder, Caglar (1978) *Economic Growth in Britain and France, 1780–1914: Two Paths to the Twentieth Century*, London: Allen & Unwin.

OECD (1990) *Economic Outlook, June 1990*, Paris: Organisation for Economic Cooperation and Development.

Pacey, Arnold (1974) *The Maze of Ingenuity*, London: MIT Press.

Pamuk, S. (1982) 'World Economic Crises and the Periphery: the Case of Turkey', Chapter 6 in E. Friedman (ed.) (1982).

Pearce, David, Markandya, Anil and Barbier, Edward B. (1989) *Blueprint for a Green Economy*, London: Earthscan.

Perez, C. (1983) 'Structural Change and Assimilation of New Technologies in the Economic Social Systems', *Futures*, October, 357–75.

Perez, C. (1985) 'Microelectronics, Long Waves and World Structural Change: New Perspectives for Developing Countries', *World Development* 13 (3) 441–63.

Phelps Brown, Edmund Henry (1988) *Egalitarianism and the Generation of Inequality*, Oxford: Clarendon Press.

Pinkney, David H. (1986) *Decisive Years in France, 1840–1847*, Princeton: Princeton University Press.

Pitelis, Christos (1986), *Corporate Capital: Control, Ownership, Saving and Crisis*, Cambridge: Cambridge University Press.

Poletayev, Andrey, V. (1987) 'Profits and Long Waves', paper presented at the workshop on long waves and life cycles, Montpellier, July 1987.

Price, Roger (1981) *An Economic History of Modern France, 1730–1914*, London: Macmillan.

Ranis, G. (1977) 'Growth and Distribution: Trade-offs or Complements?', Chapter 3 in W. Loehr and J. P. Powelson (eds) *Economic Development, Poverty and Income Distribution*, Boulder, Colorado: Westview Press.

Ray, G. F. (1987) 'The Decline of Primary Producer Power', *National Institute Economic Review*, August, 40–5.

Reich, L. S. (1985) *The Making of American Industrial Research: Science and Business at GE and Bell, 1876–1926*, Cambridge: Cambridge University Press.

Reynolds, T. S. (1983) *Stronger than a Hundred Men: A History of the Vertical Water Wheel*, Baltimore and London: The Johns Hopkins University Press.

Riddell, Robert (1981) *Ecodevelopment*, London: Gower.

Ridker,R. (ed.) (1976) *Population and Development*, Baltimore: The Johns Hopkins University Press.
Robb, A. M. (1958) 'Shipbuilding', Chapter 16 in Singer *et al.* (eds) vol. V (1958b).
Rolt, L. T. C. (1969) *Navigable Waterways*, London: Longmans.
Roncaglia, A. (1985) *The International Oil Market: A Case of Trilateral Oligopoly*, London: Macmillan.
Rosa, J. J. (1982) 'France', pp. 9–28, in Rosa, J. J. (ed.) (1982).
Rosa, J. J. (ed.) (1982) *The World Crisis in Social Security*, Paris: Bonnel Editions.
Rosen, Sherwin (1982) 'United States', in Rosa (ed.) (1982).
Rostow, W. W. (1978) *The World Economy: History and Prospect*, London: Macmillan.
Rostow, W. W. (1985) 'The World Economy Since 1945: A Stylised Historical Analysis', *Economic History Review*, May, 252–75.
Rostow, W. W. and Kennedy, M (1979) 'A Simple Model of the Kondratieff Cycle', in P. Uselding (ed.) (1979) *Research in Economic History*, 4, 1–36
Russell, Louise B. (1982) *The Baby Boom Generation and the Economy*, Studies in Social Economics, Washington DC: The Brookings Institution.
Sasaki, Naoto (1981) *Management and Industrial Structure in Japan*, Oxford: Pergamon.
Saul, S. B. (1969) *The Myth of the Great Depression, 1873–1896*, London and Basingstoke: Macmillan.
Schubert, H. R. (1958) 'Extraction and Production of Iron and Steel,' Chapter 4 in Singer *et al.* (eds) vol IV (1958a).
Schumpeter, J. A. (1934) *The Theory of Economic Development: An Inquiry into Profits, Capital, Credit, Interest and the Business Cycle*, Cambridge: Harvard University Press.
Schumpeter, J. A. (1939) *Business Cycles, I and II: A Theoretical, Historical and Statistical Analysis of the Capitalist Process*, New York: McGraw-Hill.
Screpanti, Ernesto (1984) 'Long Economic Cycles and Recurring Proletarian Insurgencies', *Review* VII (2) Winter, 509–48.
Sharp, M. (ed.) (1983) *Europe and the New Technologies*, London: Frances Pinter.
Simon, Julian L. (1976) 'Income, Wealth and Their Distribution as Policy Tools in Fertility Control', pp. 36–76, in Ridker (ed.) (1976).
Singer, Charles *et al.* (eds) (1958a) *A History of Technology*, vol. IV, *The Industrial Revolution*, Oxford: Oxford University Press.
Singer, Charles *et al.* (eds) (1958b) *A History of Technology*, vol. V, *The Late 19th Century, c. 1850–1900*, Oxford: Clarendon Press.
Soboul, Albert (1989) *The French Revolution, 1787–1799*, London: Unwin Hyman.
Solomou, Solomos (1986) 'Innovation Clusters and Kondratieff Long Waves in Economic Growth', *Cambridge Journal of Economics* 10, 101–12.
Solomou, Solomos (1987) *Phases of Economic Growth, 1850–1973: Kondratieff Waves and Kuznets Swings*, Cambridge: Cambridge University Press.
Spraos, J. (1983) *Inequalising Trade?* Oxford: Clarendon Press/UNCTAD.
Stark, T. (1963) *The Distribution of Personal Income in the UK, 1949–63*, Cambridge: Cambridge University Press.
Stewart, F. (1977) *Technology and Underdevelopment*, London: Macmillan.
Stolper, Gustav, Hauser, Karl, and Borchardt, Knut (1967) *The German Economy: 1870 to the present*, London: Weidenfeld & Nicholson.
Stowers, A. (1958) 'Watermills, 1500–1850', Chapter 7 in Singer *et al.* (eds) vol. IV (1958a).
Takayama, Noriyuki, 'Japan', pp. 71–91 in, Rosa (ed.) (1982).
Taylor, A. J. P. (1961) *Origins of the Second World War*, London: Hamish Hamilton.

Temin, P. (1964) *Iron and Steel in Nineteenth-Century America*, Cambridge, Mass.: MIT Press.

Thomas, B. (1973) *Migration and Economic Growth*, Cambridge: Cambridge University Press.

Thorp, Rosemary (ed.) (1984) *Latin America in the 1930s: The Role of the Periphery in World Crisis*, London: Macmillan.

Tomlinson, B. R. (1979) *The Political Economy of the Raj, 1914–47*, London: Macmillan.

Trebilcock, Clive (1981) *The Industrialisation of the Continental Powers, 1780–1914*, London: Longmans.

Tsuda, A. (1972) 'Wage and Salary Structure in Asian Context (2)', *Hitotsubashi Journal of Social Studies* 6 (I).

Tylecote, Andrew (1977) 'A Theory of the Price of Exhaustible Resources Supplied by Developing Countries', *University of Sheffield Division of Economic Studies*, Discussion Paper no. 77.11.

Tylecote, Andrew (1981) *The Causes of the Present Inflation: An Interdisciplinary Explanation of Inflation in Britain, Germany, and the United States*, London, Macmillan and New York: Halsted Press.

Tylecote, Andrew (1985) 'Inequality in the Long Wave: Trend and Cycle in Core and Periphery', *European Association of Development Institutes Bulletin*, I, 1–23.

Tylecote, Andrew (1986a) 'Sorting out the Haves from the Have-nots', *Guardian*, 5 February, p. 25.

Tylecote, Andrew (1986b) 'On Inequality and the Rate of Profit in the Long Wave', *Economic and Industrial Democracy*, February, 29–44.

Tylecote, Andrew (1987) 'Time Horizons of Management Decisions: Causes and Effects', *Journal of Economic Studies 14 (4) 51–64*.

Tylecote, Andrew (1989) 'The South in the Long Wave: Technological Dependence and the Dynamics of World Economic Growth', pp. 206–24 in Goodwin *et al.* (1989).

Tylecote, Andrew (1990) 'Unionisation in the Long Wave', *Sheffield University Management School Discussion Paper* no. 90.7.

Tylecote, Andrew and Lonsdale-Brown, Marian (1982) 'State Socialism and Development: Why Russian and Chinese Ascent Halted', Chapter 10 in E. Friedman (ed.) (1982).

Ubbelohde, A. R. J. P. (1958) 'The Beginnings of the Change from Craft Mystery to Science as the Basis for Technology', Chapter 23, in Singer *et al.* (eds) vol. IV (1958a).

UNCTAD (1987) *Handbook of International Trade and Development Statistics*, Supplement 1986, New York: United Nations.

Van Der Wee, Herman (1986) *Prosperity and Upheaval: The World Economy 1945–1980*, London: Viking.

Vilar, P. (1976) *A History of Gold and Money, 1450–1920*, London: New Left Books.

Vining, Daniel R. (1982) 'Net Migration by Commercial Air: A Lower Bound on Total Net Migration to the United States', pp. 333–50, in Julian L. Simon and Peter H. Lindert (eds) (1982) *Research in Population Economics*, vol. 4, London: JAI Press.

Voslensky, M. S. (1981) *Nomenklatura: Die Herrschende Klasse in der Sowjetunion*, Wien: KNO.

Wallerstein, Immanuel (1983) 'The Three Instances of Hegemony in the History of the Capitalist World Economy', *International Journal of Comparative Sociology* 24 (1–2) 100–8.

Wehler, Hans-Ulrich (1985) *The German Empire, 1871–1918*, Leamington Spa: Berg.

Weisskopf, Thomas, E. (1987) 'The Effect of Unemployment on Labour Productivity: An International Comparative Analysis', *International Review of Applied Economics* 1 (2) 127–51.

Welzk, Stefan (1986) *Boom ohne Arbeitsplatze*, Koln: Kiepenheuer & Witsch.

Wilkinson, Barry (1983) *Shop Floor Politics of New Technology*, London: Gower.

Wilkinson, R. G. (1973) *Poverty and Progress*, London: Methuen.

Willan, Thomas Stuart (1936, 1964) *River Navigation in England, 1600–1750*, London: Oxford University Press, 1936; London: Frank Cass, 1964.

Williamson, J. G. and Lindert, D. H. (1980) *American Inequality: A Macroeconomic History*, New York: Academic Press.

Williamson, O. E. (1970) *Corporate Control and Business Behaviour*, New York: Prentice-Hall.

Williamson, O. E. (1975) *Markets and Hierarchies*, New York: Free Press.

Wolpin, Miles, D. (1986) *Militarisation, Internal Repression and Social Welfare in the Third World*, London: Croom Helm.

World Bank (1985) *World Development Report, 1985*, New York: World Bank.

Index